Customer Service Management in Africa

Customer Service Management in Africa

A Strategic and Operational Perspective

Edited by

Robert Ebo Hinson
University of Ghana Business School, Ghana

Ogechi Adeola
Lagos Business School, Pan-Atlantic University, Nigeria

Terri R. Lituchy
CETYS Universidad, Mexico

Abednego Feehi Okoe Amartey
University of Professional Studies, Accra

Routledge
Taylor & Francis Group

A PRODUCTIVITY PRESS BOOK

First published 2020
by Routledge
605 Third Avenue, New York, NY 10017

and by Routledge
2 Park Square, Milton Park, Abingdon, Oxon, OX14 4RN

First issued in paperback 2022

Routledge is an imprint of the Taylor & Francis Group, an informa business

© 2020 Taylor & Francis

Library of Congress Cataloging-in-Publication Data

Names: Hinson, Robert Ebo, editor. | Adeola, Ogechi, editor, author. | Lituchy, Terri R., editor. | Amartey, Abednego Feehi Okoe, editor.
Title: Customer service management in Africa : a strategic and operational perspective / Professor Robert E. Hinson, Dr. Ogechi Adeola, Dr. Terri R. Lituchy, Professor Abednego Feehi Okoe Amartey.
Description: New York : Routledge, 2020. | Includes bibliographical references and index.
Identifiers: LCCN 2019060075 (print) | LCCN 2019060076 (ebook) | ISBN 9780367143374 (hardback) | ISBN 9780429031342 (ebook)
Subjects: LCSH: Customer services--Africa, Sub-Saharan--Management.
Classification: LCC HF5415.5 .C8363 2020 (print) | LCC HF5415.5 (ebook) | DDC 658.8120967--dc23
LC record available at https://lccn.loc.gov/2019060075
LC ebook record available at https://lccn.loc.gov/2019060076

ISBN: 978-1-03-240005-1 (pbk)
ISBN: 978-0-367-14337-4 (hbk)
ISBN: 978-0-429-03134-2 (ebk)

DOI: 10.4324/9780429031342

Typeset in Garamond
by Lumina Datamatics Limited

Contents

THEME G: CUSTOMER EXPERIENCE – ADVANCING
           CUSTOMER SERVICE IN AFRICA

Preface

In the twenty-first century, discourse on effective customer management and retention is attracting greater attention of researchers and business practitioners as the achievement of business goals depends on satisfying customer needs. Given that business organisations are established to provide products and services that the customers would perceive as valuable and satisfactory, organisations must understand the customer from a holistic perspective – *strategic and operational* – especially in a dynamic market such as Africa.

Customer Service Management in Africa: A Strategic and Operational Perspective aims to provide students (both undergraduate and postgraduate) and practitioners with in-depth knowledge and understanding of customer service management in Africa, given the changing nature of the market. This book also recognises that human capital is one of the most dynamic resources available to an organisation, internally and externally, as companies need them to thrive. Harnessing the best of the internal human resources to achieve excellent customer service and meet the goals of customer satisfaction requires a strategic and operational approach.

The introductory chapter provides readers with an overview of customer service management in Africa, while the other chapters, grouped into seven themes, discuss the core tenets of customer service. The first theme focuses on customer service as shared value. This theme exposes readers to issues relating to the definition of the customer, customer-driven organisations and discussions on ethical customer service. The second theme focuses on customer service strategy, which comprises an introduction to the strategic and operational perspective of customer service management and an institutional examination of an economics-led model of customer service strategy. The third theme discusses customer service systems with a focus on the application of digital technology and social media to enhance the customer service experience. The fourth theme discusses customer service style, with chapters on innovation and customer service, entrepreneurial customer service, leadership and customer service, teamwork and customer service, and customer service training.

The fifth theme exposes students and practitioners to the dynamics of culture in customer service delivery with chapters on organisational culture and customer service delivery, cultural influence on customer service delivery, reward and recognition systems in customer service organisations, and reward systems and customer service delivery among small and medium enterprises. The sixth theme focuses on customer service skills with chapters on emotional intelligence, twenty traits of customer service champions, professional grooming and presentation skills. The last theme concludes the book with a discussion on using customer experience to advance and improve customer service in Africa. Finally, the book provides strategic insights on effective customer service management in Africa, with perspectives from authors across sub-Saharan Africa.

Acknowledgements

The editors acknowledge the contributions of all the reviewers who gave constructive feedback to the chapter authors. The editors also acknowledge the support of the Development Policy Poverty Monitoring and Evaluation Centre of Research Excellence and Skills Development Fund at the University of Ghana.

Contributors

Awele Achi is currently a doctoral candidate in Strategy and Marketing at The Open University Business School, Milton Keynes, UK. Previously, Awele held a scholarly research position at Lagos Business School, Nigeria. His research interest lies within the fields of marketing strategy, social entrepreneurship and mixed-methods research.

Ogechi Adeola is an associate professor of marketing at the Lagos Business School (LBS), Pan-Atlantic University, Nigeria. She is also the academic director of the LBS Sales & Marketing Academy. Her research interests include tourism and hospitality marketing, strategic marketing, customer service management and digital marketing strategies in sub-Saharan Africa. She has published academic papers in top-ranking scholarly journals. Her co-authored papers won Best Paper Awards at conferences in 2016, 2017 and 2018. She holds a doctorate in business administration (DBA) from Manchester Business School, United Kingdom.

Isaiah Adisa is a private researcher working with a faculty member at the Lagos Business School, Pan-Atlantic University, Lagos, Nigeria. He studied industrial relations and human resources management at the Olabisi Onabanjo University (formerly Ogun State University), Ago-Iwoye, Ogun State, Nigeria. He graduated with second-class honours (upper division) and distinction, respectively, at both undergraduate and postgraduate studies in the same university. His interests focus on, but are not limited to, industrial relations and human resources management, organisations strategy, marketing and gender-related studies.

Abednego Feehi Okoe Amartey is the vice-chancellor and a professor of marketing at the University of Professional Studies, Accra (UPSA). He has published in several prestigious journals including a paper in the *Journal of Research in Interactive Marketing*, which was conferred the title of Highly Commended Paper by the Emerald Literature Network Awards for Excellence in 2016. He co-authored the book *Sales Management: A Prime for Frontier Marketers* in 2018 and *Customer Service Essentials: Lessons for Africa and Beyond* in 2019, published by IAP. He holds a doctor of business administration from the Swiss Management Center University. He is a fellow of the Chartered Institute of Marketing Ghana and won the award as the best CEO in the Educational Sector in Ghana Industry Awards in 2019 and CIMG Man of the Year 2018.

Thomas Anning-Dorson (PhD) is a senior lecturer at the Wits Business School, University of the Witwatersrand, Johannesburg, South Africa. His research interest spans innovation, service management, strategy and emerging markets.

Isaac K. Arthur is a lecturer of human geography in the Department of Geography and Resource Development at the University of Ghana. He holds a doctorate in Planning and Development from Aalborg University, Denmark. His research interests are in experience economy, innovations and entrepreneurship in rural areas, and urban planning and development. He has published in several peer reviewed journals and reviewed manuscripts for journals such as *CITIES, Area Development and Policy, African Geographical Review Journal,* and *Ghana Journal of Geography.* He is currently involved in the Pan-African College of Sustainable Cities project funded by the Robert Bosch Foundation, and Mobility and Sociality in Africa's Emerging Urban project funded by the Andrew W. Mellon Foundation/African Research Universities Alliance (ARUA).

Desmond Tutu Ayentimi (PhD) is associate fellow of the Higher Education Academy and a lecturer of management at the Tasmanian School of Business and Economics, University of Tasmania, Australia. He is currently the management major coordinator. His research is multi-disciplinary focussed on identifying institutional and cultural constraints and opportunities in HRM practice transfer to less developed and developing economies in sub-Saharan Africa. His research interests include multinational enterprises HRM policies and strategies in developing economies, technology and employment relations, cross-cultural management, local content policies and HRD in sub-Saharan Africa.

Samuel Benagr is a lecturer at the School of Performing Arts, University of Ghana. He did his master's in international cinema and PhD in cinema and new technologies with the Research Institute for Media, Arts and Design at the University of Bedfordshire, UK. For his undergraduate studies, he did a combined major in theatre arts and French at the University of Ghana. Benagr's research interests are in the areas of cinema and new technologies and identity construction, with emphasis on West African (Ghana/Burkina Faso) video filmmaking and spatial humanities. He is a contributing author of *Directory of World Cinema – Africa* (2017).

Emmanuel Chao holds a PhD (2014) and MSc (International Business and Management) (2010) from Norway. He is currently a senior lecturer at Mzumbe University-Tanzania. He has a wide experience in presenting papers in leading academic conferences/platforms such as Academy of Marketing, European Academy of Marketing, Marketing Science/World Marketing Congress, Info Marketing, Society of Behavioral Scientists (Canada), Industrial Marketing Association (China) and Business and Information Management. He has published several papers in a wide variety of international outlets such as *International Business Research, Journal of Global Marketing, Journal of Business to Business Relations,* and *Journal of Knowledge Management and Practice.*

Ishmael Ofoli Christian is research assistant at the Marketing and Entrepreneurship Department of the University of Ghana Business School. His research interests include consumer behaviour, customer value and services strategy.

Giacomo Ciambotti is a PhD candidate in management and innovation at Università Cattolica (Milan). He's the finance stream lead at the E4Impact Foundation, teaching financial planning in East African MBA programmes (Kenya, Uganda, Ethiopia, Rwanda, Zimbabwe). At the Università Cattolica, he's the teaching assistant of corporate strategy to MSc students in management and is also a research fellow at Alta Scuola Impresa e Società (ALTIS) (graduate school of business and society). His research focusses on management and growth strategies of hybrid organisations and social enterprises, especially in Africa. His research has been published in top journals such as the

Journal of Business Ethics, and he is also visiting scholar of the CREED centre at Sheffield Business School (UK). He also coordinates research-focused workshops in Uganda to build topics of social enterprises and ecosystem development, and foster research collaborations with African scholars.

Jimmy Ebong is a PhD/DBA candidate at SMC Swiss Management Center, Switzerland. He is a research specialist with Financial Sector Deepening Uganda (FSDU), leading FSDU's research, strategy, generating evidence and insights for programming financial sector development interventions. Previously, he served as a consultant and later as senior private sector development consultant with a private consulting firm and impact fund manager in Tanzania. He has successfully completed over 40 consultancy assignments in inclusive development approaches in Tanzania, Kenya, Zambia, South Sudan, Nigeria and Uganda. His research and publication experience covers themes of service marketing, value chains and financial inclusion. Jimmy's research interests are in the themes of impact finance, small and growing businesses, and digital financial services.

David Ehira is a graduate student of interactive media at the University of Westminster. He has been involved in transdisciplinary research efforts in cognitive technologies, marketing and the use of AI expert systems. Known for creativity and meticulous in putting ideas into motion, he is interested in the application of emerging technologies towards creating user-centred innovations for optimising business processes and enhancing service delivery systems. His current research interest lies in the use of Artificial Intelligent systems towards promoting sound mental health among employees in the UK.

J. N. Halm is an entrepreneur, author, speaker and business consultant specialising in service excellence. He has a decade of experience from Ghana's banking industry. Halm holds an MPhil in communications from the School of Communication Studies, University of Ghana and a BSc in agriculture from Kwame Nkrumah University of Science and Technology. Halm is a weekly columnist with a full-page column in Ghana's leading business newsprint, *Business & Financial Times*. He is also the author of two award-winning books, *Customer Romance* and *Service Sins*. He was adjudged the Service Excellence Leader Award at the 2019 Global Brands Awards.

Robert Ebo Hinson is a professor and head of Department of Marketing and Entrepreneurship at the University of Ghana. He is also the acting director of institutional advancement at the same institution, research associate at the University of the Free State Business School, and an extraordinary professor at the North West University Business School in South Africa. Hinson has authored/edited several books and has over 100 scientific publications to his credit. He has also served as the rector of the Perez University College in Ghana and holds two doctorate degrees: one in international business from the Aalborg University in Denmark and another in marketing from the University of Ghana. He has consulted for and trained several institutions globally in the general areas of marketing, sales and service excellence and served as well on the boards of local and international institutions.

Oserere Ibelegbu is currently a research assistant under the Management Scholar Academy programme at the Lagos Business School, Pan-Atlantic University, Lagos, Nigeria. She holds a master's degree in information science and a bachelor's degree in economics, both from the University of Ibadan, Nigeria. Her areas of research interest include but are not limited to economics of information, mobile technology and innovation, corporate social responsibility and service quality.

Dumebi Anthony Ideh holds a BSc degree (second-class upper), MSc and PhD degrees in industrial relations and personnel management from the University of Lagos. He also possesses an MBA (marketing management) degree from Ladoke Akintola University of Technology (LAUTECH), Ogbomosho, Nigeria. He is currently a lecturer in the Department of Employment Relations and Human Resource Management, University of Lagos. He has over 17 scholarly publications in reputable journals and has also authored papers presented in learned conferences. Dr Ideh is an associate of the Chartered Institute of Personnel Management, Nigeria.

Paul Katuse is an associate professor of strategic management. He has previously worked as a corporate consultant and lecturer and has been an external examiner and a visiting faculty for several universities in South Africa, Kenya, Zimbabwe, Rwanda and Uganda, among others. He has supervised graduate students and been a principal investigator. He is published in refereed journals. He belongs to several professional associations such as the Academy of Management, Africa Academy of Management, and Association of African Schools of Business (Affiliate Membership) among others. He is trained in case writing, pedagogy and online content delivery. His teaching philosophy is centred on experiential learning. His interest is in globalisation and organisations.

Sarah Kimani is a senior lecturer at the Catholic University of Eastern Africa. She holds a PhD in quality management from Victoria University of Wellington and has an MBA and a bachelor of commerce degree from the University of Nairobi. Her main fields of research are service marketing and quality management in higher education (HE). Sarah has published widely and has presented her research work in many conferences locally and internationally. She is a quality assurance expert in HE and has international appointments in the accreditation of degree programs.

Mary Wanjiru Kinoti is a certified behavioural scientist and axiologist from Boise State University, in Idaho, USA and associate dean at the Graduate Business Studies, School of Business, University of Nairobi. She holds a PhD degree in business administration from the University of Nairobi, Kenya, as well as an MBA-marketing and B COM finance and economics from India. She has co-authored book chapters for various publications including "Women Empowerment through Government Loaned Entrepreneurship Teams in Kenya" in *Research Handbook on Entrepreneurial Teams: Theory and Practice* published by Edward Elgar Publishing and *The Business Case for Climate Change: The Impact of Environmental forces on Kenya's Public Listed Companies* published by Emerald Group Publishing Limited.

Ruth N. Kiraka (PhD, Victoria University, Melbourne; MSc, Wageningen University, The Netherlands; BSc, Egerton University, Kenya) is an associate professor, Strategy & Entrepreneurship, Strathmore University, Kenya. She has published two books, journal articles, book chapters, conference proceedings, research reports, and case studies. She has also won a university teaching excellence award. She serves as an external examiner for several universities and an external reviewer for Kenya's and Namibia's Higher Education Commissions. Prof. Kiraka has been a journal reviewer for *Eastern Africa Social Science Research Review*; *International Journal of Knowledge, Culture and Change Management*; and International Academy of African Business and Development.

Yvonne Ayerki Lamptey holds a PhD in business studies from Swansea University, UK, has 7 years of teaching experience at universities, nearly 10 years of experience in human resource management practice with local and international organisations, and over 10 years of experience in corporate capacity building. She is currently a lecturer with a focus on human resource management strategy, labour relations and behaviour in organisations teaching both undergraduate and postgraduate students.

Terri R. Lituchy is currently a Fulbright Scholar in the Caribbean (2018–2020) and the PIMSA Distinguished Chair in International Business at CETYS Universidad in Mexico. Dr Lituchy holds a PhD from the University of Arizona, USA. She has also taught around the world, including in the Americas, Asia, Africa and Europe. Dr Lituchy's research interests are in cross-cultural management and international services and tourism from an organisational behaviour perspective. Dr Lituchy's current project, LEAD: Leadership Effectiveness and Motivation in Africa, the Caribbean and the Diaspora, has received many awards as well as grants. Dr Lituchy has published several books and has over 40 published journal articles and many research awards and grants.

Abel Kinoti Meru is the dean of the School of Business and the founding chair of the Academy of International Business – Africa Chapter. He is a seasoned innovation and business incubation consultant in Africa. He holds a doctorate degree in commerce from Nelson Mandela Metropolitan University, South Africa, as well as an MBA (marketing) and bachelor of commerce (accounting) degrees. He also holds a post-graduate certificate in academic practice from York St. John University-UK and international faculty programme certificate from IESE Business School, University of Navarra-Barcelona-Spain. He also has extensive training in case writing and the use of case teaching methods from the Lagos Business School, Pan Atlantic University, Nigeria and Gordon Institute of Business Science, University of Pretoria, South Africa. He is a renowned author.

Rehema Kagendo Mugendi-Kiarie is a lecturer at the School of Business, Riara University, in Nairobi, Kenya from 2016 to date. She lectures in the fields of public relations, sales and marketing with a passion for creating sales business strategies and marketing tools. She holds an MBA degree in marketing option from the University of Nairobi (2015–2013) and a BA degree in communication and public relations studies from Daystar University (2012–2008). She has previous working experience as a relationship marketing officer at SBM Bank (formerly Chase Bank Kenya LTD), a marketing/public relations executive at Redport Building Systems LTD, and as PR/administrative officer at Nairobi Net Online LTD.

Benjamin Mwanzia Mulili is a senior lecturer at the School of Business of the Catholic University of Eastern Africa. His research interests are in strategic marketing, customer care, tourism and sports marketing, as well as green marketing. He holds a DBA degree from Southern Cross University in Australia and an MBA as well as a BCom degree from the University of Nairobi in Kenya.

Justus M. Munyoki is a professor of marketing at the University of Nairobi, Kenya. He has over 15 years of postgraduate teaching, research and consultancy experience, and has successfully supervised ten PhD students and several master's level students. Prof Munyoki has attended and presented papers in numerous local as well as international conferences. He has authored over 30 articles in peer-reviewed journals, and is the author of *Social Science Research: A Handbook* and *Marketing Management: Theory and Practice.* His current interests are in the area of creativity and innovations management, marketing in the developing countries and university-industry linkages.

Thomas Katua Ngui holds a PhD in human resource management and has 20 years of teaching experience. Currently he is a senior lecturer and the director of research and innovations development at The Management University of Africa, Kenya, and a peer reviewer at the Commission for University Education, Kenya. He has previously served as deputy head of department, head of department, and acting director of the Graduate Business School at the Catholic University of Eastern Africa. He has successfully supervised many post-graduate students and is an external examiner at Machakos University and University of Kigali, Rwanda. He has previously taught at SEKU, JKUAT, KIM and CUEA. Additionally, he is a consultant and has published widely. He is a member of the Board of Machakos Municipality and a former director at Machakos Water and Sewerage Company Limited. Dr Ngui is a full member of the Institute of Human Resource Management, Kenya, and the Kenya Institute of Management. He is also a resource person with the Kenya National Qualifications Authority (KNQA).

Ebenezer G. A. Nikoi is a health and migration geographer at the University of Ghana. His research focuses on the geographies of malnutrition, as well as the dynamics of migration, security and development, and the implications of these for socioeconomic development in Africa. He is involved in the MADE West Africa Project funded by the European Union, and the MOOP Project funded by UKAID. Additionally, he is a member of the Ecohealth Network, which is a partnership between the University of Ghana and the University of Salford in the UK.

Michael Boadi Nyamekye (PhD) is a lecturer at the University of Professional Studies, Accra, Ghana. The focus of his research is in the area of innovation, non-profit marketing, service marketing and strategy. His email address is dr.bnmichael@yahoo.com.

Abolaji Adewale Obileye is a scholar currently teaching at the Department of Criminology, Caleb University, Lagos, Nigeria. He is also a doctoral student at Olabisi Onabanjo University where he obtained his master of science degree in sociology. His first degree, BSc (Ed) sociology was obtained from Tai Solarin University of Education, Ogun State, Nigeria. Due to his academic experience, he has sustained research interest in the field of entrepreneurship, sociology and criminology. This experience has led to numerous publications in the form of articles (academic/non-academic), book chapters and books.

Abdullah Promise Opute is a researcher and freelance academic and management consultant. He supervises, mentors, tutors and supports (analysis – SPSS, SEM and qualitative analysis including grounded theory analysis) students towards successful completion of their PhD researches. He also supports organisations with technical advice in several management streams. He is an examiner in several management fields at UK and African universities. He had a 'Best Paper' Award at the Academy of Marketing-Conference in 2007. His research interests include interfunctional integration, team-working, HRM, relationship management, cross-cultural management, conflict management, consumer behaviour, service management, entrepreneurship and SMEs, strategic management accounting, etc.

Olutayo Otubanjo is a senior lecturer in marketing at the Lagos Business School. He was a visiting scholar at Warwick Business School, University of Warwick (UK) and was in a similar capacity at the Spears School of Business, Oklahoma State University, USA. He holds a PhD in marketing with an emphasis on corporate identity. Otubanjo attended the University of Hull (UK) and Brunel University, London. His research interests sit at the interface between social constructionism and the elements of corporate marketing, including corporate branding, corporate identity, corporate reputation, corporate communications and corporate image.

Kenneth E. Parku is a lecturer with experience and skills in research. He works with Wisconsin International University College, Ghana. Kenneth holds a bachelor's degree and a master of philosophy in human resource management from the Wisconsin International University College and the University of Ghana, respectively. His research interests are in labour relations and public sector human resource management. Kenneth has collaborated actively with researchers in other disciplines such as public administration.

Chapter 1

Introduction to Customer Service Management in Africa: A Strategic and Operational Perspective

Robert Ebo Hinson, Ogechi Adeola, Terri R. Lituchy
and Abednego Feehi Okoe Amartey

Contents

Introduction

Customer Service Management in Africa: A Strategic and Operational Perspective is a new book that discusses all the crucial issues to consider in building customer-driven organisations. The book seeks to examine the concepts, roles and practices of customer service management and addresses critical questions such as what addresses means today, how organisations should position themselves to create value for customers and stakeholders, and how individuals representing organisations should project themselves to align with the service delivery promises made by their organisations.

Organisations sometimes erroneously operate on the notion that customers depend on them, when in reality, the reverse is true. Delighted customers are the reason any organisation stays in business. Delighted customers lead to repeat business, give positive word-of-mouth recommendations and make organisations profitable. Unless organisations also have engaged, empowered and energised 'internal customers' – employees – the achievement of external customer delight will remain a mirage.

Customer service management is one of the key pillars of today's business environment. Businesses operating in sub-Saharan Africa and other frontier markets have begun to embrace the concept of customer service management, with many incorporating the notion into their mission statements (Verhoef et al., 2009). For example, the Dangote Group states that their mission is to 'touch the lives of people by providing their basic needs'. MTN states that their purpose is to 'make our customers' lives a whole lot BRIGHTER', while Shoprite's mission is to be the consumers' 'preferred shopping destination' by retailing low-price products in an environment conducive to shopping.

Customer service management in Africa is dynamic, with companies transitioning from a transactional to a more strategic view of the customer. Customers have evolved and transformed from 'passive audiences' to 'active players' (Prahalad & Ramaswamy, 2000). Consequently, businesses are moving away from 'the old industry model that sees value as created from goods and services to a new model where value is created by experiences' (Prahalad, 2004, p. 172). Today, customers engage in dialogue with businesses and customer experience is factored into service design and service delivery for enhanced value creation (Altinay & Poudel, 2016; Melvin, 2016; Urban, 2016). This dialogue is an interactive process of learning together (Ballantyne, 2004), as it helps organisations understand the customer's or consumer's point of view, thereby improving customer experience.

Book Thematic Areas

Given the increasing recognition of the importance of value creation to customers, this comprehensive and well-timed book aims to be an essential reference on appropriate strategies for customer service management. The book highlights an organisation's customer service systems, strategies, skills and style, amongst others, as potential enablers of value creation.

The book discusses the management and delivery of customer service under seven broad themes.

Theme A: Customer Service as Shared Value

Part A discusses three topics, namely, Who is a customer?; defining a customer-driven organisation; and ethical customer service. In Chapter 2, Ayentimi opens up the book with some thought-provoking arguments on who a customer is. The chapter extends the notion of customers to include employees as a very important component of customer service management. It also discusses the scope and application of strategic customer service principles aimed at building and sustaining effective customer service systems. Ayentimi further explores the utilisation of customer service delivery systems as well the crucial role marketing research plays in the development of customer insights required to decentralise and implement customer service management programmes. The chapter lastly makes recommendations for organisations in sub-Saharan Africa (SSA). Mulili, in Chapter 3, writes on defining a customer-driven organisation by exploring how a strong customer service orientation can be developed in organisations the world over. It further identifies the main characteristics of customer-driven firms as well as the advantages and disadvantages of being customer-driven. The chapter finally provides some recommendations for African businesses on how being customer-driven can be beneficial to them. Kiraka, in Chapter 4 writes on ethical customer service, and this chapter discusses what ethics is in the context of customer service, the codes of customer service ethics in the African context, ethical dilemmas and the role of management in promoting and maintaining ethical customer service practices in Africa. Kiraka concludes in this chapter by arguing that African ethics and morality is indeed the bedrock of ethical customer service.

Theme B: Customer Service Strategy

This section of the book addresses two topics. Achi and Otubanjo explored an institutional economics-led model of customer service strategy in Chapter 5. They argue that there is no holistic model that takes cognisance of the role of environmental factors in the development of customer service strategy. Hence, the authors developed an institutional economics-led framework for customer strategy that encompasses the impact of external and internal environmental factors for a successful customer strategy. Chapter 6 by Kimani focuses on barriers to implementing customer service strategy. The chapter discusses the benefits of implementing customer service strategy, as well as approaches for implementing a successful customer service strategy. The author further argues that different approaches and tools can be used for successful implementation, such as the define, measure, analyse, improve and control (DMAIC) cycle. The barriers to implementation of customer service strategy, according to the author, may be related to structure, technology, policy, people, knowledge management and resources. Various strategies to overcome these identified barriers are also provided in the chapter.

Theme C: Customer Service Systems

This part of the book discusses customer service systems under three chapters. In Chapter 7, Katuse explores various customer service systems as well as their components. Discussions in the chapter include service charters, service blueprints, standard operating procedures and service level. Katuse further advocates that customer service systems should be linked to the specific core business of the organisation and its stakeholders. Adeola, Ehira and Ibelegbu write on the application of digital technology and social media to enhance customer service experience in Chapter 8. This chapter explores the role of emerging technologies such as artificial intelligence, chatbots, mixed-reality technologies and social media channels as key drivers to increase the value of customer experience in the twenty-first century. Strategies for evaluating customer experience are discussed, and they include social listening, reputation management and deep customer insight via Internet of Things (IoT). The authors explored various digital and mobile technologies prevalent in Africa. They further advocate that for a seamless and effective customer service experience journey, it is highly pertinent for organisations to understand the best medium to reach their audience in relation to the cultural generation to which they belong. In Chapter 9, Meru, Ciambotti, Ebong, Kinoti and Mugendi-Kiarie discuss technology and social media in customer service. The chapter presents evidence of how technology is changing the practices and strategies of customer service, particularly in Africa. The authors argue that it is important for businesses to recognise the disruptions of social media and adapt to social media dynamics.

Theme D: Customer Service Style

This part of the book focuses on behavioural styles and observable tendencies associated with customer service processes relative to varying sociocultural environments. Chapter 10 by Munyoki explored innovation and customer service. The author argues that the definition, scope and nature of what constitutes innovation may vary from one context to another. However, in all cases, innovations should aim at enhancing customer service. Consequently, innovation should not be considered as coincidental; rather, it must be a deliberate act by organisations. Munyoki further argues that innovation, in this case, requires a well-structured approach to continuously search for customers' changing requirements and experiences, which will yield innovative ways of serving customers better. Effectively, the author writes to convince readers that innovation is about taking customer service to a higher level of satisfaction. Following this, Kiraka sheds light on entrepreneurial customer service in Chapter 11. The chapter argues that entrepreneurial customer service implies new, exciting and innovative ways of serving the customer such that value is created in a responsive and friendly manner. The author presents two Kenyan cases of the public sector citizens' service centres and the private firm Safaricom's M-Pesa innovation, to effectively dissect the meaning and practice of innovative customer service. Seven sources of customer service innovation are discussed in this chapter. Nine stages of developing an innovative customer service experience are also presented ranging from idea generation, idea screening, concept development and testing, market strategy development, business analysis and service development amongst others. The chapter further outlines the managerial and practical implications for innovative customer service.

Going forward, Chapter 12 by Chao explores leadership and customer service with a major focus on how to improve leadership in order to achieve quality customer service in organisations, particularly in the context of Africa. The author argues that customer service cannot thrive without proper organisational structure and management. Therefore, the chapter postulates that most of the barriers to organisational performance can be properly addressed when proper design, implementation, control and consistent improvement in customer service delivery are put in place. This chapter specifically explores the barriers to quality service, the role of leadership in delivering excellent customer service, attaining holistic service quality and strategic leadership frameworks for delivering exceptional customer service both in public and private sectors. Additionally, Opute discusses teamwork and customer service in Chapter 13. As a result of the research gap in understanding how to operationalise customer service to maximise its benefits for organisations, the author advocates that effective teamwork in service management organisations is very key to attaining success and effective customer service. The chapter highlights the importance of optimum symbiotic interrelation in teams, thereby emphasising the core attributes of effective teamwork to include information sharing, cohesion and a sense of belonging amongst others. Opute further stresses the importance of managing team conflicts to make organisations exhibit harmonious working relationships that would enhance excellent customer service and boost organisational performance. Lastly in this section of the book, Mulili writes on customer service training in Chapter 14 wherein he emphasises that customer service training aids employees to unswervingly deliver excellent services to both internal and external customers. Based on extant literature reviews, the author discusses the components of customer service training to include product and service knowledge, knowledge of competitors' products and services, customer service skills, communication and human relation skills, emotional intelligence, digital capabilities, and handling customer complaints and conflicts. This chapter further highlights the benefits of customer service training to both the employees and the organisation at large. Also, the author briefly provided insights on how to develop a customer service training programme to include at least five steps, namely, conducting training needs analysis, establishing training objectives, selecting training methods, conducting the training, and evaluating the training programme. The chapter finally provides practical implications for service organisations in Africa.

Theme E: Customer Service Culture

This part of the book contains three chapters. Chapter 15 by Anning-Dorson, Christian, and Nyamekye discusses the relationship between organisational culture and customer service delivery. The authors propose that a right blend of excellent customer service delivery and organisational culture is key to gaining a competitive edge and creating value in both profit and not-for-profit organisations. Hence, the chapter argues that it is impossible for organisations without the right customer-focussed culture to deliver excellent customer service. The authors identify the challenges in the business environment that make it difficult to build a service-oriented culture. Consequently, organisations must take into cognisance the major factors to develop excellent customer service in line with their culture, which includes having knowledge and understanding of their target market in terms of their expectations from the overall customer experience, the strengths and weaknesses of the organisation, and the external forces that compete for resources. Anning-Dorson et al. conclude by stating that organisations must have exceptional and perceptible values that do not only benefit them but are also convenient for their customers in order to enjoy growth. Going further in Chapter 16, Adeola, Adisa and Obileye discuss customer service with reference to national culture. Situating it in Nigeria, the authors explored the influence of culture on the success of customer service delivery. Applying the five Hofstede's metrics of culture (power distance, uncertainty avoidance, individualism vs. collectivism, short-term orientation vs. long-term orientation and masculinity vs. femininity) with other cultural factors like religion, language, family, hierarchy, etiquette and customs, the authors discuss how businesses adopt a customer-oriented service delivery.

In Chapter 17, Ngui explicates the importance of reward and recognition systems in customer service organisations within the African context. Since nowadays customers are more knowledgeable and informed and, therefore, seek value for their money, the author emphasises the need for organisations to develop customer attraction and retention strategies to enable them to retain their customers, staff and suppliers. The chapter highlights the need for organisations to reward and recognise staff for outstanding performance, customers for their loyalty to the organisation's products/services, and suppliers for timely delivery of quality goods and services to the organisation. Also, Ngui discusses four theories of reward and its application to service organisations. These include Maslow's hierarchy of needs theory, Herzberg's two-factor theory, McGregor's Theory X and Y, and Adams' Equity theory. The components of a reward system, reward programs, as well as benefits of employee recognition are also discussed in this chapter. Relatedly, Ideh, in Chapter 18 empirically investigates the relationship between reward systems and customer service delivery among small and medium enterprises within the African context. Based on the Expectancy Theory utilised, the author finds that there exists a significant relationship between the rewards system and the quality of service delivery among SMEs. Ideh concludes in this chapter that excellent customer service delivery can be attained among SMEs in Africa if certain things are put in place in the reward and recognition systems for service employees. These include making the reward system fair and equitable, creating harmony between organisational goals and the reward system adopted, and shifting focus from external factors that hinder performance to internal factors that will help boost performance.

Theme F: Customer Service Skills

Chapters 19 through 22 explore successful execution of a customer service strategy based on the quality of customer service personnel. These chapters analyse training needs and customer service audit processes and define effective traits of successful customer service champions. Chapter 19 discusses the components of emotional intelligence as well as its implications in service organisations. Lamptey and Parku advocate in this chapter that the business sector is mainly of the view that customer service management is greatly influenced by emotional intelligence. This chapter further provides an understanding of the concept of emotional intelligence by discussing some theories and models of emotional intelligence, which include the Ability model, Mixed model and Trait model. The authors discuss the relationship between emotional intelligence and customer service, establishing that when organisations train their employees to develop their emotional intelligence, customers will become delighted; hence, repatronage, customer loyalty and organisational profit can be achieved. Similarly, Halm, in Chapter 20 expatiates on the 20 traits of customer service champions, using a wider scope of excellent customer service to distinguish individuals referred to as customer service champions from others. The author posits in this chapter that although customer service champions possess the traits of a leader, their leadership manifests in providing excellent customer service. The case of Walt Disney is used in this chapter as the ideal model of a customer service champion, with the author arguing that customer service champions are made and not born. Halm discusses the top 20 traits of customer service champions under four categories, namely, human (people) skills, situational awareness skills, technical skills and conceptual skills.

In Chapter 21, Halm goes further to discuss the importance of professional grooming in a service organisation with the assertion that professional grooming is a very crucial non-verbal mode of interpersonal communication in the work environment, which to a greater extent, communicates a perception about the individual. The author discusses key aspects of personal grooming for the customer service personnel, which include the hair, face, facial hair, skin, fingers and nails, oral health, clothing, footwear, exercise and dieting, amongst others. In addition, the chapter brings into limelight the cultural and religious dimensions of professional grooming, particularly within the African context. The chapter concludes by asserting the need for organisations to position the appropriate systems and structures that will ensure that service personnel, in particular, adhere to the underlining professional grooming guides. This is because the customer's decision to keep doing business with an organisation is also dependent on the appearance of its employees. Lastly, in this part of the book, Halm explicates the importance of good communication to the survival of an organisation with regard to presentation skills, in Chapter 22. The chapter discusses types of presentations, the benefits of acquiring presentation skills, and qualities of an effective presentation. Subsequently, the three phases of presentation are explained, namely, the pre-presentation phase, the in-presentation phase and the post-presentation phase. Halm further outlines the basic steps to be taken when preparing for each phase. The author also displays in this chapter how a presenter can effectively handle objections, and questions and answers sessions during or after the presentation. This chapter concludes by stating the importance of initially understanding the audience of a presentation, ensuring proper preparation by taking adequate time to rehearse the presentation and taking cognisance of cultural nuances in order to prevent having issues with any member of the audience.

Theme G: Customer Experience – Advancing Customer Service in Africa

This is the last part of the book, and it presents the final chapter on advancing the potential of the service sector in Africa through customer experience. Arthur, Nikoi and Benagr clearly discuss this focus in Chapter 23 from a conceptual perspective. The authors utilise the concept of the experience economy as a framework to argue that service-driven activities can increase customer loyalty, particularly within the context of Africa. The chapter further highlights how organisations can make good use of the increasing affluence in Africa to enhance customer experience. Strategies for enhancing customer experience in selected service sectors in Africa based on the four realms of experience are also discussed in this chapter.

Conclusion

This book presents significant insights into customer service management by applying the conceptual fields of culture, relationship management, value co-creation, innovation management, human capital management, emotional intelligence, organisational theories, leadership, systems thinking and service quality models. The book seeks to examine the concepts, roles and practices of customer service management in Africa by discussing the new definition of customer service management, explicating how organisations must position themselves to create value for customers and stakeholders, and how individuals representing organisations should project themselves to align with the customer delivery promises made by their organisations. Overall, this book will serve as a reference resource to customer service organisations in Africa.

References

Altinay U., & Poudel, S. (Eds.). (2016). *Enhancing Customer Experience in the Service Industry: A Global Perspective*. Newcastle, UK: Cambridge Scholars Publishing.

Ballantyne, D. (2004). Dialogue and its role in the development of relationship specific knowledge. *Journal of Business and Industrial Marketing, 19*(2), 114–123.

Melvin, J. (2016). Customer value facilitation: The service experience within a heritage tourism context. In U. Altinay & S. Poudel. (Eds.). *Enhancing Customer Experience in the Service Industry: A Global Perspective* (pp. 8–24). Newcastle, UK: Cambridge Scholars Publishing.

Prahalad, C. K. (2004). The co-creation of value: Invited commentary. *Journal of Marketing, 68*(1), 23.

Prahalad, C. K., & Ramaswamy, V. (2000). Co-opting customer competence. *Harvard Business Review, 78*(1), 79–90.

Urban, W. (2016). Emergent service quality during co-creation: The service provider's view. In U. Altinay & S. Poudel. (Eds.). *Enhancing Customer Experience in the Service Industry: A Global Perspective* (pp. 25–45). Newcastle, UK: Cambridge Scholars Publishing.

Verhoef, P. C., Lemon, K. N., Parasuraman, A., Roggeveen, A., Tsiros, M., & Schlesinger, L. A. (2009). Customer experience creation: Determinants, dynamics and management strategies. *Journal of Retailing, 85*(1), 31–41.

Theme C: Customer Experience – Advancing Customer Service in Africa

Conclusion

References

THEME A: CUSTOMER SERVICE AS SHARED VALUE

Chapter 2

Who Is a Customer?

Desmond Tutu Ayentimi

Contents

Introduction

Over the last decade, organisations large and small are now more than ever before operating in an environment that is driven by customer service, quality, speed to market, productivity and technology utilisation (Schermerhorn et al., 2016). Many organisations are overwhelmed as they make efforts to thrive in an environment of rapid changes in technology and persistent globalisation of business activities and markets, coupled with intense competition and customer complexities, that is, customers' relentlessness in their demand for product and service quality. The development of wide-ranging technological platforms (e.g. social media platforms) resulting in customer-to-customer interactions is increasing business complexity, which means that businesses need to create and manage customer experience and expectations (Opute, 2017). While organisations across the sub-Saharan African region might approach the demanding challenges of globalisation, technology and customer demands differently, the outcome must be the same. Each approach should be centred on moving goods and services into the hands of customers or clients in ways that create customer loyalty and for both short- and long-term profitability for the organisation. Customers just like you and several others are putting intense pressure on organisations for high-quality products, low-priced products and on-time product and service delivery. Primarily, the issue of quality products and services, low prices and on-time delivery continue to drive customer service management and forms the main concerns of customers' stories that organisations may encounter, particularly in sub-Saharan Africa. In recent times, there is a general agreement that the most frequent experience of customers across the sub-Saharan Africa region is the dissatisfaction with products or service providers, from the small corner convenience store to the large multinational enterprise as well as in public sector organisations. These customer experiences might include, but are not limited to, failure to cancel direct debits, billing errors, poor information provision and failure to fulfil or cancel transaction requests.

There were probably many times in your experience as a customer that you wondered why managers and business organisations do not get this message. Consider, for example, the case of a customer in some parts of sub-Saharan Africa, after arriving at an office to complain about a company's poor services, the customer is made to sit on a bench for two hours waiting to see a manager. This is a frequent occurrence in many public-sector organisations and some private-sector businesses and institutions across Africa. Indeed, gross inefficiency, lack of punctuality, failure to apply oneself diligently to statutory duties and incivility to customers are vices characteristic of some African employees. The occurrences of missing vouchers and files that later surface after tips are offered often occur in public offices. Reluctance to discharge official duties for flimsy excuses characterises many public and, to a lesser extent, private-sector organisations, and stealing of official time and facilities for the pursuit of private ends permeates the hierarchy of employees (see Abudu, 1986, p. 27).

In one way or the other, all organisations in sub-Saharan Africa, both large and small, must learn to master the challenges of customer service management as they transform inputs or resources into finished products and services for customers and clients. While it is common for organisations across the sub-Saharan Africa region to use productivity as the key benchmark for the measurement of efficiency in both the services and manufacturing sectors, the target for the measurement of effectiveness should be driven by 'customer value creation' (Hinson, 2017). In this regard, the outcome of a manufacturing product or service delivered should be worth more to the customer compared to the resources and effort invested in its production. For example, within a financial service-based organisation, customer value is created when an employee, such as an investment advisor, provides their clients with investment advice that leads to profitable investment transactions in the portfolio of stocks. Within this context, given the growing recognition of the significance of value creation to customers, understanding who our customers are contributes immensely to exploring effective and efficient ways of creating value to customers and improving customer experience within the wider customer service management framework. This chapter specifically focuses on 'who is a customer?' Moreover, how that understanding of who our customers are could feed into the new conceptualisation of customer service management in sub-Saharan Africa. The chapter concludes with a discussion of how organisations in sub-Saharan Africa can draw from human resource management practices (HRM) and tailor it to fit strategically with customer value creation, and by extension, customer service management. The rest of the chapters focus on the scope and application of strategic customer service principles designed to build and sustain effective customer service systems. The chapters also explore the utilisation of customer service delivery systems and the importance of marketing research to the development of customer insights needed to decentralise and implement customer service management programmes effectively for value creation.

Who Is a Customer?

In business organisations, the word 'customer' can be used interchangeably with 'client', 'purchaser', 'buyer' and 'consumer'. Whilst 'consumers' are generally referred to as the end-user of a service or a product, 'customers' are defined by their contracting for services or by their purchase of products or goods. In this sense, a 'customer' may be termed the end consumer of a product or service. This categorisation potentially differentiates true customers from vendors and resellers, who usually make purchases for the purpose of selling. In all perspectives, a customer denotes an individual or a business that purchases the goods or services produced by a business (Hinson, 2017). Fundamentally, businesses all over the world repeatedly follow the adage 'the customer is a king' or 'the customer is always right' with the notion that happy or satisfied customers are expected to continue buying goods and services from business enterprises that meet their expectations and needs. In recent times, we are witnessing business enterprises meticulously monitoring their relationships with customers and regularly soliciting feedback to learn whether existing services or products should be maintained or adjusted, or new products or services should be created to enhance the customer experience.

Practically everybody at a particular point in time buys products or services from business enterprises, and so almost everybody at least occasionally acts as a customer or a client. The centrality of every business enterprise sustenance and survival is its customers. Within the marketing domain, the customer is rooted in every dimension of the concept of marketing. The notion of marketing is built on the basic underlying assumption that customers are the central focus of a business purpose and survival. The literature highlights product innovation, customer service, speed to market, manufacturing flexibility and product or service quality as potential drivers of competitive advantage (Johansson et al., 2019; Subramanian et al., 2019). Many business enterprises have begun to exploit various opportunities by recognising the need to have systematic processes to manage customer expectations and needs to gain and maintain competitiveness (Anning-Dorson et al., 2018). This led to the conceptualisation of customer relationship management (CRM), which is a fairly new concept design to comprehensively or systematically facilitate organisation-wide customer service management (Khodakarami & Chan, 2014). Today, it is not sufficient for an organisation to simply aim for business survival; it is actually a requirement to have customer service management through improved staff training and development, benchmarking and improvement in work processes [total quality management (TQM)] to strengthen customer value creation. Since the conceptualisation of the notion of value maximisation in the field of economics, marketing researchers have consistently turned their attention to the core capabilities of the business enterprise to develop and maintain good customer relationships (Boulding et al., 2005).

Internal and External Customers

Marketers have, over the years, starved internal customers by embracing the traditional notion of customers as the buyers of business products and services and a driver of business success (Mudie, 2003). The general literature addresses two main categories of customers, namely internal customers and external customers. In the past, the notion of a customer was generally lessened to the external public, who are justified as the principal source of revenue (Hinson, 2017). Internal customers represent individual employees and groups who use or otherwise depend on one another's work in order to do their own jobs well, whereas external customers constitute those customers who purchase products and services and remain the purpose for business's existence (Schermerhorn et al., 2016; Hinson, 2017). Internal customers are the face of every organisation, and they constantly interact with external customers by demonstrating enthusiasm and integrity. A favourable internal customer experience within an organisation can spill over to positive attitudes to enhancing external customer experience and value creation. A more engaged and friendly staff with satisfying

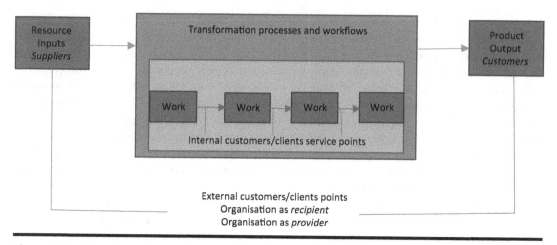

Figure 2.1 The importance of external and internal customers. (From Schermerhorn, J. R. et al., *Management: Asia–Pacific Edition,* 6th ed., John Wiley & Sons, Australia, 2016.)

workplace experiences produce high-quality products and put additional effort into improving external customers' experience (Verhoef et al., 2009). On the one hand, there is no reason for being in business without external customers. Equally, no business enterprise can survive without revenue and by extension its external customers. External customers are the reason for the development of new products or the adjustments of existing products with the ultimate aim of satisfying customers' needs and preferences.

Figure 2.1 expands the open-systems view of business organisations to depict the complex internal operations of organisations, as well as its interdependence with the external environment. In this figure, the organisation's external customers utilise the services provided or purchase the goods produced. They may be industrial customers – other firms that buy a company's products for use in their own operations – or they may be retail customers or clients who purchase or use the goods and services directly (Schermerhorn et al., 2016). Internal customers, by contrast, are found within the organisation. They are the individuals and groups who work collaboratively with members of other functional units to create that customer satisfaction outcome (Kadic-Maglajlic et al., 2018). Indeed, while both internal customers and external customers are pivotal in customer service management for business success and survival, in many business enterprises, particularly in sub-Saharan Africa, significant attention of customer service management has been centred on external customers, underestimating the importance of internal customers in the process of CRM. Eichorn (2004) notes that a successful CRM system will require an all-inclusive approach that integrates business processes, culture, information systems, organisational structure and internal leadership with the touch points of external customers.

The Neglect of Internal Customers in Customer Service Management in Africa

There are many forces other than competition, globalisation and emerging technology that are driving customer service changes in organisations (Anning-Dorson et al., 2018; Hoyer et al., 2010). Drawing from customer socialising literature, there is an emerging revolution of sorts among contemporary customers, where customer-to-customer interaction is strengthening through the arrival of social media platforms (Opute, 2017; Chan & Prendergast, 2007). The current generation of customers have consistently been unrelenting in their demand for quality products and services. Organisations that fail to listen to their customers and fail to deliver quality goods and services at reasonable prices will be left struggling in this highly competitive global business environment (Schermerhorn et al., 2016). Business enterprises have always established systems to monitor the quality of products and services delivered to their external customers as part of the commitment of providing customer satisfaction or customer value maximisation. In most business enterprises, employees act as both providers and customers to one another with the responsibility of delivering output on a regular basis (Conduit & Mavondo, 2001). Internal customer experience encompasses every aspect of a business enterprise offering, work processes, conditions of service, etc. However, only a few managers and supervisors responsible for those things have gained sustained thoughts on how their separate decisions shape the internal customer experience.

In most business enterprises in sub-Saharan Africa, when it comes to customer experience and customer value creation issues, management operations concern itself mainly on external customers. One does not need to be a rocket scientist to observe that many business enterprise managers in sub-Saharan Africa may not actively deny the significance of internal customers or employees, but many do not adequately appreciate the investment and approaches in internal customer service management that can contribute to external customer service experiences and customer value creation. Similarly, it is also noticeable that within the customer orientation and TQM literature, the focus has consistently been on the significance of external customers. The literature is generally characterised by a widespread absence of the notion that employees are internal customers and, therefore, a part of the customer service management element (Eichorn, 2004; Lukas & Maignan, 1996). There might be some notable exceptions in organisations with adages such as 'our employees are our first customers' or 'employees are our assets' (Hinson, 2017), but the reality is that such organisations may directly fail to recognise that internal customers and work processes underpin external customer service delivery, customer experience, customer value creation and customer satisfaction (Kadic-Maglajlic et al., 2018; Mohr-Jackson, 1991).

One type of business, namely the financial service sector, may know the importance and value of internal customers, especially the front desk or front-line staff's role in driving external customer service delivery, customer experience, customer value creation and customer satisfaction. For example, Gulledge (1991, p. 48) argued that 'if your front-line employees are very dissatisfied, your customers probably aren't very happy either, unless you are fortunate enough to have a few employees covering other deficiencies'. This may trigger such businesses to invest resources to develop the interpersonal and communication skills of their employees in addition to their product knowledge (Al-Zoubi & Alomari, 2017; Gulledge, 1991). This investment in internal customers by many financial institutions may have contributed to the general notion that compared to other industries and sectors, the financial sector stands tall in regard to good customer service.

Although the financial services sector can be regarded as progressive with regard to customer service performance across the world, the situation in sub-Saharan Africa is still worrying, as the financial sector still falls short of meeting many customer service quality and on-time service delivery expectations. At least in the early 1980s, some businesses across some advanced economies begun to learn new ways of delighting their external customers, leading to the acknowledgment that the needs of employees (internal customers) and work processes were pivotal in creating value for external customers, which subsequently gave rise to employee satisfaction surveys (Spinelli & Canavos, 2000; Davis, 1992). It also gave rise to internal marketing conceptualisation through the prioritisation of employees or internal customer needs and expectations (Kadic-Maglajlic et al., 2018). For example, within the tourism industry, particularly the hotel chains, employee opinion surveys have been found to represent a better indicator of external customer satisfaction compared to customer comments cards (Spinelli & Canavos, 2000; Bowen, 1996). This particular approach provides the possibility to track external customer satisfaction and experiences by examining the relationship between employees (internal customers) and their external customers. However, some business enterprises in sub-Saharan Africa do not understand why they should worry about internal customer experience and opinions. It is fascinating to note that some business enterprises collect information about their business but do not circulate the outcomes. Still others do conduct internal customer attitudes surveys annually or once every two years, but fail to make anyone accountable for failing to put the information to use (Davis, 1992; Bowen, 1996). The extent of the neglect of internal customers has not been widely documented in the literature, only a few studies (e.g. Kadic-Maglajlic et al., 2018; Al-Zoubi & Alomari, 2017; Eichorn, 2004; Bowen, 1996; Davis, 1992) have examined how internal customers can potentially impact external customers' experience and the value-addition process.

The need for business enterprises in sub-Saharan Africa to equally pay attention to internal customers is imperative as internal customers have a greater number of choices today than ever before. As part of an organisation's culture, a successful employee orientation enduringly guides the behaviours and attitudes of members of the organisation, which may implicitly or explicitly impact external customer needs and preferences. Mohr-Jackson (1991, p. 460) highlights three distinctive characteristics of positive internal customer orientation. First, a positive internal customer orientation creates additional customer value and also increases internal customer benefits. Second, internal customers can be a key source of obtaining information about external customers' needs and preferences. Third, understanding internal customers' requirements that affect external customer needs and preferences create the space to identify gaps in external customers' perceived expectations and customers' real experiences. It is essential to emphasise here that internal customer needs should be incorporated or integrated into the value creation processes within the wider value chain management framework, which involves a sequence of interdependent work processes and activities within an organisation through which value is conveyed to the external customers (Eraqi, 2006; Kadic-Maglajlic et al., 2018).

Broadening the Understanding of Customers: The Added Focus of HRM in Customer Value Creation and Satisfaction

It is important to broaden the understanding of the concept of customers so as to acknowledge the relationship and similarities between internal and external customers' needs, wants and preferences. It might sound difficult for managers and business practitioners in sub-Saharan Africa to broaden their understanding of who their customers are, particularly the inclusion of internal customers when developing and maintaining strong CRM systems. Human capital management and, by extension, market-driven HRM practices underpin internal customer service management (Meijerink & Bondarouk, 2018). It is interesting to note that the emergence of HRM has almost exclusively centred on performance against internally-set standards that was in adherence to the first industrial revolution-oriented model (Bowen, 1996; Schneider, 1994).

Importantly, the benchmark for evaluating HRM practice effectiveness consequently was subject to internally defined employee performance criteria. For example, the number of products sold, or services delivered by an employee was the basis of individual employee performance (Bowen, 1996). The HRM department in many business enterprises was operating as a provider of HR services and failed to consider the users (employees) of its services in a market context. Most importantly, HRM practices were never validated against externally-defined criteria, such as external customer value maximisation, customers' experience and customers' opinions of quality products and services. However, in recent times, we are witnessing several factors that are challenging the inward-looking focus of the first industrial revolution-oriented HRM model (Bowen, 1996). One of such factors is the TQM movement, which emerged in the early 1900s (Rahman, 2004). Even though the evolution of the concept of TQM in the 1940s was built on 'inspect for quality' after production (Dahlgaard-Park, 1999), the new concept of TQM is customer-driven, building quality into the production or service delivery processes (Dahlgaard-Park et al., 2018). The contemporary TQM approaches insist that total quality commitment applies to everyone in an organisation and throughout the value chain – 'from resource acquisition and supply chain management, through production and into the distribution of finished goods and services, and ultimately to customer relationship management' (Schermerhorn et al., 2016). Its principles include the all-encompassing objective that all organisational practices should help satisfy external customers, and organisational units must focus on satisfying their internal customers (Owusu & Duah, 2018; Schermerhorn et al., 2016). Within a contemporary TQM framework, employee fulfilment, which denotes several factors including training and career development opportunities, teamwork, performance evaluation and motivation (Eichorn, 2004), are important prerequisites in nurturing TQM commitment.

The steady growth of the services sector over the last three decades in most African economies has further challenged the inward-looking focus of the first industrial revolution-oriented HRM model. Within the service domain, quality must be established as a real-time encounter between internal customers and external customers (Hinson, 2017; Lemon & Verhoef, 2016). Therefore, quality control in this sense is a function of the HRM unit or HR department to place the right employees in external customer contact positions for quality service delivery. The literature supports the relationship between internal customers' work attitudes and external customers' satisfaction (Söderlund, 2018; Schneider & Bowen, 1993). The relationship between internal customers and external customer satisfaction has been driven by positive internal customers' attitudes trickling over on to external customers in the service encounter. If employees are recognised as internal customers and their needs and expectations are met, just as it is necessary to meet the needs of external customers, the favourable attitudes of these satisfied internal customers, in turn, will lead to more positive encounters with external customers (Wikhamn, 2019; Bowen, 1996). For example, the empirical study by Kadic-Maglajlic et al. (2018, p. 292) 'contends that the more a salesperson is willing to engage with employees from other functional units (e.g. manufacturing, accounting, finances, and marketing) in an organisation, the more likely it is that cross-functional goal compatibility becomes a successful transfer mechanism of international marketing activities to customer satisfaction outcomes'. The HRM function in business enterprises should be able to demonstrate value addition so that results can indeed be delivered to external customers. Essentially, adding value will mean engaging HRM schemes that can attract and retain talented staff who in turn support the organisation in creating value for the external customers by providing high-quality products and services (Lengnick-Hall & Lengnick-Hall, 1999).

Moving forward, the objective of business enterprises in Africa should focus on developing a well-motivated and capable workforce through the deployment of HRM practices unique to manufacturing and or a service environment. For example, services often are somewhat intangible and often produced and consumed concurrently; and in most instances, external customers are involved in co-producing the services they consume (Hinson, 2017). Thus, creating a satisfied service worker may directly lead to more positive encounters with external customers. Within the HRM literature, factors such as: work facilitation, organisational career facilitation, organisational status/reputation and new employee socialisation strengthen a positive organisational climate and employee well-being (Wikhamn, 2019; Schneider & Bowen, 1995). Importantly, these HRM dimensions generate an environment for employee well-being that can reflect in a positive service experience for external customers. For example, there exists considerable empirical evidence of the link between employee job satisfaction and external customer satisfaction (Chand, 2010; Bowen, 1996). It is also interesting to acknowledge that the level of employee turnover can affect external customer satisfaction. In business enterprises that record a high rate of employee turnover, there may potentially be a record of low customer satisfaction. For example, a customer who frequents a store or an office for a service is likely to be unhappy any time he or she establishes a customer-client relationship with an employee only to return again, and find that the employee is not working in the store or office. This kind of incidence can contribute negatively to customer renewal intentions and customer overall satisfaction. Primarily, the internal customer spill-over effect to external customer satisfaction clearly triggers a fresh perspective for business enterprises across sub-Saharan Africa to also internalise the concept of customer service management if they want to remain competitive within the global economic space.

The concept of internalising customer service management should be drawn from the role of HRM in linking employee satisfaction with the notion of the service profit chain (Bowen, 1996; Heskett et al., 1994). The notion of the service profit chain creates a relationship between employee satisfaction and internal service quality on the one hand, and customer satisfaction and customer loyalty with profitability on the other hand (see Figure 2.2). Within this relationship, the first linkage is internal service quality, which denotes the quality of work processes, systems, job design and co-workers' relationships constituting the work environment (Scotti et al., 2007; Rogg et al., 2001). The internal service quality then extends to external customers to generate customer satisfaction and customer loyalty, with a spill-over effect of profitability. It is obvious that within the service profit chain concept, HRM plays a key role within the first link – internal service quality. The service profit chain concept significantly highlights the need for businesses across Africa to reposition customer service management around its internal customers, of which the HRM department will be a critical segment in the realignment processes. Within the current market space, HRM must exhibit more of an outside-in orientation (Bowen, 1996) by paying more attention to the intangibles it delivers in support of a market focus.

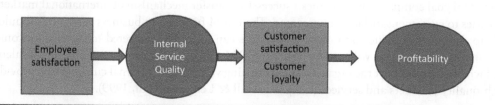

Figure 2.2 The concept of service profit chain.

Conclusion

It is now clear that when colleagues from different organisational units' place demands on co-workers, they are served appropriately as these co-workers are internal customers with wants and needs that must be fulfilled. It is also essential to stress here that just as our external customers are important, likewise are our internal customers. It is thus appropriate for business organisations in sub-Saharan Africa to internalise the notion of customers so that employees can also be part of the customer service management processes that have, over the years, targeted only external customers. In taking this new proposed approach, organisations, both for-profit and not-for-profit, have to deal with certain providers' attitudes and how work processes and co-workers' interdependence in the service delivery can be strengthened. In many instances in Africa, some inherent cultural attitudes make internal customers feel they are more superior to their external customers, particularly customers who usually have to make some form of payments. For example, gross inefficiency, stealing of official time, lack of punctuality, failure to apply oneself diligently to statutory duties and incivility to customers are vices characteristic of some African employees (Abudu, 1986). This inappropriate cultural characteristic of some internal customers (employees) within the majority of African business organisations, particularly in public-sector organisations, skews or hinders the occurrence of value-addition in the relationship between internal customers and external customers.

Internal customers may act as a hindrance as business organisations strive to achieve their marketing aims – external customer care, efficiency, greater productivity and quality. Thus, our assumptions and understanding of what it really means to be a customer remains important. The notion of customers has been explained in quite a simplistic manner, in that they are assumed to be buyers of business goods and services. However, the notion of customers must be extended to include employees as an important customer service management component. Interestingly, much of such extension in the customer service management notion may be disputed because it is considered as an altered order from the 'traditional customer' realm historically courted by marketers and business owners. Nonetheless, the reality is that the absence of internal customers in the conceptualisation of customer service management may prevent the manifestation of value-creation and value-addition to external customers. Companies in Africa might have to reconsider the concept of 'employees first, customers second'. This new conceptualisation of 'who are our customers?' needs to clarify the position of internal and external customers within the wider customer service management framework.

References

Abudu, F. (1986). Work attitudes of Africans, with special reference to Nigeria. *International Studies of Management & Organization*, *16*(2), 17–36.

Al-Zoubi, A. F., & Alomari, M. (2017). The role of internal customer in improving the quality of hotel services in Jordan: A case study of the Marriott international hotel in Amman. *International Journal of Marketing Studies*, *9*(6), 82–95.

Anning-Dorson, T., Hinson, R. E., Amidu, M., & Nyamekye, M. B. (2018). Enhancing service firm performance through customer involvement capability and innovativeness. *Management Research Review*, *41*(11), 1271–1289.

Boulding, W., Staelin, R., Ehret, M., & Johnston, W. J. (2005). A customer relationship management roadmap: What is known, potential pitfalls, and where to go. *Journal of Marketing*, *69*(4), 155–166.

Bowen, D. E. (1996). Market-focused HRM in service organizations: Satisfying internal and external customers. *Journal of Market-Focused Management*, *1*(1), 31–47.

Chan, K., & Prendergast, G. (2007). Materialism and social comparison among adolescents. *Social Behavior and Personality, 35*(2), 213–228.

Chand, M. (2010). The impact of HRM practices on service quality, customer satisfaction and performance in the Indian hotel industry. *The International Journal of Human Resource Management, 21*(4), 551–566.

Conduit, J., & Mavondo, F. T. (2001). How critical is internal customer orientation to market orientation? *Journal of Business Research, 51*(1), 11–24.

Dahlgaard-Park, S. M. (1999). The evolution patterns of quality management: Some reflections on the quality movement. *Total Quality Management, 10*(4/5), 473–480.

Dahlgaard-Park, S. M., Reyes, L., & Chen, C.-K. (2018). The evolution and convergence of total quality management and management theories. *Total Quality Management & Business Excellence, 29*(9/10), 1108–1128.

Davis, T. R. V. (1992). Satisfying internal customers: The link to external customer satisfaction. *Planning Review, 20*(1), 34–40.

Eichorn, F. L. (2004). Internal customer relationship management (IntCRM): A framework for achieving customer relationship management from the inside out. *Problems and Perspectives in Management, 2*(1), 154–177.

Eraqi, M. I. (2006). Tourism services quality (TourServQual) in Egypt: The viewpoints of external and internal customers, *Benchmarking: An International Journal, 13*(4), 469–492.

Gulledge, L. G. (1991). Satisfying the internal customer. *Bank Marketing, 23*(4), 46–48.

Heskett, J. L., Jones, T. O., Loveman, G. W., Sasser, E., & Schlesinger, L. A. (1994). Putting the service profit chain to work. *Harvard Business Review, 72*(2), 164–174.

Hinson, R. E. (2017). *Customer Service Essentials* (2nd ed.). Accra, Ghana: Sedco Publishing Limited.

Hoyer, W. D., Chandy, R., Dorotic, M., Krafft, M., & Singh, S. S. (2010). Consumer cocreation in new product development. *Journal of Service Research, 13*(3), 283–296.

Johansson, A. E., Raddats, C., & Witell, L. (2019). The role of customer knowledge development for incremental and radical service innovation in servitized manufacturers. *Journal of Business Research, 98*, 328–338.

Kadic-Maglajlic, S., Boso, N., & Micevski, M. (2018). How internal marketing drive customer satisfaction in matured and maturing European markets? *Journal of Business Research, 86*(C), 291–299.

Khodakarami, F., & Chan, Y. E. (2014). Exploring the role of customer relationship management (CRM) systems in customer knowledge creation. *Information and Management, 51*, 27–42.

Lemon, K. N., & Verhoef, P. C. (2016). Understanding customer experience throughout the customer journey. *Journal of Marketing, 80*(6), 69–96.

Lengnick-Hall, M. L., & Lengnick-Hall, C. A. (1999). Expanding customer orientation in the HR function. *Human Resource Management, 38*(3), 201–214.

Lukas, B. A. & Maignan, I. (1996). Striving for quality: The key role of internal and external customers. *Journal of Market Focused Management, 1*(2), 175–187.

Meijerink, J., & Bondarouk, T. (2018). Uncovering configurations of HRM service provider intellectual capital and worker human capital for creating high HRM service value using fsQCA. *Journal of Business Research, 82*, 31–45.

Mohr-Jackson, I. (1991). Broadening the market orientation: An added focus on internal customers. *Human Resource Management, 30*(4), 455–467.

Mudie, P. (2003). Internal customer: By design or by default. *European Journal of Marketing, 37*(9), 261–1276.

Opute, A. P. (2017). Exploring personality, identity and self-concept among young consumers. In A. Gbadamosi (Ed.). *Young Consumer Behaviour: A Research Companion*. London, UK: Routledge.

Owusu, P. A., & Duah, H. K. (2018). Evaluating total quality management as a competitive advantage tool in mobile telecommunication services in Ghana. *European Journal of Research and Reflection in Management Sciences, 6*(1), 9–22.

Rahman, S. (2004). The future of TQM is past. Can TQM be resurrected? *Total Quality Management & Business Excellence, 15*(4), 411–422.

Rogg, K. L., Schmidt, D. B., Shulla, C., & Schmitt, N. (2001). Human resource practices, organizational climate, and customer satisfaction. *Journal of Management, 27*(4), 431–449.

Schermerhorn, J. R., Davidson, P., Factor, A., Poole, D., Woods, P., Simon, A., & McBar, E. (2016). *Management: Asia–Pacific Edition* (6th ed.). Australia: John Wiley & Sons.

Schneider, B. (1994). HRM: A service perspective-toward a customer-focused HRM. *International Journal of Service Industry Management, 5*(1), 64–76.

Schneider, B., & Bowen, D. E. (1993). The service organization: Human resources management is crucial. *Organizational Dynamics, 21*(4), 39–52.

Schneider, B., & Bowen, D. E. (1995). *Winning the Service Game.* Boston, MA: Harvard Business School Press.

Scotti, D. J., Driscoll, A. E., Harmon, J., & Behson, S. J. (2007). Links among high-performance work environment, service quality, and customer satisfaction: An extension to the healthcare sector. *Journal of Healthcare Management, 52*(2), 109–124.

Söderlund, M. (2018). The proactive employee on the floor of the store and the impact on customer satisfaction. *Journal of Retailing and Consumer Services, 43*(C), 46–53.

Spinelli, M. A., & Canavos, G. C. (2000). Investigating the relationship between employee satisfaction and guest satisfaction. *Cornell Hotel and Restaurants Administration Quarterly, 41*(6), 29–33.

Subramanian, N., Gunasekaran, A., Abdulrahman, M. D., & Qiao, C. (2019). Out-in, in-out buyer quality innovation pathways for new product outcome: Empirical evidence from the Chinese consumer goods industry. *International Journal of Production Economics, 207*(C), 183–194.

Verhoef, P. C., Lemon, K. N., Parasuraman, A., Roggeveen, A., Tsiros, M., & Schlesinger, L. A. (2009). Customer experience creation: Determinants, dynamics and management strategies. *Journal of Retailing, 85*(1), 31–41.

Wikhamn, W. (2019). Innovation, sustainable HRM and customer satisfaction. *International Journal of Hospitality Management, 76*, 102–110.

Chapter 3

Defining a Customer-Driven Organisation

Benjamin Mwanzia Mulili

Contents

Introduction

This chapter examines the process involved in creating customer-driven organisations, particularly for firms operating in Africa. The chapter begins by discussing the broad concept of sustainable competitive advantage before explaining how marketing activities lead to sustainable competitive advantage. This is followed by a discussion of what constitutes customer-centricity and an identification of the key characteristics of customer-driven firms. Thereafter, the benefits that accrue from being customer-driven, as well as the associated criticisms, are discussed before providing suitable recommendations on the way forward for organisations operating in Africa.

Sustainable Competitive Advantage

Developing and maintaining a sustainable competitive advantage that leads to superior firm performance is a major concern for numerous academicians, professional consultants and business executives all over the world (Arslan & Korkmaz, 2018; Neneh, 2018; Yaacob, 2014). While every firm seeks to survive and thrive, some are more successful than others, and some even fail and exit the market (Okwo et al., 2019). In 2016, a Kenyan soft-drink manufacturer, Softa Bottling Company, closed down due to low sales. This existential threat to firms is compounded by, among others, the emergence of more demanding customers, greater global competition, increased mergers and acquisitions, rapid technological changes, and the slowdown in the growth of many economies not only in Africa but also in other parts of the world (Yunis et al., 2018). Given the dynamic nature of the environment in which contemporary firms operate, it is prudent to find ways of lowering costs and differentiating a firm's offerings. Several ideologies have been advanced in the process of addressing these concerns, and these include the total quality management (TQM) concept and business process reengineering among many others. The TQM concept emphasises external customer satisfaction through internal operational excellence, itself achieved by making continuous improvements in all operational areas (Keinan & Karugu, 2018). The aim of downsizing, restructuring and reengineering is to create lean organisations that are more efficient and effective in order to serve customers better. The appropriate ideology to use depends on the situation and the firm involved, and a firm can combine several ideologies concurrently. Further, strategies can be revised as the environment changes. Managers of firms operating in Africa should, therefore, customise the ideologies to suit their situations because ideologies crafted in a developed country may not fit fully in the context of a developing country.

A number of business ideologies, including the ones mentioned here, tend to be reactive and to concentrate on improving product and service quality by enhancing internal processes and minimising costs. However, product innovations and quality improvements are no longer sustainable approaches to achieving competitive edge. This is partially because cost-cutting measures or quality improvement approaches are generic and are accessible to a wide range of firms. On the contrary, firms have to create and sustain superior value to their customers as a way of increasing their chances of success. In other words, customer-centricity is increasingly being regarded as a way of achieving sustainable competitive advantage (Hemel & Rademakers, 2016). Superior value can be created for all stakeholders, such as the employees, shareholders and suppliers, or it can be created for the external customers only. This chapter advocates the creation of superior value for all stakeholders.

Marketing as a Source of Sustainable Competitive Advantage

Traditionally, marketing has been concerned with creating value for external customers, and this occurs when customers receive product or service offers that have more benefits (adjusted for associated risks) compared to the prices (including any costs associated with purchasing and using the products or services) that they have to pay in order to enjoy the goods or services (Ogah et al., 2018). This implies that value can be enhanced by increasing customer benefits, or reducing the associated costs, or both. Sustainability occurs when this situation is maintained for current and future customers. Superior value can then be turned into more profits by using strategies, such as premium pricing.

The provision of superior value is closely associated with firms that adopt a marketing orientation, holding that a firm's financial success is heavily depended on its ability to consistently identify, anticipate and satisfy customer requirements better than its competitors (Blythe, 2019). Marketing-oriented firms use internal and external knowledge to provide new or improved products that are needed by their clients. Although the marketing concept is challenged by other concepts, such as the societal marketing concept, its emphasis on meeting customer requirements endears it to many scholars and practitioners alike. The concept has gained an almost universal acceptance, and it is considered to constitute the heart or cornerstone of modern business (Narver & Slater, 1990). Marketing enables a firm to communicate its offers, achieve higher sales, gain a good reputation and engage in healthy competition; all these potentially lead to profitability (Mavunga, 2014). The increase in the availability of information as well as the emergence of global markets and increased competition have forced firms to adopt a customer focus. Marketing orientation is associated with better organisational performance, particularly in terms of productivity and profitability (Neneh, 2018; Yaacob, 2014). Nevertheless, this depends on environmental conditions such as the intensity of competition and the rate of market turbulence. Organisations that operate in highly competitive environments tend to be more customer-oriented than those that operate in stable environments. In order for a firm to be market-oriented, it has to emphasise the aspects of customer focus, competitor orientation, interfunctional coordination, long-term focus and profitability (Narver & Slater, 1990).

Customer-Centricity

Customers can be internal or external to the firm. Such a broad definition of customers implies that firms should develop strategies that enable them to delight both categories of customers. While external customers buy the goods and services of a firm, internal customers are the employees who produce the goods or who provide the services, and each employee can be viewed as a customer of another employee, particularly when performing cross-functional activities (Sarker & Ashrafi, 2018). Although the importance of a customer focus is acknowledged in a number of ideologies, such as the TQM concept (Keinan & Karugu, 2018), some scholars argue that customer focus should be examined on its own as opposed to being considered as a subset of another ideology (Yaacob, 2014). The marketing concept also considers customer focus to be one of its subsets, yet customer focus is a major area that deserves to be treated on its own.

Customer-oriented firms, also known as customer-driven, customer-centric or customer-focused businesses, put their customers first and design all their activities and processes around the customer. This means that they closely and patiently listen to their customers, adopt a culture that revolves around their customers, integrate customers into their businesses and provide solutions to the problems faced by customers. For instance, the Dangote Group, a business conglomerate with operational headquarters in Lagos, Nigeria, designs its products considering the needs of its customers (Adewole & Struthers, 2018). Customer-driven firms excel in after-sales service and in customer care. Therefore, customer-centric firms establish and strengthen customer relationships in the process of providing value for the customers. Safaricom PLC, which is a giant telecommunications firm based in Kenya and which is partly owned by Britain's Vodafone, is customer-driven by virtue of the wide range of products and services that it provides, such as mobile banking (M-Pesa), Internet and mobile communications. Other firms in Kenya that are highly customer-centric include East African Breweries Limited (EABL), Telkom Kenya, Bidco Africa, Co-operative Bank, Chandarana Supermarket, Old Mutual and Aga Khan University Hospital (Ngunjiri, 2018).

The customer-focus idea advocates the satisfaction of customers, but as the environment changes, there is a need to delight customers partly because the cost of acquiring new customers can be substantial and real profits arise when long-term relationships are developed and maintained with existing customers (Gichohi & Muna, 2018; Jomo & Arnolds, 2019). A variety of approaches can be used to delight customers including giving them what they expect at high standards and at low prices or giving them more than they expect in order to satisfy their latent needs. Similarly, a firm can offer unique or superior products at reduced prices, or both. Given that customers compare goods or services of one firm with those of other firms, they perceive a firm's offering to be superior when it is better than that of competitors. Customer-centric firms, therefore, seek to provide excellent customer experiences at the pre-purchase, purchase and post-purchase stages of interacting with customers. This is done by putting customers first in all their activities, listening to the customers, integrating the customers into their businesses, providing solutions to the problems faced by customers, inventing products or services that are desired by customers, providing after-sales services and building relationships with key internal and external stakeholders.

Characteristics of Customer-Focused Firms

A customer orientation is associated with superior performance, delighted customers, profitability and long-term survival (Keinan & Karugu, 2018; Yaacob, 2014). On this basis, it is important for each firm to be customer-oriented in all its activities. However, it is not clear the steps that should be taken for a firm to be customer-driven. For example, according to Day (1994), customer-driven firms have superior market-sensing and customer-linking capabilities. Such firms emphasise six main areas, namely the continuous diagnosis of current capabilities, anticipation of future needs for capabilities, bottom-up redesign of underlying processes, top-down direction and commitment, creative use of information technology and continuous monitoring of progress. Similarly, Donovan and Samler (2012) propose that customer-driven firms adopt ten steps, namely setting the service vision, gaining commitment, making the go/no go decision, segmenting the customer base, defining the success criteria, having customer feedback systems, analysing results, making the necessary changes and choosing the next area to compete in. It can be seen that there is no consensus on what constitutes a customer-driven firm. This chapter synthesises existing literature on what can be construed to be the key features of customer-centric firms. Some of these features are discussed in this section.

Develop a Customer Insight

Drucker (2012) is of the view that customers are the foundation of businesses and that they keep the businesses in existence. Marketing is simply the business seen from the customer's point of view, and a firm's existence is dependent on its ability to satisfy the needs of its customers. Customer-driven firms have listening, friendly, and empathetic service providers; these are critical for the success of the firm. Such firms also develop new offers or improve the existing ones in line with the needs, wants and priorities of their customers, meaning that they are in touch with the customers. This perspective is shared by Jomo and Arnolds (2019) who recommend that firms which meet customer needs by providing and distributing the goods and services needed by customers in the right quantity and in the right places have higher chances of success. Inks et al. (2019) refer to this as solution selling as opposed to selling goods and services. Customer needs and wants are ever-changing, and a firm must continuously adapt its products to the changing needs of the customers. Consequently, a firm must adopt a long-term approach in its operations so that it can continue to fit into the changing environment. This means that it should make long-term investments and continually innovate so as to meet the needs of its customers.

When a firm has adequate information about its clients, it is able to offer them great experiences at the awareness, purchasing and post-purchasing stages of interacting with them. Some of the approaches that can be used to collect customer information include having one-on-one interactions, engaging mystery shoppers and conducting focus-group discussions among many others. The aim is to collect comprehensive information about customers in order to understand their past, present and future needs as well as their wants, values, expectations and concerns. It is advisable to keep a register of all clients, capturing as much details as possible, such as their past purchases and any communication shared with them.

Customer-centric firms are passionate and believe in the customer. In fact, they seek to see the world from the customer's point of view, which is in line with the advice of Drucker (2012). On their part, contemporary customers have more information because of their exposure to multiple sources of information, such as the Internet and advertisements, and they compare products and services in real-time and across multiple devices. Such customers are more difficult to serve effectively. A firm should encourage its customers to communicate with the firm using a variety of methods such as emails, phone calls and social media among many others. Customer complaints, suggestions or even compliments should be treasured because they enable a firm to understand and to provide exactly what customers need thereby adding value to the customers.

Build Relationships Inside and Outside the Firm

Developing and maintaining suitable relationships with clients, suppliers, employees, local communities and shareholders of businesses can lead to sustainable competitive advantage. Since firms have many types of clients, it is advisable to develop relationships with the larger and more profitable ones that satisfy the propositions of the 80/20 Pareto Principle, which holds that a firm can have a small proportion of its customers (top 20% of total customers) who not only contribute most of the firm's profits (80% of the total profits), but who also cover the losses incurred in the process of dealing with the less-profitable customers (Koch, 2013). The relationship can entail communicating with the customers regularly, acknowledging their contribution to the firm's business, and generally getting to know them and their activities, such as the businesses they run. Besides, loyal and profitable customers can be rewarded by involving them in sales promotions and giving them goods or services at discounted prices. A firm should identify the areas that have the greatest impact on customers and then focus its resources on those areas. Further, external stakeholders, such as suppliers and distributors, should be involved in the process of developing products and services that match customer expectations, and relationships should also be developed with them. According to Amoako (2019), healthy relationships with key stakeholders lead to the generation of more revenues, an increase in customer loyalty and greater advocacy of the firm's products.

Top Management Commitment

A firm's top management should deeply believe in the importance of customer-centricity, which means improving all interactions with customers in a way that creates long-lasting and emotional relationships with them (Al-Kwifi et al., 2019). The top management should also ensure that everyone understands their role in creating an ideal customer experience, where customer experience refers to the cognitive, emotional, sensory, social and spiritual responses to all interactions with a firm. This implies that the top management should lead the process of developing relationships with customers by using methods such as having customer interaction policies that define what is expected of every customer interaction, meeting and spending time with internal and external customers regularly, seeking the input of customers when making decisions, investing resources in order to facilitate a better understanding of customers, or even being involved in serving external clients on a regular basis. That way, everything is done with purpose of serving and satisfying the customer.

Synergistic Functioning of Departments

The efficacy of the processes involved in producing goods or delivering services affects the level of satisfaction experienced by external customers. It is, therefore, important for all functions or departments to work together synergistically, not only for their own good, but also for the good of external customers. Each function should understand how its roles depend on those of other functions, and how all the roles interact to provide a pleasant customer experience. The top management should reward functions that contribute to the creation of value for internal and external customers (Teece, 2010). When interfunctional cooperation occurs, employees end up with a quality working environment (Osuagwu, 2019), which indicated by positive attitudes that the employees develop towards their jobs, colleagues and the firm. A quality working environment has great bearing on employee satisfaction. Besides, all the functions should collaborate to provide superior customer value (Gebauer et al., 2013). As such, there should be sharing of information, feedback and ideas that improve customer experiences. Where one function fails, the whole process can fail, and the customers can end up being dissatisfied. All the processes have to be continuously improved, meaning that value should be created at every point of the value chain (Mathu, 2019). Therefore, the process of developing a customer-driven organisation involves an entire firm, right from the trainees to the top management.

Besides, a marketer should have adequate information about competitors and their activities. Specifically, this is information that relates to competitors' short-term strengths and weaknesses as well as their long-term strategies and capabilities, and this should be done for both current and potential competitors (David, 2019). This information is also shared with other departments or sections, and it can be used to segment customers based on their purchasing behaviour and interests; it can also be used to develop marketing mixes that suit different customer groups. Information gathering and dissemination should be the function of all stakeholders, especially the employees who work for the firm in different functions. Further, the information is gathered through formal and informal means, and it should flow both vertically and horizontally within the firm.

Aside from competitors, the marketer needs information about developments in the broader environment, such as the political, economic, sociocultural and technological factors that affect operations of the firm. Every function must be made aware of the effects of environmental changes on the operations of the firm. Given that customers are exposed to these factors, the firm should offer goods and services that match the environmental expectations. This knowledge of the broader environment enables a firm to respond to changes appropriately, or even to predict future changes. Jaworski and Kohli (1993) emphasise the aspects of information gathering and sharing and organisation-wide response to the information obtained and shared.

Wise Use of Technology

The wise use of all types of technologies can lead to positive customer experiences. Given the wide variety of technologies that exist, the type used should be determined by its perceived contribution to a firm's operations, and by its ability to enhance customer value (Lee & Joshi, 2016). Kenyan-based Safaricom PLC has taken advantage of technology to run its mobile money business referred to as M-Pesa. Similarly, Jumia, a Nigerian e-commerce platform, connects customers, sellers and transporters. Information technology, especially the Internet, facilitates dialogue with clients as well as the keeping and sharing of information (Orayo et al., 2019). Further, the Internet enables customers to evaluate a wide range of products within a short time and to make informed purchase decisions. As such, firms can engage in online marketing to provide relevant information to customers and to reach a wider market for their goods and services. Besides, some firms, such as Apple Inc. and Amazon.com Inc., gain competitive advantage through technological innovation (Sobanke et al., 2014).

Align Performance Measurements with Customer Experience

A firm should not only know what constitutes favourable customer experience, but it should also develop measures to gauge the extent to which its employees and activities are able to provide the desired experience. Employees who excel at customer service should be rewarded, perhaps by being promoted or having their pay raised. Similarly, the top management should reward employees who increase customers' lifetime value by developing long-term relationships with them (Al-Kwifi et al., 2019). It is important to identify the metrics that can be used to measure the level of customer-centricity, and these include customer equity, customer satisfaction, customer advocacy and customer loyalty among many others. Johnson and Schultz (2004) recommend that customer-centric firms should include at least two or three of these metrics as performance indicators when reporting to the top management or to the boards of directors.

Develop a Culture of Customer-Orientation

According to Omesa et al. (2019), organisational culture is the pattern of shared values and beliefs that help individuals to understand how organisations function and that provide the individuals with the norms for behaviour in the organisations. A customer-focused culture should be driven by the top management and cascaded down to all levels. It can involve making changes in such areas as the existing processes, roles, procedures, structures and staffing arrangements, among many other areas (Al-Kwifi et al., 2019). Narver and Slater (1990) opine that managers who are led by the marketing culture should understand their competitors, and they should coordinate all functions to deliver superior value to customers.

A firm's corporate culture should be centred on employees and service to customers. This culture is then embodied in the firm's vision and mission statements, objectives, motto, culture, structure and strategy among other areas (Moodley, 2019). The customer-centric culture can be enhanced through training employees on the right behaviours to adopt when interacting with customers and rewarding employees who portray the needed behaviours. Nevertheless, culture is a difficult concept to build, maintain and change. To develop or modify a culture, a firm can begin by establishing a common goal that all employees have to work towards. This goal varies from firm to firm, but it can revolve around great customer experiences. Afterwards, the firm can define the desired values and beliefs, which are enforced through financial and non-financial rewards, and for which non-compliance can be punished. Besides, the firm can create icons, stories, rites and rituals that embed the culture into the firm (Larentis et al., 2019). For instance, storytelling can be used to describe how the firm's products solved a customer's problem, or how the firm emerged victorious in a difficult period due to its excellent customer service activities (Baker & Simmons, 2019). The top leadership should also establish the quality standards and service levels expected from the employees, such as being courteous, providing superior customer service and not making mistakes. When the top management defines the culture expected in the firm, it is likely that employees will rise to the challenge even when the standards set are very high. This can be followed by creating role models and reinforcing the traits and behaviours expected of those who adopt the customer-centric culture. Some of the personality traits that can be emphasised include passion, honesty, courage and curiosity among many others.

Learning and Continuous Development

Considering the fact that the environment is ever-changing, a firm should encourage continuous learning and development in order to enhance customer experiences and increase their lifetime value (Bonacchi & Perego, 2019). The continuous acquisition of information about competitors, environmental developments and other aspects enables a firm to build a knowledge base, or institutional memory, which can be translated into better financial performance. Employees can be encouraged to experiment with new ideas, even when the ideas look difficult to achieve. Costs incurred through the mistakes of employees can be absorbed by the firm as opposed to being passed to the employees involved. Managers should not punish employees who make mistakes in the process of taking risks. On the contrary, employees should be encouraged to learn from their mistakes (Dessler, 2016). This is partially explained by the fact that introducing new products is risky and can end up in failure, yet managers cannot afford to be risk-averse if they are to survive in a changing world.

Recruit Intelligent, High-Performing and Well-Motivated People

The attitude, communication skills, tolerance, empathy and good judgment of employees affect customer experiences. Further, Arslan and Korkmaz (2018) argue that the decisions made by employees can affect the level of customer satisfaction. When recruitment is done carefully, the firm ends up with employees who have a customer mindset, and these are the best for satisfying the needs of internal and external customers. In recruiting employees, top managers have to consider the extent to which their identity, personality and values match with the work they will be doing. It is easier for employees to change their skills than it is for them to change their identities, personalities and values. Furthermore, a firm's management should spend time tracking, motivating, training and recognising employees. Where new employees are unable to fit in with the customer-centric nature of a firm, they should be encouraged to leave the firm, perhaps by being given some financial incentives to leave (Hemel & Rademakers, 2016).

Develop a Service Vision or Service Personality

A customer-centric firm should define how its customer experiences differ from those of competitor firms (Bubakar et al., 2019). The firm can have a service promise, credo or customer charter that defines how the firm seeks to interact with its clients. An example would relate to the time taken before a customer is served. In the process, the firm makes certain promises which it seeks to fulfil. Ideally, the firm's goals should be realistic; otherwise, the firm will not be able to fulfil them, and the customers will be dissatisfied. Egerton University in Kenya has an elaborate service charter that explains the time taken to provide certain services, such as responding to customer complaints. Figure 3.1 summarises the main characteristics of customer-centric firms.

Figure 3.1 Characteristics of customer-centric firms. (From author.)

Benefits of Being Customer-Driven

Adopting the customer-focus ideology benefits a wide range of stakeholders that include the business, the employees and the external customers. A few of these benefits are explained in this section. Firstly, a business benefits by having a set of loyal customers (Budianto, 2019). Customer loyalty occurs when customers get what they need and when they realise that they are valued by the firm. The loyal customers benefit the firm by being involved in repeat purchasing, referring other customers to the firm, and sticking with the firm for long, because retention increases the lifetime value of a customer (Bonacchi & Perego, 2019; Mashenene et al., 2019). Attracting, satisfying and retaining customers enhances repeat business, customer loyalty and long-term expansion or profitability of a firm (Keinan & Karugu, 2018). Although satisfied customers may not necessarily buy again from the same firm, delighting customers plays a key role in shaping their future purchases, or even in making them loyal customers. Stewart (2019) associates customer loyalty with profitability increases. For non-profit organisations, customer loyalty translates into sustainability, which is the satisfaction of clients in the long-run and the ability to generate surpluses for running their operations.

Secondly, customer-focused firms tend to retain their current customers and to get new ones (Mashenene et al., 2019). Positive word-of-mouth advertising by satisfied customers, themselves also known as company *apostles* or customer advocates, can lead to the acquisition of more customers. This is important, bearing in mind that the rate of customer retention can affect the rate of a firm's growth. Retention occurs when the customers are satisfied. The financial performance of customer-focused firms is better, and this is often reflected in the increased profits, reduced costs, more firm growth and efficiency improvements (Keinan & Karugu, 2018). Further, innovation tends to be higher among customer-focused firms (Mukerjee, 2013). This is because such firms adopt long-term investment decisions and innovate in order to create superior value for their customers, and to earn more profits. A customer-centric firm gains competitive advantage by differentiating itself and its goods and services in a way that is difficult for competitors to displace (Bubakar et al., 2019). It also generates more information about the customers' buying behaviours, competitors' activities, market growth rates and other aspects of the market.

When a firm is customer-focused, the customers benefit from improved interaction experiences that lead to reduced waiting times and better satisfaction. Besides, customers are likely to get quality goods and services (Mokhtar, 2013). Employees benefit in the sense that they have improved and more productive work environments. As a result, the rate of staff retention increases (Jomo & Arnolds, 2019). Staff retention also benefits a firm since the firm does not have to spend money hiring and training replacements, or even relocating them to where they are needed. Staff turnover can lead to customer dissatisfaction and low productivity because clients take time to develop confidence in new employees. In some cases, business is lost when some accounts are not serviced properly while in other cases, employees can take clients away from a firm once they exit the firm.

Criticisms of Customer-Centricity

In spite of the numerous advantages associated with a customer-orientation, several criticisms have been levelled against firms that are customer-centric. Firstly, Hamel and Prahalad (1994) argue that customer-centric firms tend to narrowly focus most of their efforts on the needs of their current customers. In the process, they fail to anticipate threats from non-traditional sources such as from disruptive technologies. Failing to recognise the many actors that influence a firm's performance reduces the ability of customer-focused firms to maintain a sustainable competitive advantage.

Secondly, a customer-centric approach provides long-term benefits only when a firm's activities are not imitated or exceeded by its competitors. In some cases, every firm seeks to be customer-focused, meaning that a customer-focused approach on its own is not a source of sustainable competitive advantage. On the contrary, the adoption of a customer focus by all firms becomes a failure preventer as opposed to being a success guarantee. In this scenario, a firm should decide whether to invest its resources in an idea that does not necessarily lead to improved performance, especially when environmental factors, such as low levels of competition, do not favour its adoption. Further, customers may develop expectations that are difficult to fulfil, and some firms may find these demands too difficult to meet, particularly when switching costs are low. The firm must have adequate knowledge of the customers' latent needs (Day, 1994), and such a broad level of knowledge is only developed by proactive firms that integrate more issues than just a focus on customers.

Thirdly, sustainable advantage is best achieved by being able to learn and anticipate market trends faster than competitors. This is staying ahead of the pack, and sometimes involves staying ahead of the customers, such that the customers' needs are driven by the innovations of the firm. It is important to listen to customers' definitions of their needs, but proactive firms do more in order to make a difference. In any case, some customers do not always know what they need. According to Keinan and Karugu (2018), firms need to adopt both outside-in and inside-out strategies in the process of interacting with customers. The outside-in strategies rely on information from customers to discover their unserved or underserved needs while the inside-out strategies are from the firm and seek to uncover customer needs that even the customers are not aware they have.

Fourthly, the benefits of being customer-focused, such as improvements in sales and profits, customer satisfaction, success of new products and growth in market share tend to be short-term when compared with firms that are not customer-focused (Jaworski & Kohli, 1993). Fifthly, some of the customer retention strategies such as allowing customers to return goods if they are not satisfied with them can be costly to a firm and may not make economic sense, especially when the returns are fraudulent (Harris, 2010).

Challenges of Developing Customer-Centric Firms in Africa

In the process of implementing customer-centricity, firms in Africa are exposed to several challenges. A few are mentioned in this section. Firstly, the idea of customer-centricity is often misunderstood and, consequently, poorly implemented. This requires managers of African firms to understand and champion its implementation; they should also take time to explain the idea to their employees (Al-Kwifi et al., 2019). Secondly, implementing the idea may require training the employees, which also requires financial resources. This is constraining, particularly for smaller firms, such as micro and small enterprises (MSEs) whose incomes tend to be relatively lower. Thirdly, the idea also requires an investment in customer relationship management programs, and this can also be costly (Amoako, 2019). Fourthly, some African countries, such as Somalia and Sudan, are politically unstable and this limits the application of the customer-centricity idea. Fifthly, adopting a customer focus requires a change of culture in order to adopt a new way of working (Moodley, 2019). Some employees may resist this change, even when it is to their advantage.

Recommendations for Businesses Operating in Africa

The ongoing discourse has illustrated that adopting customer-orientation benefits firms all over the world. On this basis, this chapter makes a number of recommendations. Firstly, while there are a plethora of business theories, it is prudent to customise each theory in light of the circumstances prevailing in Africa. African scholars and practitioners should actively participate in developing theories that match the African context as opposed to relying on theories developed in the West. Ingenbleek (2019) argues that many models used in Africa suffer from comparative myopia because they are modelled after businesses found in North America and Western Europe, yet the circumstances prevailing in Africa differ from those of other parts of the world, at least in as far as the level of development is concerned.

Secondly, owing to globalisation, firms in Africa should be customer-focused. Such an orientation broadens the concept of a customer to include both internal and external customers, where the satisfaction of each category of customers is important for the long-term survival of the firm. Kenyan-based Safaricom PLC and DT Dobie have exemplary interactions with their internal and external customers. Thirdly, a firm's top management should take the lead in developing a customer-orientation (Al-Kwifi et al., 2019). This is a long-term approach that emphasises developing relationships with different stakeholders, maintaining a databank of all customers, building a culture that revolves around the customer, and encouraging interdepartmental cooperation. Fourthly, firms in Africa should take advantage of technology in their operations (Orayo et al., 2019). For instance, information technology (IT) should be harnessed, just like other types of technologies. Fifthly, continuous learning and development should be encouraged, thereby leading to the creation of learning organisations (Bonacchi & Perego, 2019). Further, each firm must carefully select who to employ so as to end up with intelligent, high-performing, and well-motivated employees (Arslan & Korkmaz, 2018). Besides, each firm should differentiate itself by defining the unique aspects that endear it to its customers, and that gives it a sustainable competitive advantage (Bubakar et al., 2019).

Conclusion

This chapter examined the concepts of sustainable competitive advantage and customer focus. On the basis of the discussion presented, African firms should invest in customer-centricity in order to reap its benefits that include creating loyal customers and easing the process of acquiring of new customers, improving financial performance and increasing rates of staff retention among many others. This investment involves taking steps to ensure that the firm understands its customers fully; it also includes building relationships with key stakeholders. The managers of African firms must be fully committed to adopting a customer focus, and a firm's departments must synergistically work together to create value for the customer. Given the importance of technology, customer-centricity involves the wise use of all forms of technologies. A firm's culture must be aligned to the interest of customers, and there should be continuous learning and development of all staff in order to be relevant in a changing environment. Furthermore, African firms should recruit intelligent, high-performing and well-motivated employees, and they should also develop service visions or service personalities.

References

Adewole, A., & Struthers, J. J. (2018). *Logistics and global value chains in Africa: The impact on trade and development.* Cham, Switzerland: Palgrave Macmillan.

Al-Kwifi, O. S., Frankwick, G. L., & Ahmed, Z. U. (2019). Achieving rapid internationalization of sub-Saharan African firms: Ethiopian Airlines' operations under challenging conditions. *Journal of Business Research.* https://doi.org/10.1016/j.jbusres.2019.02.027 (Accessed on 31 May 2019).

Amoako, I. O. (2019). *Trust, institutions and managing entrepreneurial relationships in Africa: An SME perspective.* Cham, Switzerland: Palgrave Macmillan.

Arslan, A., & Korkmaz, S. (2018). The impact of employee satisfaction and individual performance on corporate performance: A field study on education and health sectors. *Nile Journal of Business and Economics, 4*(9), 52–60.

Baker, N., & Simmons, J. (2019). Stories make the difference. In K. Kompella (Ed.). *Marketing wisdom* (pp. 127–138). Singapore: Springer.

Blythe, J. (2019). *Essentials of marketing* (3rd ed.). England, UK: Pearson Education.

Bonacchi, M., & Perego, P. (2019). *Customer accounting: Creating value with customer analytics.* Cham, Switzerland: Palgrave Macmillan.

Bubakar, M. B., Opusunju, M. I., & Mustapha, N. M. (2019). Service quality and competitive advantage in pan African Company Nigeria Limited. *Ilorin Journal of Human Resource Management (IJHRM), 3*(2), 111–120.

Budianto, A. (2019). Customer loyalty: Quality of service. *Journal of Management Review, 3*(1), 299–305.

David, A. M. (2019). Porter's competitive strategies influence on performance of mobile telecommunication companies in Kenya. *International Journal of Scientific Research and Management (IJSRM), 7*(2), 1014–1022.

Day, S. (1994). The capabilities of market-driven organizations. *Journal of Marketing, 58*(4), 37–52.

Dessler, G. (2016). *Human resource management.* London, UK: Pearson Higher Education.

Donovan, P., & Samler, T. (2012). *Delighting customers: How to build a customer-driven organization.* London, UK: Springer-Science.

Drucker, P. (2012). *The practice of management.* New York: Routledge.

Gebauer, H., Paiola, M., & Saccani, N. (2013). Characterizing service networks for moving from products to solutions. *Industrial Marketing Management, 42*(1), 31–46.

Gichohi, J. M., & Muna, W. (2018). Consumer protection measures and road safety in Nyeri County, Kenya. *American Journal of Public Policy and Administration, 3*(1), 39–52.

Hamel, G., & Prahalad, C. (1994). *Competing for the future.* Boston, MA: Harvard Business School Press.

Harris, L. (2010). Fraudulent consumer returns: Exploiting retailers' return policies. *European Journal of Marketing, 44*(6), 730–747.

Hemel, C., & Rademakers, M. (2016). Building customer-centric organizations: Shaping factors and barriers. *Journal of Creating Value, 2*(2), 211–230.

Ingenbleek, P. T. (2019). The endogenous African business: Why and how it is different, why it is emerging now and why it matters. *Journal of African Business, 20*(2), 195–205.

Inks, S. A., Avila, R. A., & Talbert, G. (2019). The evolution of the sales process: Relationship selling versus "the challenger sale". *Journal of Global Scholars of Management Science, 29*(1), 88–98.

Jaworski, B., & Kohli, A. (1993). Market orientation: Antecedents and consequences. *Journal of Marketing, 57*(3), 53–70.

Johnson, C., & Schultz, D. (2004). A focus on customers. *Marketing Management, 13*(5), 20–26.

Jomo, L. M., & Arnolds, C. (2019). An exploratory study on the impact of service quality on membership retention in medical schemes in South Africa. *International Journal of Scientific Research and Management, 7*(5), 1126–1138.

Keinan, A. S., & Karugu, J. (2018). Total quality management practices and performance of manufacturing firms in Kenya: Case of bamburi cement limited. *International Academic Journal of Human Resource and Business Administration, 3*(1), 81–99.

Koch, N. (2013). *The 80/20 Principle and 92 other powerful laws of nature: The science of success.* Boston, MA: Nicholas Brealey Publishing.

Larentis, F., Antonello, C. S., & Slongo, L. A. (2019). *Inter-organizational culture.* Cham, Switzerland: Palgrave MacMillan.

Lee, K., & Joshi, K. (2016). Importance of globalization in the information technology convergence era. *Journal of Global Information Technology Management, 19*(1), 1–5.

Mashenene, R. G., Msendo, A., & Msese, L. R. (2019). The influence of customer retention strategies on customer loyalty in higher education in Dodoma, Tanzania. *African Journal of Applied Research, 5*(1), 85–97.

Mathu, K. M. (2019). The information technology role in supplier-customer information-sharing in the supply chain management of South African small and medium-sized enterprises. *South African Journal of Economic and Management Sciences, 22*(1), 1–8.

Mavunga, G. (2014). Practicing customer service by trial and error: An investigation into the extent and nature of customer service training/education received by owners of small business enterprises in central Johannesburg. *Mediterranean Journal of Social Sciences, 5*(20), 1475–1485.

Mokhtar, S. (2013). The effects of customer focus on product performance. *Business Strategy Series, 14*(2/3), 67–71.

Moodley, V. R. (2019). Towards a culture of quality assurance in optometric education in sub-Saharan Africa. *African Vision and Eye Health, 78*(1), 1–8.

Mukerjee, K. (2013). Customer-oriented organization: A framework for innovation. *Journal of Business Strategy, 34*(3), 49–56.

Narver, J., & Slater, S. (1990). The effect of a market orientation on business profitability. *Journal of Marketing, 54*(4), 20–35.

Neneh, B. N. (2018). Customer orientation and SME performance: The role of networking ties. *African Journal of Economic and Management Studies, 9*(2), 178–196.

Ngunjiri, J. (2018). Kenyans name their top brands for quarter one. Nairobi, Business Daily, https://www.businessdailyafrica.com/corporate/companies/Here-are-Kenyas-most-loved-companies/4003102-4380280-wk188z/index.html (Accessed on 23 May 2019).

Ogah, A. V., Adah, G., & Osho, V. M. (2018). Marketing communications and tourism: Paradigm for sustainable development in Ekiti State, Nigeria. *Journal of Good Governance and Sustainable Development in Africa (JGGSDA), 4*(1), 80–88.

Okwo, H., Ezenwakwelu, C., Igwe, C., & Imhanrenialena, B. (2019). Firm size and age mediating the firm survival-hedging effect: Hayes' 3-Way parallel approach. *Sustainability, 11*(3), 1–17.

Omesa, J. E., Gachunga, H. G., Okibo, B. W., & Ogutu, M. (2019). Influence of organizational culture on implementation of strategic plans within the county governments of Kenya. *Journal of Strategic Management, 3*(1), 1–20.

Orayo, J., Maina, J., Wasike, J. M., & Ratanya, F. C. (2019). Customer care practices at the University of Nairobi (UON), Jomo Kenyatta Memorial Library (JKML), Kenya. *Library Management, 40*(3/4), 142–154.

Osuagwu, C. (2019). Market orientation in Nigerian insurance firms: A research agenda. *Archives of Business Research, 7*(4), 211–222.

Sarker, M. R., & Ashrafi, D. M. (2018). The relationship between internal marketing and employee job satisfaction: A study from retail shops in Bangladesh. *Journal of Business and Retail Management Research (JBRMR), 12*(3), 149–159.

Sobanke, V., Adegbite, S., Ilori, M., & Egbetokun, A. (2014). Determinants of technological capability of firms in a developing country. *Procedia Engineering, 69*, 991–1000.

Stewart, D. W. (2019). *Financial dimensions of marketing decisions.* Cham, Switzerland: Palgrave Macmillan.

Teece, D. (2010). Business models, business strategy and innovation. *Long Range Planning, 43*(2–3), 172–194.

Yaacob, Z. (2014). The direct and indirect effects of customer focus on performance in public firms. *International Journal for Quality Research, 8*(2), 265–276.

Yunis, M., Tarhini, A., & Kassar, A. (2018). The role of ICT and innovation in enhancing organizational performance: The catalysing effect of corporate entrepreneurship. *Journal of Business Research, 88*, 344–356.

Chapter 4

Ethical Customer Service

Ruth N. Kiraka

Contents

Introduction

Ethics are accepted norms of conduct that guide behaviour in society. It is both knowing and doing the right thing. Ethical customer service seeks to ensure that service providers do the right thing for customers. This chapter will explain the concept of ethics as it relates to customer service, explaining the importance of ethical customer service for business and the community. It will also discuss factors that influence ethical and unethical customer service practices and unpack the skills needed to resolve ethical dilemmas in customer service.

Using examples from various African settings, the chapter illustrates both ethical and unethical conduct, and makes recommendations for African managers on how to ensure ethical practices in their organisations. Finally, this chapter makes recommendations on how African managers can promote and maintain ethical customer service practices.

Defining Ethics

When researching on ethics, one will come across five connected words: values, principles, morals, virtues and ethics. These words seem interchangeable; however, each term builds on another as a staircase, to show how ethics develop (Waggoner, 2010). At the bottom of the staircase is personal *values*. These are determined by the individual who sets personalised ideas that guide their own behaviour. They may include honesty, social recognition, hard work, and being helpful and responsible. In the context of an organisation, they are the standards considered important or desirable. They may include professionalism, integrity, value for money and timeliness.

These sets of values are incorporated into *principles* – the second step of the staircase. Principles allow the fulfilment of values. They set conditions and qualifications that provide rules for conduct of values. To develop principles, one must, therefore, assign an action to go with each accepted value. For example, if one of an organisation's top values is *professionalism*, the principle may be 'always handle each client professionally'. The organisation determines what qualifies as 'professional' – from dress code, greeting, meeting venues, competence and so on. Once values are assigned relevant, meaningful principles that guide decision-making, the second floor has been reached (Figure 4.1).

The third step is establishing *morals*. Morals are concerned with defining what is right and wrong behaviour. Stories are often used to decipher between right and wrong, or to provide illustrations of what is acceptable or unacceptable conduct. Through a process of socialisation, people understand and appreciate what is right. Their conduct may, therefore, be guided by respect for doing the right thing, rather than obligation.

The climb to the fourth floor results in character traits established from the values, principles and morals determined previously. *Virtues* are character traits that 'incline us toward ethical conduct' (Waggoner, 2010). Virtues are always positive attributes. The opposite is vices. Even though people are likely to know the right thing to do, it does not necessarily mean they will act accordingly. Virtues are a necessary development because they help link knowing what is right and actually doing what is right. Morals, values and principles establish a set of attitudes adopted by a person, but a person's virtues are a 'commitment of the will to behave ethically' (Waggoner, 2010).

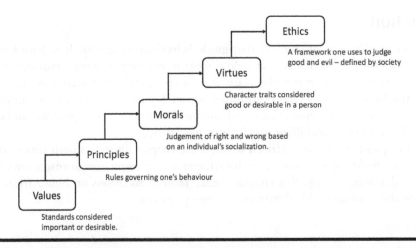

Figure 4.1   From value to ethics. (Adapted from Waggoner, J., *Ethics and Leadership: How Personal Ethics Produce Effective Leaders*, **Claremont McKenna College, Claremont, CA, 2010.)**

The final climb is a process of developing *ethical practices*. The blueprint of ethics is compiled building upon the four preceding terms and when structured well, guide a person's life and allow them to be a *good* person. The climb from level four to five is completed by combining established values, principles, morals and virtues that determine beliefs and influence actions. For individuals to have a strong ethical foundation, they must continue to use the stairs again and again until ethical practices become the norm (Waggoner, 2010).

Tullberg (2012) notes that the word 'integrity' comes from the Latin word *integer*, meaning wholeness. This wholeness is in the consistency between beliefs, words and actions. Integrity is expressed by following a personal position rather than conforming to external demands. The difference between ethics and integrity has been explained this way: an ethical person *knows* it is wrong to cheat; a person of integrity actually *does not* cheat. At integrity, there is a correspondence between knowing and doing. It is, therefore, the highest form of ethical behaviour.

Importance of Ethical Consideration in Customer Service

How then, does this debate on ethics play out in an organisation, and more specifically, when dealing with customers? Many of us may have heard of the Wells Fargo accounts fraud scandal in which the financial institution created millions of fraudulent savings and checking accounts on behalf of their clients without their consent. Clients noticed the fraud when they started to receive unsolicited credit and debit cards, as well as being charged unexpected and unexplained fees on their accounts. Obviously this is an extreme case of unethical behaviour, but if we reflect on the earlier discussion from values to ethics, it is not difficult to see where the rain started beating on Wells Fargo. Once the personal values of the leaders redefined their principles, the rules governing behaviour changed, and everything went downhill from there. In the case of Wells Fargo, the company has been fined millions of dollars, and faces additional civil and criminal lawsuits. That is the price of unethical behaviour.

Examples of everyday unethical behaviour are also common. Consider a supplier who knowingly sells a defective product, a restaurant that overcharges clients, deliberately inflating hospital bills, wrongly calibrating fuel pumps at the gas station, and the list goes on. Others are subtler and therefore harder to detect, such as a food service on a flight that has less items than stipulated, packaging that has less weight than indicated on the pack, or labelling on food items that is inaccurate and so on. The underlying driver in all these cases is that the service provider intentionally deceives the client for profit. The unfortunate reality is that these practices can go on for so long in an organisation that they are perceived to be the norm. Everyone's conscience becomes dulled to doing the right thing. Very soon, the message becomes '…but everyone is doing it…why go against the grain?' This then raises the question: What is the value of doing the right thing?

When an employee in an organisation is faced with these unethical practices, he or she may feel 'torn' between two or more options and be unable to make a decision on what to do. A person is faced with three options when they need to make a decision: to simply ignore the issue ('bury head in the sand'), to sit and complain about the issue (blame game), or to analyse the issue and take action. Ignoring an issue is likely to be the decision if the unethical practice is known to the leadership of the organisation and has been going on for a long time. Ethics promotes analysing and taking action because it is most beneficial to the individual and the greater good. An ethical person will not be '*torn*' as ethics encourages the pursuit of internal good and protects people from behaviours based on external good, such as fame, money or power. The reality of making ethical decisions is that they do not need to be defended.

From a business or organisational point of view, ethical conduct becomes important because:

1. Every society has some inescapable considerations relating to conduct, such as laws and regulations. Hence, it is important for the business to match up to these expectations, as this becomes one of the bases against which society judges that business.
2. Society considers some aspects of conduct important even though they are not regulated by legal rules, such as being courteous and respectful to clients.
3. Ethical behaviour is an important part of professionalism.
4. Organisational self-interest may be enhanced by promoting an ethical stance. There are benefits that come to the organisation due to practising ethical behaviour, especially when such an organisation is recognised in its industry as being different/superior (Newman, 2014).

In customer service, ethics is important since the service provider has the responsibility not only to think about how to handle a client, but also the impact of that engagement in the medium to long term.

Defining Ethical Customer Service

What defines ethical customer service? Ethical customer service avoids manipulation and exaggeration. It entails providing all relevant information and service that a customer needs; that is, it does not withhold important information. It is honest and not misleading. Bovee and Thill (2017) identified three mutually dependent components of ethics in a business setting: (a) personal ethics, (b) ethical leadership and (c) policies and structures. These are unpacked to the extent that they define and influence ethical (or unethical) customer service. They also relate to the previous discussion that draws on the practice from personal values to corporate ethics.

Personal ethics: Personal ethics are a guide for the right actions for an individual. They include the personal responsibility over one's choices and actions. They evolve as a person goes through the various stages of life. They are influenced by a number of factors:

Family influence: The family in which we are raised is the first voice of ethics and the place where ethical boundaries are set. Family builds our ethical foundation and contributes to our moral sensitivity.

Religious beliefs: Religion prescribes a set of values and guidelines that the followers should abide by so as to live a good moral life.

Culture: Culture is the way things are done in a particular environment. Culture is ingrained in individuals by virtue of being immersed in their environment and becomes the standard that they are accustomed to and expect others to uphold.

Experience: Events that happen in our lives determine the attitude and view that we hold about certain issues. For instance, a person who suffered a sanction for behaving unethically is likely to act ethically in the future for fear of further sanctions.

Situational factors: These may be one-off experiences that determine how we behave in a given situation. For instance, an employee who is not meeting his sales targets and risks losing his job may resort to unethical selling practices to meet his targets.

Media: TV, social media, radio. These shape our views on ethical matters through:

- The language used that either presents ethics as honourable or as mockery.
- The use of emotions to influence people's thoughts, actions and judgements.
- Past events that the media brings up so as to influence one's thoughts and perceptions (Bovee & Thill, 2017).

Leadership: Leadership has the responsibility to set policies and guidelines. It also has the obligation to ensure all employees act in accordance with the policies by leading by example. Waggoner (2010) highlights that it is not enough for leaders to do the right thing. They must explain why a specific decision and course of action is taken. To successfully implement ethical behaviour in an organisation, leaders must develop an ethics programme. This programme may include basic company information followed by ethics orientation and seminars to explain its importance. The leadership should also promote openness and participatory decision-making so that ethical issues are addressed without victimisation or intimidation. Finally, there is need to review ethical policies and practices, and address any challenges that may hinder ethical behaviour.

Policies and guidelines: These include the code of ethics of the organisation, which is a document setting out a company's values and responsibilities towards its stakeholders. They envision the excellence that individuals and society should strive for and what they can achieve. They act as a reference point for different professions and form the foundation upon which professions are built. They may provide broad statements about what constitutes unethical behaviours and penalties thereof.

Codes of Customer Service Ethics in the African Context

Udokang (2014) has argued that African ethics and morality serve as a vehicle for social order and stability in African communities. Even before the advent of colonialism and missionary initiatives in Africa, the African people always had moral codes and ethical principles that guided individuals and communities. Stability, law and order, and social harmony were maintained due to the strict adherence to normative ethical principles. He further observed that African people have a deep sense of right and wrong that has produced customs, rules, laws and traditions, which can be observed in any setting – from family to business, public service or any other form of human interaction.

If we follow Udokang's argument, therefore, the deep sense of ethical practice predates any written codes of conduct. Codes of conduct are simply written to confirm that the employee is doing the right thing. Ethical customer service should automatically exist in any situation. This suggests that people can and will behave ethically even if codes of conduct did not exist. It can, therefore, be argued that codes of ethics are written in order to develop public trust, build credibility, and in some cases, meet the demands of regulatory authorities. In other words, the audience is the external stakeholder.

Let us consider some examples of codes of ethics from African institutions.

KENYA AIRWAYS: CODE OF BUSINESS CONDUCT AND ETHICS

We value honesty and integrity above all else… Acting with integrity is about more than our Company's image and reputation or avoiding legal issues. It is about sustaining a place where we are all proud to work. Upholding these commitments is essential to our continued success as it influences how ***consumers*** feel about our services… Ultimately, it is about each of us knowing that we have done the right thing. This means acting honestly and treating each other and our ***customers***, partners, suppliers and the environment fairly, ethically and with dignity.

Adhering to this Code is essential. Our most valuable asset is our reputation… Employees shall conduct themselves in an ethical manner at all times…

This is an excerpt of the preamble of the Kenya Airways Code of Business Conduct and Ethics. Over the next 23 pages of the Code, issues of personal integrity, commercial integrity, confidentiality, information security and conflict of interest are addressed.

Source: Kenya Airways (2018)

KENYA COMMERCIAL BANK (KCB) GROUP

KCB Group is committed to creating and maintaining an environment throughout the Group in which good business ethics prevail and a trust-based internal culture is maintained. KCB Group is committed to the fundamental values of integrity, transparency and accountability and adopts a zero tolerance position to all forms of corruption, bribery and unethical business practice at the workplace.

With regard to *customers*, we are committed to the ethical treatment of the people to whom we have an obligation. Emphasis is laid on maintaining open lines of communication, which in turn yields loyalty and respect from our customers.

The code proceeds to outline KCB Group's values and value commitment, its responsibilities to all stakeholders, and provides a clear code of ethical conduct for all employees. It concludes by providing information on how and where to report any incidences of unethical behaviour and provides an online platform for making such reports.

Source: KCB Group (2018)

In addition to these codes of conduct from the corporate world, the Government of Kenya also enacted the Public Officers Ethics Act (POEA) (2003).

PUBLIC OFFICERS ETHICS ACT, 2003

The foundation of the Act is that every citizen is a customer of government services. Citizens are entitled to ethical, fair and respectable treatment from public officers.

Some of the provisions of the Act read as follows:

Part III – General Code of Conduct and Ethics

A public officer shall, to the best of his ability, carry out his duties and ensure that the services that he provides are provided efficiently and honestly.

A public officer shall:

1. carry out his duties in a way that maintains public confidence in the integrity of his office;
2. treat the public and his fellow public officers with courtesy and respect;
3. to the extent appropriate to his office, seek to improve the standards of performance and level of professionalism in his organisation;
4. if a member of a professional body, observe the ethical and professional requirements of that body;
5. observe official working hours and not be absent without proper authorisation or reasonable cause;
6. maintain an appropriate standard of dress and personal hygiene; and
7. discharge any professional responsibilities in a professional manner.

Over the next 200 pages of the Act, issues such as no improper enrichment, conflict of interest, collections and fundraising functions, care of property, political neutrality, declaration of wealth, nepotism, confidentiality and reporting improper order are addressed.

Source: Public Officers Ethics Act (2003)

In order to provide an avenue for any dissatisfied citizens to report unethical conduct by public officers in a safe and convenient environment, the Commission on Administrative Justice (CAJ) also known as the Office of the Ombudsman was established in 2011. The Office has a mandate, to investigate any conduct in state affairs or any act or omission in public administration in any sphere of Government and complaints of abuse of power, unfair treatment, manifest injustice or unlawful, oppressive, unfair or unresponsive official conduct.

Source: Commission on Administrative Justice (2019)

Looking at these codes of ethics, the key focus is on the external stakeholder, especially the customer. In practice, however, when people work, they do not hold the code of ethics in their hand to help them determine what decisions or actions to take. There is an inherent understanding of right and wrong, and a desire to do the right thing. It can be argued that the codes of ethics only confirm that the decisions taken were the right ones.

Well-written codes of ethics are therefore useful in:

- Embedding a set of ethical values (which already exist in individuals) into the organisations' goals and strategies.
- Providing support and assurance to staff as they make decisions and carry out their work.
- Consolidating and strengthening a culture of openness and integrity to facilitate a sustainable business.
- Enhancing trust and reputation among stakeholders.
- Maximising sustainability, that is the social, economic and environmental well-being of the wider society (Gilman, 2005).

The focus of a code of ethics is therefore not to penalise people for unethical behaviour, but to support, promote and strengthen a culture of ethical practice.

Why Unethical Customer Service Practices Exist

Even when people know what is right, they do not always do it. What promotes unethical conduct in customer service? In the high-pressure business environments, we see fewer acts of integrity. Below are a few examples of unethical customer service practices that are surprisingly common.

Inaccurate information to customers: There is a story of two high school students who learned in school how to test for ascorbic acid (Vitamin C) in fruits and juices. They purchased a packet of a health drink whose labelling claimed was *'filled with Vitamin C'*. On testing the drink, they found no traces of Vitamin C. They reported the matter to their high school teacher who in turn reported to the Consumer Protection Authority. The makers of the not-so-healthy drink were slapped with a hefty fine for the untruthful labelling information.

Deception: Consider this. A buyer finds an apartment she really likes with all the features she desires within her price range. When the sales agent realises how taken the potential customer is with the apartment, he starts making untruthful statements like 'there are just a few units left', or 'this is the last unit at this price range', or 'you're the fifth person to see this apartment today. If you don't make a commitment, it probably won't be available tomorrow'. Irrespective of the decision the customer eventually makes, this is deception.

Making false promises and commitments to customers: Examples of false promises and commitments have been witnessed in the digital TV and mobile telecommunications services in Kenya. Customers may make purchases with the promise of an upgrade to a better package after meeting certain requirements. When the customer asks for the upgrade as promised, the narrative changes and convoluted explanations as to why they can't get the upgrade are given. In the end, the customer loses. For those in higher education, this may be akin to promising potential students certain courses or experiences once they enrol, and then failing to deliver.

Skipping contract commitment disclosures or drawing up contracts that the customer may not understand: Needless to say, the lawyers are considered the villains here. Customers are caught off-guard and tied to commitments that are contained in the fine print. Doing so upsets customers and leads to decreased levels of customer satisfaction and declining retention rates.

Rhetoric about ethical practice with no commitment to it: On 7 April 2016, Kenyans woke up to the shocking news that one of the country's high-performing banks – Chase Bank – had been placed under receivership. This tier-two bank had won over ten regional and global awards in the preceding five years. On the bank's website and company documents, as late as December 2015, this was their commitment to customers:

> Every employee and representative of the Group has a responsibility to contribute in a positive way towards our reputation. This is through ensuring *ethical practices are always adhered to*, interactions with all stakeholders are positive, and we comply with applicable policies, legislation and regulations (Chase Bank, 2015).

As it later emerged, there were numerous undisclosed directors' loans, under-provisioning for non-performing loans, publishing of two sets of financial reports and many forms of creative accounting. So much for always adhering to ethical practices!

These are just a few examples of unethical customer service behaviour.

Udokang (2014) takes on the civilizing mission of the church as having the greatest impact on traditional African morality and ethics. Converts were made to believe that traditional customs which were the foundation of ethics and morality were paganistic and heathenish. Gatú (2016) points a finger at the Western culture, which has promoted individualism, materialism and disregard for and abuse of African traditional ethical norms which held the society together. Within the context of business, Fassin and Buelens (2011) identified a number of factors that contribute to the dissonance between knowing and doing the right thing.

The pressures and difficulties of business: The most significant problem, especially for stock-quoted companies, is the short-term evaluation on the basis of quarterly results, and consequent short-term decision-making that can lead to unethical practices.

Inconsistencies in reward systems: Even if senior managers have a genuine interest in business ethics, in most cases, it is the bottom line that ultimately counts. Reward systems are primarily based on economic results. Managers are seldom judged on their ethical behaviour. Some compensation and reward schemes are short-sighted and incorporate perverse incentives for personnel to engage in unethical conduct. It appears that in some cases, the senior management chooses to turn a blind eye to the unethical behaviour used by middle and junior management to achieve good financial results. Moreover, with the increased influence of financial considerations, major corporations are dominated by financially-oriented CEOs and senior management. They are evaluated on financial results, with bonus and stock options linked to company results. These short-term criteria in CEOs' and senior managers' reward structures totally contradict the long-term view propagated by ethical conduct.

Idealistic rhetoric in mission statements and advertisements: Communication and public relations managers like to use language that may be excessive to create an ideal organisation. Words such as 'excellence', 'world-class' and 'first-class', while well-intentioned, present an inaccurate and often unattainable reality. The letters to stockholders published in corporations' annual reports, signed by CEOs, are mostly written by public relations specialists. The letter will, therefore 'make the current top management look good, while masking some of the corporation's deficiencies and attempting to rationalize others'.

A corporate culture of selectivity in communication: Companies attempt to focus on their achievements based on their own programmes and results, according to their specific activities. Both the popular press and academic literature are selective in their choices of topics and subjects of interest. As an example of this kind of communication reduction, the debate over corporate governance codes has monopolized board discussions and focused press attention on one main topic: the publication of the remuneration packages of chief executive officers (CEO). It has diverted attention from the core of corporate governance: control and accountability. The crisis only hits the popular press when it is out of hand and expensive, and painful decisions have to be made.

Few options for the customer: Where the range of service providers is limited and switching costs for the customer are high, existing service providers can easily and unconsciously slide to unethical conduct. Competition and industry best practice tend to act as a self-regulating mechanism to help keep businesses on their toes with regard to ethical behaviour. When this check is lacking, and customers are not able to 'punish' the offending service provider by switching, unethical practices can go on unchecked for years.

Conscious or unconscious discrimination: The discrimination could be based on gender, appearance or the first communication from the customer. A customer who walks into a retail outlet and greets the attendant is likely to get better customer service. In a restaurant setting, male customers, or female customers accompanied by male companions, consistently get faster or preferential treatment over female customers. Appearance in age, dress, grooming or attractiveness also determines the level and quality of service one gets (Banaji et al., 2003).

Udokang (2014) concludes by making an urgent appeal on the need to revive African cultural values, and traditional ethical principles and institutions, as the guiding principles of our daily life and living.

Ethical Dilemmas

Ethical choices may not always be clear cut. There are some scenarios that may present real dilemmas for the decision-maker. Ethical dilemmas mean making a choice in borderline situations. Business ethics in the global market place is also not always clear. For example, is it ethical for an employee to receive a gift from a client? Does the value of the gift matter? What about the context in which it is given? Is it sufficient to have a policy for declaring gifts?

Consider the following examples adapted from Sims (1999):

Scenario 1: Admission of university students: You are involved in the admissions process in a university. You have recently learned that your senior co-worker has been violating admission requirements and admitting unqualified students. Although you have no evidence that he has been taking kickbacks for the service, you have reason to believe so. Your co-worker has been in the university for a long time and is well respected. You are unsure if his behaviour is illegal, but you believe it is not right. It denies an opportunity to an otherwise qualified applicant. What would you do?

1. Say nothing.
2. Talk to the co-worker and explain why his actions are unacceptable.
3. Find a way to justify his conduct so that you are at peace with it.
4. Report the matter to your supervisor and leave it at that.
5. Deal with the matter until the unethical practice stops.

Scenario 2: Missing information in company reports: This year has not been a very good one for your company. Sales are down significantly, which has led to the layoff of many excellent employees.

In addition, the company is facing a major lawsuit, which has the potential of bankrupting the firm. A prospective client has indicated an interest in placing a very large order which would guarantee the reinstatement of all laid-off employees and would keep them employed for quite some time. However, the client is wary about the stability of your company. To improve the client's perception of the company, the sales manager of the company, who reports to you, has removed the reference to the lawsuit in the copy of the annual report given to the potential client. You have a responsibility to ensure the accuracy of company documents. What do you do?

1. Do nothing.
2. Reprimand the sales manager, but let the issue drop after that.
3. Convince yourself that the sales manager's actions are justified.
4. Ask the sales manager to provide the client with complete information.
5. Talk with the top executives of the company, asking that the client be provided with complete information.
6. Provide the client with the complete report yourself.

Scenario 3: Lying in a speech: You have organised a corporate event for your clients to discuss the company's achievements and future directions. You have prepared a speech for your boss. However, he changes the speech to create a very rosy, but fictitious image of the company. He paints a picture of a very successful company, with multiple international partnerships and clients. He inflates the company's financial performance. He suggests where the company is going in the next two years, which is not even close to the truth. You know he is lying. What would you do?

1. Do nothing.
2. Talk to your boss about it after the event, but let the issue drop after that.
3. Convince yourself that the company might live up to the image created.
4. Suggest that you prepare an accurate company profile that provides clients with the correct information.
5. Report the matter to the chairman of the board.
6. Prepare and share accurate company information with the clients without involving your boss.

In resolving these and other ethical dilemmas the importance of the 'customer side' of the decision-making process, and powerful notion of 'duty of care' have to take centre stage. It is important to consider the specific circumstances in determining how to approach an ethical dilemma. The decisions reached must take care of the customer, and the leader/decision-maker must explain their actions to the relevant stakeholders, ensuring that care, processes and critical reflection remained central (Cranston et al., 2006).

McNeil and Pedigo (2001) identified four essential strategies for managing ethical dilemmas that may be used in ensuring ethical customer service practices. These are shown in Figure 4.2.

According to McNeil and Pedigo (2001), *marketing* is as an essential mechanism for managers in their attempts to manage the ethical content of various decisions and activities encountered in customer service. Marketing is particularly important, as it involves communicating with customers. At a pragmatic level, attention to marketing mix variables is important – type of packaging/presentation required by the end-user; promotion and advertising language used; clear, fair and transparent processes; and a pricing that is considered value for money by the customer are all essential in developing ethical business practices.

Figure 4.2 Essential strategies for managing customer service ethical dilemmas. (From McNeil, M., and Pedigo, K., *APJML*, 13, 43–65, 2001.)

Integrity is also essential in ensuring that ethical problems are handled effectively. The focus here is on the personal strength and beliefs that are necessary for ethical behaviour in business. This means taking a stand, often in difficult circumstances: 'bad ethics should not be tolerated'. Trustworthiness and honesty are pivotal. Always employ the 'golden rule': Do unto others (in this case your customers), as you would have them do unto you.

When dealing with customers across national boundaries, *cultural sensitivity*, that is, respecting the cultural values of others, is key. Caution and mutual respect are necessary to observe and respect other's cultural values. If customers feel that they are being served fairly, there is an environment that allows for the best possible outcome should any difficulties occur. If problems arise, these should be dealt with sensitivity and urgency.

The development and implementation of *formal corporate policies* is essential to prevent ongoing ethical challenges for managers involved in customer service. Formal corporate policies involve pragmatic actions at the institutional level governed by documented rules and procedures, which apply uniformly to all employees and transactions, as well as micro level actions, which are more tactical in nature and may vary depending on context. For example, a customer has lost their national identification (ID) card and wants to undertake a bank transaction. The customer is well-known to the employees of the bank, having banked at the same branch for over 30 years. A copy of the customer's ID is on file at the bank. Whereas the company policies may demand that a national identity card be produced, shouldn't the employees use good faith to assist the customer?

Faced with an ethical dilemma, White (1993) identified three steps to handle such dilemmas that would serve customer service managers well.

Step 1: Consequences assessment: In this step, the full range of consequences for undertaking certain actions both positive and negative is assessed from the customer's perspective. The considerations a service provider might take into account include assessing how the customer will be affected by actions taken, both in the short and long term, and which options are likely to produce the most benefits to the customer.

Step 2: Analyse the actions: The second step involves analysing how the options available measure up with regard to the ethical principles of honesty, fairness, equality and the dignity of the customer.

Step 3: Make a decision: Take the least harmful action as perceived by the customer, while observing ethical conduct. This suggests that if an action is beneficial from the customer's perspective, but unethical, it must not be taken. For example, in the ethical dilemma presented previously in Scenario 1, it may be perceived as beneficial by the customer (in this case the applicant) for the university to 'bend the rules' and admit him even if he is not qualified, but it is certainly unethical.

Recommendations for Africa: Role of Management in Promoting and Maintaining Ethical Customer Service Practices

In the final section of this chapter, we look at the role of management in promoting and maintaining ethical customer service practices, within an African context. As Udokang (2014) and Gatú (2016) have argued, Africans had a clear sense of morals and ethics before the advent of colonialism and infiltration of the Western culture and suggest a conscious return to those traditional ethical principles. However, since a complete reversal is not possible, and may not be entirely desirable, a healthy integration of positive Western and traditional values should be held. This is especially important as businesses become more global and interwoven, and the advent of technologies allows for new kinds of engagement that might cause ethical concerns.

Drawing on the experience of Safaricom, East and Central Africa's most profitable company, Director of Customer Operations, Jannet Atika, urges African businesses to strive to engage customers in an ethical way. Ethical customer service is the right thing to do, but it is also good for business. In an interview in 2017, she identified eight tips for African business managers that promote ethical customer service.

1. *Hire right*: Qualifications are important, but the main reason for face-to-face interviews is to ensure hiring is based on attitude and not papers. If a person is not ethical, if their moral compass is off, you can expect unethical behaviour from them, no matter what the company rulebook says. And even then, who really wants to 'police' an employee to ensure ethical behaviour?

2. *Promote collegiality*: The African society is a collegial society. Cooperation, companionship and support for each other promote collegiality. Let us use that strength to bring customer service teams together, give them a voice and access to everyone, to make them know that they are important. They can talk about what works for the customer and are appreciated for the feedback they bring, action is taken and feedback given to them. If the employees know they are valued, they have no reason to be deceitful or unethical.

3. *Execute with speed*: It is unethical to keep a customer waiting indefinitely – whether that is waiting on the phone line, waiting for a return phone call, waiting for a resolution to a complaint or anything else. Acting on feedback quickly is ethical customer service. This is one instance where the African traditional values such as caring for one another and use of technology can be very well integrated.

4. *Make some sacrifices*: Efficient and effective customer service experience can be expensive. Being ethical may sometimes come at a cost. For example, in November 2018, over 400,000 Safaricom customers were given refunds because there was a fault with one of the service providers services that resulted in double charging. The easier thing would have been to fix the problem and keep quiet about it. Refunding customers for overcharging them was the ethical and right thing to do, even when it came at an extra cost to the service provider.

5. *Think of customer experience, rather than service*: Service is for a limited time – for now, a fix. An experience, however, lingers on, and that is what people talk about. Africans are by nature storytellers. A service provider can benefit from this cultural practice by ensuring customers have positive experiences and stories to tell far and wide. Use of social media has made storytelling easier and faster. When customers are treated ethically, they are likely to talk about it for a long time, and also be loyal. Ethical customer service is, therefore, a good business strategy.

6. *Aim to make a difference*: When you serve customers ethically, especially in a business environment or sector where most players do not, you will be making a difference. Insurance companies, for example, are often perceived as villains – mean, unkind, unfair and will do anything to avoid paying a claim. Where a service provider in such a sector says to the customer – you are right, we will help you, we will settle your claim despite your delayed payments, they will undoubtedly have made a difference in the life of that customer. As an old African proverb says: *Do not follow a person who is running away.* Businesses that seek to run away from responsibility to customer should not be emulated. Ethical customer service does make a difference for the customer.

7. *Be an activist for the customer*: As a service provider, look at the services from the perspective of the customer. How would the customer like to be served? What do they want? How much are they willing to pay for it? Are they getting value for money? It's difficult to provide honest answers to these questions from the customer's perspective and still be unethical.

8. *Be open about failures*: As the African proverb goes: *Success in life depends on how you handle failures.* Things may not always go as planned. A service provider may fail to deliver a service as promised. Customers are surprisingly reasonable and understanding when information is communicated openly and in a timely manner. Even if disclosing failures may decrease sales opportunities in the short term, it will ensure that you are engaging with the right customers that will value your products and services and promote them to peers and colleagues.

Conclusion

Ethical customer service is a virtue; it is something that improves with practice. In the African context, collegiality, care for others, mindfulness, respect and social harmony are part of the culture. These values enable a given cultural group (in this case, employees in a company) to enjoy a high degree of stability to the extent that they are willing to allow their actions to be governed by dominant values and norms (code of ethics). African ethics and morality is, therefore, the bedrock of ethical customer service. The examples provided throughout the chapter illustrate how managers need to engage with their staff to ensure ethical behaviour.

References

Banaji, M. R., Bazerman, M. H., & Chugh, D. (2003). How (un)ethical are you? *Harvard Business Review, 81*(12), 56–64.

Bovee, C. L., & Thill, J. V. (2017). *Business communication today.* London, UK: Pearson.

Chase Bank. (2015). *2014 Annual report and financial statements.* Retrieved 28 January 2019 from www.chasebankkenya.co.ke/sites/default/files/ChaseBankAnnualReport 20142819.pdf.

Commission on Administrative Justice (CAJ). (2019). *About the Ombudsman.* Retrieved 28 January 2019 from http://www.ombudsman.go.ke/index.php#about-us.

Cranston, N., Ehrich, L. C., & Kimber, M. (2006). Ethical dilemmas: The "bread and butter" of educational leaders' lives. *Journal of Educational Administration, 44*(2), 106–121.

Fassin, Y., & Buelens, M. (2011). The hypocrisy-sincerity continuum in corporate communication and decision making: A model of corporate social responsibility and business ethics practices. *Management Decision, 49*(4), 586–600.

Gatú, J. G. (2016). *Fan into flame.* Nairobi: Moran Publishers.

Gilman, S. C. (2005). *Ethics codes and codes of conduct as tools for promoting an ethical and professional public service: Comparative successes and lessons.* Washington, DC: World Bank.

KCB Group. (2018). *Compliance and ethics.* Retrieved 3 December 2018 from https://ke.kcbgroup.com/about/who-we-are/ethics.

Kenya Airways. (2018). *Code of business conduct and ethics.* Retrieved 28 January 2019 from https://www.kenya-airways.com/uploadedFiles/Content/About_Us/Investor_Information/Codeof BusinessConductandEthics.pdf.

McNeil, M. & Pedigo, K. (2001). Dilemmas and dictates: Managers tell their stories about international business ethics. *Asia Pacific Journal of Marketing and Logistics, 13*(4), 43–65.

National Council for Law Reporting. (2009). *Public officers ethics act (POEA) 2003*, Chapter 183. Retrieved on 31 January, 2019 from www.kenyalaw.org.

Newman, E. (2014). *Importance of ethics in customer dealings.* Retrieved 31 January 2019 from http://corp.yonyx.com/customer-service/importance-of-ethics-in-customer-dealings.

Sims, R. L. (1999). The development of six ethical business dilemmas. *The Leadership & Organization Development Journal, 20*(4), 189–197.

Tullberg, J. (2012). Integrity – Clarifying and upgrading an important concept for business ethics. *Business and Society Review, 117*(1), 89–121.

Udokang, E. J. (2014). Traditional ethics and social order: A study in African philosophy. *Cross-Cultural Communication, 10*(6), 266–270.

Waggoner, J. (2010). *Ethics and leadership: How personal ethics produce effective leaders.* Claremont, CA: Claremont McKenna College. (Senior Theses 26). Retrieved 3 December 2018 from http://scholarship.claremont.edu/cmc_theses/26.

White, T. (1993). *Resolving an ethical dilemma.* Retrieved 3 December 2018 from www.ethicsandbusiness.org.

THEME B: CUSTOMER SERVICE STRATEGY

Chapter 5

An Institutional Economics-Led Model of Customer Service Strategy

Awele Achi and Olutayo Otubanjo

Contents

Introduction

Over the last few years, there has been a growing acknowledgement of the concept of customer service (Devasagayam et al., 2013) as a crucial element in the service sector (Mathies & Burford, 2011). The rationale for the increased attention to the subject of customer service can be credited to three basic factors. First is the increasing dynamics of customer expectations, especially in areas of logistics customer service (Daugherty et al., 2018). Today, customers are becoming complex and difficult to satisfy made possible by the paradigm shift from a seller's market to a buyer's market, and the ease of obtaining and using information is empowering customers (McDonald & Christopher, 2003).

Second, there is now an implacable change in customers' perceptions of little or no difference between product offerings; hence, markets are witnessing the preponderance of 'commodity' products (McDonald & Christopher, 2003).

Third, is the growing view of customer service importance in the attainment of high degrees of loyalty, satisfaction and generation of profits (Kiessling et al., 2016; McDonald & Christopher, 2003).

In a bid to improve market share and manage trade-offs associated with logistic costs, customer service has been acknowledged as an indispensable part of an organisation's overall marketing and logistics strategy (Theodoras, 2009). Furthermore, Verhoef et al. (2009) contend that organisations within the sub-Saharan African region and in other emerging markets have begun adopting customer service management as a key element of their mission statements. Developing an effective customer service strategy demands the holistic appraisal of marketing and logistics activities of an organisation, identifying the relevant importance-performance gaps existing in these elements (marketing and logistics), and dividing the service offered (Theodoras, 2009).

Discussing customer service strategy would require explicating what is meant by customer service. Customer service is a range of activities that organisations utilise to shape and affect the views of their customers in a service experience situation (Tablan, 2016). Mathies and Burford (2011) note that customer service is a foremost component of the service industry. Lin and Liang (2011) argue that customer service can affect customers and employees, as well as the organisation both in a favourable and unfavourable manner depending on customer outcomes. Huett (2017) argues that customer service encompasses the general assisting activities that firms render to their customers that utilise their products and services. This indicates that customer service is beyond handling customer complaints and transactions.

Customers rate the level of their customer service experience based on a service provider's ability to match their expectations (Hellén & Sääksjärvi, 2011). Alrubaiee & Alkaaida (2011) suggest that poor customer service delivery by an organisation culminates in loss of customers and low profits; this can also adversely affect corporate image. Furthermore, the managerial approach to customer strategy as research has shown over the years is either proactive or reactive (Huett, 2017; La Londe et al., 1988). Proactive strategies enable an organisation to anticipate likely questions customers could raise beforehand, ensuring that their employees are able to tackle complaints or meet customer needs (Huett, 2017). On the other hand, for a reactive strategy, when organisations are faced with a barrage of customer complaints, they should offer support rather than simply predict the likely customer issues (ibid).

Therefore, it is safe to assume that providing excellent customer service is a prerequisite for building and sustaining customer satisfaction, meeting profit targets and achieving a competitive advantage, which is all founded on the development of an effective customer service strategy. A well-defined customer service strategy should take cognisance of the different perspectives of customers, finance, operations and human resource elements in the organisation, as this is a crucial step to ensure that every employee understands their own contribution to the strategy's success (Smith, 2006).

Consequently, it becomes imperative to pinpoint the specific importance-performance gaps extant in the marketing and logistics activities of an organisation through an in-depth appraisal and delineate the services offered in a bid to design an effective customer service strategy. However, in spite of the growth of customer service literature, little attention has been paid to the strategy aspect of customer service. Given this limitation, this study shall focus on customer service strategy modelling, especially in the context of the role of environmental factor.

This paper is organised into six sections. This current first section provides a background to the study, then the second explicates and breaks down the meaning of customer service strategy into five dominant dimensions as evidenced by the authors from a review of mainstream extant literature. The third section gives a review of existing customer service strategy models. The fourth section provides an analysis of the strengths and weaknesses of the reviewed models. The fifth section introduces an institutional economics-led model of customer service strategy that considers the environment in which the organisation and customers emanate from in order to shore up the gap and limitations of the previously reviewed models. The sixth section provides a conclusion to the issues discussed in the paper.

Literature Review

Meaning of Customer Service Strategy

In the past few decades, the service sector business environment has witnessed a growing level of competition and changes (Levenburg, 2006), leading to organisations searching for innovative means of adding value to their services in order to improve organisational bottom lines (Zaino, 2002). Extant literature has credited the preponderance of attention given to customer service to its ability to create wealth and add to customers derived value (Donaldson, 1995; Christopher, 1992). Accordingly, Ko et al. (2008) argue that organisations in a bid to catch up with the present-day dynamics in different customer segments are modifying and adapting differentiated marketing strategies that are customer oriented.

Nevertheless, the review of mainstream extant literature has revealed that there is no single universal meaning that has been accrued to customer service strategy. Consequently, we have come up with a framework of five (5) dominant conceptual dimensions that help to explicate the meaning of customer service strategy based on the review of extant works, namely; *Logistic-Marketing, Human Resources Management (HRM), Technological/Internet, Customer Relationship/Intervention,* and *Strategic dimensions.* They are explicated below:

- *Logistic-marketing dimension*: This conceptual dimension of customer service strategy stems from the views of authors like Theodoras (2009), Lee and Trim (2006), Huiskonen and Pirtila (1998), and Murphy and Poist (1996) that describe customer service activities as an outcome of the logistics process and the place function in the marketing mix. The major emphasis of this dimension is the crucial nature of customer service in the logistics process. Customer service is used as an assessment tool to check the efficiency of an organisation's logistics in achieving place and time utility for products and services (Christopher et al., 1991). Furthermore, this perspective views customer service as the cord that bonds logistic and marketing activities together (Christopher, 1996).
- *Human Resources Management (HRM) dimension*: This dimension of customer service strategy is based on the works of authors Chao and Shih (2016), Jiang et al. (2015), Chuang and Liao (2010), Cutcher (2008), and Wood (2005) that views customer service strategy from a human resource standpoint. The HRM dimension argues that customer service strategy should encompass an array of human resource elements that aim to boost personnel capabilities and motives and gives room for contributing to first-rate customer service (Chao & Shih, 2016; Jiang et al., 2015).

- *Technological/Internet dimension*: This dimension of customer service strategy emerges from a technological or Internet standpoint based on a review of extant literature (e.g. Gunarathne et al., 2018; Ives et al., 2016; Eng, 2008; Levenburg, 2006; Walsh & Godfrey, 2000). In support of this dimension, several authors (Levengue, 2006; Day & Hubbard, 2003; Walsh & Godfrey, 2000) suggested that use of the Internet can facilitate enhanced customer service, cut down costs and boost customer relationships.

- *Customer Relationship/Intervention dimension*: This dimension is derived from the view of authors such as Chen (2013), Sharma (2008) and Smith (2006) who believe that customer service strategy should be built on the basis of relationship and/or intervention since the goal of relationship management is to meet customers' needs. Nonetheless, customer relation management (CRM) has become a fashionable gizmo that organisations utilise to build and sustain relationships with their markets through the in-depth use of customer analytics (Chen, 2013; Ngai, 2005). The dimension propagates the use of individualised services by identifying and tailoring services to customers' needs (Chen, 2013; Eriksson & Vaghult, 2000). Further, the dimension suggests that organisations should interfere by designing firm-level strategies during the course or at the end of relationship building to cut down cost on the mismatch between customers and the service strategy in place (Sharma, 2008). These strategies could be in the form of service process improvements, setting customer expectations and designing customer selection processes (ibid).

- *Strategic dimension*: This conceptual dimension emanates from the view of authors Lee (2004), Sinha and Ghoshal (1999) and Donaldson (1995) who view the customer service strategy from a strategic-marketing approach. The approach argues that marketing activities (in this case, customer service) are an indispensable component of the overall corporate and marketing strategy (Lee, 2004). In addition, this dimension is supported by Baker (1996) who advocated that the marketing process precedes strategy; hence, strategy emanates from marketing activities, as it involves the collection and analysis of happening data gathered from the market in an organised manner.

Table 5.1 gives an outlook of the described dominant dimensions to the meaning of customer service strategy.

Table 5.1 Dominant Perspectives on the Meaning of Customer Service Strategy

Dimensions	Contributors
Logistic-marketing	Theodoras (2009); Huiskonen and Pirtila (1998); Murphy and Poist (1996); Lee and Trim (2006)
Human Resources Management (HRM)	Chao and Shih (2016); Jiang et al. (2015); Chuang and Liao (2010); Cutcher (2008); Wood (2005)
Technological/Internet	Gunarathne et al. (2018); Ives et al. (2016); Eng (2008); Levenburg (2006); Walsh and Godfrey (2000)
Customer relationship/intervention	Chen (2013); Sharma (2008); Smith (2006); Eriksson and Vaghult (2000)
Strategic	Lee (2004); Sinha and Ghoshal (1999); Donaldson (1995)

Source: Developed by the authors.

Particularly, customer service strategy has become a popular and effectual tool for developing and sustaining profitable relationships with customers of an organisation. This has resulted in a paradigm shift from the conventional perspective of marketing to a relationship perspective that seeks the durable sustenance of relations between organisations and their customers (Gwinner et al., 1998). Sharma and Lambert (1994) contend that customer service as a component of the marketing mix is the most cost-effective method that can be employed to concentrate the marketing strategy specifically on the needs of customers in mature markets.

Customer Service Strategy Models

A variety of customer service strategy models have been put forward by different marketing scholars (e.g. Chao & Shi, 2016; Chen, 2013; Huang et al., 2015; Theodoras, 2009; Sharma, 2008; Wouters, 2004; Lee & Trim, 2006; Etherington, 2002; Huiskonen & Pirttila, 1998; Wagenheim & Reunink, 1991) to elucidate the nexus between strategy and customer service with a view to deepen the knowledge on customer service. A summary of the reviewed models of customer service strategy is shown in Table 5.2.

The review of literature indicates the dominance of three frameworks within the literature of customer service strategy models. These include explanatory, antecedents and outcome frameworks. These component frameworks of existing models on customer service strategy are comprehensively examined below.

Explanatory Framework

Models that come under this framework give a broad description of customer service strategy. For instance, the integrated assessment model of service strategy for customers by Chen (2013)

Table 5.2 Summary of Customer Service Strategy Models

Name of Models	Author(s)
Model of lifestyle and customer service strategy	Huang et al. (2015)
Model of customer service strategy options	Wouters (2004)
Model of customer service element classification	Huiskonen and Pirttila (1998)
Model of customer intervention	Sharma (2008)
Model of customer service relationships	Wagenheim and Reunink (1991)
Model of customer service policy	Lee (2004)
Model of customer service-focused HRM system	Chao and Shih (2016)
Model of customer support problems solution	Smith (2006)
Model of vertically integrated marketing and retailing strategy framework with a customer service focus	Lee and Trim (2006)
The service model	Etherington (2002)

Source: Developed by the authors.

explains how customers with different values and levels can be served by an organisation. The model breaks down customers into premium, general and static categories and presents a three-stage model that explicates how the customer categories can be served. Similarly, Wouters's (2004) model of customer service strategy options offer an explanation of the discrepancies in an organisation's capability of customer service delivery. Using a combination of the capability of suppliers' customer service and sensitivity of buyers' customer service, the model showcases a taxonomy of customer strategy options, namely customer integration, customer adaptation, logistical precision and standard customer service. Lee and Trim's (2006) model of integrating customer service strategy within a vertical-marketing framework captures the elusive nature of customer service, as it has links with other key areas in the organisation and requires trust and commitment from other areas to enable the organisation to defend itself against rivals. Lee's (2004) model of customer service policy views customer service strategy from a holistic perspective, which seeks to gather happening data (marketing intelligence) and places a customer response system to monitor the external environment. In a similar vein, Huiskonen and Pirttila (1998) advanced the Kano-led quality classification model of customer service strategy planning to explicate how customer service strategy can be classified along the lines of quality classification, attractive quality and one-dimensional quality. Furthermore, Wagenheim and Reunink's (1991) model of customer service relationships explains the various levels and components of relationships pivotal to the success of customer strategy with the goal of creating effective and efficient organisations. Sharma's (2008) model of customer intervention uses the notion of customer relationship to capture customer service by building on the importance of customisation to meet customer needs and complaints. These classifications were put forward to explain the most crucial customer service elements while also indicating the divergent nature of customer groups that are served by organisations.

Antecedent Framework

Models belonging to this framework present the predictors of customer service strategy under various circumstances. For instance, Huang et al. (2015) approach to the Kano-led model argues that lifestyle can be a predictor of the quality of an organization's customer service strategy. The Kano model was proposed in the 1980s to explicate the requirements of customer service quality and improvements of customer satisfaction (Materla et al., 2019; Kano et al., 1984). The model introduces a two-level cluster analysis to demonstrate how lifestyle can lead to customer service strategy (Huang et al., 2015). Smith's 2006 study shows that CRM strategy acts as a precursor to customer service strategy.

Outcome Framework

This represents models that underscore the outputs of customer service strategy. Theodoras's (2009) study presented food segmentation as a consequence of customer service strategy. The author utilised a cluster analysis in segmenting the market into four spectra. Etherington (2002) highlighted that an effective customer service strategy can result in and deliver personalised service to customers of an organisation. In addition, Chao and Shih (2016) developed a model to explain how customer service strategy that is underpinned by Human Resources results to firm performance in the Taiwan service industry.

Strengths and Weaknesses of the Models

Strengths: These models give a clear articulation of customer service strategy and its components. Also, the models also identify which customer groups are most profitable. Furthermore, the models demonstrate how customer service strategy can be leveraged to gain a competitive edge. The models can assist in improving decisions on customer service differentiation. In addition, the models have explicated the elements that act as precursors to customer service strategy. Lastly, the models have articulated clearly the outcomes of putting in place a customer service strategy. These outcomes include effective market segmentation and cluster analysis.

Weaknesses: While it is apparent that the models reviewed have strengths, they are also not without limitations. The models did not take into consideration other actors in the customer service delivery process, such as external environmental factors. Based on the fundamental premise of integrated assessment models, it is usually not suitable for short-term forecasts and implementation. Furthermore, by using cluster analysis, vital information from outliers (non-customer) is lost. Lastly, the models do not account for the cost implications of implementing customer service strategy on the organisational bottom line and in other non-financial measures that were not highlighted.

Given the analysis of strengths and weaknesses of the reviewed models in the study, it is safe to assume that there is not a holistic model that considers the impact and role of environmental factors in the development of a customer service strategy model. In view of this limitation, we propose an institutional economics-led model of customer service strategy that captures the unavoidable contribution of the market environment to customer service strategy. The choice of institutional economics in this study was inspired by its ability to fully accommodate institutions, such as environmental factors in the shaping of human economic behaviour.

Institutional Economics Approach

Putting in place a holistic customer service strategy is imperative because customer service is subject to perception; hence, many factors influence the outcome of a person's customer service experience (Lin & Liang, 2011; Hellén & Sääksjärvi, 2011). Thus, in this study, we adopt an institutional economics-led approach in the development of a model of customer strategy. This approach provides a platform for capturing how various elements within the economic and social environment of the organisation impact and relate to the customer service strategy of organisations.

Adopting an institutional economics perspective for the study ensures that economic and social elements are jointly considered in the development of the model. Invariably, this implies that there is an appropriate blend maintained in developing the model and the present realities on the ground (see Staniek, 2010). In addition, the approach includes three mutually exclusive components (Staniek, 2010) which are:

- Formal institutions (e.g. law and regulatory agencies)
- Set of institution-organisations (which includes competitors, organisational customers etc.)
- Informal institutions (e.g. cultural undertones, norms, networking, social capital)

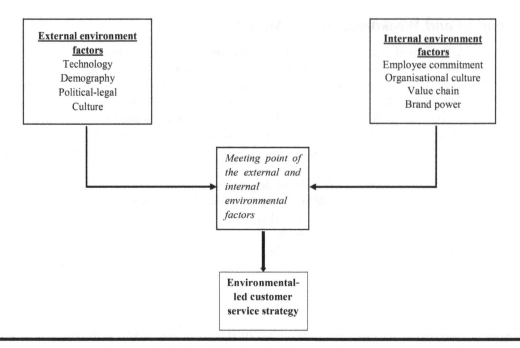

Figure 5.1   Proposed framework of an institutional economics-led model of customer service strategy. (Source: The authors.)

Bringing the above-mentioned approach into perspective, we propose a framework that shows how environmental factors (both external and internal) affect the customer service strategy of organisations (Figure 5.1).

Environmental Factors

This section discusses the various factors construed from the extant review of mainstream literature and the institutional economics as the key determinants of an environmental led customer service strategy.

External Environment Factors

Technology: With the current shape of things in today's business world, advancement in technology is a key factor in the capability of a firm to establish and engage with its customers, especially in virtual markets (Eng, 2008). The technological capability enables the firm to initiate a self-service platform for customers in a bid to ensure service consistency is delivered to customers. Accordingly, this can be in areas of website tools, functionalities and interface (ibid). Technology is constantly making firms reinvent the means and methods of conducting their marketing and branding activities (Domegan, 1996). A key issue in this environment is that there is the increasing rise of technologically savvy customers in almost all spheres of life (Fitzgerald et al., 2013); hence, organisations, especially in African settings, must continually monitor customer service strategy with the goal of acting as a customer technology company.

Demography: Demography refers to the study of knowledge in regards to populations and its dynamics, such as birth, death, income, migration etc. In developed societies, demography has become a hotbed issue (Max Planck Institute for Demographic Research, MPIDR, 2018). For organisations, engaging in the demographic analysis would support decision-making on understanding the changing composition in a population, such as that of age and gender (Lutz & Samir, 2013). This could take the form of market segmentation with the goal of designing marketing programmes (customer service strategy included) that meet customer expectations. Effective marketing is a key requirement for meeting customers' needs; hence, designing customer-oriented strategies which take into consideration customers' demographic variables and attitudes has the potential of becoming successful (Cleveland et al., 2011).

Political-legal: Changes in government priorities can lead to changes in laws relating to consumer protection, restrictions, employment etc. Furthermore, the rise in customer complaints (Tressler 2016), which is the act of expressing a dissatisfaction with a service or a product (McGraw et al., 2015), it has been suggested to be attributed to customer political orientation (Jung et al., 2017). This most likely will have implications for customer service and the implementation of organisational strategies already in place.

Culture: Culture is arguably the primary determinant of people's value, beliefs (Assael, 1995), wants, behaviour (Luo, 2009), knowledge, morals, norms, habits and other abilities (Hawkins & Mothersbaugh, 2010). Furthermore, symbols of products and services are reflective of the existing culture of a society (Cheginia et al., 2016). This explicates why it is imperative for organisations in Africa to understand the society it operates in and the targeted customers from a cultural perspective. In this regard, customer service strategy should be designed along customer values and norms. Assael (1995) notes that customer values are an outcome of a customer's culture, indicating the reason why customer values tend to be static and at the same time dynamic.

Internal Environment Factors

Employee commitment: Organisational commitment according to Greenberg and Baron (1997) is the degree an employee identifies with and engages with his organisation. Research findings have demonstrated that committed employees support and strive to ensure that service levels in the organisation do not drop by closing the 'gaps' left by others (Batt, 2002; Allen & Grisaffe, 2001). Such affective behaviour is likely to be copied by other employees to ensure customers' satisfaction (Conway & Briner, 2015). Being committed serves as a motivation for employees to key into the organisational philosophy and support the attainment of organisational goals (Dhar, 2015) resulting in positive consequences such as trust and cultural values (Nambudiri, 2012; Singh & Mohanty, 2011).

Organisational culture: Organisational culture refers to the system of shared views and beliefs by members of an organisation (Robbins & Coulter, 2005). Poor organisational culture has been suggested as one of the root causes of poor customer service in an organisation, especially in a sales context (Financial Conduct Authority, 2014). An erstwhile vice president of Goldman Sachs, Gregg Smith, in moments leading up to his resignation noted that 'Culture was always a vital part of Goldman Sachs's success. It revolved around teamwork, integrity, a spirit of humility, and always doing right by our clients. The culture was the secret sauce that made this place great and allowed us to earn our clients' trust for 143 years' (Smith, 2012).

It is the extent to which the organisation and customer requirements fit together and the fit between employees and the organisation (O'Reilly, 1989). Organisational culture is a key determinant of strategy at the workplace (Laforet, 2016; Safford, 1988). An excellent customer service delivery can be linked to a good organisational culture (Petrolino, 2018) leading to a structured behavioural pattern and fluid communication network, acting as a context for relationship marketing (Lee, 2004).

Value chain: Value chain is the range of value-adding activities an organisation in a particular industry carries out to deliver its value proposition to the target market (customers) (Miller & Jones, 2010). Value chain comprises actors and actions working together to ensure improvement in product and service delivery (Norton, 2014). Customer service is a key primary activity (Porter, 1985) in the value chain process. Stutter (2017) points out that putting customer needs at every turn in the value chain (supply chain) process ensures that services, processes and people can be aligned to meet customer expectations. Hence, developing a customer service strategy that reassures customers that their needs have been met at every stage of the value chain is imperative for success.

Brand power: The central foci of brand management is the delivery of unique and continuous customer experience with the brand (Mosley, 2007). Branding is the use of signs, symbols, logos and words to differentiate between products. Subramaniam (2009) argues that although many organisations ignore the link between customer service and brand building, leveraging on the nexus can contribute to business differentiation, customer retention and loyalty. Currently, employees are at the centre of ensuring that customers experience the brand through building a positive service attitude and evoking emotional values in a unique pattern (Mosley, 2007). Therefore, it is imperative that African organisations design *brand-aligned customer service initiatives* that ensure the brand power is visible in all customer service touchpoints of the organisation (Subramaniam, 2009).

Recommendations for Africa

Considering the implications of putting in place and operating an effective customer service strategy such as the one we have proposed in this study, the following recommendations are provided for African organisations.

First, African organisations should ensure there is a congruence between its resources and the customers' resources, especially given the unorganised and fragmented nature of the prevailing business environment. They can do this by benchmarking their strategy against best-practice organisations. This provides room for learning how they succeeded, tackling arising challenges and pinpointing exact elements that the organisation can adopt to become successful.

Second, implementing customer service strategy requires examining the human capital of the organisation, as it is key for the success of any strategic goals. Hence, success is dependent on the organisation recruiting and training the right workforce to perform at optimum levels. Doing this requires implementing improvement initiatives built on the work culture to sustain morale and attain quick wins by paying attention to customer touchpoints.

Lastly, organisations in Africa should ensure a controlling customer relationship management mechanism is running concurrently with the execution of the customer service strategy. This is important in order to create a community by sustaining customer relationships, be updated with customers' interests as it changes, improve customer service processes and increase customer lifetime value.

Conclusion

This chapter has explored customer service strategy from an institutional economics-led approach. Discussion on the meaning of customer service strategy in existing mainstream literature highlights five dimensions. These include logistic-marketing, HRM, technological/Internet, customer relationship/intervention and strategic dimensions. The ten (10) models explicating customer service strategy from different dimensions were also reviewed and further broken down into three (3) frameworks: explanatory, antecedent and outcome frameworks. The strengths and limitations of the models reviewed in the chapter were also outlined. The strengths indicated that the models were useful for articulating customer service strategy. In addition, the models showed possible predictors and outcomes of customer service strategy while also indicating how the concept can be put to use to achieve service differentiation. The limitations were that external environment actors and cost implications of the strategy were not captured in the models. Therefore, from the gap noticed in the review of models, we propose an environmental-led customer service strategy that captures the contribution of the environment in the development of customer service strategy.

The institutional economics approach was used as the theoretical lens in developing a framework that captures environmental factors in the crafting of a customer service strategy. The environmental factors were divided into external and internal factors. The external factors comprised of technology, demography, political-legal and culture. The internal factors included employee commitment, organisational culture, value chain and brand power.

In conclusion, this chapter has put forward the notion of an environmental-led customer service strategy, which signifies a pragmatic and environmental approach to its crafting. Today, this pragmatic approach is exemplified in organisations becoming determined to design and implement customer-oriented strategies that have the ability to meet customer expectations. Nevertheless, in the quest to put in place these customer service strategies, the environment, especially turbulent ones such as those in some African countries, must be taken into consideration because changes to strategies are usually driven by the dynamic nature of the environment. From a theoretical perspective, it can be seen that a link between environmental factors and customer service strategy exists; hence, we urge organisations to recognise the imperative nature of environmental factors in crafting a successful customer service strategy.

In light of this, the framework put forward in this chapter will raise some interesting exploratory research hinged on environmental factors and their nexus with customer service strategy. This will deepen the knowledge on customer service strategy and likely help to introduce instruments to measure these constructs.

References

Allen, N. J., & Grisaffe, D. B. (2001). Employee commitment to the organization and customer reactions: Mapping the linkages. *Human Resource Management Review, 11*(3), 209–236.

Alrubaiee, L., & Alkaaida, F. (2011). The mediating effect of patient satisfaction in the patients' perceptions of healthcare quality – patient trust relationship. *International Journal of Marketing Studies, 3*(1), 103–127.

Assael, H. (1995). *Consumer behavior and marketing action* (5th ed.). Mason, OH: South Western College Publishing.

Baker, M. (1996). Marketing strategy. In M. Warner (Ed.). *International encyclopaedia of business and management* (pp. 3333–3347). New York: Routledge.

Batt, R. (2002). Managing customer services: Human resource practices, quit rates, and sales growth. *Academy of Management Journal, 45*(3), 587–597.

Chao, M., & Shih, C. (2016). Customer service-focused HRM systems and firm performance: Evidence from the service industry in Taiwan. *The International Journal of Human Resource Management, 29*(19), 2804–2826.

Cheginia, F., Molanb, S. B., & Kashanifar, S. S. (2016). An examination of the impact of cultural values on brand preferences in Tehran's fashion market. *Procedia Economics and Finance, 36*, 189–200.

Chen, S. (2013). Devising appropriate service strategies for customers of different value: An integrated assessment model for the banking industry. *The International Journal of Human Resource Management, 24*(21), 3939–3956.

Christopher, M. (1992). *The customer service planner.* Oxford: Butterworth-Heineman.

Christopher, M., Payne, A., & Ballantyne, D. (1991). *Relationship marketing: Bringing quality customer service and marketing together.* Retrieved from https://dspace.lib.cranfield.ac.uk/bitstream/handle/1826/621/?sequence=2.

Chuang, C. H., & Liao, H. (2010). Strategic human resource management in service context: Taking care of business by taking care of employees and customers. *Personnel Psychology, 63*, 153–196.

Cleveland, M., Papadopoulos, N., & Laroche, M. (2011). Identity, demographics, and consumer behaviors: International market segmentation across product categories. *International Marketing Review, 28*(3), 244–266.

Conway, N., & Briner, R. B. (2015). Unit-level linkages between employee commitment to the organization, customer service delivery and customer satisfaction. *The International Journal of Human Resource Management, 26*(16), 2039–2061.

Cutcher, L. (2008). Service sells: Exploring connections between customer service strategy and the psychological contract. *Journal of Management & Organization, 14*(2), 116–126.

Daugherty, P. J., Bolumole, Y., & Grawe, S. J. (2018). The new age of customer impatience: An agenda for reawakening logistics customer service research. *International Journal of Physical Distribution & Logistics Management, 3*, 1–31.

Day, S. G., & Hubbard, J. K. (2003). Customer relationships go digital. *Business Strategy Review, 14*(1), 17–26.

Devasagayam, R., Stark, N. R., & Valestin, L. S. (2013). Examining the linearity of customer satisfaction: Return on satisfaction as an alternative. *Business Perspectives and Research, 1*(2), 1–8.

Dhar, R. L. (2015). Service quality and the training of employees: The mediating role of organizational commitment. *Tourism Management, 46*, 419–430.

Domegan, C. (1996). The adoption of information technology in customer service. *European Journal of Marketing, 30*(6), 52–69.

Donaldson, B. (1995). Customer service as a competitive strategy. *Journal of Strategic Marketing, 3*(2), 113–126.

Eng, T. (2008). E-customer service capability and value creation. *The Service Industries Journal, 28*(9), 1293–1306.

Eriksson, K., & Vaghult, A. L. (2000). Customer retention, purchasing behavior and relationship substance in professional services. *Industrial Marketing Management, 29*(4), 363–372.

Etherington, L. (2002). Prudential's customer service strategy delivers personalized service for customers. *Measuring Business Excellence,6*(4), 70–72.

Financial Conduct Authority. (2014). *Mortgage lenders' arrears management and forbearance.* Thematic Review 14/3, 1–20. Retrieved from https://www.fca.org.uk/publication/thematic-reviews/tr14-03.pdf.

Fitzgerald, M., Kruschwitz, N., Bonnet, D., & Welch, M. (2013). *Embracing digital technology. A new strategic imperative.* MIT Sloan Management Review Research Report. Retrieved from https://www.academia.edu/28433565/Embracing_Digital_Technology_A_New_Strategic_Imperative.

Greenberg, J., & Baron, R. A. (1997). *Behavior in organisations* (6th ed.). Englewood Cliffs, NJ: Prentice-Hall.

Gunarathne, P., Rui, H., & Seidmann, A. (2018). When social media delivers customer service: Differential customer treatment in the airline industry. *MIS Quarterly, 42*(2), 489–520.

Gwinner, K. P., Gremler, D. D., & Bitner, M. J. (1998). Relational benefits in services industries: The customer's perspective. *Journal of the Academy of Marketing Science, 26*(2), 101–114.

Hawkins, D. I., & Mothersbaugh, D. L. (2010). *Consumer behavior: Building marketing strategy* (11th ed.). Boston: McGraw-Hill/Irwin.

Hellén, K., & Sääksjärvi, M. (2011). Happy people manage better in adverse services. *International Journal of Quality and Service Sciences, 3*(3), 319–336.

Huang, Y., Chung, J., Lin, Y., Hsu, K., & Kao, C. (2015). Discussing the effects of lifestyle on customer service strategy with cluster analysis and Kano model: A case study on maintenance and repair of motor vehicles. *Journal of Information and Optimization Sciences, 36*(3), 247–268.

Huett, K. B. (2017). Customer service. In C. R. Scott & L. Lewis (Eds.). *The international encyclopedia of organizational communication.* London, UK: John & Wiley Sons.

Huiskonen, J., & Pirttila, T. (1998). Sharpening logistics customer service strategy planning by applying Kano's quality element classification. *International Journal of Production Economics, 56*(1), 253–260.

Ives, B., Palese, B., & Rodriguez, J. A. (2016). Enhancing customer service through the internet of things and digital data streams. *MIS Quarterly Executive, 15*(4), 1–22.

Jiang, K., Chuang, C. H., & Chiao, Y. C. (2015). Developing collective customer knowledge and service climate: The interaction between service-oriented high-performance work systems and service leadership. *Journal of Applied Psychology, 100*(4), 1089–1106.

Jung, K., Garbarino, E., Briley, D. A., & Wynhausen, J. (2017). Blue and red voices: Effects of political ideology on consumers' complaining and disputing behavior. *Journal of Consumer Research, 44*(3), 477–499.

Kano, N., Seraku, K., Takahaski, F., & Tsuji, S. (1984). Attractive quality and must-be quality. *Hinshitsu (Quality, The Journal of the Japanese Society for Quality Control), 14*(2), 39–48.

Kiessling, T., Isaksson, L., & Yasar, B. (2016). Market orientation and CSR: Performance implications. *Journal of Business Ethics, 137*(2), 269–284.

Ko, E., Kim, S. H., Kim, M., & Woo, J. Y. (2008). Organizational characteristics and the CRM adoption process. *Journal of Business Research, 61*(1), 65–74.

La Londe, B. J., Cooper, M. C., & Noordewier, T. G. (1988). *Customer service: A management perspective.* Oak Brook, IL: Council of Logistics Management.

Laforet, S. (2016). Effects of organisational culture on organisational innovation performance in family firms. *Journal of Small Business and Enterprise Development, 23*(2), 379–407.

Lee, Y. (2004). Customer service and organizational learning in the context of strategic marketing. *Marketing Intelligence & Planning, 22*(6), 652–662.

Lee, Y.-I., & Trim, P. R. J. (2006). Placing customer service strategy in the context of a vertical marketing system. *Strategic Change, 15*, 331–339.

Levenburg, N. M. (2006). Benchmarking customer service on the internet: Best practices from family businesses. *Benchmarking: An International Journal, 13*(3), 355–373.

Lin, J. S. C., & Liang, H. Y. (2011). The influence of service environments on customer emotion and service outcomes. *Managing Service Quality: An International Journal, 21*(4), 350–372.

Luo, Y. (2009). Analysis of culture and buyer behavior in Chinese market. *Asian Culture and History, 1*(1), 25–30.

Lutz, W., & Samir, K. C. (2013). *Demography and human development: Education and population projections.* UNDP Human Development Report Office. *Occasions Paper, 4*, 1–18. Retrieved from http://www.hdr.undp.org/sites/default/files/hdro_1304_lutz_kc.pdf.

Materla, T., Cudney, E. A., & Antony, J. (2019). The application of Kano model in the healthcare industry: A systematic literature review. *Total Quality Management & Business Excellence, 30*(5–6), 660–681.

Mathies, C., & Burford, M. (2011). Customer service understanding: Gender differences of frontline employees. *Managing Service Quality: An International Journal, 21*(6), 636–648.

Max Planck Institute for Demographic Research (MPIDR). (2018). *What is demography?* Retrieved from https://www.demogr.mpg.de/en/education_career/what_is_demography_1908/default.htm.

McDonald, M., & Christopher, M. (2003). *Marketing: A complete guide.* Basingstoke, UK: Palgrave Macmillan.

McGraw, A. P., Warren, C., & Kan, C. (2015). Humorous complaining. *Journal of Consumer Research, 41*(5), 1153–1171.

Miller, C., & Jones, L. (2010). *Agricultural value chain finance: Tools and lessons.* Food and Agriculture Organization of the United Nations. Warwickshire, UK: Practical Action Publishing.

Mosley, R. W. (2007). Customer experience, organisational culture and the employer brand. *Journal of Brand Management, 15*(2), 123–134.

Murphy, P. R., & Poist, R. F. (1996). Comparative views of logistics and marketing practitioners regarding interfunctional co-ordination. *International Journal of Physical Distribution & Logistics Management, 26*(8), 15–28.

Nambudiri, R. (2012). Propensity to trust and organizational commitment: A study in the Indian pharmaceutical sector. *International Journal of Human Resource Management, 23*(5), 977–986.

Ngai, E. W. T. (2005). Customer relationship management research (1992–2002): An academic literature review and classification. *Marketing Intelligence & Planning, 23*(6), 582–605.

Norton, R. (2014). *Agricultural value chains: A game changer for small holders.* Retrieved from https://www.devex.com/news/agricultural-value-chains-a-game-changer-for-small-holders-83981.

O'Reilly, C. (1989). Corporations, culture, and commitment: Motivation and social control in organizations. *California Management Review, 31*(4), 9–25.

Petrolino, L. (2018). *Inside out: How organizational culture drives customer service.* Retrieved from https://spinsucks.com/communication/organizational-culture-customer-service/.

Porter, M. E. (1985). *Competitive advantage – Creating a sustaining superior performance.* New York: The Free Press.

Robbins, S. P., & Coulter, M. (2005). *Management.* New York: Pearson Prentice Hall.

Safford, G. S. (1988). Culture traits, strength, and organizational performance: Moving beyond 'strong culture'. *Academy of Management Review, 13*(4), 546–558.

Sharma, A. (2008). Improving customer service and profitability through customer intervention in service relationships. *Journal of Relationship Marketing, 7*(4), 327–340.

Sharma, A., & Lambert, D. M. (1994). Segmentation of markets based on customer service. *International Journal of Physical Distribution & Logistics Management, 24*(4), 50–58.

Singh, R. N., & Mohanty, R. P. (2011). Participation satisfaction and organizational commitment: Moderating role of employee's cultural values. *Human Resource Development International, 14*(5), 583–603.

Sinha, G., & Ghoshal, T. (1999). Quality customer service: Strategic advantage for the Indian steel industry. *Managing Service Quality: An International Journal, 9*(1), 32–39.

Smith, S. (2006). CRM and customer service: Strategic asset or corporate overhead? *Handbook of Business Strategy, 7*(1), 87–93.

Smith, G. (2012). Why I am leaving Goldman Sachs. *The New York Times*, New York. Retrieved from https://www.nytimes.com/2012/03/14/opinion/why-i-am-leaving-goldman-sachs.html.

Staniek, Z. (2010). Diversification of institutional economics. *Warsaw Forum of Economic Sociology, 1*(1), 89–116.

Stutter, B. (2017). *3 ways to make customer service your best supply chain strategy.* Retrieved from http://www.waspbarcode.com/buzz/supply-chain/.

Subramaniam, A. (2009). *Six ways to build your brand through customer service.* Retrieved from https://hbr.org/2009/04/six-ways-to-build-your-brand-t.

Tablan, F. (2016). A catholic-personalist critique of personalized customer service. *Journal of Markets & Morality, 19*(1), 99–119.

Theodoras, D. (2009). Customer service strategy and segmentation in food retailing using the importance-performance paradigm. *Supply Chain Forum: An International Journal, 10*(2), 64–72.

Tressler, C. (2016). *Consumer complaints to the FTC increased in 2015.* Federal Trade Commission. Retrieved from https://www.consumer.ftc.gov/blog/consumer-complaintsftc-increased-2015.

Verhoef, P. C., Lemon, K. N., Parasuraman, A., Roggeveen, A., Tsiros, M., & Schlesinger, L. A. (2009). Customer experience creation: Determinants, dynamics and management strategies. *Journal of Retailing, 85*(1), 31–41.

Wagenheim, G., & Reurink, J. (1991). Customer service in public administration. *Public Administration Review, 51*(3), 263–270.

Walsh, J., & Godfrey, S. (2000). The internet: A new era in customer service. *European Management Journal, 18*(1), 85–92.

Wood, S. (2005). Leveraging diversity: A customer service strategy. *Journal of American Water Works Association, 1*, 47–104.

Wouters, J. P. M. (2004). Customer service strategy options: A multiple case study in a B2B setting. *Industrial Marketing Management, 33*(7), 583–592.

Zaino, J. (2002). Behind the numbers: IT investment boosts business-services sector. *Information Week, 917*, 79–80.

Chapter 6

Barriers to Implementing Customer Service Strategy

Sarah Kimani

Contents

Introduction

In recent years, many organisations have identified the need to become more customer-oriented. Consequently, different organisations have designed various customer service strategies that aim to improve customer service and customer satisfaction. Some of these strategies that include customer relationship management (CRM) strategies and systems cost huge amounts of money, yet their success is illusive. The purpose of this chapter is to provide an exposition of the various barriers to the implementation of a customer service strategy (CSS) in organisations. These barriers may be related to structure, technology, policy, people, knowledge management (KM) and resources. For instance, in Kenya, despite many organisations having great policies in the form of service charters, procedures and service timelines, they have not succeeded in implementing them effectively. As a result, many organisations continue to suffer from customer attrition because of failure to implement effective customer service strategies.

This chapter is divided as follows: a discussion of the benefits of implementing a successful CSS, implementation of CSS, barriers to the implementation of CSS, strategies for overcoming identified barriers and conclusion.

Benefits of Implementing Customer Service Strategy

Research findings on the implementation of CSS indicate that the more an organisation focuses on CSS, the more it is able to acquire long-term business partners (Mutea, 2013). Indeed, research in implementation of customer satisfaction strategies in a Kenyan bank indicate that the bank was able to have high customer attraction and retention, reduced marketing expenditures, lessened number of complaints and lower attrition rates (Mutea, 2013). Relatedly, successful implementation of a CSS can lead to the following benefits (Bergeron, 2001):

- Greater customer satisfaction due to ability to offer superior customer service.
- Greater business coherence linked together by higher customer satisfaction.
- An increase in the number of customers and greater customer loyalty due to the reorganisation and computerisation of business processes surrounding the customer relations life cycle.
- Improvement in customer relationships and extended relationships that generate new business opportunities.
- Better knowledge of segmenting customers, differentiating profitable customers from those who are not and establishing appropriate business plans for each case.
- Increased effectiveness in providing customer service by having complete and homogeneous information.
- Lowered costs of operations (or lower costs of servicing the customers).
- Real-time (sales and marketing) information about customer requirements, expectations and perceptions.

The above benefits then lead to high business performance, which would then lead to greater employee satisfaction and performance.

Implementing a Successful Customer Service Strategy

Successful implementation of a CSS requires everyone in the organisation to support the CSS. It also requires everyone to 'buy in' to the underlying vision that sets the path for the CSS. In many cases, organisations may have well-developed CSSs. However, the basic questions is 'how could an organisation achieve its well-developed or intended CSS?' Borrowing from the work of Berry (1999, p. 239), Akroush (2007) cites that a customer does not experience a strategy but rather experiences the execution (implementation) of that strategy. Therefore, putting the CSS into action is critical in the overall performance of an organisation.

In the implementation of a strategy, such as the CSS, different methodologies, approaches and tools can be used, but should be selected and applied appropriately for a specific strategy or process. Indeed, the successful implementation of approaches, tools and techniques depends on how well they are understood and how well they are applied in an organisational process and/or strategy (Sokovic et al., 2010).

Approaches for Implementing a Successful Customer Service Strategy

Different organisations use different approaches and tools for implementing quality management initiatives such as CSS for continuous quality improvement. These approaches might include total quality management (TQM), theory of constraints (TOC), service quality (SERQUAL), Six Sigma, business process reengineering (BPR), operational excellence or business excellence. Regardless of the approach or the tool used, each CSS initiative requires proper selection and/or a combination of different approaches, tools and techniques in its implementation process (Sokovic et al., 2010). As a guide of implementing a CSS initiative, we discuss the define, measure, analyse, improve and control (DMAIC) cycle approach as an illuminating example below.

The DMAIC Cycle

The current applications of customer service strategies in many organisations tend to coincide with the DMAIC cycle, a tool of Six Sigma. DMAIC is an acronym for five interconnected phases, namely define, measure, analyse, improve and control. It is a data-driven life-cycle approach to Six Sigma projects for implementing and improving processes (Sokovic et al., 2010). Figure 6.1 shows a simplified definition of each phase as conceptualised within a CSS initiative implementation plan. There are five stages.

- *Define* – This stage involves a justification of why the CSS initiative is needed, defining the scope of the CSS initiative and setting objectives of the CSS initiative. The stage also involves defining customers by their unique characteristics, prioritising customers and selecting the right customers to deal with (targeting customers) for the particular CSS initiative.
- *Measure* – This stage involves understanding the key metrics for measuring the CSS results. Such metrics may include customer satisfaction score (CSAT), response time and customer retention rates. The metrics should be measurable in terms of scores, percentage rates or time taken. Data from the metrics should help indicate levels of improvement or otherwise of CSS initiatives. For instance, customer retention from 3% to 5% over a four-month period may

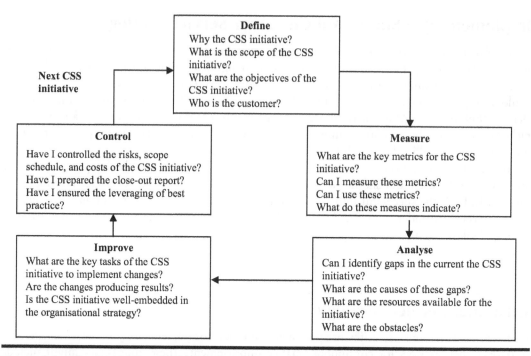

Figure 6.1   The DMAIC cycle for implementing a customer service strategy initiative. (From Sokovic, A. M., et al., *J. Achiev. Mater. Manuf. Eng.*, 43, 476–483, 2010.)

indicate improvement on customer satisfaction. Thus CSATs within the same period should also correlate with the customer retention rate, holding other factors constant. More importantly, this stage should also measure or differentiate customers by their value (measure), behavioural characteristics and needs against the performance of the CSS initiative. Today, those organisations that have the capabilities to leverage petabytes of data they have on their customers and markets are likely to grow their customer bases (Camarate & Brinckmann, 2017). Moreover, huge data and analytics can add value internally by equipping customer service managers with deep insights to better serve their current customers (Camarate & Brinckmann, 2017).

- *Analyse* – This stage involves identifying gaps in the current CSS initiative and the causes of these gaps. The gaps model of service quality, for instance, (Zeithaml et al., 2009) identifies customer gaps that are largely caused by four (4) provider gaps. These provider gaps are caused by not knowing what customers expect (GAP 1), not selecting the right service designs and standards (GAP 2), not delivering the service designs and standards (GAP 3) and not matching performance promises (GAP 4). Thus, this stage should not only identify the gaps in CSS and their causes, but also analyse the available resources for successful implementation of the CSS initiative. The process of analysing should also help identify any obstacles to the CSS implementation. Moreover, analysis should also take care of customer interactions to ensure their cost-effectiveness and efficiency with regard to the CSS initiative.
- *Improve* – In this stage, the key tasks (objectives) of a CSS initiative should be reviewed to check if it is producing expected results. The metric results would be good indicators of the level of improvement achieved.
- *Control* – This stage aims to sustain the gains derived by the CSS initiative, reducing the costs and risks, and ensuring the leverage of best practice.

After the control stage and with the successful implementation of the particular CSS initiative, the subsequent stage is to move to the next CSS initiative. And the cycle moves through the five stages again leading to the process of continuous improvement of CSS.

Regardless of the approach, findings of research work by Akroush (2007) with managers of service organisations on marketing strategy implementation, of which CSS belong, suggests five important factors in its implementation. These are superior customer service competencies, supportive organisational culture, internal marketing, adaptive organisational structure and management of the external business environment. Thus, the approach should take into consideration how these factors may affect the success of a CSS initiative.

Within the banking sectors in Kenya, several factors have been found to affect implementation of CSSs. They include changing consumer tastes and preferences, volatility of the technological environment, limited involvement of lower management, low staff motivation and poor teamwork (Mutea, 2013). These factors may be regarded as barriers and are discussed in the next section.

Barriers to Successfully Implementing Customer Service Strategy

Many barriers exist that impede the successful implementation of a CSS. This subsection discusses six key barriers.

Structure-Related Barriers

Under structure-related barriers, we identify two types of barriers: product-oriented structures and functionalism or departmentalism.

Product-Oriented Structures

Product-oriented structures are those that focus on products and/or transactions as opposed to customer-oriented structures (customer orientation) that emphasise on customer satisfaction and building long-term relationships. The product-oriented structures emphasise on continuous improvement of product quality instead of focusing on better solutions to solve customer problems (Kagira & Kimani, 2010) and often leads to marketing myopia.

In customer-oriented structures, customers become partners with the firm. The aim of this partnership is to have long-term commitments for maintaining those relationships with quality, service and innovation. Customer-oriented organisations have put in place processes that capture customer requirements that have been dubbed '*Voice of the Customer* (VOC)' (Gaskin et al., 2010). With technology, *Virtual Customer Communities* (*VCCs*) or 'online social networks' have also been developed that support customer requirements in many ways. For instance, VCCs support mass-customisation strategies that allow customers to become co-designers of their products and services. Indeed, organisations that have embraced customer orientation view customers as 'actively co-creating and re-creating value with organisations' (Romero & Molina, 2011). In Kenya, Unaitas Bank emphasises on 'membership'. The bank calls its customers 'members'. Many other organisations are today referring to their suppliers and other stakeholders as 'partners'. However, the level of involvement of such partners and the value of the partnership in the performance organisations remain unclear.

Despite the opportunities and benefits for embracing customer orientation, the practice has remained largely product orientated (Ryals & Knox, 2001). However, in the recent past, several factors have obliged and enabled firms to reorganise their structures around their customers. Such factors include the widespread changes in business processes, growth of the services sector and the availability of cost-effective software solutions to the challenges of 'mass-customisation' (Ryals & Knox, 2001). Although these factors, in some way, are facilitating the shift from product management to a customer focus, the shift is not yet eminent. While this shift might be easy with the small-scale organisations, it might be more difficult with larger firms.

To facilitate this shift, the necessary changes should impact the ways that organisations view their customers and how they treat them, how they are themselves organised and how they measure and reward success (Ryals & Knox, 2001).

Functionalism/Departmentalism

Poor interdepartmental coordination and lack of cross-functional integration are key barriers to effective CSS implementation. A lack of departmental and interdepartmental coordination in an organisation often leads to decreased productivity, complicate processes and delay the completion of tasks. In order to coordinate the efforts of an entire organisation, the organisation requires a systematic integration of its processes that ensure accountability within the organisation. Implementing this type of process allows interdepartmental coordination throughout the organisation among employees. Signs and symptoms of poor coordination and lack of cross-functional integration are delays, duplication of tasks, inflexibility, loss of data and poor communication.

Technology-Related Barriers

For effective implementation of a CSS, there should be appropriate technology and effective data management systems in place. A technical support and implementation specialist should provide the technical vision, strategy and leadership for design, while overseeing the technical implementation of the CSS as needed. This specialist should provide customer support for both internal and external customers, including application troubleshooting and problem resolution. Many technology-related barriers abound in many organisations because of the following factors:

- *Inappropriate technology that supports the customer service strategy.* Often, due to limited resources, some organisations tend to go for less appropriate or poor-quality technology that often fails to support effective implementation of a CSS. Perhaps, the best approach to negotiating for the best technology is to look at the long-term corporate and CSS and how the particular technology (solution) will support it.
- *Inadequate and/or poorly qualified technical support and implementation specialists.* There should be adequate staff with the right qualifications and with adequate time available to dedicate to managing, supporting and updating the technology that supports the CSS.
- *Inadequate training (for all employees) on the technology that supports the CSS.* The training needs for implementing the CSS should be assessed early on in the process to determine how users should be introduced to it. The costs and time necessary for training should be rolled into the budget and deployment plan, taking into consideration the need for customised training to various learning types, to get the best possible value from it. Moreover, organisations should have adequate resources for technology training, not only for implementing the CSS, but also

for managing it going forward. Thus, organisations whose employees possess superior knowledge and skills to be able to analyse changing customers' needs are more likely to be successful.

■ *Integration issues.* The technology that supports the CSS needs to be evaluated from the perspective of existing processes. Many organisations assess the compatibility and integration of a new solution as an afterthought, which often leads to failure in implementation.

■ *Scepticism about the new technology.* Those who advocate for the status quo will resist the new technology often because of their limited understanding of how the new change can benefit the organisation. When organisations fail to communicate to the users how the new technology will make their roles more efficient, then scepticism sets in.

■ *Changes in market trends.* In Kenya, for instance, one of the current trends in the telecommunication sector is the rise of text messages. The trend has been caused by the telecom firms selling cheap SMS bundles, with Safaricom leading with 95.2% market share in SMS (Mumo, 2017). Within the banking sector, one of the trends in the South African banking market is the ongoing transformation of the four universal banks (Barclays Africa, Standard Bank, Nedbank and FirstRand) to address changing customer, regulatory and technology needs (Camarate & Brinckmann, 2017). These banks have made substantial investments in digital transformations, which form part of their strategies to improve risk management and cost-efficiency, as well as enhance customer-centricity. The key operational trends these banks have adopted are the implementation of emerging technologies to replace old systems, strong focus on cyber and IT resilience, and digitisation of front and back-office operations. At the same time, they have prioritised customer expectations fulfilment through electronic channels (Camarate & Brinckmann, 2017).

When appropriate technology and effective data management systems are in place, then the system would be able to generate high-quality data and information that would lead the management to make the right decisions and conclusions.

Policy-Related Barriers

Many organisations have clear policies and performance measurement systems in almost all their functional areas, such as human resources policies (hiring and promotional policies, leave policies, and education policies), and financial management policies (auditing policies, financial reporting policies, internal control and risk management policies, and procurement policies). However, how such policies help organisations to improve performance is still unclear. In some cases, it seems that some of these policies have been put in place to help organisations to get accreditations or certifications, such as ISO 9000, rather than customer satisfaction (or quality improvement). Thus, gaps occur with regard to such policies because organisations are very quick to fix the gaps by developing further policies and guidelines. However, the major problem is that such policies are not well implemented or are never implemented at all. An organisation might, for instance, have a customer satisfaction measurement questionnaire in place that is reviewed and administered regularly. However, information from the survey is rarely communicated within the organisation and/or the specific functional area(s). Moreover, when it is, it is often distributed via memos or protocols that tend to 'disappear' in the other paperwork required to run the business on a daily basis (Osarenkhoe & Bennani, 2007). In such a case, we find that such an organisation over-relies on policies instead of the outcome of the policies or how the policies may help the organisation to improve customer service.

People-Related Barriers

The people-related barriers are influenced to a large extent by the following factors:

Poor Organisational Culture

Organisational culture defines the core beliefs, values, norms and social customs that govern the way people act and behave in an organisation. It is the sum of shared philosophies, assumptions, values, expectations and attitudes that bind the organisations together (Singh & Kant, 2008). Organisational culture is also defined as shared perceptions of organisational work practices within organisational units that may differ from other organisational units (Van den Berg & Wilderom, 2004). Although there exists many types of cultures such as power-oriented, rule-oriented, and performance-oriented (Westrum, 2004), it has been argued that the best companies have organisational cultures that are characterised by task autonomy, external orientation, interdepartmental coordination, human resource orientation and improvement orientation (Van den Berg & Wilderom, 2004). Nevertheless, many organisations tend to have cultures that lack job autonomy, have an inward-looking perspective and lack interdepartmental coordination. Many also lack an ongoing improvement orientation.

The implementation of CSS requires an organisational culture that is adaptive and responsive to change needed by the strategy since organisational culture has been found to be integral to effective strategy implementation. It has also been opined that those cultures that can help organisations anticipate and adapt to change are associated with superior performance (Parry & Proctor-Thomson, 2003). Thus, for successful implementation of CSS, organisational culture should be supportive of the strategy, and adaptive to changes in the environment. The culture should be characterised by proper coordination within departmental units. Moreover, a transparent organisational culture with an emphasis on effective communication, empowerment, teamwork, coordination, customer focus and continuous improvement may provide a good foundation for implementing a CSS. There should be *'passion for the customer'* within the organisational culture. An important issue to note is that 'cultures do not change by mandate; they change by the specific displacement of existing norms, structures and processes by others. The processes of cultural change depend fundamentally on modelling the new values and behaviour that you expect to displace the existing ones' (Burger et al., 2007, p. 34).

Inadequate Top Management

The organisational issues of culture, communication, management metrics, commitment and participation all lie with the top management. These issues may enhance or impede implementation of a CSS. Indeed, as companies attempt to reorientate themselves around customers, the top management's support and commitment become a critical factor. If individual employees will commit themselves and come to terms with changing cultural norms in the context of a new CSS, top management must be at the forefront to support the strategy. There are a number of studies (Martiny, 1998; Braganza & Myers, 1996; Ryals & Knox, 2001) that show that the commitment of senior management is critical to the success of a new strategy. Indeed, a META Group report (1998) reinforces this by singling out the Chief Executive Officer's (CEO) involvement as a key success factor for CRM projects (Ryals & Knox, 2001).

Thus, a top management culture that fails to support CSS and poor communications within organisations are key barriers to CSS implementation. Other barriers relate to inadequate knowledge and skills of top management with regard to CSS implementation. Where top management lacks knowledge and competence in implementing a particular strategy, have poor creativity, and are risk-averse, then, it is likely that implementation of CSS may fail.

Inadequate top management is also characterised by a poor sense of integrity, lack of performance orientation, self-serving nature with an inward looking perspective, lack of focus and follow through, and lack of vision. Such characteristics then yield corruption and impunity that impede successful implementation of any strategy. Because these characteristics are common among leaders of many African organisations, efforts to improve and/or implement CSS often fail. This is because many employees who would implement such strategies often look up to the top management for guidance on how to behave with regard to accountability, integrity, performance and commitment.

Poor Communication

The quality of communication, as discussed later in this chapter, is an important aspect of the CSS/ initiative. Secretive, closed attitudes towards information as well as failure to successfully communicate the CSS and its implications to employees, customers and the stakeholders can lead to failure. Thus, an effective internal communication strategy needs to be in place so that there is '*buy-in*' to the initiative led by the top-management team (Ryals & Knox, 2001; Mabin et al., 2001).

Inadequate Skills for Implementing Customer Service Strategy

In many organisations, implementation skills are lacking or are inadequate. These skills relate to the following (Bonoma, 1984):

- *Diagnostic skills*: These skills help to determine the causes of implementation problems.
- *Identification skills:* These skills help to determine where the implementation problems occurred.
- *Implementation skills:* These skills can be categorised into four:
  - *Interacting skills:* Those implementing CSS should show empathy and have an ability to understand how others feel. They should also have good bargaining skills.
  - *Allocating skills:* Good implementers should have the abilities to schedule tasks and budget time, money and other resources efficiently.
  - *Monitoring skills:* Good implementers make efficient use of information available to correct any problems that arise in the process of implementation.
  - *Organising skills:* Good implementers exhibit the ability to create a new informal organisation or network to match each problem that occurs.
- *Evaluation skills:* These are monitoring skills that help to track and evaluate CSS actions.

From the above set of implementation skills, we find that the people skills dimension is diverse. It also entails managing the social structure of a relationship across the various functions for effective implementation of a CSS.

Inadequate Internal Marketing

Internal marketing is a process of motivating and empowering employees of a company to work as a team to provide superior customer satisfaction (Kotler & Armstrong, 2006, p. 260). The key elements of internal marketing are employee commitment (involvement in, identification with, and attachment to their organisation); job satisfaction and trust in management; employee security; employee empowerment; extensive training; information sharing; generous rewards (that are contingent on organisational performance); and reduced status/power distinctions (Bansala et al., 2001).

A research study investigating marketing strategy implementation success factors in service organisations in Jordan identified the practice of internal marketing as a major issue that enabled employees to perform their service roles and actualise the intended marketing strategy into reality (Akroush, 2007).

Knowledge Management Barriers

KM is a people-related barrier that has emerged as an integral part of customer strategy. KM is seen as deliberate and systematic coordination of an organisation's people, technology, processes and organisational structure in order to add value through reuse and innovation (Singh & Kant, 2008).To achieve this coordination, an organisation creates, shares and applies knowledge and best practices into its corporate memory with the aim of fostering continued organisational learning (Dalkir, 2005). Indeed, KM facilitates the flow of knowledge and sharing to improve the efficiency of individuals and hence, the organisation's business or CSS.

Although businesses today have realised the competitiveness of KM, many organisations, particularly in Africa, still lag behind with integrating KM in their business processes. Some of the reasons why KM has not been implemented in these organisations are not different from the barriers to implementation of a successful customer strategy. They include inadequate top management commitment, inappropriate organisational structure, poor technological support, poorly defined implementation methodologies and unsupportive culture (Singh & Kant, 2008). One example of KM can be seen in Kenya, as the government has recently engaged in 'huduma number' project, which is conducted by the National Integrated Identity Management System (NIIMS) and involves collecting biometric data of Kenyans. The NIIMS then generates a unique number that will enable Kenyans to access government services. It is expected that the 'huduma number' will be the only identification document Kenyans will need and this is seen as a step forward in data management in Kenya.

Limited Resources

Often, organisations fail to have adequate resources not only for implementing a CSS but for managing this strategy going forward. These resources are in terms of human resources (adequacy in numbers and in capability), financial resources, technological and technical resources, physical and infrastructural resources, and intellectual resources. In Kenya for instance, the higher education sector faces a number of limited resources such as an inadequate number of teaching staff (human resources), most of whom do not have qualifications in PhD. There are also inadequate learning and teaching facilities (including classrooms and laboratories), which often make the implementation of the newer methods of learning and teaching difficult. The limited government funding in most public universities means that many universities are handicapped to put up new teaching and learning facilities and infrastructure (Kimani, 2015).

Strategies to Overcome the Identified Barriers

In order to implement a CSS effectively, an organisation may adopt the following strategies:

Emphasising Quality

Many organisations have adopted quality management systems that are drawn from the TQM movement, the European Framework for Quality Management (EFQM) excellence model, the balanced scorecard (BSC) framework, the Malcolm Baldrige National Quality Award (MBNQA), the ISO 9000 series, the BPR, the SERVQUAL framework or the TOC (Kimani, 2015). Although these frameworks and models have been adopted with the aim of improving quality, many have failed to do so. Recently, Barnard (2010) conducted an analysis of a representative sample of research studies using TQM, Six Sigma, Lean, BSC, BPR, organisational transformation, out-sourcing initiatives, new product launches, MRP/ERP, TOC and other IT projects. The results of the study indicated that 50%–80% of the quality initiatives conducted using these models failed to meet the original objectives, stopped before completion, or even caused organisation performance to decay. In Kenya, for instance, many universities are ISO 9000 series certified. Yet, a number of these universities are suffering from poor quality management issues that revolve around resources planning and management. Issues related to missing marks and incomplete grades are therefore not uncommon in the ISO 9000 certified universities (Kimani, 2015).

Thus, in order to improve quality that may result in superior customer service, organisations must start with a clear and official implementation plan of the *specific quality initiative* and inform all the relevant employees (such as the academic staff) about the when, where, how and why they should adopt the specific quality initiative. Moreover, all employees should be given education and continuous training of the quality system adopted to help implement the quality initiative. For instance, in universities, academic staff should be trained on assessment of high-impact prac-tices (HIP) or engaged learning practices that are associated with student success (Kilgo et al., 2015; Kimani, 2015).

Managing Customer Service

A number of organisations such as banks do have customer service managers and service charters. In Kenya, many organisations including the government ministries, corporations, county govern-ments and public service commissions all have service charters that define expected service standards. Moreover, most of the county government service charters are available online. The challenge is that most of these organisations do not have a person responsible for managing customer service. Such a person would ensure that what is promised in the service charter is delivered. But many organisa-tions may perceive such a position as an unnecessary cost. However, having personnel responsible for ensuring service excellence assures customers (and the organisation) of accountability for any service failures. Some of the duties and responsibilities of such a personnel would include:

- Developing customer care programme(s), policies and procedures, and ensuring their implementation;
- Defining and communicating customer service standards contained in the charter and in customer service policies and procedures;
- Developing and sharing reports on the evaluation of the level of customer satisfaction on a quarterly or half-yearly basis;
- Developing measures for identifying and measuring quality service improvements, produc-tivity and profitability;
- Identifying and implementing strategies to improve quality of service, productivity and profitability;

- Planning, prioritising and delegating work tasks to ensure proper functioning of the customer service department;
- Directing the daily operations of the customer service team;
- Overseeing the achievement and maintenance of agreed customer service levels and standards,
- Ensuring that the necessary resources and tools are available for quality customer service delivery;
- Handling complex and escalated customer service issues;
- Analysing relevant data to determine customer service outputs;
- Co-ordinating and managing customer service projects and initiatives;
- Reviewing and assessing customer service contracts;
- Reviewing customer complaints procedures and tracking customer complaint resolution processes; and
- Monitoring accuracy of reporting and proper management of database information.

Investing in People

Organisations need to invest in people. People, in this case, imply both employees and customers. On the one hand, employees need to be trained on customer service excellence. They also need continuous training of the quality management system that their organisation has put in place to ensure excellent service. In a university, for instance, academic staff and administrators should be trained on the academic management system (AMS) put in place by their university. Similarly, in an organisation using a CRM system, employees should not only be able to define what CRM entails, but also indicate the benefits they derive from using such a system. More importantly, employees should have the skills and capability to manage the customer service management system. Customers, on the other hand, need to be continuously trained on how to use the quality system in place. In a university setting for instance, students using an AMS should be trained on how to use it to register for semester course units, and get their grades and fee statements. For those taking online courses, they should be trained on how to use their portals for maximum benefits. Nevertheless, feedback on the use of the system should be obtained regularly from both the employees and customers. The feedback should be compiled in form of a report and presented to the relevant authorities.

Maintaining Dialogue with Customers

Organisations must have a person responsible for developing and maintaining long-term relationships with customers. Today, organisations are communicating with customers in various ways such as Facebook, Twitter, Instagram and many other social media forums. Organisations should be able to segment their customers so that they can define the best ways to interact with them. For instance, an organisation can identify the VIP customers that have a professional interest in a particular field and create a webpage for such professionals where they can share experiences and ideas that may provide benefits to customers and the company. Organisations must also have systems in place where they are able to collect information on unsatisfied needs, complaints and complements. Such information should be analysed regularly and then shared with all the key constituents (customers, suppliers, producers, employees, distributors, governments, marketing facilitators and financial intermediaries). Where possible, it should be made available online.

Due to advances in technology, many banks in Kenya provide customers with the digital systems to access funds through their mobile phones and other services. Through the digital systems, they are able to maintain dialogue with their customers. In South Africa, TymeDigital (a subsidiary of the Commonwealth Bank of Australia) also provides similar services (Camarate & Brinckmann, 2017).

Communicating Relevant Information

When implementing CSS, it is critical that relevant information be communicated clearly through the right channels in order to minimise communication gaps. Communication gaps exist between management and customers, management and staff, and management and systems (Osarenkhoe & Bennani, 2007). Where communication gaps exist, management may be unable to execute their strategy in the way intended. Internally, management must communicate and explain the purpose of implementing a CSS. Consequently, all employees at all levels should clearly know what the CSS that the organisation is implementing means to them and their customers. For instance, to enhance empathy and understanding as part of a customer-focused strategy, an organisation can create internal forums for cross-functional communication about the same. Moreover, a clear definition of the strategy should be available on the company's intranet and on their home page. Furthermore, management must consistently communicate the customer service strategic priority of the organisation cross-functionally. Externally, an organisation should keep key customers and constituents informed about the CSS that they are implementing. Moreover, an organisation can give such customers access to online information regarding their own company and/or any contracts and tenders. Such access would ensure a two-way communication with the external customers, promoting openness and transparency.

Measuring Customer Satisfaction

Organisations must have clear standards for measuring customer satisfaction at different functional areas. The measurement of the level of customer satisfaction should not be sporadic but quite systematic and specific (Osarenkhoe & Bennani, 2007). Measurement can be done daily by issuing customers a satisfaction survey, and reporting the results weekly or monthly. However, the officer in-charge of every functional area must be held responsible for any urgent action that may be required from the survey feedback. As such, the officer in-charge should pre-review the survey feedback on a daily basis to respond to the urgent issues and report out the information to customers and employees regularly.

Evaluating the Customer Service Quality Management System

Having a customer service quality management system in place is not enough. The quality management system/initiative should be reviewed periodically and the effect of the use of the quality management system should be continuously reported to all employees. This report should be in terms of the success and/or failure of the system in relation to the organisation's objectives and/or specific departmental/functional goals. The report should be a critical report that aims at quality improvement and not a report to stamp compliance.

Conclusion

There may be many barriers to the implementation of a successful CSS. However, if the customer service problems can be correctly identified and an appropriate CSS approach can be selected, then it can be implemented to solve issues and meet strategic objectives. Again, the organisation should verify that the CSS initiative will properly remedy the problem and ensure all major barriers to its implementation have been identified and addressed. After addressing the barriers, management should ensure the commitment of all leadership to making the implementation successful. Moreover, the responsible personnel for CSS should provide a detailed plan of the implementation of the strategy and its proper coordination. If these steps are taken and partnerships are built with internal and external stakeholder, then the desired impact of a CSS can be realised.

References

Akroush, M. N. (2007). Marketing strategy implementation success factors: A qualitative empirical investigation of service organisations in Jordan. *Jordan Journal of Business Administration*, *3*(3), 391–411.

Bansala, H. S., Mendelsonb, M. B., & Sharmac, B. (2001). The impact of internal marketing activities on external marketing outcomes. *Journal of Quality Management*, *6*(1), 61–76.

Barnard, A. (2010). Continuous improvement and auditing. In J. Cox & J. Schleier (Eds.), *Theory of constraints handbook* (pp. 403–454). New York: McGraw-Hill.

Bergeron, B. (2001). *Essentials of CRM: Customer relationship management for executives.* New York: John Wiley & Sons.

Bonoma, T. V. (1984). Making your marketing strategy work. *Harvard Business Review*, March Issue, *62*, 69–76.

Braganza, A., & Myers, A. (1996). Issues and dilemmas facing organisations in the effective implementation of BPR. *Business Change and Re-engineering*, *3*(2), 38–51.

Burger, J. M., Webber, C. F., & Klinck, P. (Eds.). (2007). *Intelligent leadership: Constructs for thinking educational leaders.* Dordrecht, the Netherlands: Springer.

Camarate, J., & Brinckmann, S. (2017). The future of banking: A South African perspective. Strategy&. Retrieved from www.strategyand.pwc.com

Dalkir, K. (2005). *Knowledge management in theory and practice.* Burlington, VT: Elsevier Butterworth-Heinemann.

Gaskin, S. P., Griffin, A., Hauser J. R., Katz, G. M., & Klein, R. L. (2010). Voice of the customer. In J. N. Sheth & N. K. Malhotra (Eds.), *Wiley international encyclopaedia of marketing.* Chichester, UK: John Wiley & Sons.

Kagira, E. K., & Kimani, W. S. (2010). *Marketing principles and practices: An African perspective* (2nd ed.). Nairobi: Mashel Publishers.

Kilgo, C. A., Ezell S., J., & Pascarella, E. T. (2015). The link between high-impact practices and student learning: Some longitudinal evidence. *Higher Education*, *69*(4), 509–525.

Kimani, S. (2015). Exploring quality of learning and teaching experiences in higher education using the theory of constraints: Kenya and New Zealand. PhD Thesis, Victoria University of Wellington, Wellington, New Zealand. Retrieved from http://researcharchive.vuw.ac.nz/xmlui/bitstream/handle/10063/4878/thesis.pdf.

Kotler, P., & Armstrong, G. (2006). *Principles of marketing* (11th ed.). Upper Saddle River, NJ: Pearson Prentice Hall.

Mabin, V., Forgeson, S., & Green, L. (2001). Harnessing resistance: Using the theory of constraints to assist change management. *Journal of European Industrial Training*, *25*(2/3/4), 168–191.

Martiny, M. (1998). Knowledge management at HP consulting. *Organisational Dynamics*, *27*(2), 71–77.

Mumo, M. (2017, October 4). Trends in Kenya's telecoms sector. *Business Daily.* Retrieved from https://www.businessdailyafrica.com.

Mutea, E. (2013). Implementation of customer satisfaction strategies in Kenya Commercial Bank. MBA thesis, University of Nairobi, Nairobi, Kenya. Retrieved from http://erepository.uonbi.ac.ke/handle/11295/59732

Osarenkhoe, A., & Bennani, A. (2007). An exploratory study of implementation of customer relationship management strategy. *Business Process Management Journal*, *13*(1), 139–164.

Parry, K. W., & Proctor-Thomson, S. (2003). Leadership, culture and performance: The case of the New Zealand public sector. *Journal of Change Management, 3*(4), 376–399.

Romero, D., & Molina, A. (2011). Collaborative networked organisations and customer communities: Value co-creation and co-innovation in the networking era. *Journal of Production Planning & Control, 22*(4), 1366–5871. doi:10.1080/09537287.2010.536619.

Ryals, L., & Knox, S. (2001). Cross-functional issues in the implementation of relationship marketing through customer relationship management (CRM). *European Management Journal, 19*(5), 534–542.

Singh, M. D., & Kant, R. (2008). Knowledge management barriers: An interpretive structural modelling approach. *International Journal of Management Science and Engineering Management, 3*(2), 141–150.

Sokovic, A. M., Pavletic, B. D., & Pipan, K. K. (2010). Quality improvement methodologies – PDCA cycle, RADAR matrix, DMAIC and DFSS. *Journal of Achievements in Materials and Manufacturing Engineering, 43*(1), 476–483.

Van den Berg, P. T., & Wilderom, C. P. (2004). Defining, measuring, and comparing organisational cultures. *Applied Psychology: An International Review, 53*(4), 570–582.

Westrum, R. (2004). A typology of organisational cultures. *Quality and Safety in Health Care, 13*(Suppl II), 22–27. doi:10.1136/qshc.2003.009522.

Zeithaml, V. A., Bitner, M. J., & Glemler, D. D. (2009). *Services marketing: Integrating customer focus across the firm* (3rd ed.). Boston, MA: McGraw-Hill.

THEME C: CUSTOMER SERVICE SYSTEMS

THEME C: CUSTOMER SERVICE SYSTEMS

Chapter 7

Customer Service Systems

Paul Katuse

Contents

Introduction

Customer service systems are a set of principles or procedures which indicate how, when, with what a customer is served. These systems entail organised schemes or methods of service. This chapter elaborates on service systems for service-based organisations. The discussion will specifically be centred on service blueprints, service charters, SOPs and service levels. Several examples of how organisations seek to serve their stakeholders as they deliver their services are given.

Service Charter

Service charter can be viewed as a legal framework that governs the service delivery of an organisation to its customers (Macaulay, 2018). A service charter communicates the major functions of the business, that is, the business model. A service business charter lays out the commitment of business to incorporate all stakeholders in executing its mission. Often the service charter may indicate business boundaries with respect to business unilateral, multilateral and international confines of trade. The public and private sectors are confined to service delivery by the service charter under the accountability of their respective stakeholders. Charter and Tischner (2017) assert that the approach to public charter can be subdivided into either private or public sector depending on its scope. Therefore, the structure of a service charter, public or private, must outline the framework of service delivery to the customers by the business.

Components of Service Charter

An organisation's service charter should be the first face of the contract the firm wishes to have with its customers. Picciotto (2017) points out that the components of an organisation's charter should clearly entail the mission, objectives and mandate. These components, however, are diverse with regard to the scope of operation of the organisation. The Kenyan government, for example, requires that organisations, government parastatals and private players have their service charter communicated to their relevant stakeholders (Mang'era and Bichanga, 2013). In most Kenyan public institutions, the service charter is more like a creed and serves as a promise to the customer and an accountability statement for the institution (Republic of Kenya, 2015).

The components of a service charter for different firms may be similar, even though the specifics may be different. According to Reim (2015), the components of a service charter are universal and may have few variations depending on the jurisdiction of an organisation. These components usually include a commitment to service provision, a purpose statement, service charter mandate statement, mission and vision statements, core values, stakeholder responsibility, customer obligation and product portfolio. The particular components used may be based on the core business of the organisation. The following are definitions of the major components of a service charter.

Commitment to Service Provision

The service charter of any organisation should be an open declaration of service delivery. Public and private organisations are expected to commit to their stakeholders' expectations. The commitment should legally bind the organisation to service delivery. According to Tukker (2017), it is worth noting that commitment to service delivery cannot be jeopardised at any given time and could attract legal action from the stakeholder in the event of breaching the commitment. Therefore, commitment to service delivery as laid down in a service charter should represent a deliberate move by an organisation to fulfil its mandate to its stakeholders (Australian Government, 2018).

Purpose Statement

A service charter shows the rights, privileges and obligations of organisations, both private and public. Service charters clearly state the organisation's purpose of the operation. The purpose statement should be elaborate and submitted to the registrar of companies for verification and authentication. The purpose statement should be within the confines of the law to ensure that no illegal businesses are in operations. The scope of the purpose statement should be confined to the nature of operation of an organisation. Therefore, a private service charter should only operate within the confines of private jurisdictions while those registered as public organisations should confine their purpose statement to the stipulations engraved in the law and the mandate granted to them by the state. Reim (2015) asserts that the purpose statement needs to be well coined to erase any form of vagueness. Service charters should be built around the purpose statement to ensure that all the subsequent activities of the organisation are relevant and appropriate. The purpose statement in the service charter should form the framework for assigning responsibilities to internal constituents of an organisation. Clear understanding of the purpose statement by the workforce will help deliver the organisation's mandate.

Statement of Service Charter Mandate

A service charter mandate statement is a statement meant for the consumption of an organisation's stakeholders. It is a deliberate communication by an organisation to make known to its customers and stakeholders their intention and motive to deliver their mandate, to achieve the organisation's vision and mission, to maintain and enhance the organisation's standards of service delivery, and possibly, the organisation's commitment to continuous improvement of service delivery. Charter and Tischner (2017) assert that the mandate of a private or public organisation is ingrained in the service charter. In the case of a public sector organisation, the mandate should be constitutional or through government executive provision. The mandate should highlight key aspects of the areas that the organisation aims at directly impacting, scaling it up from minor to a major scope. According to Veselovsky (2015), the service charter should lay out the organisation's primary mandate, pointing out the stakeholders and partners that an organisation undertakes to serve through its mandate. The mandate of an organisation should incorporate its operational framework, which provides a guideline to the stakeholders of the responsibilities and obligations of the firm and the customers. Public organisations are required to communicate their operational mandate to their stakeholders in an attempt to clarify their operational space and limit. The statement of mandate should be carefully conducted to avoid cases of overstepping the provisions of the law in regard to the operations of an organisation. The mandate should be well-communicated to the stakeholders to ensure that the company is kept in check on its progress and fulfilment of its obligations (Mukesh, 2001).

Vision and Mission Statement

Vision statements should reflect the stakeholder's interest while also considering the intended customers. They should be designed in such a way that it incorporates all the stakeholders' interests and provides a clear picture of the short and long-term business projections. The vision statement is critical in bringing investors on board for companies (Public Administration Select Committee, 2008). A good mission statement should have clear outcomes linking the organisations intentions to the stakeholders expectations. These outcomes should be attainable within the strategic planning period of the organisation.

The mission of an organisation is its legal justification for its existence. Reim (2015) defines the mission statement as the narrow business level objective statement. The mission statement in a service charter should form a blueprint for the realisation of core business objectives. A mission statement is an imperative tool for the induction of employees into the company. Therefore, organisations should be very clear in their mission statement. Charter and Tischner (2017) assert that the inclusion of a mission statement creates a harmony of thoughts and erases imminent confusion in carrying out an organisation's mandate. The connection between the vision and mission statement helps the company work with clear time frames to achieve its objectives (Emily, 2008).

Core Values

Core values are the fundamental beliefs of an organisation. They are guiding principles which determine the way workers conduct themselves as they carry out their professions. Reim (2015) asserts that a service charter is meant to serve the stakeholders of an organisation is based on the organisation's beliefs. Therefore, an organisation must incorporate the legal and moral obligation of the company to its stakeholders in the formulation of its core values. Firms are obligated to uphold moral standards in carrying out their businesses and protect their stakeholders from any form of exploitation. Organisations are professional entities, and as such, the core value component of the service charter should portray a high standard of professionalism. Picciotto (2017) points out that core values should incorporate equity in handling different stakeholders and avoid any form of discrimination. Public companies are open to the members of the public for scrutiny, and hence they are obligated to ensure that there is a fair ground for all stakeholders. Discriminatory agenda based on gender, religion, race or any other factor should be addressed in formulating the core values.

Responsibility to Stakeholder Statement

A service charter is usually a commitment document that binds a company to service delivery to stakeholders. The stakeholders in any organisation can be categorised into internal and external categories. The internal stakeholders' category is composed of investors, employees and the management. According to Tukker (2017), public and private companies have an obligation to their internal constituents and as such, there should be transparency in the statement of these obligations. Investors in any organisation are key financiers of the company's undertakings. Therefore, both private and public organisations are mandated to come up with a clear road map to realise the expectation of investors. Wang (2015) emphasises that companies should adopt a remuneration approach that will ensure that investors' dividends are paid on a timely basis. It is worth noting that any attempt to frustrate investors may expose an organisation to financial woes. Secondly, the management of a company is a crucial component in carrying out the implementation of a business model. The investors are obligated to the financial remuneration of the management team regarding salaries and allowances. A company should ensure that it adopts a proper and competitive remuneration package for the management for a smooth running of the business. Employees are people mandated to ensure that the vision of the company is implemented at different levels and therefore, firms have a legal obligation to reward their employees equitably. A company is obligated to incorporate its remuneration packages in employment contracts to erase confusion among its employees (Berkowitz and Muller-Bonani, 2006).

The external stakeholders' category comprises of the customers, the general public and the government. According to Tukker (2017), a public company should make known to the general public its obligation to customers. The public declaration of commitment to upholding the customers' expectation acts as a checkoff point for the company. Public companies are legally obligated to communicate this information to ensure there is no breach of the commitment. Private companies are also mandated to come up with a declaration of their legal obligation to their customers. However, in the case of a private company, Wang (2015) notes that the declaration is limited to its stakeholders. It is worth noting that in the event of flouting a service commitment as laid out in the service charter, customers can file a case against a company. Therefore, it is imperative to ensure that all the declarations made are within the provision of the company. Companies are warned against overstating their obligations to their customers to avoid cases of conflict. Public and private companies in Kenya, for example, are mandated by the constitution to pay their taxes and comply with the legal provisions laid out by the constitution in all their undertakings. Public companies must file their financial returns to the general public. On the other hand, private companies are mandated by the service charter to report their annual financial returns to their stakeholders (Okello, 2010).

An example of a Stakeholder Statement from the Bank of Kigali's website states *'Over the years, BK has demonstrated the capabilities of increasing shareholders' value by providing the best financial services and achieving the company's valuation securities.'* (Bank of Kigali, 2019). The Bank of Kigali has linked its mission to the vision and clearly identified their primary stakeholder – the shareholder.

Statement of Customer Obligations to the Company

Customer obligations are the specific expectations organisations have of their customers. Reim (2015) asserts that customers are obligated to uphold all the best practices as laid out by the companies. Customers are obliged to adhere to the company's rules and regulation in any dealing involving the two parties. Customers are mandated to follow the right procedures while handling any case with the organisation.

The service charter should provide a framework for direct interactions between a company and its customers. Interactions should include critiques and feedback on major components of products. Customers are also obligated to report any cases of product misrepresentation in the market. Public and private companies are faced with counterfeits and misrepresentation, and as such their customers should assist by giving feedback identify cases of fraud.

According to Picciotto (2017), customers are expected to pay for deliverables in a timely manner in case a company has provisions of credit buying. Customers are expected to buy products as a way of supporting organisations. Private and public companies expect their customers to consume their products safely in light of the preservation of the environment. The service charter should communicate all these requirements to facilitate proper communication with its external stakeholders (Weiser, 1997).

Product Portfolio

A service charter should communicate the range of deliverables that a company deals in. The product communication should be done in a very elaborate way since miscommunication may dent a company's image to the public. Tukker (2017) asserts that the public should have a preview of the products and explanation of different features of the product communicated to them. Public companies are obliged to make the communication of their products to the general public while a private company can limit its product access to its desirable audience. However, it is imperative that a service charter communicates the firm's line of products as an obligatory requirement and as a measure to curb any counterfeit (Spiros, 2005).

Service Blueprints

A service blueprint is an illustrated presentation which helps visualise the relationships between different service components, including people, props (physical or digital evidence) and processes. These are the ones directly linked to the customer points of service. Different scholars have devised different approaches to solving business-level problems. Customer feedback and complaints are part and parcel of this mechanism of identifying the problems to be solved. Service blueprints have over the years been used as ideal mechanisms for formulating customer-oriented solutions. A service blueprint deploys a cascading approach to service delivery that directly connects with customer requirements. Scholars have realised that the consumer-centred approach to problem-solving has been effective in the implementation of new business models and innovations. According to Macaulay (2018), a proper service blueprint should incorporate all business processes and functions. Customers are more interested in the flexibility and reliability presented by a business model (Rao and Raju, 2005). Therefore, a complex service blueprint may fail to address customer's expectation, hence failing in delivering the ultimate business model. An elaborate service delivery model should be formulated with the key focus being the business-end customers. The design of service blueprint should incorporate customer processes, employee's direct contact, the invisible process, support components and stock levels. The formulation of the service blueprint should be focused on building these foundations to create a holistic business model.

Components of a Service Blueprint

The components of a service blueprint entail:

The Visible Front Phase

The front phase of an organisation is an imperative component of a service blueprint. Customers perceive an organisation to be what it represents on its façade (Barlow and Moller, 1996). An organisation's front phase is mainly composed of its employees who are at the contact level. These employees interact directly with the customers, and whatever representation they offer may build or destroy a business. The importance of handling customers is emphasised by Picciotto (2017), who notes that customers are perceived to be very delicate, and any mishandling may render a business out of operation. Therefore, a business should carry out intensive training of its contact employees on issues of customer relations. Moreover, employees should be equipped with the requisite technical knowledge to execute public relations mandated at the contact level. They should also be people of integrity and a high standard of morals since any case of underhandedness would dent the image of a company to the general public (Wang, 2015). The discussion on how private and public companies handle their front end cannot be assumed since they are diverse in composition and scope of operation. Public companies are linked to a broader business audience. Therefore, public companies are more susceptible to misrepresentation at their front end. Private companies are usually in control of their operational space since it is only limited to a micro-audience. However, the challenges of keeping up with the demands of their customers are more or less the same to public companies. Veselovsky (2015) asserts that private companies should ensure that their contact persons are well equipped with interpersonal knowledge to handle customers.

Invisible Business Processes

The invisible business processes are deliberate actions executed by the contact persons in light of delivering services to customers (Mukesh, 2001). The processes associated with the invisible actions include escalation of customers' complaints to the relevant personnel or order preparation. Osadchy (2015) points out that the success of the invisible deliberate actions arouses customer satisfaction and creates loyalty among them. Contact persons should be well motivated so that they can take the deliberate actions that end up boosting the service blueprint of an organisation. However, it is worth noting that firms need to develop an identity-oriented culture for full optimisation of service blueprint directives. Developing a sense of ownership among the employees through inclusion in major business processes is great leverage for any business (Peltier, 2016).

Customers' Service Paths

The service blueprint has been argued by Barlow and Moller (1996) to be the best tool for harmonising processes to facilitate good customer experience. Customers are focused on their experience from placing an order on a product through to the checkoff system and final delivery of the product. Therefore, the service blueprint should be tailored in a way that it incorporates the major components of a product utility chain. Cascio (2018) opines that companies should focus on eliminating all the hurdles in their supply chain to ensure that products have time utility attached to them. Delays in processes have a negative impact on customers and may affect their trust in a company's processes. Charter and Tischner (2017) argue that companies have to carry out a feasibility study on their processes as a countermechanism to allow rectification of major problems associated with product chain. The processes involved in the design of a product to its actual assembling into a final deliverable should be harmonised to suit the dictates of customers. Companies must work with processes managers to ensure that process turnaround time is greatly minimised to ensure the satisfaction of the clients.

Support Processes

According to Reim (2015), a company's blueprint not only relies upon the contact persons, but also the support team. The support team is a vast team that works in the background. The support team is usually composed of the technical team that is tasked with ensuring that a company's system is well maintained. The support team should work in harmony with other units of the company to ensure that all the systems are operational. The support team should ensure that systems used by a company are updated and secure. Customers are concerned with the security of their data presented to the company (Tukker, 2017). Therefore, data security and authenticity should be handled with utmost care. The support team should liaise with other departments to ensure that all processes are geared towards customer service delivery. Public and private companies have a wider scope of operations. Customers should be the core focus of any business, and hence, all departments should be evaluated on metrics of upholding this requirement (Weiser, 1997).

Stock-Level Synchronisation

A customer service model should be focused on delivering products to its end customers. A certain accepted level of preparedness must be maintained at a competitive level to ensure there is a balance between supply and demand forces. Wang (2015) asserts that stock levels at any company should be ingrained in the confines of quality and quantity. This level of preparedness by the company must be based on product research to ensure that the products meet the customers' expectations. Customers expect that companies should provide products that meet all the dimensions of utility. Customers are not only interested in the end products, but also the processes involved until products reach them.

Harmonisation of the Front and Back End

There exists a thin line between the front desk and operations of any organisation. Service blueprints ensure that the front end is subsequent to the operations. Generally, in business, the front end should replicate the deliberate business decisions made in the background to provide the best customer services. Charter and Tischner (2017) opine that the success of any company relies on the harmonisation of the front and back ends in full realisation of the business- and corporate-level objectives. The front end should replicate the internal face of the business to the outside stakeholders. The processes at the front end should ensure that customers are fully satisfied with the services provided to them by the organisation. Peltier (2016) asserts that companies should ensure that processes involved in running the back end are well organised to avert internal conflict.

Physical Justification of a Company

The organisation's physical layout gives some 'presence' to an organisation as customers are interested in the physicality of a company. Reim (2015) asserts that companies should create confidence in customers with physical infrastructures. Companies that do not have physical premises may instil fear in the customers. Therefore, companies should invest in physical infrastructure to ensure that customers can derive confidence in the operations of the company. Osadchy (2015) asserts that public and private companies should have a physical location as a reference point. Physical premises and assets such as vans and delivery logistics are some of the physical capital that a company should own. They add up to the organisation's service delivery efficiency.

Waiting Time and Processes Turnover Time

Time spent waiting may in itself give a customer a positive or a negative perception of the company. Companies should ensure that all queue processes have a manageable turnaround process time. Processes should not overlap each other, and the time allocated for each process must be well calculated (Emily, 2008). Processes should be streamlined to work in a sequence that allows proper time management. Firms should work on time allocation with key considerations given to product development (Public Administration Select Committee, 2008).

Service Blueprint Assessment, Review and Feedback

A private company should allow its stakeholders to review the document within a workable time frame to allow them to internalise major clauses while giving their independent opinions on the same (Cascio, 2018). Public companies have a wider scope of stakeholders and should ensure that piloting is done for timely submission of reviews. According to Charter and Tischner (2017), upon completion of reviews, the steering team should consolidate the information gathered for analysis and implementation. In regards to evaluation, a service charter should also allow customers to rate a company's service delivery indexed against given metrics. There are different ways of measuring service quality, such as SERVQUAL and QUALITOMETRO. Wang (2015) asserts that communication paths will be effective in handling customer feedback and complaints on a timely basis if there is an internal framework for handling the complaints raised by customers since failure to address them may present a major loophole to competitors. Public and private companies should focus on responding to customer feedback as a way of creating trust among their clientele (Barlow & Moller, 1996).

Handling of Administrative Bottlenecks

Administrative bottlenecks are those impediments which make it hard for business operations to be conducted effectively. According to Picciotto (2017), the operation of a business should scale up to full accessibility by all stakeholders to the company's management. The internal operations of a private and public company should provide a room for diagonal, horizontal and vertical communication among its employees (Wang, 2015). Macaulay (2018) asserts that organisations that have a bureaucratic approach to management are more likely to fail while the liberal managerial style is more likely to succeed. Therefore, the service blueprint should be well designed to erase any case that may compromise the swiftness in rolling out the operations.

Management and Employees Mandate Statement

A service blueprint should lay out the mandate which governs the management and support employees. Management is mandated to communicate major business strategies to the support employees to ensure harmonisation of an organisation's goals. Subsequently, the support team should implement the strategies in their area of operation with a full commitment to a company's mission. According to Wang (2015), management should exercise authority to ensure that the support team performs its contractual obligations. However, it is worth noting that the management should handle the support team with utmost professionalism to avoid cases of micro-management.

Customer and Organisation Steered Actions

According to Peltier (2016), a service blueprint should be very elaborate to draw lines between customer championed actions against organisation's mandate. Berkowitz and Muller-Bonani (2006) emphasise that there ought to be a symbiotic relationship between a company and its customers. Firms should be under constant review of their service charter to align their actions with their customer commitment statement and to ensure that they do not overstep their mandate. Strategists argue that companies must ensure that they are constantly committed to innovative means of improving customer expectations. Customers are obligated by the provisions of a service charter to question major business development and quality metrics deployed by companies in undertaking their product delivery mandate. Wang (2015) notes that the line between customer-oriented actions against company-oriented action should be well defined to ensure that all the parties involved play their role effectively.

Level of Independence of the Company

Companies are regarded as independent entities that have the legal capacity of a natural man. Therefore, directors of a company should work with the full knowledge that the company's interests are different from their interests. Macaulay (2018) asserts that a majority of firms collapse when the directors merge their interests with that of the company (Veselovsky, 2015). Companies should uphold transparency in reporting of financial reports at the end of a fiscal year. Moreover, service charters should incorporate a roadmap for officiating audits on the business to ensure that the bookkeeping process is completely independent of management interest (Charter and Tischner, 2017). According to Picciotto (2017), a public company should, therefore, ensure that it has full autonomy in all its operations to comply with the legal framework that governs the interplay of companies while private companies should be monitored as a control mechanism since any form of breaching of their level of independence may result in operational problems (Berkowitz & Muller-Bonani, 2006).

Standard Operating Procedures

Standard operating procedures (SOPs) are a set of step-by-step instructions put in place by an organisation to assist employees to carry out complex routine operations. SOPs are composed of the general functional layout, policies and ethical framework that bind stakeholders of an organisation towards the provision of the quality deliverable. Cascio (2018) asserts that the statement of SOPs is a component of the top management and as such proper consultation of stakeholders should be conducted to ensure that the document meets the desired standards. Public and private companies are required by the law to synchronise their SOPs within the legal framework to avert cases of employees' oppression.

Components of Standard Operating Procedures

The design of an SOP should put into consideration the major components of a company. Organisations are mainly composed of investors, management and employees. An SOP statement should incorporate processes played by all the stakeholders that will ultimately deliver the organisational objectives. Therefore, SOPs should consider basic procedures, administrative layout, customer relations and the legal framework (Berkowitz & Muller-Bonani, 2006).

Procedures and Operations

The realisation of a company's corporate- and business-level objectives relies on the operational framework adopted. The operations of a company should have a top-down layout that facilitates the smooth running of the organisation. Firms should ensure that all their departments are within the confines of its service blueprint as a control mechanism to ensure uniformity in an organisation. According to Reim (2015), companies should ensure that its top management, middle-level and general support employees are well accustomed to basic operational procedures adopted. Companies should ensure that all the inputs required for production activities are delivered within the required quantities and time. Tukker (2017) asserts that the production level of operation should dictate all subsequent processes in a business chain. The SOP at the operation level should layout procedures to be adopted in the acquisition of production equipment to complement production within the budget and quality constraints. Organisations should carry out procedural analysis of all its production procedures to ensure that they are lean.

Employee Hiring and Orientation

Hiring is a complementary process that helps in realising the organisation's objectives while fulfilling human resource requirements. The hiring process holds a company liable for financial obligation to persons hired. The SOP dictates that companies should follow the right procedure in their hiring process to avoid a mismatch of labour. The SOP allows consultations among departmental heads before the implementation of hiring. The company should have clear procedures that govern their hiring process to allow inclusivity while averting cases of discrimination in the hiring process and averting any imminent problems that may arise from a procedure lapse. According to Macaulay (2018), basic SOPs are well defined to complement the HR department in carrying out employee orientation programs. The statement of the SOP must clearly state the procedure to be adopted in terminating the services of any employee and ensure that all the labour provisions are upheld (Berkowitz & Muller-Bonani, 2006).

Financial Management

Companies have a financial obligation to their suppliers, employees and the government at large. The financial obligation must be managed to ensure that a company remains solvent. The statement of an SOP should lay out a framework for handling all the finances that are available to the company. Cascio (2018) points out that companies should have accountable persons in the finance department to ensure that there is smooth management of all financial resources. SOPs enacted should ensure that a company is in control of all accounts receivable and payable to avoid cases of deficits. It is worth noting that any form of miscalculation may result in massive losses for the company. Peltier (2016) asserts that the SOP should also have a provision that allows for continuous auditing of accounts by external auditors to ensure that there is accountability and transparency in the handling of a company's liquidity.

Job Design

Implementation of an organisation requires decomposition of the vision into small tasks. The management of any company should incorporate a strategic and analytic approach to designing major functional areas in the company. The SOP should map out all the tasks required to accomplish the vision into jobs. Subsequently, the jobs should be mapped to job descriptions that can be assigned to relevant persons in the job market. The job design function of the SOP should be conducted by experts since any mismatch may replicate into financial responsibilities to the company. The job description should fall under the confines of the labour laws and proper remuneration adopted.

Marketing and External Communication

Marketing entails the process of identifying customer wants and needs and fulfilling them in a better way than rivals would. In the process of identifying and fulfilling those needs, an organisation interacts with its external environment, hence, the necessity of communication. According to Veselovsky (2015), companies directly interact with the external environment for product marketing. The SOP of any given company should outline procedures on which platforms and forms of communications should be used in deploying the marketing mandate. The SOP should provide a balance between the cost implication and benefit deduced from any form of communication. Reim (2015) asserts that marketing procedures should be well defined to ensure that the company's product is well represented in the marketplace. The SOP should ensure that the marketing department reviews the press releases and forms of communication intended to promote a company's products. It should also formulate a proper mechanism for allocating price tags on the product to ensure that products are neither overpriced nor underpriced. The quotes presented to the market will impact the competitive level of the company. The SOP should provide clear communication of the product guarantee through warranties and formulate a procedural framework to achieve reliability in executing the warranties. Product warranties should be well calculated to ensure that customers get quality after-sale services while curtailing any form of tampering with products that may attract replacement, thus financially impacting a company. The SOP should lay out the formula to be deployed in adopting a branding technique that will uniquely communicate to the market.

Legal Framework

The SOP must lay out the legal framework to be deployed in handling critical matters in the company. The procedures to be included in a legal framework of a company's SOP should include the control over accessibility to copyright information, as well as the confidentiality and privacy level of a company. According to Reim (2015), the SOP should also address the legal approach to employee handling, especially in regards to information safety. The top management should ensure that the SOP is clear in the handling of any legal dispute that may arise in undertaking a company's mandate. The dictates of an SOP should specify whether to contract a legal officer on a temporary or permanent basis. Legal provisions of an SOP should be limited to a specific area, but should be diverse in the handling of matters business.

Service-Level Agreements

A service-level agreement (SLA) is a contract between the organisation offering the service and the customer receiving the service. Tukker (2017) defines the SLA as the obligation that an organisation has to its clientele to provide quality products. The SLA of any company should factor in quality, quantity, accessibility and availability of products. The SLA can be subdivided into service-based SLA and multidimensional SLA. Customer-based SLAs cover individual contractual agreements between a customer and a company. The dictates of this agreement are that the company should provide reliable services on a timely basis, adhering to the quality parameters of the contract. In the event of any foreseeable inconveniences, the company should communicate with the customer for the adoption of necessary alternatives.

Peltier (2016) defines a service-based SLA as a general agreement between a company and the consumer of it services that the former is obligated to provide reliable service to the customers with a holistic approach. The provisions of a service-based SLA ensure that no particular customer gets preferential treatment over the other. According to Osadchy (2015), a multidimensional service agreement can be categorised into three tiers: corporate, customer and service level. Corporate level incorporates a portfolio of services that are less prone to changes, and as such the company can offer the same service update to its customers. Customer-level-based multidimensional SLAs cover service delivery obligation to a particular group of customers without consideration of their service subscription. Service-level multidimensional SLAs confine a company's services to specific issues that a certain group of customers is experiencing.

Components of the Service-Level Agreement

Definition of Services

The composition of an SLA should be primarily built around service provision. A company should carefully package its products while ensuring that the package is appealing to the customers. According to Wang (2015), the agreement on the service to be extended to the customers should be carefully crafted to avoid overpromising the customers. The company should ensure that it clearly states components of its products to the customer to help the latter evaluate the product. The service agreement should communicate the extent to which it applies to avoid vagueness. Customers should be allowed to evaluate the provisions of the contact before consenting.

Definition of Service Performance Level

According to Reim (2015), an SLA must articulate its performance capabilities with all factors held constant. The service provider should ensure that the services offered to the contracting customer are reliable and meet the required threshold. A good example is the Internet service agreement in which a customer may be subscribing to a higher bandwidth but ends up getting a lower bandwidth in the long run. The Internet service provider, in this case, has breached the contractual framework and risks legal actions. Therefore, it is imperative that companies practice a high level of transparency in the sealing of SLAs. Otherwise, occasional failure to uphold the agreed terms may be frustrating to the customer and attract legal actions (Cascio, 2018).

Continuous Management of Services

Continuous management of service entails the process whereby the organisation constantly supports the customer service to ensure that quality in the service provision is maintained. According to Reim (2015), companies are mandated to carry out a continuous assessment of their services to the customer to ensure that they comply with the agreed parameters of the SLA. The level of performance achieved on a regular basis should be well recorded, and a report of the same submitted to the customer. In case of discrepancies, a company is obligated to explain to the customer with a well-laid plan to correct the problem enacted. According to Peltier (2016), statistics must be provided to the customer on a regular and timely basis so that they may review them. In the event customers feel unsatisfied with the services provided to them, they can opt to terminate the agreement and claim their compensation. Therefore, companies should be keen on service delivery to eliminate quality issues. Negative reports may dent the public confidence in a company, hence the risk of losing clientele.

Problem Reporting Framework

SLAs should have an elaborate framework for problem reporting. The agreement obliges a contracting company to report problems associated with its services to a client. Picciotto (2017) asserts that reports must be submitted on a timely basis to allow the customer to seek alternatives if need be. The service provider has a legal obligation to provide timelines for corrective measures. Therefore, companies should adopt proper communication plans to avoid miscommunications with the client. In the event of a foreseeable breakdown, a customer should be informed in advance.

Response Time

A service response time is the agreed standard of response time between the organisation which is offering the service and the customer who receives the service. According to Macaulay (2018), an SLA must stipulate the response time that a company requires to address issues reported by a client. The SLA should have a clear time frame for conducting an assessment of issues reported by the client. Customers should demand a provision of fixed timelines for correction of the same and provision of a report of the problem by the service provider. Companies should ensure that all the provisions of the contract are upheld within the required timelines to avoid frustrating the customer.

Actions for Failure to Deliver

The SLA should be formulated to provide an action plan in the event of a service provider's failure to fulfil the contract. Customers should be keen on the actions stipulation to avoid cases of deliberate understatement of action clause. The clause should ensure that a customer is empowered to implement drastic corrective measures such as termination of the contract. According to Wang (2015), service providers should work on an open agreement that obliges them to deliver the provisions of the contract. The contract should have legal provisions to ensure that customers are not subjected to under provision of services. Customers must ensure that service providers are held responsible for any breach of contact. Otherwise, all parties to the SLA have a legal obligation to uphold the provisions of the contract. The definition of major components of an SLA should address all aspects of the relationship between the service provider and customers. However, litigation should be the last resort in the handling of conflict arising from the contract. Unless the service provider fails to uphold key proponents of the contract, parties to an SLA should deliberate on issues at a personal level.

Conclusion

Business operations of firms are associated with wide scope of customer service systems. Customer service systems should be linked to the specific core business of the organisation and its stakeholders' expectations. Stakeholders should be involved in all phases of a company's life cycle from inception to maturity. Proper documentation of the company should be done as a prerequisite to its operations. Documentation should adopt a waterfall methodology that will entail mission and vision statements as key pillars of company formation. Subsequently, key processes should be incorporated in the service charter as a blueprint for the realisation of business- and corporate-level objectives. Stakeholders should ensure that all the components of a service charter are addressed as a preliminary phase of company formation.

The statement and definition of a service blueprint should be of the essence in the realisation of a clear framework required for full functionality of a business. The service blueprint development should be discussed with full inclusivity of stakeholders. The clarity in the statement of a service blueprint will form the basis for a stable organisation. The legal operands of a company must be put into consideration as a mechanism to ensure that the operations of a company are within the confines of the laws.

Finally, the provision of all the documents stated herein should be legally binding, hence, full commitment to any declaration is imperative. Therefore, companies should be tailored to uphold their commitment to both internal and external stakeholders. In conclusion, companies should be keen on transforming their business models into businesses. The profitability of a business venture is of key concern to its stakeholders.

Bibliography

Aguiar, M. (2017). Implementation of public health policy and its challenges in the digital age. *Brazilian Journal of Public Administration, 51*(6), 1104–1121.

Agyapong, A., Afi, J. D., & Kwateng, K. O. (2018). Examining the effect of perceived service quality of health care delivery in Ghana on behavioural intentions of patients: The mediating role of customer satisfaction. *International Journal of Healthcare Management, 11*(4), 276–288.

Ahn, M. (2012). Effective public policy delivery system in the age of information overload – The role of imagery on citizen perception and compliance of public policy. *The Korean Social Science Journal, 39*(1), 1–17.

Ajulor, O. (2018, February 9). The challenges of policy implementation in Africa and sustainable development goals. *International Journal of Social Sciences, 3*(3), 1497–1518. https://dx.doi.org/10.20319/pijss.2018.33.14971518.

Anabila, P., Kumi, D. K., & Anome, J. (2019). Patients' perceptions of healthcare quality in Ghana: A review of public and private hospitals. *International Journal of Health Care Quality Assurance, 32*(1), 176–190.

Australian Government. (2018). *Client Service Charter*. Canberra Act 2600: Department of Infrastructure, Regional Development and Cities.

Bank of Kigali. (2019, February 21). Retrieved from Bank of Kigali web site: https://www.bk.rw/investor-relation.

Barlow, J., & Moller, C. (1996). *A complaint is a gift*. San Francisco, CA: Berett-Koehler Publishers.

Berkowitz, P. M., & Muller-Bonani, T. (2006). *International labour and employment law – A practical guide*. Chicago, IL: ABA Publishing.

Cascio, W. (2018). *Managing human resources*. New York: McGraw-Hill Education.

Charter, M., & Tischner, U. (2017). Towards sustainable business. In *Sustainable solutions*, New York: Routledge, 77–97.

Discovery Medical Health Scheme. (2019). *About Discovery Health Medical Scheme*. Retrieved 24 March 2019 from Discovery Health Medical Scheme: https://www.discovery.co.za/medical-aid/about-discovery-health-medical-scheme.

Discovery. (2019). *Discovery Vitality*. Retrieved 24 March 2019 from Discovery: https://www.discovery.co.za/vitality/how-vitality-works.

Emily, A. (2008). *Crafting effective mission and vision statements*. Saint Paul, MN: Fieldstone Alliance.

Gambarov, V., Sarno, D., Hysa, X., Calabrese, M., & Bilotta, A. (2017). The role of loyalty programs in healthcare service ecosystems. *The TQM Journal, 29*(6), 899–919.

Ghana Health Service. (2017). *The Patients Charter*. Retrieved 24 March 2019 from Ghana Health Service: http://www.ghanahealthservice.org/ghs-subcategory.php?cid=&scid=46.

Government of Ghana (GoG). (2009, November). *Government white paper on the single spine pay policy*. Accra, Ghana: Cabinet, GoG.

Hopkins, S. A., Nie, W., & Hopkins, W. (2009). Cultural effects on customer satisfaction with service encounters. *Journal of Service Science, 2*(1), 45–56.

International Committee of the Red Cross (ICRC). (2019, February 20). https://www.icrc.org/en/doc/resources/documents/misc/icrc-mission-190608.htm. Retrieved from The International Committee of the Red Cross (ICRC) web site: https://www.icrc.org

Kenya Power. (2019, February 21). http://kplc.co.ke/content/item/33/safety-watts. Retrieved from Kenya Power web site: http://kplc.co.ke

Korto, P. (2014, December 1). The effects of frontline health workers' discretion on the implementation of the free maternal healthcare policy by the Ghana health service: The case of la general hospital. Unpublished Masters Thesis, Ghana Institute of Management and Public Administration, Accra, Ghana.

Kwateng, K. O., Lumor, R., & Acheampong, F. O. (2018). Service quality in public and private hospitals: A comparative study on patient satisfaction. *International Journal of Healthcare Management, 12*(4), 251–258. doi:10.1080/20479700.2017.1390183.

Lee, K. (1982). *Policy making and planning in the health sector*. London, UK, and Sydney: Croom Helm.

Macaulay, S. (2018). Non-contractual relations in business: A preliminary study. In M. Granovetter, R. Swedberg, M. Granovetter, & R. Swedberg (Eds.), *The Sociology of Economic Life* (pp. 198–212). New York: Routledge.

Mang'era, J. O., & Bichanga, W. O. (2013). Challenges facing the implementation of citizen's charter: A case study of Kisii Level 5 Hospital -KENYA. *Interdisciplinary Journal of Contemporary Research in Business, 4*(12), 242–260.

Mukesh, J. (2001). *Excellence in government*. New Delhi: Atlantic Publishers and Distributors.

Okello, A. (2010). *Managing income tax compliance through self assessment*. Nairobi, Kenya: International Monetary Fund.

Osadchy, E. A. (2015). Development of the financial control system in the company in crisis. *Mediterranean Journal of Social Sciences, 6*(5), 390.

Parliament of Ghana. (1996, December 30). *Ghana Health Service and Teaching Hospitals Act*, Act 525 of 1996. Accra, Ghana: Assembly Press.

Parliament of Ghana. (2012, October 9). Public Health Act, Act 851 of 2012. Accra, Ghana: Assembly Press.

Parliament of Ghana. (2016, September 19). *Tobacco control regulation* (L.I. 2247 of 2016). Accra, Ghana: Assembly Press.

Peltier, T. R. (2016). *Information security policies, procedures, and standards: Guidelines for effective information security management.* Boca Raton, FL: CRC Press.

Picciotto, S. (2017). *Rights, responsibilities and regulation of international business.* New York: Routledge.

Public Administration Select Committee. (2008). *From citizen's charter to public service guarantees: Entitlement to public service.* London, UK: House of Commons.

Rao, T. V., & Raju, R. (2005). *Power of 360 degree feedback – Maximising managerial and leadership effectiveness.* New Delhi, India: Sage Publications India.

Reim, W. P. (2015). Product–Service Systems (PSS) business models and tactics – a systematic literature review. *Journal of Cleaner Production, 97*, 61–75.

Republic of Kenya. (2015). *Customer service charter.* Nairobi, Kenya: The State Corporations Advisory Committee (SCAC).

Spiros, G. (2005). Product portfolio management and corporate performance in the banking sector. *International Journal of Bank Marketing, 23*(1), 5–7.

Tukker, A. (2017). *New business for old Europe: Product-service development, competitiveness and sustainability.* Abingdon, UK: Routledge.

Veselovsky, M. Y. (2015). Development of financial and economic instruments for the formation and management of innovation clusters in the region. *Mediterranean Journal of Social Sciences, 6*(3), 116.

Wang, Y. W. (2015). Service supply chain management: A review of operational models. *European Journal of Operational Research, 247*(3), 685–698.

Weihrich, H. C. (2010). *Management: A global and entrepreneurial perspective* (13th ed.). New Delhi, India: Tata McGraw-Hill.

Weiser, C. R. (1997). Encouraging customer feedback. In Gower, *Handbook of customer service* (pp. 253–267). Burlington, VT: Gower Publishing Limited.

Chapter 8

Application of Digital Technologies and Social Media to Enhance Customer Service Experience

Ogechi Adeola, David Ehira and Oserere Ibelegbu

Contents

Introduction

'In an era when companies see online support as a way to shield themselves from costly inter-actions with their customers, it's time to consider an entirely different approach: building human-centric customer service through great people and clever technology' (Smaby, 2011).

Customer service transactions have come a long way since the pre-telephone era, when customer service operations in stores and business centres were conducted in face-to-face interactions. A great milestone in customer service operations was crossed with the invention of the telephone in 1876 and switchboards in 1894 (Edosomwan et al., 2011).

Telephones gained in widespread use and led to the introduction of call centres in the 1960s. Private automated branch exchange systems increased customer service operations efficiencies, but the ability to resolve customer service issues was limited to the working hours of the weekday (Ries, 2011).

In 1967, the customer service industry invested in an efficient and cost-effective means for working with clients when the American Telephone and Telegraph (AT&T) company introduced the 1–800 prefix. This toll-free number system allowed customers to make direct calls to customer service departments without being routed through a middleman (Treacy & Wiersema, 2007).

With the rise of the Internet in the early 1990s, customer service operations became available on a 24/7 basis. By 1996, the growth of Internet usage had spread exponentially. All enterprises, regardless of size, could provide and maintain a digital platform to offer personalised customer service experiences through electronic mail and chat links (Ross, 2016).

The subsequent proliferation of social media platforms like Facebook and Twitter allowed customer-oriented businesses to connect with their customers and meet their needs through a more personalised means, generally referred to as *social media customer service* (Odhiambo, 2012). The advent of mobile apps, self-service options, artificial intelligence (AI), chatbots and the like has created a new paradigm of customer service delivery: client representatives or customer service agents in any time zone and on any social media platform can provide effective customer service (Melo & Machado, 2018; Osterwalder & Pigneur, 2009).

In a bid to win the largest market share, some companies are enhancing their customer service systems by integrating available technologies (Porter, 2001). Amazon, for example, has fully adopted and deployed the use of a virtual personal assistant, marketed as *Echo* or *Alexa*, to create a seamless customer experience in their online marketplace. In 2005, Amazon created Amazon Prime which, for a nominal annual fee, provides free next-day delivery on most items, as well as benefits such as free or low-cost video streaming.

It is increasingly evident that innovations and advances in technology will continue to be a critical component of customer/firm interactions. Organisations are no longer limited to certain locations where interactions can take place; customers no longer have to travel to stores to shop for products or learn about services, or spend hours on the phone to conduct transactions with a customer agent. Technology-based interactions are key criteria for long-standing business success in the twenty-first century (Meuter et al., 2000; Van den Bergh, 2016).

For consumers, the fusion of technology and customer service cannot come soon enough. The array of technological platforms has created an appetite for multitasking and an increasing demand for information by both 'digital immigrants' (a cohort of users born before the wide-spread use of technology, usually 1980 and earlier) and 'digital natives' (born into the personalised technology era), who expect digital devices to be easy to use to provide and manage access to information (Prensky, 2009).

More recent cultural generations (e.g. Millennials and Gen Z) demonstrate a higher standard for customer service: a zero-tolerance for faulty apps, greater expectations for an increasing level of personalisation, and a preference for self-service applications (Forbes, 2018b). Their demand for speed and simplicity has obvious consequences on the adoption of technology to a customer service process (Meuter et al., 2000). Organisations that hope to remain relevant must consider this generational shift in customer service attitudes, demands and expectations of innovative technologies.

This chapter will discuss emerging customer service technologies that improve customer service experiences and ways to provide real-time evaluation of these experiences using sentiment analysis via social listening, reputation management and deep insight analysis via the Internet of Things (IoT). A current understanding of Africa's emerging digital technologies and the varying expectations of their use by cultural generations will be described along with the implications of the application of these technologies within a customer service context. The subsequent section then discusses the implication of these emergent technologies. The conclusion summarises the issues related to customer satisfaction and the use of digital technologies.

Customer Service Technologies

'Specifically, artificial intelligence has become the top priority for Fortune 500 companies— and with AI; you can take customer service to a whole new level' (Suthur, 2018).

Innovative digital engineering has reshaped the landscape of customer care with the application of real-time analytics, cognitive computing and proactive engagement tools (Hesse, 2008). Evolving technologies aimed at promoting proactive customer service experiences include chatbots, AI and augmented reality (Solis, 2013). This digital revolution has been embraced by the Millennial generation, which places considerable value on the mobile technologies and social media that have taken over the customer experience space.

Chatbot

Conversational services (e.g. Facebook Messenger) and virtual assistants (e.g. Apple's Siri, Amazon's Alexa, United Bank of Africa's Leo) continue to re-engineer the customer service experience to meet the high demands and expectations of digital citizens (Sotolongo & Copulsky, 2018). The key deliverable of conversational chatbots, a unified solution to multifaceted problems, is characterised by personalisation, enhanced customer experience and rapid responsiveness (Thompson, 2018). It is predicted that conversational chatbot technology will evolve rapidly, introducing applications that help customers make informed decisions that create an immersive brand engagement experience (Copulsky, 2019).

Chatbots have been designed to function as intelligent robotic digital assistants that resolve customer queries using natural language processing mechanisms (Garbade, 2018) that understand human prompts and respond with appropriate customer feedback (Shawar & Atwell, 2007). Although chatbots may be unable to handle some specialised requests, with the help of an AI algorithm reinforcement they can 'learn' to understand and respond to more complex tasks. At present, the most common chatbot interactions involve basic enquiries such as password retrieval and editing personal details, issues easily and rapidly resolved by drawing from established databases that can be retrieved in real time. The advantage of this approach is to free up organisational human resources so that they can focus on more value-added tasks (Daniel et al., 2018).

When chatbots are included in an e-commerce website or messaging channel such as Twitter, connected devices can understand and respond to users' enquiries using conversational capabilities. For example, SAMI (ServiceNow Automated Messaging Interface), launched in 2018 by Stanbic IBTC Bank in Africa, assists customers in checking their balances, accessing frequently asked questions and opening an account (mTransfersHQ, 2018). Chatbots in retail organisations have become the new channel for delivering a customer service experience and maintaining relationships by answering support questions, even when used in a physical store. An example of a chatbot in retail is the Loystar NG Bot, which helps individuals discover local brands in the country and shop for food, beverages, flights, hotels and fashion items (Olawale, 2018).

Mixed Reality (Virtual and Augmented Reality)

With the adoption of cutting-edge technologies like virtual reality (VR) and augmented reality (AR), brick-and-mortar retail stores are now able to provide customers with a virtual shopping experience that can mimic the in-store experience, giving them a competitive advantage over online retail stores (The Telegraph, 2018). As brick-and-mortar retailers seek to push the boundaries of customer service and the shopping experience by creating personalised shopping models, more retail operations are beginning to adopt an innovation known as concept stores equipped with VR and AR technologies (Bonetti et al., 2018). For example, in 2001, Apple opened its first retail store, a brick and click system that integrates a physical store (the brick) with online shopping (the click) to create a showroom concept where consumers can purchase products or be able to see and feel products that they can purchase later online. Other organisations like Tesla and Samsung have followed suit (Forbes, 2018a). Amazon Go utilises IoT technology to provide customers with an experience of shopping with no checkout lines or cashiers. With the use of smart retail technologies, retailers can now attract prospects and convert them to shoppers. Using VR and AR technologies, brick-and-mortar retailers have been able to establish a valuable customer experience for its consumers amidst the strong competition from online stores.

Social Media Channels

The proliferation of ubiquitous computing and the evolution of the Internet have given rise to the rapid scale of interest in social-media-driven customer engagement systems. The introduction of Web 2.0, microblogging sites like Twitter and networking sites like Facebook, MySpace and LinkedIn have transformed customer service engagements from informational to conversational (Jenkins et al., 2018).

Beyond the adoption of social media for promotional campaigns, social media has become a strong influence on how firms and institutions relate with their clients. Over 1.5 billion people are active social media users, making it the most efficient and cost-effective mediums for customers to channel their issues and make enquiries (Malthouse et al., 2013). For example, Instagram has developed a 'contact' button, which helps customers lodge their complaints and queries directly on the platform. With this application, customers can easily get in touch with firms or companies without being redirected out of the Instagram page.

Social media has revolutionised branding and communication strategies, as firms worldwide can control their presence and voice within the global marketplace while retaining local relevance and profitability. Small and Medium-scale Enterprises (SMEs) can now think like Fortune 500 companies as they adopt strategic, proactive social media strategies that increase customer satisfaction by creating positive brand sentiment, customer loyalty and engagement, while at the same time increasing revenue for the organisation (Baird & Parasnis, 2011).

Live Chat

This type of customer service experience is rendered in real time via a dialogue system that allows customers to post questions, comments and concerns about an organisation's product or services, then receive immediate feedback from the customer service department (Wirtz et al., 2010). A live chat option on any organisation's website creates a marketing advantage of converting browsers into buyers. It is one of the fastest and most widely accepted technologies for businesses today. Companies that intend to reduce communication latencies can deploy live chat as a unified communication provider.

For small to mid-sized businesses with limited staff capacity, live chat is a strategic tech tool to help the company provide the level of personalisation that customers require to retain their loyalty (Corbae et al., 2003). While the usefulness of live chat for customer services differs based on the industry and company size, this service can be offered by any organisation that invests in the necessary technological infrastructure (Keller, 2001). For example, business-to-consumer (B2C) entities generally have larger customer base and customer traffic than business-to-business (B2B) firms, which implies that live chat is more beneficial to B2C users. However, research has shown that the B2B user base is almost twice that of B2C. Some non-profit and B2C organisations do not readily adopt live chat due to the cost of setting the required technological infrastructure and scaling the maintenance over time (Miller, 2012).

Self-Service Sites

Self-service portals provide customers with answers to frequently asked questions, a system that saves the organisation time and resources (Meuter et al., 2000). These knowledge-based portals suggest or implement solutions that do not require interaction with a representative of an organisation. This approach helps organisations provide immediate access to common and similar fixes of service issues generally experienced by customers. A good self-service portal helps the organisation reduce customer service costs, enhance customer engagements and increase positive customer recommendations that earn brand loyalty and visbility, thereby aiding business growth (Casaló et al., 2008). Whereas other digital marketing channels such as blogs and discussion forums are intended to resolve specific queries, reliable and responsive self-portals disseminate information that answers the most frequently asked questions. A company can also provide links to external customer service experts that contribute to the knowledge base and provide comprehensive support. This helps maximise organisational resources required to resolve all customer queries (Van Riel et al., 2001).

Discussion Forums

Discussion forums are online communities which facilitate information sharing (videos and documents) about an organisation's services or product, while at the same time resolving queries and generating feedback and suggestions about the organisation's products or services. They provide a unique insight into customers' expectations of a company's products and services and translate customers' expectations into new growth opportunities. Early pioneers of discussion forums designed them to disseminate information (e.g. troubleshooting a tech problem) that would only describe or answer queries about an organisation's product or service. However, discussion forums have now become a platform for conversational engagement where customers could provide feedback or exchange information about a product or service (Kaplan & Haenlein, 2010).

With the evolution of social media and other messaging platforms, the use of discussion forums began to decline; however, organisations still utilise discussion forums because they are useful in understanding patterns and interests based on trending topics in the online community. Discussion forums offer multiple advantages:

- They are a veritable market research source when formulating the creation of a business approach for future products and services (Shim et al., 2002).
- They are knowledge-based platforms which help an organisation's clients validate or affirm the quality of their existing products and services.
- The online community connects customer service agents with customers who share similar experiences or challenges and offer solutions or feedback (Mangold & Faulds, 2009).
- An established discussion forum builds trust and efficient communication as it promotes brand loyalty and builds customer advocacy.
- Discussion forums play a crucial role in gaining and sustaining customer engagement, especially at the pre-purchase stage of the customer buying cycle. Authentic and positive customer videos and comments help potential customers evaluate various products and services, building confidence in the value of an organisation's website and customer service capabilities (Andersen, 2005).

Research has shown that the customer loyalty that organisations enjoy is significantly related to the level of customer engagement enjoyed on the discussion forum and online communities (Darley et al., 2010).

A major benefit of discussion forums is its use as a strategic tool to help in product design and evaluation. What begins as a simple discussion can go in multiple and unexpected directions, the outcome of which can be the creation of strategic indicators for planning and decision making by the organisation (Nambisan & Nambisan, 2008). New product development benefits from discussion forums that serve as market research pools from which designers can clearly discern which components of a product offer greater value for customers. For consumers, discussion forums serve as a medium to affirm the quality of a brand and participate in a poll or opinion ratings to record their level satisfaction with or loyalty to a brand (Kotler & Armstrong, 2010).

Customer Experience Evaluation Strategies

Social Listening

In order to increase competitive business advantage and enhance customer experience value, organisations currently look beyond their own websites to gather as much data as they can across all social media platforms and the Internet. To achieve this, they use social listening tools to monitor and analyse customer-generated content and textual information posted on their competitors' social media sites as well as on their own social media platforms. The data collected is then transformed into actionable knowledge for decision-makers (He et al., 2013). Customer service analytics serve as a strategic resource which provides more than query handling capacity to making proactive decisions that would ultimately enhance the customer experience.

Social listening tools such as Mention, Brandwatch and TweetDeck search all social media platforms to analyse aggregated customer interactions, transactions and feedback which provide a comprehensive picture of customers' purchasing behaviours and post-purchase satisfaction experiences. Consolidating such analyses with their own databases allow businesses to leverage this social media content as a powerful tool to construct and deliver exceptional customer service. Driven by actionable insights, strategic decisions based on customer satisfaction experiences help to create favourable business outcomes for the organisation (Stodder, 2012).

Analytic software uses predictive techniques to access call centre notes, demographics, social media and other data silos to uncover actionable data that provides predictive insights. Companies that use customer service analytics, therefore, are prepared to act on insights systematically and take a broader view of the customer experience to outperform other companies financially (Bose, 2009). Analyses help to identify high-loyalty customers in order to create cross-sell and up-sell opportunities targeted towards increasing revenue. Real-time mechanisms identify current issues that have a positive or negative impact on customer satisfaction and help to formulate appropriate responses to those experiences (Nyce, 2007; Rygielski et al., 2002).

Reputation Management

The escalating interest in social media has created seemingly unlimited platforms – blogs, electronic discussion forums, chat rooms, message boards, product review and discussion web sites, online retail sites, social networks and media repositories – for customers to post impressions and comments about an organisation and its products or services (Ward et al., 2010). This places a heavy responsibility on organisations to maintain a positive reputation by analysing and responding to the perceptions of consumer-generated media about a brand's corporate identity.

Several reputation management tools (e.g. Sprout Social, Trust Pilot, Reputation Loop) are being used to monitor public perceptions of the reputations of organisations and their brands, and create policies and strategies that respond effectively to negative publicity. Tesla, a leader in the race to autonomous driving, is an example of the way negative publicity can be addressed to minimise damage to a corporation's reputation. Tesla, well-known for its swift response to customers' concerns and queries via the social media channels, enjoyed a positive perception and public trust of the brand, but in 2013 when Tesla Model S was involved in a fire incident, the brand risked being mired in negative publicity. In response to this incident, Tesla CEO Elon Musk immediately addressed the issue via Twitter and Facebook and, with permission, published the related mail correspondence with the owner of the car involved in the incident. Musk's prompt, personal intervention and full transparency bolstered Tesla's brand reputation by assuring customers that they could depend on a personal relationship with Tesla (Consumer News and Business Channel–CNBC, 2018).

Deep Customer Insight via the Internet of Things

The interconnection of digital technologies, otherwise known as IoT, has opened up opportunities for business organisations to offer consumers personalised product offerings based on real-time, big-data insights into their consumer habits and behaviours. This has been proven to create an engaging customer experience value rather than flooding customers with poorly timed advertisements (Koesters, 2018). For example, Amazon's Alexa smart home assistant is connected to the owner's Amazon account. Based on recent Amazon purchases or transactional activities, when the owner is in need of a product and unsure about what to purchase, Alexa can provide a personalised recommendation. The IoT system connects with the owner's Amazon account to deduct the cost of an item as soon as it is placed in the shopping cart or subtracts it when it is returned. The Amazon connection is discontinued when the owner tells Alexa they have finished shopping (Forbes Insights, 2018).

Netflix, another leading pioneer in the use of IoT to promote effective customer experiences and satisfaction, delivers personalised movie recommendations to their users using real-time AI algorithms to monitor and analyse their customers' reviews, search queries and most-watched movies to adequately predict viewing preferences that would be of interest to the users (Smith, 2017).

The key insight to be drawn from the Netflix and Amazon examples is the fact that they do not operate under the assumption that the customers understand the value of their data, but consistently work to help them realise and understand the value of receiving immediate, personalised recommendations based on real-time insights driven by the IoT.

Because the IoT thrives on building a reliable cloud infrastructure with sophisticated IoT sensors, organisations willing to adopt this technology trend must be willing to invest in the acquisition and continuous maintenance of the underlying network infrastructure and technological devices required to create a continuous, seamless customer service experience.

Digital Technologies in Africa

Mobile technologies are driving Africa's digital economy, with creative innovations making significant improvements in how the continent's organisations do business. Important examples of such innovations support banking, customer service, insurance and even agriculture.

Mobile Banking: A mobile banking platform allows customers to check their account balances, access their account statements, transfer funds, pay bills and purchase airtime. Mobile banking services are offered via a Java app or SMS (short message service) platforms available on smartphones.

Mobile Money: This innovation is increasingly popular across the world and particularly in Africa. It is a payment system that enables users to create an electronic wallet on their mobile phones through which payment for goods and services can be made and funds can be transferred (Okafor, 2017). It supports a cashless policy that reduces cash circulation within an economy to a bare minimum. Unlike mobile banking, mobile money systems do not require a bank account; however, a mobile money wallet can be funded through a money banking app. Examples of mobile money services in Africa include Paga, PocketMoni, EazyMoney, QikQik, M-Pesa and U-Mo.

Fintech: Coined from the term 'financial technology', fintech provides automated delivery of financial services and products using chatbots and AI platforms that help organisations and individual customers manage their financial transactions. Fintech software is operated via computers or, more commonly, smartphones. The fintech industry in Africa is on the rise, striving to provide better customer service experiences. Examples of fintech start-ups include Piggybank.ng (a mobile savings platform) and Jumo.world, which supports credit and savings plans (Ngwa, 2019).

Insurtech: Insurtech technologies automate the delivery of affordable and accessible insurance products for low- and middle-income households, the rural population and Millennials (Founder 360° Team, 2019). Bluewave, which offers micro-insurance products, and Pula, which offers farm insurance, are examples of Africa's insurtech start-ups.

Chatbots: Chatbots are computer-based text messages meant to simulate person-to-person conversations. This allows businesses to respond to many customers quickly, consistently, and at the same time (Awosanya, 2018). Various sectors and brands are increasingly using chatbots to improve customer experience. The banking sector, for example, uses chatbots to assist customers to perform banking transactions. Nigeria's education sector offers SimiBot, an interactive learning assistant that helps students prepare for the Unified Tertiary Matriculation Examination (UTME) and Post UTME. SimiBot also assists students in making informed career choices (Awosanya, 2018).

Farmcrowdy: Nigeria's foremost digital agricultural platform links farmers with farm sponsors who can use their phones and computers from any part of the world to get involved in the process and business of agriculture without physically stepping onto farmland (Farmcrowdy, n.d.). Farmcrowdy empowers farmers in the rural areas by training them on mechanised farming, as well as providing improved seeds, farm inputs and a market for their harvested produce, advantages that help Africa's farmers to expand their capacity to cultivate more acres, thereby increasing crop production and food security.

Market Segmentation by Cultural Generations

It is crucial for customer service organisations to understand the phenomenon of generational cultures. Each generation has unique experiences, expectations, demographics, values and lifestyles that invariably influence their purchase behaviours (Williams & Page, 2011). Five generational groups currently exist within the consumer market: Veterans (aka The Silent Generation), Baby Boomers, and Generations X, Y (Millennials), and Z.

Veterans: This group is also referred to as the pre-depression generation, born before 1930. They are conservative and altruistic in nature, and their quest for material goods has drastically reduced with age. They are concerned about their health, financial and personal security, aging and the disposition of valued properties (Bailor, 2006; Branchik, 2010). More than other generations, veterans seek information through newspapers, magazines and print or television/radio ads. They value face-to-face communication and personal service; only a few use the Internet (Williams & Page, 2011).

Baby Boomers: Members of this generation were born between 1945 and 1964, a period of increased post-World War II birth rates (Williams & Page, 2011). As a rule, they are workaholics and optimistic. They have increased disposable incomes, are more tech-savvy and spend more on technology compared to other generations. Baby Boomers enjoy browsing and shopping online and prefer Facebook as a social media platform (Quicksprout, 2016). Boomers browse the Internet to search for information and depend more on sites that offer text rather than graphics and images (Rempel, 2009).

Generation X: Members of the "Gen X" generation were born between 1965 and 1980 and are frequently referred to as the forgotten generation (Lister, 2019; Quicksprout, 2016). They make family their utmost priority and seek a perfect balance of personal life, family and work (Lager, 2006; Williams & Page, 2011). They are well-educated despite the fact that they are sceptical, dissatisfied with almost everything and relatively liberal (Williams & Page, 2011). Members of this generation have a higher purchasing power than any other generation, and that will increase as they age (Quicksprout, 2016). They like Facebook and Twitter; they embrace technology adoption and use them more than Baby Boomers but less than Millennials (Lister, 2019). They can be reached through direct e-mailing, digital videos, Facebook, Twitter, blogging and educational sites.

Generation Y: Also called The Millennials, this cohort was born between 1981 and 2000. They are slowly taking over the workforce as they outnumber retiring Baby Boomers (Lister, 2019; Williams & Page, 2011). They were born into a period of rapid technological advancement, are highly tech-savvy and have a strong online presence (Quicksprout, 2016). They are image-driven, optimistic, goal-oriented, open-minded and in need of peer acceptance and social networking (Himmel, 2008). They are the majority of online shoppers and are attracted to innovations. They read product reviews and make good use of rewards and loyalty programmes (Lister, 2019). As a result, they can be mostly reached through mobile marketing and social media sites.

Generation Z: This newest generation, also referred to as Gen Z, iGeneration, or Post-Millennials, was born between 2001 and 2020 (Quicksprout, 2016). Individuals in this generation are showing signs of being the new conservatives, accepting traditional beliefs and having concern for the family unit. Like Millennials, they have a need for peer acceptance. They are self-controlled and responsible and hope to change the world and make a positive impact on humanity (Williams & Page, 2011). They do not care about being loyal to certain brands; rather, they are more interested in quality. They can be best reached through social media such as Snapchat and YouTube, but not Facebook, as there has been a decline in their Facebook usage. They prefer and enjoy utilising multiple digital media platforms concurrently (Quicksprout, 2016).

Implications for Africa

Access to and use of mobile devices and Internet infrastructure in sub-Saharan Africa has increased dramatically over the past decade, introducing new possibilities for the use of emergent technologies amongst small- and medium-enterprise organisations across the urban-rural and rich-poor communities (Evans, 2019). An emerging body of research shows that the growing access to mobile devices, along with the push to build the required network infrastructure in developed areas of Africa, has brought tangible economic benefits to small- and medium-sized organisations. However, the potential barriers to effective development and adoption of these technologies in underserved cities and rural settlements in sub-Saharan Africa are the skills gap and limited network infrastructure (Aker & Mbiti, 2010; Evans, 2018).

Skills gap: The use or adoption of machine learning and natural language processing algorithms is not a core competency in most IT departments and is at present a nascent skill in Africa (Mbwilo et al., 2019). Although simple, well-developed conversational chatbots are being used across most e-commerce applications, and only a few organisations can afford the cost of training their personnel to develop the skills needed to provide the technical services available with more complex emergent technologies.

Network infrastructure: Most emergent technologies rely on seamless connections to 3G and 4G networks which are limited if available at all in Africa's rural settlements or underserved cities (Gwaka et al., 2018; Pejovic et al., 2012). It is, therefore, imperative that organisations that would adopt these technologies in Africa should take into account the cost of infrastructure, the demographics of their target audience(s) and personnel development training or personnel acquisition required for a stable implementation.

Conclusion

For a seamless and effective customer experience journey, this study advocates that organisations understand the cultural generation where their market segment falls in order to identify the shift in consumers' attitudes and expectations in consonance with the required emergent technologies and social media channels that would adequately meet their customers' expectations.

For example, the application of technologies like AI chatbot, AR and VR in building and managing a customer experience journey, especially for the Millennials and Gen Z will give organisations a competitive advantage over their competitors in adapting to their customers as a leading provider of customer value. Overall, emphasis must be placed on having an effective brand reputation strategy using reputation management tools, if the organisation will maintain sustained revenue and profitability as well as increase its market share.

References

Aker, J. C., & Mbiti, I. M. (2010). Mobile phones and economic development in Africa. *Journal of Economic Perspectives, 24*(3), 207–232.

Andersen, P. H. (2005). Relationship marketing and brand involvement of professionals through web-enhanced brand communities: The case of Coloplast. *Industrial Marketing Management, 34*(3), 285–297.

Awosanya, Y. (February 21, 2018). *How Nigerian brands and startups are creatively using Chatbots to improve customer experience.* Retrieved 28 August 2019 from https://techpoint.africa/2018/02/21/chatbots-in-nigeria/

Bailor, C. (2006). Elder effect. *Customer Relationship Management, 10*(11), 36–41.

Baird, C. H., & Parasnis, G. (2011). From social media to social customer relationship management. *Strategy & Leadership, 39*(5), 30–37.

Bonetti, F., Warnaby, G., & Quinn, L. (2018). Augmented reality and virtual reality in physical and online retailing: A review, synthesis and research agenda. In *International AR & VR conference: Empowering human, place and business through AR & VR* (pp. 119–132). London, UK: Springer-Verlag.

Bose, R. (2009). Advanced analytics: Opportunities and challenges. *Industrial Management & Data Systems, 109*(2), 155–172.

Branchik, B. J. (2010). Silver dollars: The development of the US elderly market segment. *Journal of Historic Research in Marketing, 2*(2), 174.

Casaló, L. V., Flavián, C., & Guinalíu, M. (2008). The role of satisfaction and website usability in developing customer loyalty and positive word-of-mouth in the e-banking services. *International Journal of Bank Marketing, 26*(6), 399–417.

CNBC. (2018). Elon Musk sent an email to Tesla employees about another fire in its factory on Sunday. Retrieved 4 March 2019 from https://www.cnbc.com/2018/06/18/elon-musk-mailtesla-factorypaint-shop-fire-sunday.html.

Copulsky, J. (2019). Do conversational platforms represent the next big digital marketing opportunity? *Applied Marketing Analytics, 4*(4), 311–316.

Corbae, G., Jensen, J. B., & Schneider, D. (2003). *Marketing 2.0: Strategies for closer customer relationships.* Berlin: Springer Science & Business Media.

Daniel, F., Matera, M., Zaccaria, V., & Dell'Orto, A. (2018). Toward truly personal chatbots: On the development of custom conversational assistants. In *Proceedings of the 1st International Workshop on Software Engineering for Cognitive Services* (pp. 31–36). New York: ACM.

Darley, W. K., Blankson, C., & Luethge, D. J. (2010). Toward an integrated framework for online consumer behavior and decision making process: A review. *Psychology & Marketing, 27*(2), 94–116.

Edosomwan, S., Prakasan, S. K., Kouame, D. Watson, J., & Seymour, T. (2011). The history of social media and its impact on business. *The Journal of Applied Management and Entrepreneurship, 16*(3), 1–13.

Evans, O. (2018). Digital agriculture: Mobile phones, internet & agricultural development in Africa. *Mathematical Methods, Models and Information Technologies in Economy*, 75–90. Retrieved from https://mpra.ub.uni-muenchen.de/90359/1/MPRA_paper_90359.pdf

Evans, O. (2019). Repositioning for increased digital dividends: Internet usage and economic well-being in sub-saharan Africa. *Journal of Global Information Technology Management, 22*(1), 47–70.

Farmcrowdy. (n.d.). Earn profits. Empower farmers. Retrieved from farmcrowdy.com

Forbes. (2018a). The store as 'Software': How apple reimagined retail – Again. Retrieved 17 February 2019 from https://www.forbes.com/sites/jonbird1/2018/07/01/the-store-as-software-how-apple-reimagined-retailagain/#119de83e423f

Forbes. (2018b). Ten customer service/customer experience predictions for 2019. Retrieved 2 June 2019 from https://www.forbes.com/sites/shephyken/2018/12/16/ten-customer-servicecustomer-experience-predictions-for-2019/#5962b8126178

Forbes Insights. (2018). IoT is building higher levels of customer engagement. Retrieved 3 June 2019 from https://www.forbes.com/sites/insights-inteliot/2018/06/14/iot-is-building-higher-levels-of-customer-engagement/#4a42f53a7d87

Founder360° Team (2019, July 10). These 4 insurTech startups are disrupting an 88-year-old industry in Kenya. Retrieved 28 August 2019 from https://founder360mag.com/these-4-insurtech-startups-are-disrupting-an-88-year-old-industry-in-kenya/

Garbade, M. J. (2018) A simple introduction to natural language processing. Retrieved from https://becominghuman.ai/a-simple-introduction-to-natural-language-processing-ea66a1747b32

Gwaka, L. T., May, J., & Tucker, W. (2018). Towards low-cost community networks in rural communities: The impact of context using the case study of Beitbridge, Zimbabwe. *The Electronic Journal of Information Systems in Developing Countries, 84*(3), e12029.

He, W., Zha, S., & Li, L. (2013). Social media competitive analysis and text mining: A case study in the pizza industry. *International Journal of Information Management, 33*(3), 464–472.

Hesse, B. W. (2008). Enhancing consumer involvement in health care. In J. C. Parker & E. Thorson (Eds.), *Health communication in the new media landscape* (pp. 119–141). New York: Springer Publishing Company.

Himmel, B. (2008). Different strokes for different generations. *Rental Product News, 30*(7), 42–46.

Jenkins, H., Ford, S., & Green, J. (2018). *Spreadable media: Creating value and meaning in a networked culture*. New York: NYU Press.

Kaplan, A. M., & Haenlein, M. (2010). Users of the world, unite! The challenges and opportunities of social media. *Business Horizons, 53*(1), 59–68.

Keller, K. L. (2001). *Building customer-based brand equity: A blueprint for creating strong brands* (pp. 3–27). Cambridge, MA: Marketing Science Institute.

Koesters, J. (2018). Connected marketing: How IoT is revolutionizing customer engagement. Retrieved 3 June 2019 from https://www.digitalistmag.com/customer-experience/2018/03/23/connected-marketing-how-iot-is-revolutionizing-customer-engagement-05994564

Kotler, P., & Armstrong, G. (2010). *Principles of marketing*. Harlow, UK: Pearson education.

Lager, M. (2006). X ways. *Customer Relationship Management, 10*(11), 28–32.

Lister, M. (August 22, 2019). *Generational marketing: How to target millennials, gen X, & boomers*. Retrieved 27 August 2019 from https://www.wordstream.com/blog/ws/2016/09/28/generational-marketing-tactics

Malthouse, E. C., Haenlein, M., Skiera, B., Wege, E., & Zhang, M. (2013). Managing customer relationships in the social media era: Introducing the social CRM house. *Journal of Interactive Marketing, 27*(4), 270–280.

Mangold, W. G., & Faulds, D. J. (2009). Social media: The new hybrid element of the promotion mix. *Business Horizons, 52*(4), 357–365.

Mbwilo, B., Kimaro, H., & Justo, G. (2019). Data science postgraduate education at university of Dar es Salaam in Tanzania: Current demands and opportunities. In P. Nielsen & H. C. Kimaro (Eds.), *International conference on social implications of computers in developing countries* (pp. 349–360). Dar Es Salaam, Tanzania: Springer International Publishing.

Melo, P. N., & Machado, C. (Eds.). (2018). *Management and technological challenges in the digital age.* Boca Raton, FL: CRC Press.

Meuter, M. L., Ostrom, A. L., Roundtree, R. I., & Bitner, M. J. (2000). Self-service technologies: Understanding customer satisfaction with technology-based service encounters. *Journal of Marketing, 64*(3), 50–64.

Miller, M. (2012). *B2B digital marketing: Using the web to market directly to businesses.* New Jersey: Que Publishing.

mTransfersHQ (September 18, 2018). *Banking ChatBots in Nigeria.* Retrieved 21 August 2019 from https://medium.com/mtransfers/banking-bots-in-nigeria-21a3e6c8600e

Nambisan, S., & Nambisan, P. (2008). How to profit from a better virtual customer environment. *MIT Sloan Management Review, 49*(3), 53.

Ngwa, E. (January 24, 2019). *5 African FinTech Startups to Watch in 2019.* Retrieved 28 August 2019 from https://www.afrohustler.com/5-african-fintech-startups-watch-2019/

Nyce, C. (2007). *Predictive Analytics White Paper.* Retrieved from http://www.the-digital-insurer.com/wp-content/uploads/2013/12/78-Predictive-Modeling-White-Paper.pdf.

Odhiambo, C. A. (2012). *Social media as a tool of marketing and creating brand awareness: Case study research* (Master's Thesis). Vaasan Ammattikorkeakoulu University of Applied Sciences. Retrieved from https://swsu.ru/help/pdf/Christine.A.Odhiambo.pdf.

Okafor, P. (September 20, 2017). Mobile money – Transfer money pay bills on mobile phone. Retrieved 27 August 2019 from https://www.naijatechguide.com/2012/02/mobile-money-transfer-money-pay-bills.html

Olawale, W. H. (2018, June 12). The rise of chatbots in Nigeria. Retrieved 21 August 2019 from https://chatbotslife.com/the-rise-of-chatbots-in-nigeria-55490cc58484

Osterwalder, A., & Pigneur, Y. (2009). *Business model generation.* Self Published.

Pejovic, V., Johnson, D. L., Zheleva, M., Belding, E., Parks, L., & Van Stam, G. (2012). Broadband adoption|the bandwidth divide: Obstacles to efficient broadband adoption in rural sub-Saharan Africa. *International journal of communication, 6,* 25.

Porter, M. E. (2001). Strategy and the internet. *Harvard Business Review, 79*(3), 62–78.

Prensky, M. (2009). H. sapiens digital: From digital immigrants and digital natives to digital wisdom. *Innovate: Journal of Online Education, 5*(3), 1.

Quicksprout (2016, July 8). *How to reach your perfect customers with generational marketing.* Retrieved 27 August 2019 from https://www.quicksprout.com/generational-marketing/

Rempel, C. (2009). Marketing to different generations, *Security Dealer & Integrator, 31*(2), 34–36.

Ries, E. (2011). *The lean startup: How today's entrepreneurs use continuous innovation to create radically successful businesses.* United States: Crown Books.

Ross, D. F. (2016). *Introduction to e-supply chain management: Engaging technology to build market-winning business partnerships.* Boca Raton, FL: CRC Press.

Rygielski, C., Wang, J. C., & Yen, D. C. (2002). Data mining techniques for customer relationship management. *Technology in Society, 24*(4), 483–502.

Shawar, B. A., & Atwell, E. (2007). Chatbots: Are they really useful? In *Ldv Forum, 22*(1), 29–49.

Shim, J. P., Warkentin, M., Courtney, J. F., Power, D. J., Sharda, R., & Carlsson, C. (2002). Past, present, and future of decision support technology. *Decision Support Systems, 33*(2), 111–126.

Smaby, K. (2011). *Being human is good business.* Retrieved 3 June 2019 from http://alistapart.com/article/being-human-is-good-business/

Smith, A. (2017). *How to create a customer-obsessed company like Netflix.* Retrieved 3 June 2019 from https://www.forbes.com/sites/anthonysmith/2017/12/12/how-to-create-a-customer-obsessed-company-like-netflix/#2a1594066d22

Solis, B. (2013). *WTF?: What's the future of business?: Changing the way businesses create experiences*. Hoboken, NJ: John Wiley & Sons.

Sotolongo, N., & Copulsky, J. (2018). Conversational marketing: Creating compelling customer connections. *Applied Marketing Analytics, 4*(1), 6–21.

Stodder, D. (2012). Customer analytics in the age of social media. *TDWI best practices report*. Renton, WA: TDWI.

Suthur, S. (June 14, 2018). *Top 7 ways AI will delight your customers and improve branding*. Retrieved from https://acquire.io/blog/ai-delight-customers-improve-branding/

The Telegraph. (2018). *The future of retail*. Retrieved from https://www.telegraph.co.uk/business/tipsfor-the-future/future-of-retail/

Thompson, C. (2018). Assessing chatbot interaction as a means of driving customer engagement. Bachelor's thesis. Retrieved 20 October 2019 from https://www.theseus.fi/bitstream/handle/10024/158152/Final%20Thesis%20Chris%20Thompson%20theseus%20-%20After%20Language%20Check%20theseus.pdf?sequence=1&isAllowed=y

Treacy, M., & Wiersema, F. (2007). *The discipline of market leaders: Choose your customers, narrow your focus, dominate your market*. New York: Basic Books.

Van den Bergh, J. (2016). *The awareness and perception of cloud computing technology by accounting firms in Cape Town*. Master dissertation, University of South Africa, Pretoria.

Van Riel, A. C., Liljander, V., & Jurriens, P. (2001). Exploring consumer evaluations of e-services: A portal site. *International Journal of Service Industry Management, 12*(4), 359–377.

Ward, M., Webber, J., & Graziano, D. M. (2010). U.S. Patent No. 7,720,835. Washington, DC: U.S. Patent and Trademark Office.

Williams, K. C., & Page, R. A. (2011). Marketing to the generations. *Journal of Behavioral Studies in Business, 3*(1), 37–53.

Wirtz, B. W., Schilke, O., & Ullrich, S. (2010). Strategic development of business models: Implications of the Web 2.0 for creating value on the internet. *Long Range Planning, 43*(2–3), 272–290.

Chapter 9

Technology and Social Media in Customer Service

Abel Kinoti Meru, Giacomo Ciambotti, Jimmy Ebong,
Mary Wanjiru Kinoti and Rehema Kagendo Mugendi-Kiarie

Contents

Introduction

Gradually, traditional media is being overtaken by disruptive and rapidly changing technologies driven by social media among others. The same applies to business models and business strategies globally. As a result, firms are increasingly changing the way they interact with their customers. Offering the best service to customers is undoubtedly the lifeline and hence most important aspect of a business. As such, customer service management is relevant for a business aspiring to become competitive. Since the advent of the Internet, businesses have resorted to using social media to communicate and interact with their customers. It is inextricably true that businesses worldwide are using social media strategically to keep tabs on their customers through photos and status update postings on platforms such as Facebook and Twitter among others, making social media a vital tool and a more convenient way to keep in touch with the customers. Husain et al. (2016) noted that social media has witnessed an exponential growth in the millennium and that at the present information age, social media marketing has become part of doing business. Social media represents one of the most transformative impacts of information technology on business, as it drastically changes how consumers and firms interact. Therefore, companies nowadays increasingly compete for consumers' attention and engagement with their brand in the social media space.

This section contributes to the discussion regarding disruptive transformation of customer service brought about by social media. The article presents evidence of how technology is changing practices and strategies of customer service with a focus on the African context. Notably, digital transformation is acting as a trigger in turning customer service improvements into an urgent imperative. This chapter argues that businesses need to recognise disruptions of social media and adapt to social media dynamics (Deloitte, 2013). Worldwide, businesses cannot forget to focus on the need for contemporary and up-to-date customer service strategies and tools. Companies that integrate social media in their customer-centric business models will be able to appropriately take advantage of agility brought about by technologies and succeed in providing modern customer service. Adopting new business models that integrate social media requires new competencies. Appropriate responses to online reviews and posts about a company's products and (or) services demonstrates strength in a company's communication and enable a company to persuade potential customers, acquire them and even successfully retain them, thus improving a company's performance.

Customer Service

Most definitions of customer service focus on practices, strategies, and technologies that companies use to manage the relationship between a business and an existing or potential customer. Customer service and service management are even more important for businesses that deal in services, especially, because of the unique characteristics of services. 'The key to the success of a service enterprise lies in the quality of services they deliver' (Mbise & Tuninga, 2016). Competing on value, meeting and exceeding customers' expectations, saving customers' time and effort, and generosity are additional precepts that need to be added to fundamental precepts in service marketing. While service quality and efficiency are two important trajectories of corporate strategy (Calabrese & Spadoni, 2013), quality of services could be a single competitive strategy for enterprises (Mbise & Tuninga, 2016). Because of the difficulty in defining and measuring quality of services, the focus of initiatives to satisfy a customer should be on enabling customers to 'experience the various tangible elements associated with the service' (Mbise & Tuninga, 2016).

Quality is 'the extent to which a product or service meets and/or exceeds customer expectations' (Sebastianelli & Tamimi, 2002). As noted by Mbise and Tuninga (2016), 'quality of a service can only be defined from the perspective of the consumer and occurs at the point where the consumer comes into contact with the service'. In addition, 'perceived service quality is the degree and direction of discrepancy between the consumers' perceptions and expectations' (Mbise & Tuninga, 2016). Satisfaction and service quality are connected but disparate. Satisfaction can be described as the difference between how a person feels after experiencing a service, compared to the feeling before experiencing a service. Satisfaction can also be described as 'a function of relative level of expectations and perceived performance' (Mbise & Tuninga, 2016).

Service performance is a concept derived from service contracts to refer to the performance of the service provider. In service marketing and marketing management, management's own proclamations concerning their services and service quality are a replica of the concept of objective service performance (OSP) advanced by Prince and Khaleq (2013) and Gijsenberg et al. (2015). Management's own proclamations are often expressed in the mission and vision statements of service providers and associated marketing materials. Sometimes proclamations are made in online references to the service provider. OSP is a level of service performance that management perceives can be attained or can be provided. This is a call for management to strive and measure up to their own proclamations.

According to Luo and Qu (2016), Prince and Khaleq (2013) and Mbise and Tuninga (2016), quality of service is more difficult to define, measure and manage. The quality of service will either enhance or degrade customer loyalty to a brand and eventually the entire business. A business that proves to be responsive to customer complaints, as well as appreciation and continuously delivers services that offer memorable and lasting experiences to consumers is likely to gain a clear competitive advantage.

Information technology has played a critical role in businesses for several decades (El Sawy & Bowles, 1997; Ray, Muhanna, & Barney, 2005). Technology adoption is changing the way of interacting and engaging customers. Deloitte (2013) further notes that the main forces that are changing the role of customer service are rapid adoption of technologies, changes in customers behaviours, and market competition. Rapid adoption of technologies includes the increased use of social networks, mobile applications and smartphones, analytics, and cloud computing. Changes in customer behaviours can be seen in iterative research on specific products and services online, reading of reviews of previous buyers, use of smartphones as shopping assistant, following up favourable brands or stores online or watching demos before product purchases, thus enhancing the ease of market accessibility. Increased competition in the market of many industries has occurred as companies are reinventing themselves with innovative business models that make them more agile and relevant.

The adoption and usage of social media platforms and related tools in customer service and the growth of e-commerce platforms are clear manifestations of how adoption of technology is changing interactions with customers. According to Sarma and Choudhury (2015), the most popular social media platforms are blogs, microblogs, opinion mining, content community sites (YouTube), social networking sites (Facebook), social news, sites dedicated for feedback, virtual social world, collaborative projects (Wiki), social bookmarking and voting sites. They further classify collaborative social media and social bookmarking as collaborative social media, while the rest are categorised as expressive social media. Statista (2018) data predicts that by 2019 social media users worldwide will reach 2.77 billion and grow to 3.03 billion by 2021. This will represent nearly half of the global population. This implies that enterprises dealing with goods and services that will not seize the opportunity for online marketing using social media will continuously lose customers, and such enterprises may exit their respective markets in the long run.

Social media usage is still low in Africa. According to Statista (2018), as of January 2018, only Egypt, having 39 million users, appeared in the top 11 countries with the most Facebook users. India claimed the first place with 294 million users, ahead of second-ranked United States with 204 million Facebook users. The low usage of social media in Africa implies that in this era of globalisation, African businesses can still benefit from social media by targeting the bigger global market. On the other hand, African businesses must adopt marketing strategies that use social media in order to grow usage of such platforms.

The incredible growth of e-commerce platforms is affecting companies' performances in customer services in many ways. Nowadays, all size product companies need to have very high-quality customer service, able to respond quickly to customer queries. Social media platforms like Facebook and Twitter are pervasively used to quickly and responsively provide customer services, thereby increasing enterprise performance, especially when customer service metrics are used to measure performance. In emerging markets like China, social media networks like WeChat, Sina Weibo and Renren dominate their local market. Similarly, Mouthshut and Pagayguy dominate markets in India (Ilavarasan et al., 2018). WeChat (referred to as Weixin in Chinese) belongs to Tencent a Chinese top tech firm, which by early March 2018, had reached 1 billion monthly users, mainly drawn from China, slightly below the 1.5 billion monthly users of Facebook, becoming the largest social network in China, offering online medical appointments, money transactions, requests for food and dating services (Atkinson, 2018). It is modelled similar to WhatsApp.

The best-cited example of social media among the developing countries is in Kenya, where, the giant telco, Safaricom (K) Limited, operates a social networking service, known as Bonga platform. The platform leverages on the robust Mpesa mobile money transfer platform, focussing on a three-pronged strategy: pay (money transfer), play (gaming) and purpose (chat) as the key drivers (Bright, 2018). Bright (2018) further notes that users on the Bonga platform have an option of using either Bonga Sasa (for instant messaging and money transfer), Bonga Baraza in case of funds drive, or Bonga Biashara to build social network commerce. The name of Bonga platform was changed in 2019 to Zwuup (sound made by a passing item). The success of local social media platforms in China and India carries huge implications for Africa. One lesson that social media platforms in Africa can draw from the example of China and India is that users tend to appreciate local content like that of Bonga and WeChat on a platform that is efficient like Facebook and Twitter.

A 2018 Adobe report shows that artificial intelligence (AI) is the lead enabler on real-time experiences to over 2.5 million people worldwide actively engaging through online social media networks like WeChat, Facebook, Instagram and Sina Weibo. AI comes in the form of basic automation including the ability to respond to questions and machine learning (making decisions from big data), as well as computer programmes without human intervention, through neural networks among others (RWC, 2017). In a nutshell, AI uses multiple technologies to sense (computer vision and audio processing), comprehend (natural language programming and knowledge representation) and act (machine learning and expert systems) to yield solutions, such as virtual agents, identity analytics, cognitive robotics, speech analytics, recommendation systems and data visualisation (Purdy & Daugherty, 2016), which is also the domain of cognitive computing. An IBM (2017) report shows that AI and cognitive computing supplement human capacity in analysing and building a firm's competitive position, since cognitive systems can make sense out of big data, enable one to make informed decisions and unlock gaps between humans and machines. Cognitive computing is defined as 'information systems that understand, reason, learn, and interact through continually building knowledge and learning, understanding natural language, and reasoning more naturally with human beings than traditional programmable systems' (IBM, 2017).

Changes in customer behaviours as a second transformation force is related to how customer cultures, demographics and technological capabilities are turning customers into smart actors. Serving this emerging category of smart customers requires higher transparency and business responsibility and creates a demand for better service quality, low cost and immediate responsiveness (Deloitte, 2013). Trends are moving towards a category of customers who are informed, complaining immediately if something goes wrong and are ready to fight the battle with the company (Agnihotri et al., 2012). Customers are pervasively using social networks and associated mobile applications and smartphones to complain instantly whenever and wherever they are dissatisfied. This calls for enterprises to have immediate and real-time responses if they are to provide customer service that matches modern demands.

Finally, in the current world, market competition is higher than in the past. Companies that take advantage of technology are succeeding to beat their competitors. Companies in this era are reinventing themselves with innovative business models, which are based on providing services and products online. Companies that are progressing are taking advantage of globalisation and technology development and are serving a bigger customer base by serving them online. Some examples are Facebook, Google, TripAdvisor, Amazon and Apple. Serving global customers online changes how businesses approach customer service and manage customers. Modern customer service management needs to take into considerations the relevance of correct processes and reduced turn-around time so as to benefit from the challenge posed by technology advancement. Thus, new strategies of customer service management are required to bring customer service as a new marketing and strategic tool to gain a sustained competitive advantage against competitors (Campbell, 2003).

Customer Service as a Servicing Tool: Multiple Customer Interfaces and Integration

Quality customer service represents a more and more important tool to gain customer satisfaction, customer loyalty and customer retention (Verhoef et al., 2009). From developed and developing countries, there is clear evidence of how customers are increasing the use of apps, tools and devices simultaneously. They use multiple channels at the same time to solve their issues on services, and they expect a high-quality response. As a consequence, companies are turning customer services into multi-channel interaction providers (Deloitte, 2013) to provide seamless customer experience irrespective of the channel used. Different tools such as social media, website platform and e-commerce are required to complement and be aligned together in the overall strategy of the business. Companies need to implement web 2.0 interfaces and smart automation to balance human and automated interaction, experimenting with new innovation on the technology frontline. The interface has to be efficient and effective to ensure well-synchronised processes of query and automated reply to some basic enquiry.

An important change in the customer service is the integration of the customer service in the customer touchpoints, which are the moments when the customers engage the companies from the first contact to the delivery of product/service and finally to customer care. These touchpoints catalyse the opportunity to satisfy customers and gain their loyalty as a basis for customer retention. In African countries especially, integrating customer service in these touchpoints is actually crucial, as the African ecosystem is composed of informal relationships, community ties and mutual trust agreements. The success of the touchpoint thus is extremely connected to how the customer perceives the enterprise in meeting his/her needs. Integrating customer service into the touchpoints allows also the company to obtain feedback and finally adopt the product/service to the customer's needs. Then, companies need to design models of customer services integrated into an overall service experience that can not only solve the customer's needs but that can also create a relationship with the customer, delighting him/her to give full-feedback that can be reused in the customer engagement process (Gummerus et al., 2012). For instance, by modifying the product/service delivery, increasing the product quality, or taking into consideration customers' feedback into the research and development process.

Customer service is clearly becoming a driver towards increasing the company's value in product/service delivery. Adobe (2018) defines customer experience 'as the complete set of interactions and engagements a customer has with a brand, with both online touchpoints (click, view and transact) and offline touchpoints (physical experience)'. The Adobe digital trends report further shows that offering multiple touchpoints enhances customer experience, among other factors. The user-generated content for social media is created or co-created using either opinion mining (sentiment analysis), netnography or machine language processing tools (Misopoulos et al., 2014), which are the domains of AI. This evidence brings us directly to the second way of using the customer service, as a marketing tool.

Customer Service as the New Marketing: Customer-Centric Models and Social Media

Customers are changing their behaviours and expectations on the quality of the product/service, the cost and the customer care, as the bundle of services available around the product/service delivery (Hölbing et al., 2009). Companies are also turning their business models into customer-centric models. The basic idea is that all processes are built around the customers' needs and aim to establish a new culture based on the delivery of a bundle of services to the consumers (Hölbing et al., 2009).

All the technologies and mechanisms should be aligned with this new model. Social networks in this way play a critical role. The goal is to leverage these social channels into a marketing strategy that creates brand awareness, increases sales of products and services, and gets the brand closer to its customer community. Information within the social network must be aligned and interplay in a systematic way. Social media then helps directly to grow businesses (Mangold & Faulds, 2009). Social media platforms can be used to grow business by boosting brand awareness (generating more loyalty and satisfaction), marketing products or services (photos, video, advertisement and contents) and 'listening' to customers queries and questions.

New Competences of the Customer Service

An alignment between technologies and new strategies with business models that are customer-centric is required (Hölbing et al., 2009) for companies to prosper. Technologies such as social media platforms and apps present both challenges and opportunities for businesses adopting customer-centric models. Today, companies have to grow in customer advocacy. Social media and other relevant tools such as customer relationship management (CRM) in this way represent relevant solutions to strategically manage customer care. Moreover, a customer should not be viewed in isolation, but as a subunit of a bigger market. This bigger market is the community from which the customer hails. Viewing the customer as part of a community enables a company to strategise appropriately to use the customer as an entry point into the community, thus growing the customer base. Viewing the customer as a unit of a community is particularly relevant in informal economies, where social ties play a strong role.

Africa for instance, is characterised by many social enterprises that aim to solve social needs by creating strong relationships and partnerships with local communities and associations through social initiatives, work-integration practices and customer-centric orientation that ultimately contribute to customer satisfaction and loyalty. In this ecosystem – strongly based on mutual trust, informality and loyalty – managing the customer relationship becomes a key activity.

Other capabilities developed are related to operations in customer care. Today managers have to oversee social interactions and engage with applications, connected experiences, and events that enrich the customer experience. The design of these tools should reflect the customer-centric strategy: managing multiple channels in a complementary way to become strategic in the continuous pursuit of competitive advantage. In summary, strategic alignment in this new era between customer-centric orientations, and new capabilities and processes, are the key success factors to adapt and transform customer service to the current disruptive change. Within this journey, technology innovation and integration in multiple-channels solutions represent the root to take following the shape in customers' behaviours and expectations. However, Ilavarasan et al. (2018) point out that social media's effects on customer service may vary based on account of market divergence, economic situation, cultural differences, penetration rate, legal framework, accessibility and also the nature of the content generated. Therefore, caution should be exercised when one is generalising studies or examining social media and customer service, since these dynamics and the technological landscape are constantly changing.

Social Media, Word of Mouth and Customer Service

Historically, consumers use word of mouth (WOM) to communicate their experiences of using products, as well as evaluations of their experiences (Yang et al., 2012). Through WOM, customers can easily copy others' buying patterns, share ideas, express appreciation or dissatisfaction, and moreover, endorse a product or service. However, due to time, distance and perceived customer distortion of facts, WOM is limited, compared to social media. The most important strategy in this new era is strongly related to social media management. There is increased use of social media for customer service and marketing by the customers of organisations (Kaplan & Haenlein, 2010).

Hamilton et al. (2016) highlight the role of social media in value creation by demonstrating the relationship between customer interaction, satisfaction and immersion and customer value. Customer value is in the form of lifetime value, influence value and knowledge value. Lifetime value is the profit attributed to the entire future relationship with a customer. Customer influence value is a perceived utility of what social media networks offer to a customer, as perceived by the customer. Knowledge value is the perceived empowerment obtained from attaining knowledge about a product.

Various studies of online reviews of tourism (Rogerson & Visser, 2011) and destinations in Africa (Mkono, 2012; Kladou & Mavragani, 2015) as well as reviews of hotels and restaurants (Mkono, 2012) demonstrate how online reviews can be used as a powerful managerial tool to create and co-create value, and consequently improve business performance. A positive response to online reviews (Phillips et al., 2015) does not only instil confidence in prospective and potential customers but also enhances customer retention (Reichheld et al., 2000). In the context of the tourism and associated services industry, management has used online reviews to gauge market patterns (Banerjee & Chua (2016), consumer behaviour (Cohen et al., 2014), customers service experience, customer's satisfaction with various service components and expectations of service quality, to improve service management (Ebong, 2017).

An Adobe (2018) report on digital trends shows that technology-oriented firms' priority is on optimising customer experience/service and creating the content enabling the same, inferring that there is a correlation between investment in integrated technological platforms and success or failure of a firm, since it is directly linked with customer service. In this new trend, the younger generation is more likely to use brands' social media sites because they grew up in the mobile world. Electronic word of mouth (eWOM) enables seamless sharing of information from everyone to everyone (E2E), as opposed to merely consumer to consumer (C2C), business to consumer (B2C) or business to business (B2B). The best way of understanding social media in customer service is by examining online reviews.

Bolton et al. (2013) conducted a study to understand the youth in Generation Y and their use of social media. There is an association of usage of social media with the growth of Generation Y populations. This finding is particularly significant for Africa where the population is growing rapidly (United Nations, 2019). The findings of this study point towards an African future with many users of social media. Although African businesses currently use social media mainly to reach out to their global customers, the findings of the study by Bolton et al. (2013) serves to highlight a future where such businesses will have a significant number of users to target with social media marketing and customer service.

Online reviews act as e-WOM. e-WOM is a form of informal marketing that can become viral if the message is persuasive. In e-WOM, the focus is on person-to-person contacts that happen on the Internet. Cheung and Thadani (2010) define e-WOM communication as 'Any positive or negative statement made by potential, actual, and former customers about a product or a company via the Internet'. Evolution of e-WOM is inspired by the advent and advance of the Internet (Cheung & Thadani, 2010) which is making it possible for consumers to share product experiences. Managers can apply e-WOM to ascertain customers' service experience and perceptions of service quality, and from such analysis, derive practical implications for marketing strategy and management.

While e-WOM is a fairly new discipline, in its short lifespan, e-WOM has demonstrated its importance, especially in consumer marketing and the great impact it can have on influencing consumers' decision-making (Hu et al., 2008; Cheung & Thadani, 2010; Yang et al., 2012). Literature on harnessing the power of social media in customer service within the African context is growing but is still limited to online firms that market their products to online consumers (Samarov, 2015). By inference, opportunities for value creation and co-creation using social media are growing, following a similar pattern of growth in online marketing. Within the African context, online marketing is more prevalent in tourism and destination marketing (Rand et al., 2003) as well as retail marketing (Reardon et al., 2003; Weatherspoon & Reardon, 2003) as compared to other spheres of product or service marketing. The rise in the application of online reviews in retail marketing is particularly driven by a rising trend in multinational chains of supermarkets (Reardon et al., 2003; Weatherspoon & Reardon, 2003) investing and expanding across the continent.

Saffu et al. (2008) studied strategic value and electronic commerce adoption among small- and medium-sized enterprises in Ghana. Their study revealed that organisational support, as well as managerial productivity can be used to predict how the organisation perceives the value of adopting e-commerce. The study also found that perceived usefulness of e-commerce, systems compatibility, as well as external (peer) and organisational (internal) pressure also determine the adoption of e-commerce. These findings point towards the importance of peer learning in enhancing the adoption and usage of e-commerce and social media platforms by African businesses. In addition, the findings of the study regarding the perceived usefulness of e-commerce in driving the adoption of African businesses implies that although usage of platforms such as Facebook in businesses is still low, this usage will increase as more and more African businesses learn about the strategic relevance of social media in customer service.

Online Reviews and e-WOM for Customer Service Management

The utility of online reviews in service management is particularly expressed in how the views and opinions of previous customers can sway decisions of potential customers; how the impact of reviews from renowned reviewers may have more devastating or beneficial effects on a business; comparison of value expectation; ascertaining customer's expected service quality and perceived service quality (Prince & Khaleq, 2013; Gijsenberg et al., 2015) based on multiple service traits; and managements' proclamation of services offered, a concept known as OSP. The ultimate utility of online reviews lies in how management can use reviews to strategise for delivering the best quality services.

Online service reviews are considered to be strong communication instruments (Duan et al., 2008). Reviewers may evaluate the subject being reviewed from their personal perspectives and may also express their opinions on the subject (Duan et al., 2008). Past customers may also express their experiences regarding service or product failures in their reviews. Often, when let down, clients narrate very 'descriptive, persuasive and credible story, often motivated by altruism or, at the other end of the continuum, by revenge' (Ebong, 2017; Sparks & Browning, 2010). The concern for management should be when narratives of a customer's previous experience with a service failure sway the decision of a potential customer. This is how a business begins to lose customers. When management does not address clients' concerns adequately, the trend of negative narratives swaying decisions of customers may continue to drive down business performance.

A reviewer's quality, exposure and product coverage are related to the effects of online reviews. According to Chevalier and Mayzlin (2006), the impact of reviews from a renowned reviewer is greater than such impacts from a less well-known reviewer. Both satisfied and disgruntled customers post reviews, and therefore the average rating does not necessarily show the totality of good and bad aspects of a product (Hu et al., 2008). Many positive reviews serve to significantly reduce consumer's uncertainties and hence increase sales and revenues (Yang et al., 2012). The volume of reviews adds to the power of the reviews in influencing the consumer (Liu, 2006; Chen et al., 2004).

Customers attain a perception of service quality after reading posts of other reviewers (Hu et al., 2008). Reviews enable customers to form their own expectations of service quality. Once customers have formed their expectations of service quality, customers validate their own perceptions and expectations of service quality against the actual service quality they have experienced as evidenced by reviewers' statements. Management can use online reviews, whether positive or negative, to create and co-create value (Akaka et al., 2013). Value creation means making something out of nothing using human effort and ingenuity. In management, business value is an informal term that includes all forms of value that determine the health and well-being of the firm in the long run. Business value often embraces intangible assets not necessarily attributable to any stakeholder group. Co-reading value means to involve others in creating value. The view centred on customers means involving customers to create value. Co-creating value with customers means identifying what the customers want and involving customers in the co-creation of the experience, before or after the actual experience itself. Creating value, as well as co-creating value improves value in the service and enables making such values known to the potential customers through online means such as search engine marketing. Value creation and co-creation make services and products more visible and easier to find for existing and potential customers (Murphy & Kielgast, 2008).

Conclusion

Technology is changing practices and strategies of customer service, particularly in the areas of adopting new technologies, adapting to fast changes in customers behaviours, and becoming competitive in the market. Although usage of social media is still low in Africa, African businesses can still benefit from social media by targeting the global market and servicing international customers. Companies that adopt business models that will take advantage of new technologies will succeed in providing effective customer service. Businesses have to adopt multiple customer interfaces to be able to provide a fast quality response. Because customers are changing their behaviours and expectations on the quality of the product/service, companies must adopt customer-centric business models. Adopting customer-centric business models comes with new demands for competencies, which require investments to upgrade skills, equipment, technology and related applications. Customer-centric business models should seek to respond and address customer complaints and compliments on social media as well as address and respond to issues raised through reviews and e-WOM.

A positive online review is likely to lead to more customers for a business. Negative reviews have negative consequences for a business if such reviews are left unaddressed. Management can use online reviews to instil confidence in prospective and potential customers, and retain old customers (Reichheld et al., 2000). Reviews can also help Management improve service by gauging market patterns (Banerjee & Chua, 2016), consumer behaviour (Cohen et al., 2014), customers service experience, customer satisfaction with various service components and expectations of service quality. Management should proactively respond and adequately address negative reviews (Phillips et al., 2015), as the response of management may cancel the potential impact of a negative review. Service experience is considered as a sum of experiences encountered with different aspects of services. This is why management should strive to deliver quality across all aspects of the business. Because preferences for specific aspects of services differ from customer to customer, management should identify elements of services that most customers consider to be important and prioritise addressing such elements of services that they offer.

Management can use online reviews for a number of managerial and strategic functions (Xu et al., 2013) including service quality evaluation and management; creation, co-creation, and communication of value; as well as targeting and prioritising service improvement. Because services are difficult to define, measure and manage, management can use online reviews, also known and e-WOM, to properly assess their services.

References

Adobe. (2018). *Digital intelligence briefing: 2018 digital trends.* Retrieved 11 July 2018 from https://www.adobe.com/content/dam/acom/en/modaloffers/pdfs/0060629.en.aec.whitepaper.econsultancy-2018-digital-trends-US.pdf

Agnihotri, R., Kothandaraman, P., Kashyap, R., & Singh, R. (2012). Bringing 'social' into sales: The impact of salespeople's social media use on service behaviors and value creation. *Journal of Personal Selling & Sales Management, 32*(3), 333–348.

Akaka, M. A., Vargo, S. L., & Lusch, R. F. (2013). The complexity of context: A service ecosystems approach for international marketing. *Journal of International Marketing, 21*(4), 1–20.

Atkinson, S. (2018). WeChat hits one billion monthly users: Are you one of them. Retrieved 11 July 2018 from https://www.bbc.com/news/business-43283690

Banerjee, S., & Chua, A. Y. (2016). In search of patterns among travellers' hotel ratings in trip advisor. *Tourism Management, 53*, 125–131.

Bolton, R. N., Parasuraman, A., Hoefnagels, A., Migchels, N., Kabadayi, S., Gruber, T., Loureiro, Y. K., & Solnet, D. (2013). Understanding generation Y and their use of social media: A review and research agenda. *Journal of Service Management, 24*(3), 245–267.

Bright, J. (2018). Safaricom rolls out Bonga social networking platform to augment Mpesa. Retrieved 11 July 2018 from https://techcrunch.com/2018/04/30/safaricom-rolls-out-bonga-social-networking-platform-to-augment-m-pesa/

Calabrese, A., & Spadoni, A. (2013). Quality vs productivity in service production systems: An organization analysis. *International Journal of Production Research, 51*(22), 6594–6606.

Campbell, A. J. (2003). Creating customer knowledge competence: Managing customer relationship management programs strategically. *Industrial Marketing Management, 32*(5), 375–383.

Chen, P. Y., Wu, S. Y., & Yoon, J. (2004). The Impact of Online Recommendations and Consumer Feedback on Sales. *Proceedings of the International Conference on Information Systems.* Washington DC: Association for Information Systems, 711–724.

Cheung, C. M. K., & Thadani, D. R. (2010). The state of electronic word-of-mouth research: A literature analysis. *PACIS Proceedings.* Retrieved 5 August 2016 from http://aisel.aisnet.org/cgi/viewcontent.cgi?article=1149andcontext=pacis2010

Chevalier, J. A., & Mayzlin, D. (2006). The effect of word of mouth on sales: Online book reviews. *Journal of Marketing Research*, *43*(3), 345–354.

Cohen, S. A., Prayag, G., & Moital, M. (2014). Consumer behaviour in tourism: Concepts, influences and opportunities. *Current Issues in Tourism*, *17*(10), 872–909.

Deloitte. (2013). The digital transformation of customer services: Our view point. Retrieved 12 July 2018 from https://www2.deloitte.com/content/dam/Deloitte/nl/Documents/technology/deloitte-nl-paper-digital-transformation-of-customer-services.pdf

Duan, W., Gu, B., & Whinston, B. A. (2008). Do online reviews matter? – An empirical investigation of panel data. *Decision Support Systems*, *45*(4), 1007–1016.

Ebong, J. (2017). A qualitative analysis of service experience, perceptions of service quality and service management. *International Journal of Qualitative Research in Services*, *2*(4), 280–294.

El Sawy, O. A., & Bowles, G. (1997). Redesigning the customer support process for the electronic economy: Insights from storage dimensions. *MIS Quarterly*, *21*(4), 457–483.

Gijsenberg, M. J., Van Heerde, H. J., & Verhoef, P. C. (2015). Losses loom longer than gains: Modeling the impact of service crises on perceived service quality over time. *Journal of Marketing Research*, *52*(5), 642–656.

Gummerus, J., Liljander, V., Weman, E., & Pihlström, M. (2012). Customer engagement in a Facebook brand community. *Management Research Review*, *35*(9), 857–877.

Hamilton, M., Kaltcheva, V. D., & Rohm, A. J. (2016). Social media and value creation: The role of interaction satisfaction and interaction immersion. *Journal of Interactive Marketing*, *36*, 121–133.

Hölbing, K., Künstner, T., Marsch, C., & Steinkrauss, N. (2009). Next-generation customer service: The new strategic differentiator. Booz and Allen Inc. Retrieved 27 June 2018 from https://www.strategyand.pwc.com/media/file/Next_Generation_Customer_Service.pdf

Hu, N., Liu, L., & Zhang, J. J. (2008). Do online reviews affect product sales? The role of reviewer characteristics and temporal effects. *Information Technology and Management*, *9*(3), 201–214.

Husain, S., Ghufran, A., & Chaubey, D. S. (2016). Relevance of social media in marketing and advertising. *Splint International Journal of Professionals*, *3*(7), 21–28.

IBM. (2017). Accelerating enterprise reinvention: How to build a cognitive organization. Retrieved 12 July 2018 from https://www-01.ibm.com/common/ssi/cgi-bin/ssialias?htmlfid=GBE03838USEN

Ilavarasan, V., Kar, A., & Gupta, M. P. (2018). Social media and business practices in emerging markets: Still unexplored. *Journal of Advances in Management Research*, *15*(2), 110–114. https://doi.org/10.1108/JAMR-05-2018-111

Kaplan, A. M., & Haenlein, M. (2010), Users of the world, unite! The challenges and opportunities of social media. *Business Horizons*, *53*, 59–68.

Kladou, S., & Mavragani, E. (2015). Assessing destination image: An online marketing approach and the case of TripAdvisor. *Journal of Destination Marketing & Management*, *4*(3), 187–193.

Liu, Y. (2006) 'Word of mouth for movies: Its dynamics and impact on box office revenue. *Journal of Marketing*, *70*(3): 74–89.

Luo, Z., and Qu, H. (2016). Guest-defined hotel service quality and its impacts on guest loyalty. *Journal of Quality Assurance in Hospitality and Tourism*, *17*(3), 311–332. doi:10.1080/1528008X.2015.1077185.

Mangold, W. G., & Faulds, D. J. (2009). Social media: The new hybrid element of the promotion mix. *Business Horizons*, *52*(4), 357–365.

Mbise, E. R., and Tuninga, R. J. (2016). Measuring business schools' service quality in an emerging market using an extended Servqual instrument. *South African Journal of Business Management*, *47*(1), 61–74.

Misopoulos, F., Mitic, M., Kapoulas, A., & Karapiperis, C. (2014). Uncovering customer service experiences with Twitter: The case of airline industry. *Management Decision*, *52*(4), 705–723. https://doi.org/10.1108/MD-03-2012-0235

Mkono, M. (2012). A netnographic examination of constructive authenticity in Victoria Falls tourist (restaurant) experiences. *International Journal of Hospitality Management*, *31*(2), 387–394.

Murphy, C. H., & Kielgast, C. D. (2008). Do small and medium-sized hotels exploit search engine marketing? *International Journal of Contemporary Hospitality Management*, *20*(1), 90–97.

Phillips, P., Zigan, K., Silva, M. M. S., & Schegg, R. (2015). The interactive effects of online reviews on the determinants of Swiss hotel performance: A neural network analysis. *Tourism Management, 50,* 130–141.

Prince, P. R., & Khaleq, Z. B. (2013). Assessment of gap between service quality expectation & perception: A study on the walk-in guests' of economic hotels in Cox's Bazar, Bangladesh. *The IUP Journal of Marketing Management, 12*(3), 7–26.

Purdy, M., & Daugherty, P. (2016). Why AI is the future of growth. Accenture. Retrieved 12 July 2018 from https://.accenture.com/lv-en/_acnmedia/PDF-33/Accenture-Why-AI-is-the-Future-of-Growth.pdf

Rand, G. E. D., Heath, E., & Alberts, N. (2003). The role of local and regional food in destination marketing: A South African situation analysis. *Journal of Travel & Tourism Marketing, 14*(3–4), 97–112.

Ray, G., Muhanna, W. A., & Barney, J. B. (2005). Information technology and the performance of the customer service process: A resource-based analysis. *MIS Quarterly, 29*(4) 625–652.

Reardon, T., Timmer, C. P., Barrett, C. B., & Berdegue, J. (2003). The rise of supermarkets in Africa, Asia, and Latin America. *American Journal of Agricultural Economics, 85*(5) 1140–1146.

Reichheld, F. F., Markey Jr, R. G., & Hopton, C. (2000). E-customer loyalty-applying the traditional rules of business for online success. *European Business Journal, 12*(4), 173.

Rogerson, C. M., & Visser, G. (2011). African tourism geographies: Existing paths and new directions. *Tijdschrift voor economische en sociale geografie, 102*(3), 251–259.

RWC. (2017). Global emerging markets and artificial intelligence. https://www.rwcpartners.com/uk/wp-content/uploads/2017/05/17.05-RWC-Emerging-Frontier-Markets-Q2-Investor-Letter.pdf. Downloaded on. 12 July 2018

Saffu, K., Walker, J. H., & Hinson, R. (2008). Strategic value and electronic commerce adoption among small and medium-sized enterprises in a transitional economy. *Journal of Business & Industrial Marketing, 23,* 395–404. http://dx.doi.org/10.1108/08858620810894445

Samarov, E. (2015). *Value creation and value co-creation in the consumer sphere: Online retail context.* Doctoral dissertation, University of Pretoria, South Africa.

Sarma, A. D., & Choudhury, B. J. (2015). Analyzing electronic word of mouth in social media for consumer insights: A multidisciplinary approach. *International Journal of Science, Technology and Management, 4*(1), 978–990. https://pdfs.semanticscholar.org/2074/5e67a4c04da9c6414f8cf9fa5b415ae194d8.pdf. Downloaded on 13 July 2018

Sebastianelli, R., & Tamimi, N. (2002). How product quality dimensions relate to defining quality. *International Journal of Quality & Reliability Management, 19*(4), 442–453.

Sparks, A. B., & Browning, V. (2010). Complaining in cyberspace: The motives and forms of hotel guests' complaints online. *Journal of Hospitality Marketing and Management, 19*(7), 1–39.

Statista. (2018). Number of social media users worldwide from 2010 to 2021 (in billions). Retrieved 11 July 2018 from https://www.statista.com/statistics/278414/number-of-worldwide-social-network-users/

United Nations. (2019). World population prospects 2019. Retrieved 26 October 2019 from https://population.un.org/wpp/

Verhoef, P. C., Lemon, K. N., Parasuraman, A., Roggeveen, A., Tsiros, M., & Schlesinger, L. A. (2009). Customer experience creation: Determinants, dynamics and management strategies. *Journal of Retailing, 85*(1), 31–41.

Weatherspoon, D. D., & Reardon, T. (2003). The rise of supermarkets in Africa: Implications for agrifood systems and the rural poor. *Development Policy Review, 21*(3), 333–355.

Xu, J. D., Benbasat, I., & Cenfetelli, R. T. (2013). Integrating service quality with system and information quality: An empirical test in the e-service context. *MIS Quarterly, 37*(3), 337–352.

Yang, Y., Wang, C., & Lai, M. (2012). Using bibliometric analysis to explore research trend of electronic word-of-mouth from 1999 to 2001. *International Journal of Innovation Management and Technology, 3*(4), 337.

THEME D: CUSTOMER SERVICE STYLE

THEME IV: CUSTOMER SERVICE STYLE

Chapter 10

Innovation and Customer Service

Justus M. Munyoki

Contents

Introduction

Organisations the world over are increasingly realising the importance of quality customer service as a way of remaining relevant in an increasingly competitive world. Serving customers well implies that the firm has to come up with relevant approaches that are not only superior, but also makes the firm more competitive than its competitors. Innovation has become a very important way of ensuring that firms come up with new ways of doing things, or simply 'doing things differently'. Innovation is about trying to do better in a particular context. Innovation of whatever nature not only makes firms come up with better ways of serving customers, but also reduces the cost of doing business, as it aims at coming up with cost-effective and efficient ways of doing business. Customer service is about ensuring that the service meets customers' needs and expectations, which is expressed in terms of customer satisfaction. Organisations, therefore, need to meet the customer expectation threshold level by adopting not only appropriate, but relevant innovations. Innovation should ensure that the customer is treated with dignity, sensitivity, honesty, fairness and a welcoming attitude. Customer service quality may be measured using indicators such as reliability, responsiveness, assurance and empathy. This chapter presents a detailed assessment of the role that innovation plays towards customer service. It puts emphasis on the various approaches to innovation, both in the developing as well as in the developed countries. This is important because as Aubert (2004) explains, innovation levels differ from economy to economy, and developing countries experience more difficulties in adopting innovations because of various inherent limitations.

The chapter provides a balanced view of how to use innovation, whether technological or otherwise, to enhance customer service. Special reference will be made on the African context and experiences, as it is in Africa where industries need, more than ever before, to realise that firms exist not just to make profit but to serve customers better. Africa is also very dynamic with a huge diversity of customer profiles and a growing youth population, which means that firms operating in Africa must adopt innovative ways of doing business, both at the production level as well as at the customer contact level. The author argues that the definition, scope and nature of what constitutes innovation may differ from one context to another, but should in all cases, aim at enhancing customer service. The author argues that innovation must be a deliberate attempt by firms and industry to do things better, but should not be seen as coincidental. It requires a well-thought-out and structured approach to continuously search for customers' changing requirements and experiences, and come up with innovative ways of serving those customers in a more superior way than before. The author seeks to convince the reader that innovation is about taking customer service to a higher level of satisfaction.

The Concept of Innovation

Innovation as a concept implies newness, that is, anything that comes to market as new as a result of thinking and creativity. In a sense, nearly everything we use today was at some point an innovation. The laptops, mobile phones, iPads and tablets being used today are all examples of innovation. A product that has been in use for a long period of time and is no longer seen as new by the market ceases to be an innovation. At that point, the organisation tries to come up with another product or modify the existing one so that customers may see it as new. This could be done through modification of the existing product, extension or by just adding new flavours, colours or designs. Innovation and creativity go hand in hand, and it is almost impossible to talk about innovation without talking about creativity. Gurteen (1998) considers creativity as the process of generating ideas, and innovation as the sifting, refining, and most critically, the implementation of those ideas. According to him, creativity is about divergent thinking involving generation of ideas, while innovation is about convergent thinking, putting the ideas into action.

Innovation will not just manifest, but rather it requires some catalyst to make it happen. The catalyst comes in the form of creativity. However, for there to be creativity, there needs to be the right environment of freedom, positive challenge, resources and group support. By definition, innovation refers to anything that is new. The Organization for Economic Cooperation and Development (OECD) defines an innovation as *'The implementation of a new or significantly improved product, a new process, a new marketing method, or a new organisational method in business practices, workplace, organisation, or external relations'* (OECD, 2010). This definition seems to lay emphasis on newness by whatever form. Thus, for anything to be considered an innovation, be it a product, idea or process, there must be an element of newness. This may be clearer in the developed world where, because of their technological advancement, it is easier to come up with something new. In a developing economy like those in most African countries, many innovations are in existence elsewhere for a long period of time before being introduced in the developing world. However, this is changing as more African companies are moving towards innovation in areas such as solar power, generators, building materials and telecommunications. M-PESA money transfer technology, for example, is an idea that emanated from Kenya with Safaricom Plc. In Ghana, there are very good innovations in the textile industry.

Importance of Innovation in Organisations

Innovations offer benefits to the country, to the firm, to the customer and to the general public as well. It is beneficial to all stakeholders by the way in which it offers benefits. Some of the ways by which innovation is important to a country include contributing to national growth, facilitating growth of the enterprise, serving customers better, becoming more competitive, responding to technological changes, motivating staff and reducing the cost of doing business.

Contributing to national growth: Innovations contribute heavily towards growth in a nation. This is because innovation increases efficiency in carrying out operations, which leads to cost reduction and time saving, as well as enabling the firms to come up with new products. Countries that have advanced and recorded growth in various areas grow largely because of innovation. Every country thus will experience economic growth if they engage in innovative ways of doing business. Kenya's growth in the construction industry and telecommunications sector is largely as a result of innovation.

Facilitating growth of enterprise: Innovation in many ways helps organisations to grow and become more competitive. Innovation has seen many companies grow and expand in ways that would not have been possible otherwise. Growth of enterprise will be experienced when the firm comes up with new products that attract new customers. Innovation also increases customer satisfaction level, and those customers talk positively to others through word of mouth, which makes the company increase its customer base.

Becoming more competitive: Companies often use innovations to compete by coming up with new products and services that are superior to those of the competitors. Companies that have developed new products are better competitors than those that do not have new products. Innovation leads to efficiency in customer service delivery. In order to deal with competition, Mabati Rolling Mills (MRM) had to introduce various forms of iron sheets that are very attractive to the customers. This has enabled the firm to compete very favourably amongst its leading competition. Some of the innovative products from MRM include the use of aluminium-zinc coating technology under license by BIEC International, Inc. to make aluminium-coated iron sheets branded as Zincal®. This is recognised all over the world as the most advanced technology for delivering extended service life to steel (Mabati Rolling Mills website, https://mabati.com/contact-us/, 2018)

Serving customers better: Innovation is very important for the economic development of a county. This is because innovation enables a country to come up with new ways of doing things, new products and new services that lead to improved performance, and spur economic development. Customers are always looking for new experiences with new products. They easily get bored by seeing everything, in the same way, the traditional way. Customers want to see something that excites them. This is what innovation is about. This is why it is important for companies to continuously come up with innovations that make the customers want to consume new innovations. The government of Kenya introduced the *Huduma* Service, which concentrates government services under one room, and uses the e-citizen services to serve citizens. The word '*Huduma*' is a Swahili word meaning 'service'. The Government of Kenya has come up with *Huduma* Service Centres in all the major towns in Kenya and plans to have the services extended to all the current 47 counties in Kenya. This has greatly enhanced efficiency in service delivery in Kenya.

Responding to technological changes: Innovations can come up as a response to changing technologies as way of survival. Given that technology is always changing, firms must be able to come up with new products that respond to those changes. Technological changes are inevitable, and companies must always look for innovative ways of responding to the technological changes in order to survive and grow. Unless a company aligns its operations with the changing technology, it will be difficult to grow. In the eighties and early nineties, many government offices were using manual typewriters, and in some cases, electric typewriters, which did not have memory to store information. They were very slow and inefficient. With time, these have been replaced with computers that have higher storage capacity, are faster, and more efficient. There are many technological advances taking place all over the world, especially in the area of technology, and use of energy-saving sources of power. In Germany, a Munich-based start-up has taken advantage of the strong Bavarian sun in the summer to test the final development of the charging system of its Sion car, an all-electric solar vehicle that lets you charge it as you drive. Note that Germany is working towards putting one million electric cars on the road by 2020, and the government said in April 2018 that it was ready to offer support to companies that make batteries for electric vehicles (Reuters, 2018).

Motivating staff: Innovation can lead to staff motivation in organisations. Staff always try to get something new that can make them do things in a different way. The emergence of mobile phones brought a new way of doing things, and with it a lot of excitement among staff. Staff become more motivated when they are allowed to use innovative ways to solve problems in the organisation, because they feel that their contribution is being appreciated.

Reducing cost of doing business: Innovation is about better things, efficiency and reduced cost. A firm that becomes innovative in the way it does things cuts down the cost of doing business in a very significant way. There are time-saving and fewer losses as a result of innovation. For example, with the introduction of mobile banking, it has become very easy to for individuals to transact business without necessarily going into the banking halls, meaning that the bank can afford to do with fewer counter tellers, hence reduced cost. Use of automatic teller machines in the banks has also led to efficiency in the banking halls, with reduced queues for counter services.

Factors That Facilitate Innovations

Innovation comes as a response to certain triggers, which include shortage of resources, increased competition, changes in customer needs and preferences, and government policy.

Limited resources: A company that faces limited resources will be forced to come up with innovative ways of utilising limited resources. This is how people have been able to come up with ways of growing vegetables in hanging gardens rather than planted in the ground.

The person will come up with an innovative way of putting soil with manure in a gunny bag and then placing it or suspending it outside along the verandah of the apartment where he/she lives and harvest the vegetables from there. Various companies have come up with money-maker pumps that help to pump water from one point to another, especially in the dry areas. Solar panels have also been introduced to heat water in places where other sources of power are either not available or there is limited power supply. Thus, lack of resources can be a major trigger of innovation.

Increased competition: Competition makes organisations think about new ways of survival in a competitive environment. Without competition, companies tend to be complacent and lack innovation and creativity. Competition in Kenya has made universities come up with very innovative programmes that are market-driven in order to survive in the highly competitive environment. The University of Nairobi, for example, has in the last 10 years introduced market-driven programmes such as MSc in Marketing, MSc in Entrepreneurship and Innovations Management and MSc in Project Management, among many other programmes (University of Nairobi, 2018). The university has also introduced open and distance learning in almost all programmes in order to enhance accessibility for students from any part of the world, instead of relying purely on on-campus training, which is limited to the physical location.

Changes in customer needs and preferences: Changes in customer preferences make customers move away from the usual consumption pattern, and may even discontinue the use of a particular product altogether. This means that the company must come up with other products that respond to changing customer needs and preferences.

Government policy: When the government of Kenya banned the use of plastic bags in 2017, companies that had been thriving on plastic bags found themselves in an awkward position and risked closure because they had nothing to produce. However, within no time, companies came up with a solution – production of alternative packaging materials such as biodegradable paper and other reusable materials such as clothes that were compliant and acceptable by the National Environment Management Authority (NEMA) regulation. NEMA is the government agency in Kenya responsible for checking to ensure that organisations meet certain environmental standards and to guard against environmental contamination as a result of human activity.

Forms of Innovation

Deloitte Development LLC (2015) discusses 10 types of innovations, under the 10 types of framework, which are structured into three categories: configuration, offering and experience.

Configuration: Under this category, three types of innovation exist, namely profit model, network, structure and process, which are discussed below.

Profit model: The focus here is on how organisations make money. Organisations exist to serve customers, but the profit motive remains a key factor. Organisations need to have innovative ways of making money. In Kenya, M-PESA, a mobile phone-based money transfer, was launched in 2007 by Vodafone for Safaricom and Vodacom, the largest mobile network operators in Kenya and Tanzania. It has since expanded to other countries such as Afghanistan, South Africa and India. The M-PESA service, which has been hailed all over the world as a very innovative idea, has contributed heavily towards the profitability of Safaricom. In fact, in 2018 Safaricom reported a revenue of Kshs

224.5 billion (~$2.24 billion) in which M-PESA revenue was Kshs 62.9 billion as customers had moved from traditional payments to M-PESA. The results were driven by innovations in data and mobile money (M-PESA). The company's profitability has more than doubled as a result of this innovation (Bankelele, 2018).

Network: According to the model, companies can benefit a lot by working closely with others in ways that are of mutual benefit to both. No company can survive and sustain itself by working alone. Working with others creates networks that can spur growth in the company's profitability. Networks have been known all over the world to contribute to success among organisations. The issue of strategic alliances, for example, makes companies work closely together, tapping from the combined strength of one another, which creates synergy.

Structure: This deals with aligning a company's talent with its assets. This leads to more efficient utilisation of resources. For innovativeness to make sense in organisations, there is a need to align an organisation's activities and key competence areas with its assets. For example, Equity Bank in Kenya has aligned its key talents with its resources, so that employees are hired and given the necessary resources. The bank puts a lot of emphasis on developing leadership capabilities at all levels of the organisation by sponsoring employees to some of the world's leading business programmes, such as those at Harvard and Wharton Business Schools (Equity Bank, 2018). The bank also gives scholarships to bright students to go to high school and university, as well as a chance to work in the banks, so that they can develop their talent (Mang'eli, 2019).

Process: Innovation needs also to focus on the process that goes on as an organisation makes products. Efficiency and effectiveness are very important in managing a process. How much time does a process take? What has the company done to minimise losses?

Offering: Under this category, we have product performance and product system.

Product performance: This requires a company to come up with innovative ways of producing products that offer superior service to the customer. This will enhance customer satisfaction and loyalty.

Product system: A company needs to have complementary goods and services to support the existing ones, and to offer customers a wide variety of product choice.

Experience: This category comprises service, channel, brand and customer engagement.

Service: Service delivery is very important in product offerings. A company needs to offer innovatively superior services to support its offerings. For example, Startimes sells decoders and follows-ups with the customers to ensure that they are properly fixed and managed. The company, which was formed in China in 1988 and entered the Kenyan market in 2002, has a very strong customer care team with a call line that is operation day and night (Startimes, 2018). Similarly, Davis and Shirtliff, a leading water technology firm in Kenya, has been quite innovative over the years. One of its most recent innovations include the ultra-filtration and reverse osmosis water treatment processes equipment, which is now manufactured at the company's Nairobi factory (Davis & Shirtliff, 2019).

Channel: The channel used to get goods and services to customers is of major interest, as it can affect customer satisfaction levels. Whether one uses direct or indirect channels and how the channel is managed should be innovative enough to enhance customer satisfaction. Debonair, a leading pizza food chain in South Africa with presence in other African countries, has a very innovative way of delivering orders directly to the customers within specified geographical areas. The company delivers meals to offices once an order is placed.

Brand: This is about a company offering a wide variety of brands that cut across several sectors. For example, Virgin extends its brand into sectors ranging from soft drinks to space travel. Coca-Cola has started producing water (Dasani brand) to take care of the increasing number of health-conscious customers who may not like soda. The company also manufactures sugar-free soda and low-calorie options such as Coke Zero (Coca-Cola, 2019). BIDCO Africa manufactures up to 70 brands cutting across six product categories, namely: oil and fats, baking products, detergents and laundry soaps, personal care and beauty, hygiene, and animal products. These include famous brands like Kimbo, Cowboy, Elianto corn oil, and Chipsy cooking oil (BIDCO Africa, 2019).

Customer engagement: Engaging customers and interacting with them can go a long way in enhancing customer satisfaction. Placing personalised attention to the customer can help in bringing the customer closer to the company

Customer Service in Organisations

This subtopic focuses on understanding what customer service is about the indicators of quality customer service in organisations and gives specific examples of how quality customer service helps organisations to grow. This is very important, particularly in the African continent where due to various limitations, customer service satisfaction levels are still rather low.

Organisations are always engaged in customer service in one way or another. Customer service is about meeting a customer's needs through desired services. Customer service may take various forms: giving information, packaging, transport, delivery to the customers, providing security, providing the right environment, etc.

Customers are always in search for information. It may be information about product availability, about the price, or about usage. It is, therefore, necessary that organisations have the right information on various issues about a product. Customers will walk into a shop with numerous questions such as the user benefits, where it was made from, expiry date and ways in which the product is regarded as superior to those others. Unless the person serving the customer has the right information, the customer will go away dissatisfied, because their questions were not sufficiently answered. Customers are always in search for information, which depends on the complexity and value of the product. The more complex and unfamiliar a product is, the more information the customer will seek. Simple, inexpensive and familiar products that customers use on a daily basis such as bread do not elicit a lot of questions; thus, the informational need for these products is low. Customers of such purchases may, therefore, not require as much customer care as far as information is concerned as compared to purchasers of products that are of high value, are unfamiliar, and are complex such as a generator. Companies need to be equipped with the right information if they are to offer services to the customer.

Another area of customer service is after-sales services. This includes making follow-ups about the maintenance of equipment and other facilities that a customer may have bought. For such equipment, it is important for a company to make follow-ups and ensure that the customer is able to use the product properly with few difficulties. The company should keep regular contact with the customer to check if the customer is satisfied, or if there are issues that he/she would like to have addressed. For example, Startimes media, a digital television company and suppliers of TVs and TV decoders, maintain contact with the customers to find out if the customers are comfortable with the product, or if assistance may be needed. The company regularly will call its customers using a customer service line and find out if the customer is satisfied with the services. This gives confidence to customers (Startimes, 2018).

There are times when a customer buys a product and expects it to be delivered to his/her house or office. In this case, the company offers to deliver the product to the customer either at some additional cost or the cost is factored into the purchase price. This is very important, especially in cases where the customer does not have the means or time to go for the product. A number of supermarkets such as Naivas in Kenya deliver items purchased by customers to the parking areas around the supermarket, up to about 200 meters away from the supermarket. Tuskys and Naivas supermarkets in Kenya deliver furniture and other equipment to customers, provided they pay some subsidised transport fee. This is very convenient for the customers, as they may not get a parking space around the supermarket. Debonairs Pizza company has a delivery service that enables them to deliver meals to offices using motorbikes, a service that is very convenient to the customers.

Customer service can also be in the form of customer experience through provision of good working environment, such as avoiding slippery floors, making sure that rooms are properly ventilated, and ensuring that bathrooms are working properly. In the hospitality industry, customer service includes how well a customer is received on arrival, room services and services in and around the hotel. Having a good swimming pool that is very well maintained is part of the customer service, as is provision of Wi-Fi Internet services in the rooms. Thus, a customer who visits a hotel and finds unwelcoming receptionists who do not even offer a glass of refreshment may feel unwelcomed and a bit uncomfortable at the hotel. Worse is if the customer goes to the room and finds there is no warm water, the television is not working, and sockets have no power. To add, the customer may try to call for maintenance work or a change of room and may be met with apathy or neglect. This is an extreme case of poor customer service. Good customer service in such a case requires that the room is properly checked and prepared before the customer arrives, and when the customer finally arrives, he/she should be treated very well right from the reception to the room itself. In public offices, it is common for one to find very complacent officers at the reception who are not in a hurry to assist the customer. The person may be busy just making a telephone call and is least bothered by the presence of the customer, which is very unfortunate.

Importance of Customer Service

In many ways, customers are key to the operations of any enterprise, and organisations exist to serve customers. Without customers, an organisation would find it hard to justify its existence. Organisations succeed not because of the beautiful buildings they have, not because of the facilities they have, and not because of the products they have. They exist because they have customers. Hence, putting up buildings and other facilities, or developing new products must start with the customer. Customer service is therefore very central to an organisation. Some of the areas in which customer service is important include:

- *Increased profitability.* Good customer service can make customers not only buy more, but also refer others to the company. This leads to increased profitability to the company.
- *Increased market share.* Customer service may lead to increased market share because a company that offers good customer service is able to retain customers and therefore grow.
- *Increased customer satisfaction.* Serving customers well makes them more satisfied, which may make them become more committed to the company's brands. When customers are satisfied, the company spends less time serving them, as they rarely complain or ask many questions unless they are faced with a new situation.

■ *Enhanced company image.* A company that serves its customers well is mentioned favourably by the customers, which enhances the company image. This can help to build trust and confidence among potential customers.

■ *Reduced cost of searching for new customers.* When a company maintains good customer service, existing customers will refer other customers by word of mouth, which is an inexpensive way to win customers. Thus, it is important for the company to try and retain its customers and cut the cost of searching for new ones.

■ *Can enhance product life cycle.* Good customer service can maintain a product life cycle because it maintains customers who keep buying the product for many years. This is why brands like Coca-Cola have thrived for decades.

■ *Enhanced word of mouth promotion.* Satisfied customers talk positively about the company, which in return helps to draw more customers to the company.

The issues addressed above have a direct contribution towards organisational growth. This is because the organisation will have happier and satisfied customers. With these types of customers, it becomes easier to serve them and reduces costs as there will be fewer complaints. Customer service allows a company to sell more products or services at reduced costs, and thus increases its market share.

Linking Innovation with Customer Service

This part focuses on the link between innovation and customer service. Emphasis will be on the fact that innovation is about serving the customer better, at a higher level.

Customer service is about listening and understanding the customer in such a way that one is able to serve that customer. Customer service is very important, as it helps an organisation not only to attract, but to retain customers. One indisputable fact is that customer needs are ever changing and require innovation to keep pace with new preferences and needs. A company that is able to identify customer needs and therefore serve them better enhances customer satisfaction. Safaricom, for example, was able to come up with the now almost world-famous M-PESA service, that has revolutionised banking in Kenya.

Practical Experience

The author presents a brief practical experience on innovation and customer service targeting specific industries in Kenya. In Kenya, there is strong evidence of innovation in nearly all the sectors of the economy. The determination by companies to survive and grow in the highly competitive environment has made many companies seek innovative ways of serving their customers. For the sake of simplicity, we focus on three areas: fast-moving goods, construction industry, and the informal sector (*Jua Kali sector*).

The Fast-Moving Goods Sector

In this category, two cases are presented: BIDCO company and Azuri Health. BIDCO is a leading cooking oils manufacturer in Kenya, which has introduced very innovative ways of serving customers after realising that consumer preferences and technology are always changing. Founded in 1970, the company has continued to expand, and today it has grown into a multinational consumer goods company with presence across 16 countries in East Africa, Central Africa and Southern Africa. Its product portfolio includes oils and fats, baking products, detergents and laundry soaps, animal feeds, food and drinks, personal care and beauty.

In order to save time and energy, BIDCO keeps up-to-date with the latest production equipment and processes that help the company to serve its customers better. This has seen the company become very popular, not just in Kenya, but across the region. Innovation has helped to reduce production and manufacturing costs, which translates into value for customers.

Azuri Health, a small dried fruit company in Kenya, was established in 2010 and has come up with very innovative way of processing mangoes and other fruits and packaging them as dried fruits, elongating their shelf life. This was after the company realised that mangoes were ripening on seasonal basis and nearly all of them ripened at the same time, creating excess supply and reducing the prices to a minimum, as many mangoes were going to waste. The company started buying mangoes from farmers and sun-drying them before packaging them for sale. This process of drying the mangoes and other fruits using the natural heat of the sun in the open may be seen to be an innovation. This results in the longer shelf life of the fruits, which can last up to one year.

The Construction Industry

In the construction industry, companies are coming up with innovative ways of serving their customers. In the example of Mabati Rolling Mills, which was started in 1961 and is today the leading manufacturer of metal-coated and painted steel roofing solutions in Kenya, the CEO Mr Andrew Heycott cites three reasons for the success of the company:

1. Its customers have the knowledge, satisfaction and trust in both the company and the leading product brands the company stands behind.
2. The company has always strived to be at the forefront of steel coating technology and was the first company to offer a superior aluminium-zinc coating system under license from BIEC. This technology is acknowledged to be far superior to traditional galvanised coatings and offers superior performance to corrosion over the long term.
3. The company takes great pride as part of the Safal Group of Companies in employing, developing and nurturing the highest calibre workforce who all form part of the MRM Family (Kenya Engineer, 2016).

The second point given by the CEO is very important for any company. Companies must always try to benefit by coming up with superior technology that serves customers better. This is what MRM has capitalised on, and the rewards have been evident in the company's growth.

Superior aluminium-zinc coating iron sheets come in many sizes and shapes that fit customer preferences. According to Manu Chandaria, the founder and chairman of the Safal Group in which Mabati Rolling is the company's flagship business believes innovation is important to remain at the forefront of the steel roofing industry. This is why Mabati Rolling Mills went into alu-zinc coating and simultaneously introduced multicolour on the iron sheets, which has seen the sales more than triple. According to Chandaria, as quoted in the Kenya Engineer (2016):

> Competition makes you think twice how you will continue with that market share. It's not that easy. But if there is no competition you will be lazy and lousy. To be lazy and lousy is the easiest way to be, but to be on the top, on your toes all the time, is most difficult.

Informal Sector

In Kenya, the informal sector contributes to about 35% of the country's GDP and nearly 80% of employment (Institute of Economic Affairs, 2016). This sector thrives mainly through innovation. The sector comprises mainly young men who are involved in the making of various kinds of products ranging from wheelbarrows, boilers, 3-point energy-saving cooking stoves, metal boxes and so on. Women are also involved mainly in making African baskets for sale both locally and abroad.

Innovation in Basketry in Africa

Basketry is a thriving informal business in many parts of Africa and is almost exclusively a business for women who are mainly the weavers. Men, however, may come in as middlemen when it comes to selling the baskets. Women, either individually in their houses or in organised groups, are involved in making very innovative baskets. These baskets, usually made from sisal or dried banana stem wastes, come in all forms in terms of size, shape and colour. Some women use synthetic twines to strengthen them, but most baskets are made from local materials. Even the colour is made from local dyes made from special trees.

Conclusion

This chapter has provided an elaborate discussion about innovation, creativity and customer service. The author has presented a strong argument in support for continuous innovation, especially within the African continent, where the level of innovation is still low.

Innovation needs to be adopted by all companies in response to various market dynamics, which include changing customer needs and preferences, government policy, competition and changing technology. Benefits of innovation are many, and innovation indeed has benefits to a nation, the company and the customers.

Finally, the author has demonstrated that Africa is on the right path, with innovation taking place in both the formal as well as the informal sectors.

References

Aubert, J. E. (2004). *Promoting innovation in developing countries: A conceptual framework*. Washington, DC: World Bank Institute report, July 2004.

Bankelele. (2018). *Safaricom 2018 results, driven by M-pesa and data growth*. Retrieved 9 May 2019 from http://bankelele.co.ke/2018/05/safaricom-2018-results.html.

BIDCO Africa. (2019). *Products*. Retrieved from https://www.bidcoafrica.com/our-brands/

Coca-Cola. (2019). Retrieved 18 December 2019 from https://www.cnbc.com/2019/10/18/coca-cola-ko-earnings-q3-2019.html

Davis & Shirtliff. (2019). Retrieved 15 February 2019 from https://www.davisandshirtliff.com/water-treatment/product/787-dro4-0-5

Deloitte Development LLC. (2015). *The ten types of innovation*. Retrieved from https://doblin.com/dist/images/uploads/Doblin_TenTypesBrochure_Web.pd.

Equity Bank. (2018). Senior management. Retrieved from https://www.equitybankgroup.com/about/senior-management

Gurteen, D. (1998). Knowledge, creativity and innovation. *Journal of Knowledge Management*, 2(1), 5–13.

Institute of Economic Affairs. (2016). *Economic burden of the informal sector*. Retrieved from http://www.Keww.ieakenya.or.ke/number_of_the_week/economic-burden-of-the-informal-sector.

Kenya Engineer. (2016). Retrieved 15 December 2019 from https://www.kenyaengineer.co.ke/page/76/?
p=y136gdisq

Mabati Rolling Mills. (2018). website, https://mabati.com/contact-us/

Mang'eli, I. (2019). *Equity Group Foundation celebrates top KCSE Wings to Fly scholars*. Retrieved from https://
www.capitalfm.co.ke/thesauce/equity-group-foundation-celebrates-top-kcse-wings-to-fly-scholars/

Organization for Economic Cooperation and Development (OECD). (2010). *The OECD innovation Study,
getting ahead start on tomorrow*. Paris: OECD. Retrieved 15 October 2018 from https://www.doblin.
com/dist/images/uploads/Doblin_TenTypes Brochure_Web.pdf

Reuters. (2018). *This solar Powered car chargers as you drive*. Retrieved from https://nypost.com/2018/08/07/
this-solar-powered-car-charges-as-you-drive.

Startimes. (2018). *Startimes Kenya customer care team – with you 24/7*. Retrieved 15 February 2019 from
https://aptantech.com/2016/11/startimes-kenya-customer-care-team-with-you-24/7

University of Nairobi. (2018). *Listing of programmes offered in UoN*. Retrieved 20 February 2019 from http://
www.uonbi.ac.ke/uon_programmes_type

Chapter 11

Entrepreneurial Customer Service

Ruth N. Kiraka

Contents

Introduction

Customer service entails engagement with the customer before, during and after a purchase, while innovative customer service seeks to spur organisations to constantly find new ways to add value to customers. This chapter will define innovation and describe sources of innovation in the customer service context. It will also outline creative customer service process, explaining how customer service innovations are developed, and the managerial and practical implications of innovation in customer service.

By examining two innovative customer service case studies in Kenya as examples, this chapter draws lessons that may be used by other service providers, both in the public and private sectors.

Defining Innovation in the Context of Customer Service and Its Value

Customer service entails the engagement with the customer before, during and after a purchase. The aim is to enhance customer experience (*Entrepreneur Handbook*, 2018). Kaufman (2009) defined customer service as the act of *creating value* for the customer. This suggests that customers are driving change in the way organisations provide services to them by defining what is valuable to them. Organisations, therefore, need to be responsive to these changes just to survive. To generate new business ideas for serving customers better and differently, however, creativity is needed.

Creativity is a mental process involving the generation of new ideas/concepts or even creating new associations between existing concepts. Creativity is critical because it leads to superior business ideas (Satell 2018). Innovation is the application, implementation and commercialisation of these new ideas to lead, in this case, to superior services. An innovative customer service environment seeks to spur organisations to constantly find new ways to add value to customers (Kaufman, 2009).

Innovative customer service proffers value to an organisation in the following ways:

1. *Improves quality* of a service;
2. *Creates leaner structure* – layers of management or administration may be collapsed for quicker responsiveness to client needs;
3. *Generates prompt and imaginative* solutions to problems;
4. *Allows for less formality in structure and style* – leading to better communication and quicker decision-making; and
5. *Builds greater confidence* inside and outside the organisation in its ability to cope with change (Golkar, 2017; Lessl et al., 2018; Stock et al., 2017).

The day-to-day serving of customers and the deployment, maintenance and refinement of customer experience are junctures in need of an entrepreneurial spirit. Having a system of entrepreneurial customer service means that employees are allowed to derive creative solutions when it comes to the minute details of serving the customer (Solomon, 2018).

Identifying Sources of Innovation

Peter Drucker (1985) identified seven sources of innovation that may be relevant when considering innovative customer service. The first was the *unforeseen* – the unexpected success, unexpected failure or unexpected event in the business environment. Failure can be a strong driver of innovation and, consequently, can achieve repeated success. Indeed, some of the most successful companies are those that learn from their mistakes and turn failures into opportunities.

The unforeseen success of Kenya's leading mobile telecommunications firm Safaricom and its mobile money transfer service M-PESA, has led to many innovations. Started only as a money transfer service, it has moved to offer a wide range of services and products to customers, cheaply, easily and in every corner of the country (*see the case study for details*). Solomon (2018) refers to this as anticipatory customer service – servicing *unexpressed* needs and desires that a customer has not voiced. It is one element that drives entrepreneurial customer service.

The second source of innovation is one based on a *process need*. Krell (2017) notes that the process of innovation represents a better way to do something, arguing that meaningful innovation should make the world a better place and benefit the greatest number of stakeholders possible. In this respect, two examples of process innovation by the Kenyan Government are worthy of mention. The government implemented two key processes to enhance customer service – Huduma Centres and e-citizen. *Huduma* is a Swahili word meaning 'service'. Huduma Centres are one-stop citizen service centres that provide an array of National Government Services in a single location. There are 52 such service centres all over the country that are easily accessible to everyone. They offer up to 55 different government services, including issuance of birth certificates, national identification cards, driver's licenses, business licenses, registration of companies and welfare associations, registration for statutory deductions, student loan applications for government funding and many others. Almost all government department services can be offered through these centres, meaning the process of getting multiple government services is made faster, easier and cheaper. Services that would have taken several hours or days to be accessed can easily be accessed in a single day or within minutes, as processes have also been improved and shortened. Subsequent sections of this chapter provide more examples. The second process innovation, e-citizen, is a platform that allows one to get a number of services and conduct a number of transactions with the government online. A number of services available at the Huduma Centres are also available via the e-citizen platform, such as renewal of driver's license, payment of student loans, filing tax returns for individuals and corporate institutions, and application for passports. Foreigners also use the same platform to apply for a Kenyan visa. The Huduma Centre initiative has won several global accolades and continues to hold its place as one of Kenya's best public service innovations.

The third source of innovation according to Drucker (1985) is the imbalance between reality and what was expected – or what Harreld (2014) refers to as a *performance gap*. A performance gap will most likely result in dissatisfied customers, leading to the need to innovate. Behind a performance gap often lies a lack of proper market intelligence on customer needs and preferences. The Huduma Centres initiative was driven by feedback from citizens on poor public service delivery, which was also costing the government millions of shillings in lost revenue.

A fourth source of innovation is the *dynamics of industry and market structure*. Industry and market structures that have been relatively stable for many years can suddenly disintegrate. Malerba (2006) noted that changing market structure driven by demand invariably results in innovation. Consider, for example, the convergence in technology. One is able to receive voice, data and video feed through their computer or mobile phone. The telecommunications, music and film industries have converged. Even the simplest smartphone today allows one to access multiple services. Innovations are therefore being pushed as customers demand even more innovative products and services that converge multiple functions at low prices.

Fifth, the changing *demographics structure* is also driving the need for innovative customer service. Johnson et al. (2018) have argued that aging is an engine of innovation and business development. The Baby Boomers (born between 1946 and 1964), Generation X (born between 1965and 1982), Generation Y or Millennials (born 1982 and early 1990s) and Generation Z or the iGeneration (born in the later 1990s and onwards) all represent different customer tastes and preferences. One example of differences among these generations is an affinity for online shopping. Whereas this is gaining popularity among the Generations Y and Z and among the affluent members of society, many customers in Generation X and earlier, as well as those more accustomed to traditional shopping, are very suspicious of it. There is a perception among the older generation that online payment platforms are insecure and lack the social experience of actually going to a retail outlet to shop. At the other extreme, as online shopping gains traction among the younger generation, online shopping platforms and service providers will be pushed to be increasingly innovative in their service offering as customers will demand more for less.

On demographics, Pettinger (2005) made a case for gendered customer service, arguing that enacting certain forms of femininity is fundamental to the gendering of customer service and is directly related to enhancing sales. Additionally, she argues that the 'service culture' of say, a retail outlet aimed at an older and more affluent lifestyle segment involves more developed forms of customer service than a cheap, high-fashion outlet. Ethnicity, religion and cultural demographics also impact what she refers to as aesthetic labour. Thus, the social and cultural attributes, skills and knowledge of employees are brought into the service and have a bearing on the creativity of the services they offer.

The sixth source of customer service innovation is changes in *perception, mood and meaning*. Customers decide what will be a successful innovation or not driven by the superior experiences that the innovation offers. The customers' perceptions, mood or meaning that they attach to an innovation such as 'useful', 'beneficial', 'superior' or 'better' will determine whether they use the service or not (Vogt, 2013). When social media and the use of multiple mobile applications first hit the market, platforms and applications were perceived to be for the youth. Today, older people including senior citizens have Facebook, Twitter, Instagram and Snapchat accounts. They are also forming WhatsApp groups for both social and professional engagements, have their professional profiles on LinkedIn, and the list goes on. Perceptions about these platforms and their usefulness have changed and the customer service experience is being enhanced.

The last source of customer service innovation is *new knowledge*. New knowledge generated both from research and practice about customer needs and expectations are likely to drive service innovation (Malerba 2006). The numerous innovations that have driven the growth and success of M-PESA have largely been drawn from research. Customers receive additional features on their SIM cards that allow them to use an ever-increasing diversity of services – from financial transactions to password voice commands.

Creating an Innovative Customer Service Environment

According to Kaufman (2009), at the heart of creating an innovative customer service experience is a shift in mind-set. It is not enough to train staff. They need to think creatively to apply what they learn. He notes that three dimensions – education, creativity and evolution – are necessary for a superior service culture. As new issues arise in a service situation, an employee who is perceptive and well-informed will recognise the new opportunity and apply the principles learnt for a positive outcome.

Solomon (2018) adds that the elements that drive entrepreneurial customer service include:

1. Self-reliant, self-driven teams. Teams should be given an opportunity to review customer-facing business processes regularly to determine if the customer's expectations are being exceeded, not just met;
2. Employees who look for new processes that improve customer-related productivity. This includes reviewing the number of customers being served and the cost of serving them;

3. Management and staff who think and act innovatively. Innovation is not just about new services but new ways of doing things as well – more efficiently, faster or in a way that is more satisfactory to clients; and

4. Intrapreneurs who are encouraged to thrive. Those who innovate should be rewarded irrespective of how their innovations turn out. Each failure brings opportunities to learn and do things better in the future. As the African proverb says: Success depends on how you handle your failures.

The preceding argument points to the important role of management in creating an innovative customer service environment. Emerald Group (2008) and Heskett (2007) point to five important aspects:

1. Giving financial backing to innovation by spending on research and development, market research and risking capital on new ideas.

2. Giving employees an opportunity to work in an environment where the exchange of ideas on innovation can take place.

3. Directing recruitment policy towards appointing employees with the necessary skills to do innovative work, where appropriate. This may be particularly important where innovation involves technological changes and adaptations.

4. Identifying specific managers to be responsible for obtaining information from outside the organisation about innovative ideas and communicating it throughout the organisation. Innovative customer service is everyone's responsibility and each individual should reflect on how customer feedback impacts the way they deliver services.

5. Strategic planning, setting targets for innovation, and, where possible, rewarding success.

Developing an Innovative Customer Service Experience

In 1982, Booz Allen Hamilton developed an eight-stage process of developing innovations which include: (i) idea generation; (ii) idea screening; (iii) concept developing and testing; (iv) marketing strategy development; (v) business analysis – cost, profits; (vi) product/service development; (vii) market testing; and (viii) commercialisation. This was further developed by Alam and Perry (2002) into a ten-stage model: (i) strategic planning; (ii) idea generation; (iii) idea screening; (iv) business analysis; (v) formation of cross-functional teams; (vi) service and process design system; (vii) personnel training; (viii) service testing and pilot run; (ix) test marketing; and (x) commercialisation. In their work, Alam and Perry (2002) focussed on the need to be customer-oriented in product and service innovations. This work was further developed by Trott (2011). Although there have been variations in the works of different authors, the underlying concepts have remained largely the same. Borrowing from these works, nine steps in service design and development are discussed below. The steps are shown in Figure 11.1. The steps are illustrated with examples from the design and development of the Huduma (Service) Centres in Kenya by the National Government. The Huduma Centres Programme aims to transform public service delivery through an innovative customer service experience by providing citizens access to various public services and information from one-stop shops. The centres provide services through integrated technology platforms. Each service centre is located within one building, possibly on one floor, making it possible for service seekers (including persons with disabilities) to access it conveniently. Citizens are able to get services such as the issuance of national identity cards, birth certificates, registration of business names, application of business licenses, drivers' licenses, police abstracts and more than 50 other services from one location.

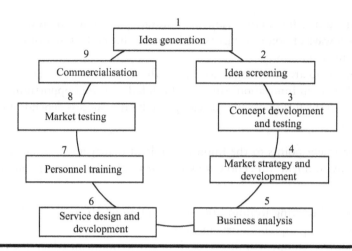

Figure 11.1 Service development cycle. (Adapted from Booz-Allen Hamilton. *New Product Development,* Booz, Allen, Hamilton, New York, 1982.)

Idea Generation

This is the first stage of a new service development process. In the case of the Huduma Centres, the Kenyan Government in 2013 decided to invest public resources in a programme informed by the belief that improved service delivery would lead to the realisation of Kenya's Vision 2030. The programme required numerous government ministries, departments and agencies to come together as stakeholders to negotiate and agree on how this 'one-stop' shop model would provide the services they were offering independently, and how this would affect their operations. Significant buy-in was therefore required. The programme was incorporated into the country's system of planning, budget, disbursement, procurement, accountability for results and value for money. In order to ensure quality and access to public services, the Huduma Programme specifically aimed at transforming the public service towards a people-centred, professional, efficient, transparent and accountable service, which would meet global standards and best practices. To this end, the presidency through the Ministry of Devolution and Planning spearheaded the Huduma Kenya Programme as a flagship project under the Kenya Vision 2030 (Kobia & Oliech, 2016).

Idea Screening

Idea generation creates a large number of ideas which then necessitates screening to reduce the number of ideas into an attractive, and manageable number. With the Huduma Centres, the starting point for the development of the centre was to find which services could be devolved from the parent ministry, department or agency to the centre. Ideas were evaluated against the following criteria:

1. Extent of existing or potential demand for the service;
2. Ease of getting the service;
3. Current challenges in service delivery that the innovation would address;
4. The value for money; and
5. Ability to offer the service online (Kobia & Oliech, 2016).

An initial 20 services were identified. This number was increased to 55 services by 2017.

Concept Development and Testing

Attractive ideas need to be developed into a service delivery concept and then tested. The service concept is an elaborated version of the idea expressed in meaningful consumer terms, for example accessibility, convenience, speed and affordability. For each of the services that was identified to be devolved to the centres, the entire service delivery process was mapped out and process designs were developed. For example, prior to the Huduma Centres and e-citizen, the process of renewing a driver's license was as shown in Figure 11.2.

This process had several challenges. First, was the time taken to renew the license. It could take several hours to a full day to get this done. Second, was the number of customer service staff required. There would be about ten counters, but in most cases, only two to three would be staffed at any one time, making service delivery slow and tedious. Third, the stickers would sometimes run out. In Kenya, one can renew a license for either a year, or three years. Most drivers would prefer the three-year renewal, but sometimes the stickers were not available, forcing some to renew for just one year and repeat the tedious process the following year.

To address these challenges, both online (e-citizen) and offline (Huduma Centre) processes of renewing a driver's license were developed and tested in the market. The focus was on the benefits – speed, convenience, affordability and accessibility.

Market Strategy Development

The new service managers developed a preliminary marketing strategy for introducing the services at the centres into the market. Using a multiplicity of channels, advertising was done countrywide in different local languages to ensure the information was available to everyone. In cases where services were available both off and online, this was also communicated.

Business Analysis

For the government, the business analysis was in the cost savings and efficiency in service delivery that the innovation brought. In cases where both online and offline service provision was available, tracking was done to see which was more popular and why. Initially, citizens were sceptical of the online platforms given that this was the first time the government was utilising such platforms on a large scale. However, as stories of ease of use and convenience became common, the online platforms gained traction. Customers could be served faster, cheaply and at any time, since the online services were available 24/7. The Internet penetration in the country is at 89.4%, which means that most citizens can access the services at a fraction of the cost of physical access.

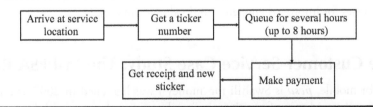

Figure 11.2   Process of renewing a driver's license prior to Huduma Centres and e-citizen.

Service Development

The service development stage answers the question of whether the service is technically and commercially feasible in the long-term (Trott, 2011). Once the service was successfully tested and the benefits were clear, the focus moved to the back-end support to ensure the system was able to handle multiple transactions, downtimes were limited, the user interface was friendly, and payment platforms were secure.

Personnel Training

Before testing the service in the market, personnel training was essential. In this stage, personnel were trained on the use of the service – so that they could answer any questions from the citizens. They conducted some mock service delivery and made improvements as required.

Market Testing

The purpose of market testing is to learn how consumers and service providers react to handling, using and purchasing the actual service and how large the market is (Entrepreneur, 2019). In the case of a government service like renewing a driver's license, this was not difficult to ascertain, since the number of people with licenses is known and the government is the only service provider. Sooner or later, everyone must renew their license. However, feedback on the citizen's satisfaction was still critical as was the assessment as to whether the government was achieving its objective with this innovation.

Online service or a combination of online and offline delivery process was developed for all the services identified. Some of the services, such as getting a Certificate of Good Conduct, have both an online and offline component. While most of the process may be done online, a citizen must still visit a Huduma Centre for fingerprinting. However, this activity now takes about 10 minutes, as opposed to the several hours it took previously.

Commercialisation

Market testing provides enough information to make a final decision about whether to launch the new service into the market and how to do it, as well as provides the impetus for setting up a framework to monitor the performance of the innovation (Kim et al., 2011). With the service centres, it was evident that the prospects were good, and the returns worthwhile. The government established five forms of the 'one-stop-shop' channels as platforms for integrated service delivery: Huduma Centres, Huduma Web Portal, Huduma Mobile Platform, Huduma Call Centre and Huduma Payment Gateway. The physical Huduma Centres increased from one in 2013 to 52 in 2017, while the number of services offered increased from 20 to 55 over the same period.

The government continues to keep an eye on the performance of the centres and gets citizen feedback. Any word of mouth or written feedback is useful in adjusting the service delivery innovation and processes for improved efficiency and value for money.

Innovative Customer Service Case Study: The M-PESA Revolution

M-PESA (**M** for mobile, *pesa* is Swahili for 'money') was launched in 2007 as a mobile phone-based money transfer and microfinancing service. Users can deposit, withdraw, transfer money and make payments easily with even the most basic mobile device. Users are charged a small fee for these transactions. M-PESA spread quickly and today has over 30 million customers in ten countries. It is by far the most successful mobile-phone-based financial service in the developing world. The service has been lauded for giving millions of people access to formal financial services. Below is a description of some of the key customer service innovations in the last ten years.

The M-PESA Revolution That Keeps on Giving

In the mid-2000s, the then CEO of Safaricom encouraged a small team of people to focus on building innovative products for customers. Innovation was one of the pillars on which Safaricom was built. The innovations needed to be exciting and value-adding for customers. Vodafone became aware of the opportunity to get a grant from the Department for International Development in the UK – which was looking for companies interested in developing services to help the unbanked. Safaricom set about creating straightforward financial services that people could easily use from a basic feature mobile phone.

In Kenya, and other parts of Africa, the breadwinner typically travels to an urban area for work while their family stays in the rural area. In order to send money to their relatives, people travelled for days to get home or sent the money through a bus driver. These people did not have access to financial services, and in rural areas, there was little, if any, traditional banking infrastructure. If people did use banks, the cost took a big chunk out of their wages. Safaricom took a chance and re-engineered the financial system to focus on transmitting money from one phone to another. The idea was to have a 'branch' on every street corner, so there was need to recruit a huge network of agents. The company spent $10 million in the first year to establish this network. The aim was that customers would visit an agent with cash, then, through a series of short message service (SMS), convert that money into electronic funds that securely sat on their SIM cards. Through SMS, they could transfer that money to anyone else, who would then visit their local agent and withdraw that cash. The transaction needed to take place in seconds, have very low transaction cost, and the system needed to be very easy to use on the most basic mobile phone. In March 2007, the innovation that came to be known as M-PESA was launched (Vodafone Group, 2017).

More than 10 years on, and M-PESA continues to innovate for customers. It has evolved far beyond its roots of person-to-person money transfers. The service now plays an important role in the broader economies of several countries and is used for a wide variety of essential transactions, including the payment of household bills and salaries, the distribution of pension payments, and disbursement of agricultural subsidies and government grants. M-PESA customers can pay for goods and services both at retail stores and online. They can also transfer money to and from their bank accounts. Services such as M-Shwari, M-Pawa and KCB M-PESA (microloan products) provide interest-bearing mobile savings and small loans in partnership with Commercial Bank of Africa and Kenya Commercial Bank. M-Tiba (meaning M-Health) allows customers to send, save and spend funds on medical treatment at partner clinics and hospitals (Vodafone Group, 2017).

Next the new M-PESA platform dubbed G2 (for M-PESA second-generation platform) was launched to offer versatile integration capabilities that systems developers could take advantage of to create excellent M-PESA transactions across the different industries they serve. This was a key factor in the G2 platform. The platform allows consolidating the different interfaces that developers are interested in to enable innovation around M-PESA. Most of these are about the payment transactions, covering both disbursements (business to customers – B2C) and service payments (customer to business – C2B and business to business – B2B). These and other features are available via secure application programming interfaces (APIs) that allow for third-party applications to easily plug into M-PESA (Safaricom, 2018a).

M-PESA has been very successful mainly because of its simplicity of use and device agnostic nature, working equally well on the newest devices as it does on antiquated and low-quality brands. The API rides on the same concept, providing open interfaces over standard protocols through web services. Unlike the old system (G1) where a lot of workarounds had been done to automate payment experiences, developers can now hook directly to the core M-PESA and get creative with the systems they run. Let's look at the payments use cases below:

1. *Automated Payment Receipt Processing*: Imagine the different scenarios that require customers to pay and have it processed instantly! Before G2, this was handled purely through instant payment notification (IPN). As the name indicates, IPN was only for notification processing. The use cases for payment processing are numerous – from utility bills to m/e-commerce, and the future is likely to get even more interesting. With the new system, the notifications are taken a notch higher by incorporating an optional payment validation step for Paybill. This allows the payment recipient (merchants) to confirm the incoming payment. This significantly reduces errors that may occur during a transaction as the validation API allows the recipient to confirm any of the payment parameters, including account, amount and sender.
2. *Automated Payment Disbursements*: Many systems that process receipts also require outward payments processing. This ranges from employees' salary disbursements to paying other merchants that accept M-PESA payments. This feature was only available via web portal for B2C with limitations on capacity, making it unsuitable for large disbursements. With the new platform, developers can have this done via API, thus, the B2C API process has become seamless.
3. *Automated Payments Reversal*: Even with an elaborate system, there is always a unique case that calls for a reversal such as when a customer has made a payment for services that the merchant is no longer able to render. The best way to handle this is to have a reversal process that the merchant can adapt based on their internal processes. G2 supports secure payment reversal automation for such cases.

Looking at the above use cases, one can see the vast opportunity presented by the open interfaces. The future that was once thought very distant of machine-to-machine payments is here and now. The only limitation to the adaption is the developer's imagination (Safaricom, 2018a).

Other recent innovations include:

M-Tiba (M-Health): This is a service on the mobile phone that allows the customer to put funds aside for healthcare. Funds stored in M-Tiba can only be used to pay for services and medication at specific health facilities. The healthcare providers contracted by M-Tiba are checked for quality, availability, and cost of services to ensure they are committed to better healthcare for all. Given the popularity of M-Tiba among customers, healthcare providers are increasingly requesting to participate in the scheme which is good for customers.

Jitambulishe: This Swahili word means 'identify yourself'. It is a voice biometrics service that allows a customer to enrol their voice and use it to access services such as PUK, M-PESA PIN, Sim replacement, and unlocking an M-PESA account conveniently using the voice as the password. It replaces the need for a PIN as password (Safaricom, 2018b).

DigiFarm: Safaricom has ventured into the agri-business space by developing programmes aimed at facilitating delivery of solutions to farmers countrywide. It offers two products: *Digifarm* (for smallholder farmers) and *Digifarm for Enterprise* (for cooperatives that buy produce).

The *Digifarm for Enterprise* ensures that when a farmer takes the produce to a collection centre, for instance, the facility has a Bluetooth-enabled weighing scale. The system takes details of the produce and corresponds it with the farmer, since through the programme, Safaricom already has the farmers' registration and identification details. The farmer gets an SMS notification of how much he has delivered. This gives one an idea of how much payment to expect, while the collection centre also easily keeps tabs of what it has received. The system effectively eliminates manual record-keeping by farmers and the cooperatives. From an enterprise point of view, it ensures that a processing manager sees how much is collected and from which farmer. The system is also integrated into stock management for the cooperative societies so that the enterprises involved can easily issue stock to farmers on credit and deduct the cost of the stock from the farmers' earnings.

Digifarm on the other hand, is a business solution that addresses small-scale farmers' matters using a simple mobile device that does not need to be a smartphone. Market research has identified significant issues that hamper smallholder farmers' productivity, and which the programme is expected to address. These include poor farm profiling; farmers not knowing what, where, and when they should grow crops; lack of agricultural extension services; lack of information on costs; affordability and quality of farm inputs; and lack of access to local and international markets, most of which are controlled by brokers and middlemen. After a farmer is registered in the system, he can start learning different aspects of agriculture and agribusiness that touch on most of these issues from the comfort of his home through the platform. A farmer can learn about crop and farm management, record keeping, pest and disease control, livestock production, proper ways to market their produce, and other agricultural extension services; all which effectively increase yields and harvests, according to Fredrick Kiio, Head of Agribusiness at Safaricom (Maina, 2018).

In concluding this chapter, one more discussion is important: the managerial and practical implications of innovative customer service. This is discussed below.

Managerial and Practical Implications for Innovative Customer Service

Drawing on the preceding discussions and the two case studies, this section discusses the implications for management in promoting innovative customer service.

Shift in mind-set: As argued by Kaufman (2009), nearly all current performance management models are stacked against innovation. This includes confining such activities to an 'R&D' function. If innovation is to be fostered in the conventional organisation, the role and practices of management require innovation as well. But what does this mean? Drawing on the deliberations of a colloquium held at the Harvard Business School, Heskett (2007) made the following summation: 'Innovation is directly proportional to the attitude and commitment of senior management. The CEO must have vision and fortitude to stand before the board and defend the opportunity to explore and fail'. In the case of M-PESA, the CEO led the initiative – identified innovators, and provided the resources and space to innovate. For the Huduma Centres, the Head of State led the initiative, recruited a Cabinet secretary, formed a task force, and pushed for finances and stakeholder engagement to realise his dream.

Allocation of resources: Resource allocation is a core activity in creating an innovative customer service environment. Solomon (2008) and Emerald Group (2008) made the case for adequate resource allocation to a broad range of innovation projects. In the case of M-PESA, the initial allocation was USD10 million. Although the data on the budget allocation for setting up Huduma Centres may not be available, Kobia and Oliech (2016) are categorical that the only way such a large-scale project succeeded in less than two years was the direct top-level government support and goodwill, and the accompanying budget prioritisation.

Having innovation intent: Picking on the M-PESA innovation, Safaricom's CEO noted that innovation was and still is one of the company's pillars. The mission and value statement mention innovation as one of the core drivers of the company (Safaricom, 2018c). This points to innovation intent, which is then supported by finances and top management as discussed previously.

Monitoring innovation: As discussed in the commercialisation stage of the service development cycle, integration, monitoring and evaluation is a part of innovative service delivery. With the Huduma Centres, deliberate programmatic improvements are being undertaken to establish key impact indicators on both the supply and demand sides of the Huduma Programme (Kobia & Oliech 2016). At Safaricom, Net Promoter Score (NPS) and brand consideration scores are used to track customer satisfaction with new products and services. For the M-PESA platform whose objective is to drive financial inclusion, customer usage and revenue indicators help to manage this aspect of innovation. In terms of social innovations, they use numbers of active users/subscribers to gauge the impact and success of new products and services (Safaricom, 2018c).

Allowing for open innovation: The M-PESA case study discussed previously is a good example of open innovation. The firm does not limit innovation to the company's staff. Indeed, there are many opportunities for anyone to innovate and sell their innovation to the firm. The Safaricom Academy, a collaboration between Safaricom and Strathmore University, is a case in point. The academy provides talented mobile application developers and graduates an opportunity to further develop their skills and set up businesses. The goal is to build capacity in mobile application development to ensure local developers can provide locally relevant innovative solutions. This is done through short courses, as well as a two-year Master in Mobile Telecommunications and Innovation Programme. Additionally, Safaricom launched a venture capital fund named Safaricom Spark Fund in 2014 to stimulate innovation even further. The fund aims to support the successful development and scale-up of high-potential, 'late seed' to 'early growth' stage, information and communication technology (ICT) start-up companies in Kenya through investment and in-kind support, such as mentorship, technical assistance and access to Safaricom services such as SMS, SSD, cloud hosting and marketing opportunities (Safaricom, 2018c).

Customer-centric innovations: Most of Safaricom's services/products have Swahili names that Kenyans like and identify with. Even the tagline is in Swahili, as is the company name 'Safari' which means 'a journey' (but which interestingly has found its way into the Oxford dictionary). As it continues to innovate more services and use names that are readily identifiable and easy to read, more customers can identify with the brand and patronise the services. At the Huduma Centres, the focus is on customer access, high customer service standards and customer dignity. As this is being achieved, the Kenyan government is proceeding to provide an even broader range of services using these centres (Huduma Kenya, 2018).

The outcomes of innovative customer service include:

Maintaining customer loyalty: In Kenya, Safaricom is not the cheapest service provider, but it has the highest market share at 65.4% as of October 2018. Customers are accustomed to it. It started off as a bottom-of-the-pyramid service provider, was affordable and attracted a large market share of customers who could otherwise not afford a mobile phone or airtime. Although with time its tariffs have increased, customer loyalty remains strong. The customers are loyal because they believe they are getting the best service, and there's always something new happening that will add value to them.

Economies of scale: In this case, cost per unit of output decreases as volumes increase. At Safaricom's 10th anniversary in 2017, it was observed that the service provider was processing 529 transactions per second, and 614 million transactions per month. Such extensive use of its services means that, first, its systems must always be reliable, and second, that the cost per transaction is very low (Safaricom, 2018b). At the Huduma Centres, over 30,000 citizens are served daily and collections are at USD120 million annually (Huduma Kenya, 2018). The cost per transaction is reduced, which makes services affordable for all citizens.

Conclusion

This chapter has discussed the meaning and practice of innovative customer service using case studies exclusively from the African context. From a public sector organisation, the Huduma Centres, the possibilities and importance of innovation in customer service, even in the delivery of public sector services where competition is non-existent, can be observed. Safaricom's M-PESA, on the other hand, is largely a private company, and the case study has unpacked its never-ending journey of innovation. As soon as one innovation is up and running and the firm can exploit it, it is time to explore a new one. Both enterprises serve the majority of the Kenyan citizens, and despite being in different sectors, we can draw similar lessons regarding their innovations. As they continue to serve many people depending on them, they need to provide more resources to support further innovation. At the scale of their operations, innovation is not a choice, it is a requirement for them to thrive and continue to grow. Managerial and practical implications for promoting an innovative customer service experience have also been outlined.

References

Alam, I., & Perry, C. (2002). A customer-oriented new service development process. *Journal of Services Marketing*, *16*(6), 515–534.

Booz Allen Hamilton. (1982). *New product development*. Booz, Allen, Hamilton, New York.

Drucker, P. (1985). *Innovation and entrepreneurship: Practice and principles*. New York: HarperCollins Publishers.

Emerald Group. (2008). Improving customer service: How employees and innovation hold the key. *Strategic Direction*, *25*(1), 5–9.

Entrepreneur Handbook. (2018). *What is customer service?* Retrieved 31 January 2019 from https://entrepreneurhandbook.co.uk/what-is-customer-service/

Entrepreneur. (2019). *Market testing*. Retrieved 31 January 2019 from https://www.entrepreneur.com/encyclopedia/market-testing

Golkar, G. (2017). *6 Benefits of a strong customer service culture*. Retrieved 31 January 2019 from https://www.vocalcom.com

Harreld, J. B. (2014). *Executing strategy*. Boston, MA: Harvard Business School Publishing.

Heskett, J. (2007). What is management's role in innovation? *Working Knowledge: Business research for business leaders series*. Boston, MA: Harvard Business School Publishing.

Huduma Kenya. (2018). *Huduma Kenya programme*. Retrieved 31 January 2019 from https://www.hudumakenya.go.ke/analytics.html

Johnson, J. H., Parnell, A. M., & Lian, H. (2018). Aging as an engine of innovation, business development, and employment growth. *Economic Development Journal, 17*(3), 32–42.

Kaufman, R. (2009). Change in service mindset needed. *The Business Times.* Retrieved from http://ronkaufman. com/wp-content/uploads/2014/01/Article_Business_Times_ ChangeinServiceMindset_110114-1.pdf

Kim, S. K., Lee, B. G., Park, B. S., & Oh, K. S. (2011). The effect of R & D, technology commercialization capabilities and innovation performance. *Technological & Economic Development of Economy, 17*(4), 563–578.

Kobia, M., & Oliech, D. (2016). *The case of Huduma Kenya programme in Kenya.* Ottawa, CA: Commonwealth Association for Public Administration and Management.

Krell, E. (2017). Deeper thoughts (and fundamental questions) about innovation and disruption. *Baylor Business Review*, Fall, 4–7.

Lessl, M., Trill, H., & Birkinshaw, J. (2018). Fostering employee innovation at a 150-year-old company. *Harvard Business Review Digital Articles, 12*(17), 1–5.

Maina, S. (2018). *Safaricom's digiFarm aims to put more coins in farmers' pockets through technology.* Retrieved 30 October 2018 from https://techweez.com/2018/07/23/safaricom-digifarm-more-coins-farmers/

Malerba, F. (2006). Innovation and the evolution of industries. *Journal of Evolutionary Economics, 16*(1), 3–23.

Pettinger, L. (2005). Gendered work meets gendered goods: Selling and service in clothing retail. *Gender, Work and Organization, 12*(5), 460–478.

Safaricom. (2018a). *M-PESA Application Programming Interfaces (API).* Retrieved 30 October 2018 from https://www.safaricom.co.ke/business/corporate/m-pesa-payment-services/m-pesa-api

Safaricom. (2018b). *M-PESA.* Retrieved 30 October 2018 from https://www.safaricom.co.ke/#m-pesa-module

Safaricom. (2018c). *Our material matters: Innovation.* Retrieved 31 January 2019 from https://www. safaricom.co.ke/sustainabilityreport_2017/our-material-matters/innovation/

Satell, G. (2018). Set the conditions for anyone on your team to be creative. *Harvard Business Review Digital Articles, 12*(5), 7–11.

Solomon, M. (2018). *For a customer service culture to thrive, an entrepreneurial mindset is essential. Forbes.* Retrieved from https://www.forbes.com

Stock, R. M., Jong, A., & Zacharias, N. A. (2017). Frontline employees' innovative service behaviour as key to customer Loyalty: Insights into FLEs' resource gain spiral. *Journal of Product Innovation Management, 34*(2), 223–245.

Trott, P. (2011). *Innovation management and new product development.* Harlow, UK: Pearson Education.

Vodafone Group. (2017). Vodafone marks 10 years of the world's leading mobile money service, M-PESA. Retrieved 30 October 2018 from https://www.vodafone.com/content/index/media/vodafone-group-releases/2017/m-pesa-10.html

Vogt, D. (2013). *Innovation Perception from a Customer Perspective Recognition, Assessment, and Comprehension of Innovations.* Unpublished doctoral dissertation, University of St. Gallen, Switzerland.

Chapter 12

Leadership and Customer Service

Emmanuel Chao

Contents

Introduction

Customer service is central to an organisation's success (Hsiao et al., 2015), but in a framework of organisations, customer service cannot emerge without proper structure and management. This is even more important when it comes to public organisations where there is always less incentive and an increase in the problem of corruption. Leadership carries an important part in transforming the concept of service quality and influences the process and the quality of customer interactions (Chuang et al., 2012). To develop and cultivate that mindset, every company needs to put efforts into refined hiring processes, constant employee training, and growing leaders who will set the tone for other team members to follow (Lewis, 2017).

This chapter addresses how to improve leadership in achieving better service quality in both public and private companies. Much of the organisational performance impediments within sub-Saharan Africa (SSA), for example, can be well addressed within the framework of proper design, implementation, control and continuous improvement in the way customer service is delivered.

The services markets of SSA are small compared to those in developed markets, with SSA as a whole accounting for only 1.8% of global services value-added in 2014 (Powell, 2017). However, the service sector output in the region has grown rapidly in recent years (Powell, 2017). SSA services value-added increased at a compound annual growth rate of 6.3% during 2005–2014, outstripping world services sector growth (2.6%) by a significant margin (World Bank, 2016). While there are no specific data on the informal sector's contribution to the SSA services economy, estimates suggest that the overall SSA informal sector is large and services activities generally account for a substantial share of its output and employment (Powell, 2017). With important sectors such as transport, communication and tourism, there are continuous changes in the entire value system of the customer service in SSA. Apart from its growth, the customer service sector in SSA contributes a significant amount each countries' employment and general economy.

This chapter will also explore the impediments to quality service, role of leadership in quality service and achievement of holistic quality service. Further, the chapter provides some strategic leadership models for providing efficient and effective customer service delivery.

Leadership and Customer Service Overview

Customer service does not occur in a vacuum, but in an atmosphere of interaction. The interactive nature of service creation and delivery makes the coordination to important and central features (Chen et al., 2015). In addition to simultaneous production and consumption (Skaggs & Huffman, 2003), heterogeneity, volatility and intangibility are often the characterising features of customer service.

Dynamics and the unpredictable nature of interactions make the control process an enormous task for leaders (Skaggs & Galli-Debicella, 2012). In this type of atmosphere, the leader depends on the intuition and flexibility of the employees to serve the customers. Further, such an atmosphere requires the employees to learn through trial and error. Effective leaders in service firms often encourage frontline employees to learn through trial and error and to adapt their future behaviours accordingly (Bowen & Ford, 2002). Leaders in these situations display central features of servant leadership, such as acceptance and tolerance and provide support and continuous guidance to their staff. Servant leaders' developmental, self-reflective and altruistic orientation makes them more effective than transformational leaders in modifying all aspects of employees' service performance

Customers in service organisations frequently come into direct contact with and participate in service production. These interactions not only increase the uncertainty that service employees must face but also make it difficult for leaders to effectively monitor and control each step of the process (Skaggs & Galli-Debicella, 2012). Instead, leaders in such situations must rely heavily on frontline employees' spontaneity and initiative. Beyond co-producing services with customers, frontline employees must also frequently resolve unexpected problems.

Using a measure of employee involvement that included items pertaining to participation, Liao and Chuang (2004) found positive relationships between unit-level involvement and aggregates of employee-rated service performance as well as customer-rated service quality.

Customers are the lifeblood of a business, so the happier they are, the better for the organisation. Customer service is defined as an organisation's ability to meet the needs and desires of its customers. Excellent customer service is a vital part of marketing for enterprises. It is the ability of an organisation to consistently exceed the expectations of its customers. Customer service is displayed in the presentation of the organisation and facilities as well as in the attitude, knowledge and behaviour of the organisation's employees. Customer service begins before a customer arrives and ends long after the customer leaves the organisation.

Customer satisfaction is often linked to customer service, and customer service is a major factor in customer retention and word-of-mouth referrals. Customer retention is important to the bottom line. Research shows that it costs three to five times more to replace a customer than it does to keep a customer (Gallo, 2014). Companies can succeed in gaining a competitive advantage through better provision of customer services. Numerous studies (Emery & Barker, 2007; Ugboro & Obeng, 2000; Ahearne et al., 2005) have also linked leadership behaviours with customer satisfaction. Kim (2002) suggests that a leader's use of a more participative management style will result in higher levels of satisfaction among his or her employees. Jaussi and Dionne (2003) also determined that leaders play a part in subordinate satisfaction, especially if they behave in unconventional ways.

Customer Service Leadership

Achieving customer service requires the proper calibration of customer expectation. Such expectations come from different sources (Kotler & Keller, 2012) and differ from one customer to the other. Further, such expectations determine the level of customer satisfaction. Ensuring that customer expectations are achieved is an important part of service leadership. Customer service leadership requires dedication, and when well-practised, it becomes a source of competitive advantage to the firm. Customer leadership should thus be an integral part of corporate strategy.

Innovation and creativity, when applied to leadership, can make a firm more competitive in their services, by positively influencing employees, thus creating improved service delivery. Leadership by example is a highly effective way of communicating the service values to the employees. In other words, leaders need to be ahead or to be at the centre of the service innovation. For example, rather than hosting a seminar on treating customers with care, a CEO can demonstrate it through caring for the internal customers – the employees. In this way, the behaviour modelled by the leader can be imitated by the employees.

Customers tend to compare the perceived with expected service. If the perceived service is below the expectation, customers are disappointed. To achieve customer satisfaction, the service offering should exceed the expected level. The service-quality model provides the main requirements for delivering high quality service. It identifies five gaps that cause unsuccessful delivery:

1. Gap between consumer expectation and management perception: Management does not always have a correct perception of what the customer needs. For example, the university management may think that the students need more study time, but students may actually be in need of quality teaching materials.
2. Gap between management perception and service-quality specification: Management might correctly perceive customers' wants, but not set a performance standard.
3. Gap between service-quality specifications and service delivery: This gap will likely emerge when the employees lack the capacity or the willingness to meet the specified service standard.
4. Gap between service delivery and external communications: This is the gap that is generated when there is lack of consistency between what is communicated (promised) and what was actually received. The management must strive to align the messages that are delivered and the services that are delivered.
5. Gap between perceived service and expected service. This gap occurs when there is a mismatch between what was delivered and what a customer expected.

Corporate leaders should have an in-depth assessment of these gaps and ensure that they are well addressed. This requires a continuous process and timely feedback.

Creating Better Customer Service

When seeking to create a better customer service culture, leaders should observe the following:

1. *Provide Goals and Expectations*: Employees should be given clarity on what is expected to be delivered to customers and how. For example, how much time it takes to serve a customer inquiry or how the customer should be served. Specification of expectation should also be in relation to the customer service level. Performance measurement should be well specified and communicated. This means that the employee should have a clear understanding of how their efforts are measured and what is involved in determining success.
2. *Provide the Tools to Deliver the Expectations*: The employees require having appropriate tools and training for effective customer service delivery. These tools could include software, policies/guidelines and appropriate knowledge of product and customer service. When these

tools are in place and are ensured to be working appropriately, they will facilitate a conducive environment for customer service. When the employees have all relevant tools, the customers will enjoy better and timely services.

3. *Provide Practical, Relatable Training*: Use of existing successful cases and real examples that have happened in the organisation will provide an in-depth insight into how employees should handle situations. The use of role-play can also be helpful in providing practical examples of how to handle situations.

4. *Provide Opportunities for Shared Learning*: Corporate leaders have a key role in terms of leading the employees to engage on appropriate means for delivering effective customer services. Their experience learned from other members or units within the organisation should be shared. Regular training should be conducted and the emphasis should be on providing positive and negative cases. Leaders have a key role in building the knowledge-sharing culture within the organisation.

Customer Service: Public and Private Sector Perspectives

Service in the private sector is both solution and profit-driven (Haskett, 1994), but the services in the public sector are centred on serving the community/citizens. This has a serious implication when it comes to quality improvement because, under a well-functioning marketing system, the private sector firms have incentives to improve the quality and match with the market dynamics so as to maintain their market share.

Customer service in the public sector is often complex as compared to the private sector, even though there is an existing functioning market. In the public sector, the satisfaction of service offering to one group may likely lead to the dissatisfaction of another one. Often the complexity does not arise from the service delivery, but from the measurements, developments and evaluation of service delivery. To resolve such complexity, the managers in the public service often tend to rely on the internal rather than external evaluations. Citizens may, for example, have one opinion, and politicians, business groups and policy advocacy organisations may have another. To enhance the objectivity of such evaluations, public service leaders should optimise the combination of both internal and external feedback.

Conversely, the private sector can focus its efforts on meeting the expectations of their biggest stakeholder (Swinscoe, 2015), the customers as customers give private firms a reason for existence. With the improved global service measures that rank the customer experience by providing opinions, the service leaders in the private sector work in broader value ecosystems. Rating agencies, customers' online opinions, timely digital surveys and other forms of feedback collection often tend to expand the bases for the standards development and evaluation of private sector service. Markets often control the implementation of customer service in the private sector, but such control is limited in the public sector.

The decision-making structure for the public service sector is internally centred, thus, it is often long and complex, with limited flexibility in the adoption of new improvements. This is, however, possible to overcome through decentralisation and public–private partnerships. The public services that are offered though the privatised state-owned organisations tend to perform better.

The organisational incentives school of thought suggests that in the public sector, the last claimant of the residue (profit) is the public, not an individual. This means that there is no strong incentive for public servants to put efforts in ensuring a better service level because they perceive that there is no extra benefit, unlike in the private sector. Using the incentive-based systems through recognition and regular feedback on performance will enable the leaders in the public service sector to achieve better results. Further, introducing or putting into active use the existing tools for evaluating performance will enhance the provision of better services in the public sector.

Service Leadership: Strategic Perspective

Customer service strategies in the private sector are more highly developed than those in the public sector. In borrowing private sector service management ideas, public sector actors must confront a host of operational and political implications that are not easily dissociated from the management strategy and tactics.

Vision and Mission

It is important for leaders to indicate clearly the organisation's vision for customer service and communicate it constantly to the employees. It is very easy for the customer service to be applied in an ad hoc manner if the employees have no guide or standard.

Goal Setting

Service leadership should be focus driven. It is easy to maintain consistency when there is a focus in the service offering. Customer service leaders should be able to communicate their expectations of customer service to their employees, showing that it is a priority.

Customer service goals and standards must not be set arbitrarily, but should be established based on customer research data (Goodman, 1993). Goals must also be measurable and verifiable.

- Use customers to identify goals: Asking customers what they want is the most important part of setting customer service standards and goals. Methods for determining customer needs include face-to-face interview of key customers, focus groups, polling frontline service employees, questionnaires and min-groups of key stakeholders and decision-makers.
- Performance plans based on goals: Individual performance plans, which can include both retention-level standards and target-level goals, should be reviewed carefully at the beginning of the performance period to ensure that plans are aligned with organisational goals. Evaluating the proposed plans also allows managers, teams and individuals to determine the feasibility of attaining the goals that were set.

Monitoring and Control of Customer Service

Overview

Monitoring and controls are essential elements for effective management of customer service. Effective customer service requires proper monitoring and control of the activities that are involved in service delivery. This is more important in the service sector due to heterogeneous and interactive nature of service.

Key performance indicators that are used by the organisation, the customer feedback, and rating agencies are some of the important controls within the private service sector. The service leaders in the private sector have more push to optimise the value of the information received and use it to improve the service delivery compared to those in the public sector.

Big data analytics is another growing area that produces the opportunity for obtaining better insight and control in the service industry. The service leaders in both the private and public sector should be able to optimise the power of these new data tools for enhancing decision-making and service improvement.

Developing Operational Standards

Developing standards is important in order to create a basis on which to compare performance. The development of standards process should consider customers' expectations and use primary data, such as survey, secondary data and reports. The process needs to be participatory at the firm level, ensuring that the employees are involved in the process. The process can be conducted by using the workforce available within the organisation, but in some cases, there could be a need to bring in consultants.

Implementing the Standards

The implementation of standards is very critical for the improvement of a service. One of the major stumbling blocks in this area is resistance to change. It is relatively easy to implement standards when they are developed inclusively by all affected stakeholders. Additionally, a stage-wise or incremental implementation will provide the opportunity to learn the critical challenges before embarking on the full organisation implementation.

The measuring system can be implemented by:

■ Identifying the goals that need to be measured
■ Developing performance indicators to measure the service or outcomes established in the goal-setting process
■ Involving employees in order to create trust and buy-in
■ Using multiple measures and inputs
■ Providing flexibility
■ Providing feedback
■ Analysing data

Measuring the Service Performance

Measuring service performance is often challenging in the public sector, but with the use of technology and dedicated leadership, the quality of service delivery will improve. Leading the service delivery in the public sector requires designing incentives for customers (citizens) to provide feedback and the service delivering agents to be committed. It is not easy to achieve this due to the nature of the public sector, but continuous efforts will earn improvement. Another avenue is for strategic public-private partnership, such as engaging consultants or outsourcing some of the functions that are not core to the organisation. Independent third-party agencies such as researchers and NGOs can be used to measure and control the public sector service delivery. Customer service leaders in the public sector thus need to be sensitive to the information that they receive and use it to improve the level of service delivery.

Evaluating the Standards

Standards should be evaluated to ensure that they keep pace with changes in the environment. The evaluation should include both the internal and external stakeholders. For objective evaluation, it is also important to involve a third party.

The following are some examples of effective evaluation methods:

- Provide a continuous feedback mechanism for both employees and customers (e.g. suggestion box, regular meeting)
- Monitor the employee performance and match with the expectations
- Ask feedback from your customers
- Hire undercover shoppers to report customer service experience
- Monitor continuously
- Review the comments and complaints

When there is no relationship between the external and internal performance evaluation, the private sector manager will opt for the external evaluation because their loyalty is aligned towards the customers. On the other hand, the public sector must be more discerning with evaluations as the performance improvement may satisfy one group or sector and lead to the dissatisfaction of the other. To a great extent, the service managers in the public sector can focus more on the internal rather than the external measures of service (Kelly, 2005). Whether it is the internal or external performance measure that is adopted, the important consideration is whether customers (citizens for public sector) are better off.

Improving the Standards

The reason behind the evaluation is to improve the standards. The leaders in the service sector should ensure that the outcome of the evaluation is reflected in standards' improvement. It is also important that the improvement be continuous and should not necessarily wait for the evaluation. The performance scores advance the goal of customer satisfaction (Kelly, 2005), thus service leaders should use performance data to improve internal processes and retain customers.

Other Strategic Issues on Customer Service Leadership

Market Segmentation and Targeting and Positioning

Segmentation in service offering: This is more common in the private sector than in the public sector: Firms conduct market segmentation in order to identify profitable customers. They partially shape preferences and expectations as an integral part of customer relations, just as they have grown increasingly sophisticated in their ability to harvest information regarding the preferences of customers. Customer service management is one component of a broader strategic focus (Fountain, 1999).

Further, service quality in the private sector correlates highly with the socioeconomic status of customers. Many firms target particularly lucrative customers, either those who have a record of spending over a certain amount with the firm or those whose demographic profiles show high potential for spending (Fountain, 1999).

Targeting and positioning are essential elements when it comes to service delivery in the private sector. The service leaders should identify and select target customers.

The service leaders should also make critical decisions relating to how to position the service offerings in the markets. Some will like to be followers, others leaders, but in each selected position, the service leaders need to ensure that it is well integrated in the customer service strategy.

Boundary Management

Engaging the external stakeholders and customers in service improvement is one of the key issues in today's service industry. Organisations operate in constant interaction not only with the internal, but also with the external stakeholders. With increased technology advancements, the intensity of interaction between the firm and its stakeholders is at its highest point. This means leaders can optimise the modern tools for attracting even external members to bring ideas and feedback. Customer delivery process and its innovation propensity is thus not just an affair of the organisation and customers, but it also involves the ecosystem of all stakeholders.

Service Client Charter (Service Plan)

The generic name for service plan in the public sector is the 'service client charter' which has been used as a tool for ensuring that public organisations are delivering to their customers what was promised. Most public organisations, especially in developing countries, have adopted this tool as a status quo, rather than a tool to assess the organisation's performance. The client service charter/plan has thus become an internal document that customers are mostly not aware exists. For the private sector organisations, a client service plan can be used for internal purposes because, in a perfect working market, the invisible market hand will push firms to optimise the service quality in order to survive. In the public sector, however, this is not the case because there is competitive pressure for survival, thus there is always a need for a well-functioning guide that customers can use for evaluation of service delivery. Lack of this communication can also impede the service quality in the public sector. This chapter, however, will not provide extensive information on client service plan/charter.

Customer Service Leadership Implications for Small and Large Firms

Customer service leadership has implications when it comes to the size of the firm. With small firms it becomes flexible for supervision and maintaining the atmosphere of control for the front desk customers. Such advantages, however, are reduced with larger firms as the multiple communication layers which arise from the growth of the firm makes it even more challenging to maintain the quality. Further, customer service creativity is challenged by the growth of the firm. When the organisation grows, the decision-making process should be synchronised to match with such changes. Flattening the structure will enable a better decision-making process and empower the value delivery. Flattening or decentralising decision-making comes at the expense of controlling everything. Continuous feedback mechanisms are therefore important for ensuring better quality customer service. Investing in technology that will enable quick reporting and feedback or the provision of real-time data will empower the leaders in the service sector. This applies to both the public and private sector. For example, in Tanzania most citizens were not complying to pay some of the taxes due to poor coordination and long ques (World Bank, 2015). With the introduction of e-government payment gateways, it became easy for the citizens to pay at any place and anytime via the mobile payment systems. Such power of providing flexibility to service consumers added an advantage for employees to focus on the most critical tasks. Further, leaders can easily monitor service interactions due to real-time data availability.

It is thus possible to enjoy the benefit of the small firms when it comes to leading the service provision even when the organisation has grown by reducing the bureaucratic structures and optimising technology. In other words, maintaining the easy control of the service delivery process that takes into account both the customers and the employees need to be given priority. Another issue to consider is the implications for value delivery based on the growth strategy.

Leadership Features for Effective Customer Service Delivery
Involvement

The literature on change management suggests that one of the ways to lead the change is to involve those who are affected in the earlier stages. This is the same case when it comes to service leadership. It is important that all the employees are engaged as a team in the development of customer service delivery. This type of atmosphere will provide the opportunity for continuous innovation and constructive feedback on the current interventions. Further, this generates a sense of ownership that eases the adaptation process. The leader in such an ecosystem is not perceived as one who knows it all, but someone who coordinates the continuous process of service creation and delivery.

Feedback

Feedback works best when it relates to a specific goal. Establishing employee performance goals before work begins is the key to providing tangible, objective and powerful feedback. Feedback should reflect the following features:

- Timely: To have an effective customer service programme, employees need feedback on a daily basis regarding their performance on reaching their customer service goals. If improvement needs to be made in their performance, the sooner they find out about it, the sooner they can correct the problem.
- Appropriate: Feedback should be given in an appropriate manner that will help to improve performance. Since people respond better to information presented in a positive way, feedback should be expressed in a positive manner.

Proactive

Service improvement should be taken as a proactive rather than just a reactive activity. This is only possible when the public service organisations engage in the art of continuous improvement, which in most cases is not feasible without customer-centred leadership.

Waiting for a problem and then solving it will be too late for any organisation that is customer-oriented. This is only possible when the service leaders are innovative and future-oriented. Continuously seeking feedback, understanding the customer expectations and using such information to improve all the potential bottleneck areas will do better for the organisation.

Insight

The employees should have in-depth information on the service that they are offering to their customers. This is gained through continuous training and interactive leadership. Leaders in the service sector should also acquire such insight so as to be able to influence the employees to do the same.

Holistic

The organisation should function as a single unit when it comes to service offering and delivery. In this manner, all the service touch points will work towards the common goal of delivering good service experience to the customer. The task of the leaders in the service sector is to ensure that the purpose and actions of the organisation and all the activities that lead to service delivery are centred on the customer.

Commitment

The willingness to go an extra mile in achieving service delivery is what makes the distinction between ordinary and extraordinary organisations. Commitment is only feasible when the customer becomes the focal point of the organisation's business and when the organisation functions in a holistic fashion in delivering the service.

Culture

Building a service culture does not happen in a single day or accidentally. This should flow from the organisational strategic plan backed up by continuous improvement, training, motivation and sometimes enforcement. The efforts are definitely worth it because once this framework is in place, it shapes and directs all the service actions.

Listening

Service leaders should not only talk but must be willing to listen and understand the concerns and feedback from the internal and external organisational stakeholders. The leader should always be ready to learn and leverage the acquired knowledge towards improvement of the service delivery.

Motivation

Frederick Herzberg's two-factor theory of motivation in marketing research (Herzberg, 1987; Naumann & Jackson, 1999) is applied to help identify and theorise antecedent factors of relationship quality. Two categories of factors are identified in the two-factor theory, 'hygiene' factors and 'satisfiers'. Hygiene factors are those attributes that are expected by the customers as minimum requirements. Lack of hygiene factors will lead to dissatisfaction; however, having them will not necessary enhance customer satisfaction.

Leaders in the customer service delivery should take into account the different approaches for motivating employees. Motivational factors can also be viewed in terms of financial and non-financial classification. A leader can demonstrate a huge potential by exploring the different possibilities for optimising the non-financial motivation. The process of a customer encounter with employees who are delivering the services should be structured in such a way that it provides an experience for both parties. Internal recognitions may yield more positive impact than an increase in pay. Leaders in the service sector should also be at the forefront of discovering and optimising the various options for motivating the employees and even customers who contribute to the service improvement of the organisation (boundary management approaches). Rather than leaders pointing out was done wrong, they can appreciate what was done right. These recognitions can be done in terms of certificates of recognition, public praise and other related approaches.

Innovation and Openness

Continuous innovation is what drives the competition of today's service sector. Innovation is broad in terms of its dimensions. For example, it could be the process of innovation, which can lead to time reduction, or it could be through the improvement of service experience when the customer interacts with service offerings. In whatever format and shape the innovation may take, a leader in the service sector should be able to foresee and seize the innovation opportunity.

In the public sector, especially in developing economies, there is a lack of service innovation, which makes it difficult to provide better services. With improved service innovation, a level of public service in some of the public organisations has started to make some progress in service delivery based on segmentation. For example, Mhimbili Hospital of Tanzania has fast-track options for the patients who pay extra money to get faster service. This again adds extra incentives for the doctors who will be paid much better allowances and thus reduce the employees' turnover. Most doctors tend to get additional work at other private centres for more income, especially when the corruption loopholes are closed. By implementing such innovations, service leaders in the public sector can make their organisations more efficient and competitive.

Impediments to Customer Service

Service delivery is often not a smooth undertaking. It faces several challenges, which can arise from multiple sources. There are, thus several factors that can hinder effective customer service (Thomas, 2009). This section explores some of the common factors that can hinder customer service delivery.

Bureaucracy

Red tape and bureaucracy are what characterises the service delivery, especially in developing economies. It is possible to reduce this when the layers of interactions between the customer and the service are reduced. Use of technology that allows online payments with minimal or no human interactions makes it better. E-health adaptation in Tanzania enhanced the revenue collection of the public hospital and improved the efficiency of service delivery.

Bureaucracy works in a different direction of customer service. One of the challenges, which can confront a large organisation, is the increase of red tape when it comes to decision-making. When the organisation continues to grow, it has an adverse impact on decision-making due to increased decision-making layers. Such decision layers can lead to a communication breakdown in terms of understanding.

For example, when a customer is sent to another employee to handle his/her case, there could be a possibility of improper interpretation of the original need or requirement. Alternatively, if the communication decision-making layers are short, it is easy to handle the client on time with proper feedback. When it comes to the public sector, this problem can be heightened, as there are still bottlenecks, especially in developing countries. Using a client service charter can reduce some of these issues, as there is a clear guide for handling bottlenecks, but it cannot completely resolve issues brought on by the organisation's structure. Addressing the problem of bureaucracy can be done through flattening decision-making. An alternative mechanism is the case tracking where each specific customer case is assigned a specific individual who can track it to completion.

Over- and Underworked Staff

Overworked staff can be a result of having too few workers, too much workload, rapid organisation growth or all of these occurring at the same time. Overworked staff will lead to poor service quality due to deterioration of energy level. This is detrimental to both staffs and customers. In the private sector where competition is high, this problem can immediately lead to customer switching and ultimately result in poor performance. In the public sector, this is a very significant problem, especially in developing countries. With a growing population, that is not proportional to the developments of the service delivery methods, a significant part of the population does not or inadequately receive services. The utilisation of technology and restructuring of the service delivery methods will assist in improving the situation.

Underworked staffs have a similar, but opposite effect on customer service. If the staffs are underworked, they will feel less challenged, underappreciated and unimportant. The work-time theory suggests that work tends to expand to fit the amount of time allocated. When staffs are underworked, they will tend to take more time to deliver the same service, which will lead to a longer time for customer service. This problem exists more in the public sector where jobs tend to be inadequately specified. In some public offices, there are those who are doing too much (understaffed) and those who are doing too little (overstaffed).

Non-Caring Culture and Lack of Accountability

The workplace culture can have a significant impact on customer service delivery. An organisation that does not have a good internal customer care atmosphere will likely have poor external customer service provision. Inadequate working conditions for public workers, especially in developing countries, leads to poor service provision to their clients. Transforming the caring culture by promoting responsibility and accountability is important for achieving a positive impact on customer service provision. Where there is a lack of accountability, there will be no serious efforts from staffs to ensure that quality service is provided to customers. Tacking or tracing systems which make it possible to link specific employees with services provided is a key for ensuring a high level of accountability. The tracking system will provide the organisation with very essential information. This information should be used for correcting and training those who are performing poorly as well as recognising those who are doing outstanding work.

Insufficient Working Tools

When the working tools are poor, customer service will be poorly provided. This will lead to dissatisfaction and poor compliance for the public sector consumers. For example, where there are poor recording systems, it is not easy to track customer records. This challenge can be addressed by the provision of better tools and constantly updating the existing tools.

Inadequate Communication of Customer Value

Staffs should have adequate knowledge of the service they are providing and should also be able to communicate the same in an appropriate manner to the customers. If staffs have never been taught the value of customers to the organisation, they could likely not deliver the appropriate service to them.

Lack of Incentive

Appropriate incentives motivate the staffs to go an extra mile in delivering the appropriate service to customers. Lack of incentives will, in most cases, work in the opposite direction of quality service. These incentives can be financial or non-financial and, in most cases, work as the motivation tool. In public sectors of most developing economies, there are poor or inadequate incentives. This renders the efforts for better service provisions insignificant.

Conclusion

Leadership plays a significant role in ensuring a good performance of customer service; thus, without a proper leadership, there is no quality customer service. The service leaders need to ensure that the employees have relevant skills that are required to deliver quality service that meet customers' expectations.

Achieving customer satisfaction requires a proper calibration of customer expectation. Such expectations come from different sources (Kotler & Keller, 2012) and differ from one customer to the other. Further, such expectations determine the level of customer satisfaction. Ensuring that customer expectations are achieved is an important part of service leadership.

Due to the complex nature of customer service, designing proper mechanisms for service delivery will depend on the sector. Leading the service delivery in the public sector requires designing incentives for customers (citizens) to provide feedback and the service delivering agents to be committed. It is not easy to achieve this due to the nature of the public sector, but continuous efforts will earn improvement.

Customer service leadership in any sector requires dedication, but when well-practised it becomes a source of competitive advantage to the firm. Customer leadership should thus be an integral part of corporate strategy.

References

Ahearne, M., Mathieu, J., & Rapp, A. (2005). To empower or not to empower your sales force? An empirical examination of the influence of leadership empowerment behaviour on customer satisfaction and performance. *Journal of Applied Psychology, 90*(5), 945.

Bowen, J., & Ford, R. C. (2002). Managing service organizations: Does having a 'thing' make a difference? *Journal of Management, 28*(3), 447–469.

Chen, Z., Zhu, J., & Zhou, M. (2015). How does a servant leader fuel the service fire? A multilevel model of servant leadership, individual self identity, group competition climate, and customer service performance. *Journal of Applied Psychology, 100*(2), 511.

Chuang, A., Judge, T. A., & Liaw, Y. J. (2012). Transformational leadership and customer service: A moderated mediation model of negative affectivity and emotion regulation. *European Journal of Work and Organizational Psychology, 21*(1), 28–56.

Emery, C. R., & Barker, K. J. (2007). The effect of transactional and transformational leadership styles on the organizational commitment and job satisfaction of customer contact personnel. *Journal of Organizational Culture, Communications and Conflict, 11*(1), 77.

Fountain, J. E. (1999). *Paradoxes of Public Sector Customer Service.* (Faculty Research Working Paper Series, R99-03). Cambridge, MA: Harvard University.

Gallo, A. (2014). The value of keeping the right customer. Retrieved 15 March 2019 from https://hbr.org/2014/10/the-value-of-keeping-the-right-customers

Goodman, J. A. (1993). Preventing TQM problems: Measured steps toward customer-driven quality improvement. *National Productivity Review, 12*(4), 555–571.

Haskett, J. L., Jones, T., Loveman, G., Sasser, Jr, W. E., & Schlesinger, L. A. (1994). Putting the service-profit chain to work. *Harvard Business Review, 72*(2), 164–174.

Herzberg, F. (1987). One more time: How do you motivate employees? *Harvard Business Review* (September–October), 5–16. https://www.academia.edu/35421607/One_More_Time_How_Do_You_Motivate_Employees_Harvard_Business_Review.

Hsiao, C., Lee, Y.-H., & Chen, W. J. (2015). The effect of servant leadership on customer value co-creation: A cross-level analysis of key mediating roles. *Tourism Management, 49*, 45–57.

Jaussi, K. S., & Dionne, S. D. (2003). Leading for creativity: The role of unconventional leader behavior. *The Leadership Quarterly, 14*(4–5), 475–498.

Kelly, J. M. (2005). The dilemma of the unsatisfied customer in a market model of public administration. *Public Administration Review, 65*(1), 76–84.

Kim, S. (2002). Participative management and job satisfaction: Lessons for management leadership, *Public Administration Review, 62*(2), 231–241.

Kotler, P., & Keller, K. L. (2012), *Marketing Management*, Global Edition 14th ed., London, UK: Pearson Education Limited.

Lewis, J. (2017). *5 Tips for effective leadership in customer service*. Retrieved 14 April 2018 from https://www.providesupport.com/blog/tips-for-effective-leadership-in-customer-service/

Liao, H., & Chuang, A. (2004). A multilevel investigation of factors influencing employee service performance and customer outcomes. *Academy of Management Journal, 47*(1), 41–58.

Naumann, E., & Jackson, D. (1999). One more time: How do you satisfy customers? *Business Horizons, 42*(3), 71–76.

Powell, J. (2017). *The sub-Saharan African services economy: Insights and trends*. (Working Paper ID-046) Office of Industries, US. International Trade Commission (USITC).

Skaggs, B. C., & Huffman, T. R. (2003). A customer interaction approach to strategy and production complexity alignment in service firms. *Academy of Management Journal, 46*(6), 775–786. http://dx.doi.org/10.2307/ 30040668

Skaggs, B. C., & Galli-Debicella, A. (2012). The effects of customer contact on organizational structure and performance in service firms. *Service Industry Journal, 32*(3), 337–352.

Swinscoe, A. (2015). *How to implement an effective proactive customer service strategy*. Retrieved 13 July 2018 from https://www.forbes.com/sites/adrianswinscoe/2015/02/02/how-to-implement-an-effective-proactive-customer-service-strategy/#30d7db5b650e.

Thomas, M. (2009). *8 Barriers to Outstanding Customer Service*. Retrieved 30 October 2018 from https://www.entre-propel.com/customer-service/8-barriers-to-outstanding-customer-service/.

Ugboro, I. O., & Obeng, K. (2000). Top management leadership, employee empowerment, job satisfaction, and customer satisfaction in TQM organizations: An empirical study. *Journal of Quality Management, 5*(2), 247–272.

World Bank. (2015). Tanzania Economic Update, why should Tanzanians Pay Taxes?, Retrieved on 21 October 2019 from https://www.worldbank.org/content/dam/Worldbank/document/Africa/Tanzania/Report/tanzania-economic-update-why-should-tanzanians-pay-taxes-the-unavoidable-need-to-finance-economic-development.pdf.

World Bank. (2016). *World development indicators 2016 (English)*. World Bank Group: Washington, DC.

Chapter 13

Teamwork and Customer Service

Abdullah Promise Opute

Contents

Introduction

The importance of pursuing a customer-focused strategy has been increasingly lauded in marketing literature (e.g. Homburg et al., 2011; Khlebovich, 2012). Theoretically, the customer orientation concept suggests that organisations should focus on understanding and meeting customers' product or service needs and expectations towards achieving customer satisfaction and retention (e.g. Liao & Subramony, 2008; Homburg et al., 2011; Pekovic & Rolland, 2016).

Drucker (1954) commented that the only reasons why businesses existed was to innovate and satisfy customers at a profit. Six decades on, the notion forwarded by Drucker has not only been validated but has also expanded in its implementation. Customer satisfaction has gained central importance, and closeness to customers and has become immensely strategic for company success. To achieve market success and sustain a competitive advantage, managers must invest in customer orientation (Pekovic & Rolland, 2016). Indeed, companies aiming to be competitive in the market can no longer relax, but must become active and engage with the customer. Essentially, they need to adopt a proactive approach in attending to customers' needs (Kennedy et al., 2003), an operational logic that is pertinent given that customer retention has become more challenging. There is a need for further knowledge development regarding the proactive initiatives that organisations are adopting to respond to customer retention challenges (Kennedy et al., 2003; Homburg et al., 2011; Liao & Subramony, 2008).

For more than four decades, the continuance intention theory has been recognised as a core foundation in the service management discourse (e.g. Berry, 1980; Abbas & Hamdy, 2015). The underpinning notion in this theoretical perspective is that acquiring and retaining customers is becoming increasingly challenging and crucial to companies. Undoubtedly, this challenge is intensifying as the marketplace boundary narrows due to globalisation. Consequently, service organisations are increasingly under pressure to find ways of responding effectively to this growing challenge.

One such response that service organisations are adopting is attention to customer service (Macaulay & Cook, 1995; Hall, 2002). Emphasising its importance, scholars point to the criticality of customer service to the well-being of an organisation, and also flag a major gap in the understanding of how to operationalise customer service to maximise its gains for organisations (see also, Abbas & Hamdy, 2015). Inspired by this gap, this chapter aims to contribute to the discourse on customer service, and forwards the notion that service management organisations would achieve market success and sustain competitive edge if they focus on customer service. Recognising the central importance of teamwork in organisational dynamics (e.g. Opute, 2014; Hinsz, 2015; Gounaris et al., 2016), this chapter proposes a teamwork perspective that draws from diversity management, affective behaviour, and conflict management theories to understand teamworking and effective customer service. Thus, this chapter heeds the advocacy for more contributions on the discourse of team dynamics and conflict issues in the services setting (e.g. Opute, 2014; Gounaris et al., 2016; Opute & Madichie, 2017).

Next, customer service is explained and core initiatives/attributes are pinpointed. Following that, teamwork, conflict in teams, and antecedents of conflict are explained, as well as a guide for harnessing teamworking and customer service is presented. Thereafter, the conclusion is presented as well as the implications for service management practitioners and research agenda.

Customer Service: Definition and Core Customer Service Indicators

Acquiring and keeping customers is a critical success road path for services organisations (Abbas & Hamdy, 2015; Hall, 2002). On this plausibility, services organisations are increasingly recognising the pertinence for directing their resources towards improving customer satisfaction – a customer outcome that is a major cause of customer service switching (Liang et al., 2013). Thus, service organisations are focusing on customer service towards customer satisfaction and retention. The rationality for this focus has been reiterated in customer service discourse. For example, it is argued that the cost of acquiring new customers is five times more expensive than customer retention efforts (Keaveney, 1995). Hall (2002) collates health services management insights that lend support to that argument (see Table 13.1). It is obvious, therefore, that the intention to continue (i.e. customer retention) is a critical concern for service companies (Liang et al., 2013; Abbas & Hamdy, 2015).

Table 13.1 Statistics about Customer Service in the Services Industry

S. No	Statistical Facts	Source
1	Customer dissatisfaction costs the average practice 10.6% of its annual revenue.	Treacy and Wiersema (1995). *Customer Intimacy*
2	Most customers who have a bad experience with your practice will not tell you. But they will tell, on average, 10 other people.	Wellemin (1997). *Successful Customer Care*
3	Retaining a customer costs only 20% as much as adding a new one.	Baggett (1994). *Satisfaction Guaranteed*
4	You can increase sales by 30% by providing excellent customer service to your existing customers.	Hall (2002). *Excellent Customer Service: Don't try to practice without it*

Customer service is defined as including customer focusing initiatives that a company adopts to make the customer feel trusting, secure, relaxed and well-disposed towards the company, its staff and the products and services that the company provides (Hall, 2002; Abbas & Hamdy, 2015). In other words, customer service involves operational efforts that an organisation makes to show that it takes the customers seriously, cares about them, understands their needs and is committed to satisfying their service needs. Customer service includes services that a company, through its employees, provides for its customers before, during and after a service (or product) purchase. Excellent customer service is more critical today than ever before (Hall, 2002); therefore, an organisation that values its customers must embrace a practice culture that aims at creating loyal and satisfied customers, and this culture must be evident organisation-wide. This implies that all the staff of the organisation must reflect this culture in their interdependent relationship with other team members (Abbas & Hamdy, 2015; Macaulay & Cook, 1995).

The degree of attention that an organisation gives to the customers impacts the customers' satisfaction and their propensity to switch to another provider (Abbas & Hamdy, 2015; Liang et al., 2013). When the interactions with customers are positive, customers will stay and bring others. On the other hand, negative experiences would not only cause customer service switching, but generate bad word of mouth. As customers become increasingly informed, the bar on service expectations reflects a linear trend. The implication for organisations is that the customer service culture must respond accordingly – excellent customer service is required and must reflect high levels of professionalism, quality and efficiency.

To maximise customer service gains, organisations must ensure critical customer service initiatives/attributes are part of their operational culture (Macaulay & Cook, 1995; Liang et al., 2013; Abbas & Hamdy, 2015; Hall, 2002). Four of these initiatives/attributes are explained below.

Attentiveness: The ability to carefully listen to customers is of critical importance in ensuring effective customer service. Organisations that are keen on showing their customers that they value them and are committed to understanding and attending to their needs must pay attention to individual customer interactions, taking into consideration not only their language and terms in describing the problems, but also being mindful and attentive to the feedback coming from them.

Knowledge of the Product/Service: A central characteristic of services is that its delivery and consumption take place simultaneously with customers directly interfacing with employees.

It is, thus, imperative that forward-facing employees in the company have a deep technical knowledge of how the service works. Knowing the company's service offer from front to back is critically important for forward-facing employees to enable them to offer suitable assistance to customers when they encounter problems.

Clear and Positive Communication: Customers are interested in getting responses that boost their service satisfaction and derive value from service, both during the actual service delivery, as well as post-service delivery. Forward-facing employees of the company must be conscious and aware of the fact that communication could impact positively or negatively on the customer and his/her evaluation of service encounter. The communication habit of the forward-facing employees may translate positively or negatively to customers, depending on contextualisation and presentation; therefore, caution must be taken when communicating with customers. Forward-facing employees must not only communicate clearly to customers but should also keep their communication simple and leave nothing to doubt. Further, on the positivity of communication, forward-facing employees must be aware that non-verbal communication (body language and tone of voice) also impacts positively or negatively on communication recipients (Opute et al., in press). Thus, care must be taken in the interface with customers to ensure that negative non-verbal communications are avoided.

Effective Team Alignment: Organisations are constituted of individuals who, in spite of their differences, are supposed to harmonise effectively towards achieving a goal defined by the organisation. The reality, however, is that dysfunctional behaviours are often the norm in team dynamics. A careful team management strategy is therefore required to achieve team synergy (Opute, 2012, 2014). A company that values its customers must exhibit clear customer-focused values that prompt customers to feel special and important. Critical in ensuring customer-focused values and the customer service goal is a functioning and goal-congruity-driven team. A customer-service-oriented organisation must ensure symbiotic interrelation between team members, because that is a critical team behaviour for achieving the purpose-driven interdependence and cooperation that would aid customer service.

To achieve such a team climate and customer climate impact, identifying and managing the dysfunctional indicators in teams should also be given due attention in the customer initiatives of an organisation. Organisations need to manage team dynamics to achieve a friendly atmosphere that reflects not only openness of team members amongst themselves, but also towards the customer. This is also critical for ensuring that information is willingly shared accurately, timely and consistently. It is also important that team members know their tasks and how to perform them and can take ownership and responsibility for customer issues. Team members should also be interested in knowing what is going on beyond their own individual responsibilities towards ensuring satisfactory service encounters with customers.

Teamwork, Conflict in Teams, Antecedents of Conflict in Teams, and Harnessing Teamworking and Customer Service

Teamwork

Renowned management theorist Drucker (1909), in his book *Management: Tasks – Responsibilities – Practices* comments that 'people are our greatest assets' (p. 300). While the substance in that view is incontestable, leveraging the inherent assets is contingent on the ability of the organisation to strategically optimise the symbiotic inter-relation between workgroups and teams. Harris and Harris (1996, p. 23) defined teamwork as '... a work group or unit with a common purpose through which members develop mutual relationships for the achievement of goals/tasks'. Impliedly, teamwork is when individuals work cooperatively for a common goal by utilising their skills and knowledge and aligning their interdependence to achieve that common goal. Organisations with effective teams are more likely to meet deadlines, and team members take responsibility for their actions. As elaborated by Macaulay and Cook (1995), in the customer's view, poor customer service is a core indicator of a weak team, and this is often reflected in the left hand not knowing what the right hand is doing, failure to meet (or revise) commitments and a lack of ownership for actions.

In the modern-day marketplace, as organisations strive to convince and win customers' loyalty, integrative teamwork and synergistic teamwork have become strategic *sine qua non*. This strategic pertinence draws from the operational rationality that a functioning team drives innovation and creates an outcome that is greater than the addition of individual team members' resources (Nurmi, 1996; Opute & Madichie, 2017) For a service setting, this pertinence for strategic alignment in teamworking is more compelling, given the plausible reason of concurrency in service delivery and consumption. In addition to re-echoing the critical importance for optimal harmonisation of a team in the service context, contemporary insight from the Nigerian frontier market (Opute & Madichie, 2017) point to a higher pertinence, especially for a professional service organisation with a small range of clients (customers) that contribute significantly to the company's well-being. For service organisations with such strategic customer base, failure to ensure symbiotic interrelation in the team cannot be an option, as doing that would have immense negative performance consequences, increase the danger of losing strategic clients, as well as aid a team climate where dysfunctional behaviour and tension thrive (Opute & Madichie, 2017).

Interdependence is a core feature in teamworking. Strategic to optimising the interdependence relationship benefit is an alignment drive that motivates a 'we' culture in team members' behaviours (McManus, 2000; Opute, 2012). Optimising interdependence in teams has featured in several streams of academic discourse, for example in sports management (e.g. Opute, 2012, 2015; Chelladurai & Saleh, 1980), organisational management (e.g. Laughlin, 2011; Hinsz, 2015; Laughlin et al., 2008) and relationship management (e.g. Opute, 2014; Le Meunier-FitzHugh & Piercy, 2007; Opute & Madichie, 2017). Recognising that maximising strategic linking depends on effective symbiotic interrelation (Opute, 2012), the teamwork view described in this chapter follows the foundation that the relationship between team members thrives on good social interrelation and positive feedback (e.g. Opute, 2012; Chelladurai & Saleh, 1980).

Effective cohesion amongst team members must therefore be ensured. Cohesion is the degree of attraction members feel towards one another and the team (Bollen & Hoyle, 1990) or 'it is a feeling of deep loyalty, of esprit de corps, the degree to which each individual has made the team's goal his or her own, a sense of belonging, and a feeling of morale' (Beebe & Masterson, 2000, p. 122).

Beside cohesion, another critical indicator of effective teamwork is effective communication, a team feature that plays a significant role in creating, shaping and strengthening the bonds and belonging (Friedley & Manchester, 2005), and addressing everyday intercultural conflict episodes (Ting-Toomey, 1988). To optimise this enabling function, information communicated must be timely, accurate and purpose-tailored to support role function. Effective teams not only have effective communication internally but also assure consistency of communication with customers (Macaulay, 1993).

Conflict in Teams

One core difficulty that impedes teamwork, interdependence alignment and synergistic outcome is conflict. Conflict is 'an intense disagreement process between a minimum of two interdependent parties when they perceive incompatible interests, viewpoints, processes and/or goals in an interaction episode' (Ting-Toomey et al., 2000, p. 48). Teamwork literature distils three conflict typologies: relationship, task and process conflicts (e.g. Kotler et al., 2006; Opute et al., 2013; Opute, 2014). Conflict has a destructive impact on organisational dynamics and impedes effective communication and cohesion in teams. The conflict elements sensitised in this chapter relate to relationship and task conflict. These dimensions of conflict have also been referred to as affective and cognitive conflicts (e.g. Amason, 1996) or emotional and task conflicts (e.g. Ross & Ross, 1989).

The distinction between relationship and task conflicts is valid because they impact differently on the workplace (Rahim, 2002); hence, scholars have increasingly not only intensified empirical attention but also the advocacy for more illumination of these conflict typologies (e.g. Rahim, 2002; Jehn et al., 2010; Opute, 2014; Opute & Madichie, 2014). Relationship conflict concerns conflict over interpersonal issues, such as personality clashes (Tjosvold et al., 2006; Jehn et al., 2010; Opute, 2014). Relationship conflict can diminish group loyalty, workgroup commitment and willingness to stay in the group and organisation, and job satisfaction (e.g. Jehn et al., 1999; Medina et al., 2005). On the other hand, task (or cognitive) conflict occurs when two or more members of the team disagree on their task or content issues (e.g. Rahim, 2002; Jehn et al., 2010). Task conflict is often similar to issue conflict, which is a state where 'two or more social entities disagree on the recognition and solution to a task problem' (Rahim, 2002, p. 210). High levels of task conflict impede task completion, and thus negatively impact on organisational performance (Jehn et al., 1999).

Antecedents of Conflict in Teams

In the discourse on conflict in organisation and its management, scholars have pinpointed several antecedents of conflict in teams, such as cultural diversity (e.g. Kotler et al., 2006; Opute, 2014; Opute & Madichie, 2016, 2017; Oerlemans & Peters, 2010), reward diversity (e.g. Opute, 2012; Opute et al., 2013; Le Meunieur-FitzHugh & Piercy, 2007), structural factors (e.g. Barki & Hartwick, 2001; Ephross & Vassil, 1993), *inter alia*.

To contribute to the understanding of teamworking and customer service, this chapter is underpinned by the diversity management theory. Extant literature captures diversity as the primary factor that undermines workgroups synergy (e.g. Kanter & Corn, 1994; Opute, 2014). Indeed, Opute (2014) contends that diversity is one central factor that influences interaction and harmonisation in teams. Diversity implies the differences with regard to a common attribute that forms a basis for perceiving oneself to be different from another (Harrison & Klein, 2007; Van Knippenberg et al., 2004). The discourse on team diversity and organisational performance distils two outcomes. On the one hand, the positive information perspective of diversity forwards that group performance would improve positively due to knowledge and skills, variety and creativity, when diversity is conceptualised as heterogeneity (e.g. Jehn et al., 1999; McLeod et al., 1996). A contrast is suggested by the social categorisation perspective (Tajfel & Turner, 1986), which proposes that due to diversity, interpersonal differences impact negatively on groups due to ingroup–outgroup differentiation (e.g. Ayub & Jehn, 2014; Jehn et al., 1999; Tajfel & Turner, 1986; Opute, 2014, 2015). The conceptualisation of diversity in this chapter concurs with the latter perspective and adds that when such diversity and conflict implications are effectively managed, team (or group) psychological enhancement (Opute, 2012, 2014) and organisational performance (Opute, 2012; Cox & Blake, 1991; Opute & Madichie, 2014) would be achieved.

With regard to the social categorisation perspective, core team diversity features relate to culture, perception, orientation and knowledge differences (Opute, 2017, 2014; Hofstede et al., 2010; Opute & Madichie, 2016). Cultural diversity relates to differences in norms, values and

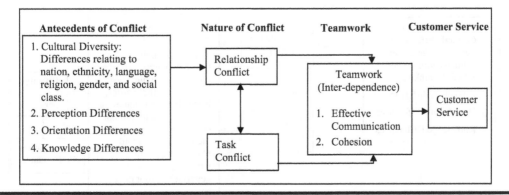

Figure 13.1   Nature and antecedents of conflict in teamwork setting.

ways of doing things, while perception diversity relates to differences in the way things are viewed and perceived. On the other hand, orientation diversity refers to differences in focus, and knowledge diversity implies differences in technical background. As Guillaume et al. (2013) note, there is still a surge in the drive to enhance the understanding of how, when and why workgroup diversity affects work outcomes. The conceptual view forwarded in this chapter (see Figure 13.1) suggests that features of diversity can fuel relationship conflicts, which on its part, intensifies task conflict, culminating in dysfunctional teamworking and ineffective customer service.

Harnessing Symbiotic Teamworking and Customer Service

To compete effectively in today's marketplace, organisations must embrace an operational strategy that enables them to win the customer's loyalty. Appropriate measures must be put in place to ensure customer service. In lieu of the pertinence for such operational strategy, this chapter offers a psychological framework (summarised in Figure 13.2) that utilises affective behaviour theory to enhance customer service understanding and teamwork association. Achieving effective teams requires that organisations employ appropriate strategies to drive team-building initiatives. Specifically, this chapter sheds light on teamwork, dysfunctional influence of conflict and how such conflict could be managed to optimise customer service and organisational performance. Recognising the signs of team effectiveness and timely identification of problems are core team management steps that organisations who care for their customers take (Macaulay, 1993).

Organisations must manage conflict to sustain organisational efficiency and effectiveness (Tjosvold, 2008; Opute, 2014). Conflict management implies the process by which parties to a conflict attempt to negotiate real or imagined differences to a mutually acceptable settlement (Faure & Rubin, 1993). The discourse on conflict management suggests two typologies. The first is resolving conflict internally (e.g. Fisher et al., 1991) or through a third party (de Reuver & van Woerkom, 2010; The Netherlands Organisation for Scientific Research, 2007). In this third-party conflict management strategy, the third party is the intervention hub in the conflict management process.

The extent to which an organisation's efficiency and effectiveness is sustained would hinge on the constructiveness of the conflict management strategy (Leung, 2008; Opute, 2015). This approach is critical in addressing the multiple diversity (cultural, perception, orientation and

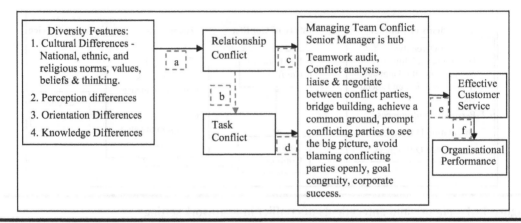

Figure 13.2   Intervention framework for managing team conflict and driving customer service and organisational performance. (Author. Facts collated from referenced sources.) Key: a = Diversity Features that drive relationship conflict; b = Relationship Conflict drives task conflict escalation (boundary fencing, no role flexibility); c and d = Relationship and Task Conflicts are carefully analysed; e = Constructive Conflict Management would lead to Effective Customer Service; and f = Effective Customer Service would contribute to improved Organisational Performance.

knowledge) effect on relationship conflict and feed-off impact on task conflict (Opute, 2014). Thus, this chapter proposes an intervention strategy where a neutral member of the organisation – senior manager (the conflict management hub) – oversees and implements the team conflict management strategy. This approach is constructive and would drive team psychological well-being upon which organisational efficiency and effectiveness is sustained. The plausible reason is that as the neutral party, the senior manager has no emotional attachment to the conflicting parties and can, therefore, maintain an objective position in addressing the conflict issues. Furthermore, given that humans are emotional, conflict parties would favour this conflict management approach.

A leadership intervention strategy involving a senior manager as the conflict management hub is pertinent. Management must, therefore, not only endorse, but also actively engage in addressing the conflict features that drive dysfunctional team behaviour and outcome. As shown in Figure 13.1 and further enhanced in Figure 13.2, an effective proactive strategy to address the relationship and task conflicts is to adopt an intervention approach that recognises the importance of these guides:

1. A senior manager that works closely with the team members. The senior manager, who is the conflict management hub, must be seen as neutral by the team members. Humans are emotional, and conflict thrives on emotions; therefore, the importance of the neutrality factor cannot be underestimated, as this plays a critical role in conflicting parties accepting the conflict resolution outcome.

2. Mitigating the negative influence of conflict in the team requires a proactive strategy that recognises the importance of analysing team conflict. A personal audit tool must, therefore, be used to analyse teamwork climate, expose dangers and initiate actions for adaptability towards enhancing customer service and organisational performance.

3. Conflict analysis should involve engaging intensively with the diversity-induced features that significantly drive relationship conflict. Doing that is critical because these diversity features build the norms, values, beliefs, thinking and way of doing things that shape the mindset

and response from individuals. These diversity features feed into relationship conflict and significantly exert a negative effect on team outcomes (Opute, 2014; Opute & Madichie, 2014). This is because heightened emotions distract team members from the task at hand (Jehn & Bendersky, 2003; Opute, 2014) as well as impede goodwill and trust between team members (Curseu & Schruijer, 2010; Opute, 2014). When goodwill and trust between team members is impeded, emotional outbursts and conflict transformation are further plausible outcomes.

4. Finally, since relationship and task conflicts are positively correlated (Rahim, 2002), the conflict management hub must identify the core conflict features, antecedents and escalation, as well as the transformation capacity and leverage emergent cues to drive symbiotic interrelation in the team. To effectively do that, a combination of procedural justice, motivation and sensibility skills would be needed. Absolute fairness must be ensured in the way conflict episodes are managed, for a contrary approach may lead to conflict parties displaying emotional outbursts when they perceive the conflict resolution effort to be unfair to them. Thus, sensitivity skills are also required for effective resolution. Lastly, the conflict management strategy must embrace a motivational problem-solving approach that involves observing teamworking actions and also encourages dialogue, tolerance and willingness to see issues from a different angle. To achieve the target of ensuring a common ground and goal congruity focus towards effective customer service and organisational performance, the conflict management hub must embrace liaising, message transmitting and negotiating skills to drive harmonious team behaviour that reflects the willingness of team members to understand things from each other's view and psychological safety of team members. Thus, leveraging the personal audit and conflict analysis outcomes, the conflict management hub (senior manager) must help the conflicting parties to negotiate and prompt them to lay aside their differences and misunderstandings to focus on working harmoniously.

Conclusion

In this section, this chapter underlines the core conclusions. Also, attention is drawn to strategic initiatives that organisations can utilise to optimise customer service and organisational performance. Conceptually, this chapter draws attention to the importance of ensuring effective teamworking towards achieving effective customer service and organisational performance. For these customer service and organisational performance targets, this chapter underlines the pertinence for optimum symbiotic interrelation in team. Core characteristics of effective teamworking include information sharing (or communication) that reflects timeliness, accuracy and consistency, as well as cohesion.

The goal of businesses is to succeed and generate profit. Profit generation, however, does not simply refer to financial gain, but also implies the ability of employees to ensure and maintain harmonious working relationships with colleagues, clients and subordinates (Tarricone & Luca, 2002). Given that conflict is a norm in organisations (Opute, 2014; Tjosvold, 2008), this chapter also underlines the strategic importance of managing team conflict. Justified on its persuasion, problem-solving and negotiation suitability, and effectiveness in minimising the negative effects of conflict on emotional well-being (Pazos, 2012; Opute, 2014; Opute & Madichie, 2017), the senior manager intervention strategy is forwarded in this chapter towards effectively managing team conflict.

Recommendations on Customer Service Management

To develop and maintain team commitment, focus and strength, effective and constructive teamwork requires careful management and application (Macaulay & Cook, 1995). Working together is a *sine qua non*, especially for service organisations, as its benefits are highly visible to the customer (Macaulay & Cook, 1995). Thus, organisations must constantly nurture and strengthen their team foundation. Drawing from affective behaviour foundation, this section offers relevant customer service management recommendations for organisations in Africa.

It is critically important for service organisations to adopt a customer orientation approach. To achieve effective customer service, service management organisations in Africa must focus on integrated teamworking. Thus, a situation whereby team members work as disparate individuals must be avoided, as such a situation would be apparent to the customer. Serving the customer is a challenging task, especially in a service setting where service delivery and consumption happen concurrently. Service organisations must avoid situations where team members don't seem to understand what is going on outside their immediate responsibilities. Constructive customer service management requires that service organisations motivate optimum symbiotic interrelation amongst team members. Towards that, suitable intervention strategy must be utilised to address conflict and animosity between team members. Transferred animosity to the customer must be avoided.

To establish a common ground for customer profitability, organisations must maintain effective customer service. In their study of the services industry in Nigeria, Opute and Madichie (2017) described the challenges organisations have in profitably satisfying customers in a context coined as a frontier market. Noting that most African economies may show characteristics that fit the frontier market description, it is recommended that organisations in the sub-Saharan African context should strategically organise teamworking in their organisations towards optimising synergies in order to create the best customer experience and value for their customer segments.

A McKinsey Report (2012) profiling of African consumers (demographics, behaviour and needs) underlines the huge potentials in Africa for businesses and investors – Africa is the world's second fastest growing region after Asia. Furthermore, the report documents that since Africa's population is the youngest in the world, a large percentage of the population belongs to the new consuming class that is highly educated, high earning and digitally savvy. Like their global counterparts, these new consumers are brand and quality conscious, and seek out the latest trends while maintaining financial prudence. To profitably satisfy customers of this type, service organisations must ensure a service strategy that allows them to stay above or at least even with the competition in the market. To achieve that, service organisations in Africa must ensure harmonised and integrated teamworking. The management must ensure optimal symbiotic interrelation and enforce measures for effectively resolving differences amongst team members – be they relationship or task-related.

For service organisations whose main customer segments are in Africa, a strategic orientation that recognises and embraces the understanding of identity theory and associated intricacies is pertinent. Africans have a tendency to exhibit highly social identity congruence behaviour, especially for high involvement products (Wanki, 2019). As a result, the preference formation of Africans for such high-involvement products is highly influenced by social group identity factor. It is, however, evidenced too that social identity congruent consumption behaviour may be moderated by acculturation (Wanki, 2019; Opute, 2017) and socialising (Opute, 2017). Consequently, personal identity may moderate social-identity-induced consumption behaviour. Organisations must be aware of these consumption propensities and must devise a holistic approach of responding to such consumer behaviour. Profitably satisfying customers has become very challenging in today's ever-dynamic marketplace. Achieving an effective strategy requires that the core functional silos in organisations (e.g. accounting and marketing) harmonise and symbiotically interrelate towards responding effectively to customers' stimuli. Managers who care for their customers must embrace effective teamwork and leverage the gains to strengthen the quality of customer service.

Research Agenda

Teamwork and social interdependence are critical features of successful businesses (Tarricone & Luca, 2002). Achieving the business performance synergy of teamworking requires more from team members than the traditional mix of industry-specific knowledge and skills. Critical additional skills include problem-solving, communication, collaboration, and interpersonal and social skills (Tarricone & Luca, 2002). Grounded in this additional skills foundation, this chapter contributes to the customer service discourse from the purview of teamwork association. Specifically, this chapter offers a psychological perspective that draws from diversity management and affective behaviour theories to highlight an intervention modus for effectively responding to conflict features towards ensuring effective communication (information sharing) and cohesion in teamworking, optimised customer service and improved organisational performance.

Future research should aim to enhance this discourse on the affective behaviour perspective of teamwork and customer service. Empirical investigation of the proposed conceptual lens would contribute to enhancing knowledge in this area. Specifically, future research should utilise quantitative or qualitative tools or a combination of both to shed light on this intervention strategy, conflict management impact and customer service outcome. According to insights from the services sector in Nigeria (Opute & Madichie, 2017), optimising the performance impact of intervention strategy hinges on the extent to which the intervention strategy is carefully aligned to the nature of service activity. Future research should illuminate this service nature contingency by exploring various service settings. Finally, future studies should test the proposed conceptual framework as well as the service nature contingency argument pinpointed earlier in various African countries.

References

Abbas, H. A., & Hamdy, H. I. (2015). Determinants of continuance intention factor in Kuwait communication market: Case study of Zain-Kuwait. *Computers in Human Behaviour*, 49, 648–657.

Amason, A. C. (1996). Distinguishing the effects of functional and dysfunctional conflict on strategic decision making: Resolving a paradox for top management teams. *The Academy of Management Journal*, 39, 123–148.

Ayub, N., & Jehn, K. (2014). When diversity helps performance: Effects of diversity on conflict and performance in workgroups. *International Journal of Conflict Management*, 25(2), 189–212.

Baggett, B. (1994). *Satisfaction guaranteed: 236 ideas to make your customers feel like a million dollars*. Nashville, TN: Rutledge Hill.

Barki, H., & Hartwick, J. (2001). Interpersonal conflict and its management in information system development. *MIS Quarterly*, 25(2), 195–228.

Beebe, S. A., & Masterson, J. T. (2000). *Communicating in small groups: Principles and practices*. 6th ed., New York: Longman.

Berry, L. L. (1980). Services marketing is different. *Business*, 30(May), 24–29.

Bollen, K. A., & Hoyle, R. H. (1990). Perceived cohesion: A conceptual and empirical examination. *Social Forces*, 69(2), 479–504.

Chelladurai, P., & Saleh, S. (1980). Dimension of leader behaviour in sports: Development of a leadership scale. *Journal of Sport Psychology, 2*, 34–50.

Cox, T. H., & Blake, S. (1991). Managing cultural diversity: Implications for organizational competitiveness. *The Executive, 5*(3), 45–56.

Curseu, P. L., & Schruijer, S. G. L. (2010). Does conflict shatters trust or does trust obliterate conflict? revisiting the relationship between team diversity, conflict and trust. *Groups Dynamics: Theory, Research and Practice, 14*(1), 66–79.

De Reuver, R., & van Woerkom, M. (2010). Can conflict management be an antidote to subordinate absenteeism? *Journal of Managerial Psychology, 25*(5), 479–494.

Drucker, P. F. (1909). *Management: Tasks – responsibilities – practices.* New York: Harper and Row Publishers.

Drucker, P. F. (1954). *The practice of management.* New York: Harper & Row.

Ephross, R. H., &Vassil, T. V. (1993). The rediscovery of real-world groups. *Social Work with Groups, 16*(1–2), 15–25.

Faure, G. O., & Rubin, J. Z. (1993). *Culture and negotiation.* Newbury Park: Sage.

Fisher, R., Ury, W., & Patton, B. (1991). *Getting to yes: Negotiating agreement without giving in.* 2nd ed., New York: Penguin Books.

Friedley, S. A., & Manchester, B. B. (2005). Building team cohesion: Becoming 'We' instead of 'Me'. Spring, available at: www.nationalforensics.org/journal/vol23no1-16.pdf.

Gounaris, S., Kalliopi, C., Boukis, A., & Perks, H. (2016). Unfolding the recipes for conflict resolution during the new service development effort. *Journal of Business Research, 69*(10), 4042–4055.

Guillaume, Y. R., Dawson, J. F., Woods, S. A., Sacramento, C. A., & West, M. A. (2013). Getting diversity at work to work: What we know and what we still don't know. *Journal of Occupational and Organizational Psychology, 86*(2), 123–141.

Hall, R. (2002). Excellent customer service: Don't try to practice without it. *The Hearing Journal, 55*(7), 34–36.

Harris, P. R., & Harris, K. G. (1996). Managing effectively through teams. *Team Performance Management: An International Journal, 2*(3), 23–36.

Harrison, D. A., & Klein, K. J. (2007). What's the difference? Diversity constructs as separation, variety, or disparity in organizations. *The Academy of Management Review, 32*(4), 1199–1228.

Hinsz, V. (2015). Teams as technology: Strengths, weaknesses, and trade-offs in cognitive task performance. *Team Performance Management, 21*(5/6), 218–230, https://doi.org/10.1108/TPM-02-2015-0006

Hofstede, G., Hofstede, G. J., & Minkov, M. (2010) *Cultures and organizations. software of the mind: Intercultural cooperation and its importance for survival,* 3rd ed., McGraw-Hill, New York.

Homburg, C., Müller, M., & Klarmann, M. (2011). When should the customer really be king? On the optimum level of Salesperson customer orientation in Sales encounters. *Journal of Marketing, 75*(2), 55–74.

Jehn, K., & Bendersky, C. (2003). Intragroup conflict in organizations: A contingency perspective on the conflict-outcome relationship. *Research in Organizational Behaviour, 25*, 189–244.

Jehn, K. A., Northcraft, G. B., & Neale, M. A. (1999). Why differences make a difference: A field study of diversity, conflict and performance in workgroups. *Administrative Science Quarterly, 44*(4), 741–763.

Jehn, K. A., Rispens, S., & Thatcher, S. M. (2010). The effects of conflict asymmetry on workgroup and individual outcomes. *Academy of Management Journal, 53*(3), 596–616.

Kanter, R. M., & Corn, R. I. (1994). Do cultural differences make a business difference? Contextual factors affecting cross-cultural relationship success. *Journal of Management Development, 13*(2), 5–23.

Keaveney, S. M. (1995). Customer switching behaviour in service industries: An exploratory study. *Journal of Marketing, 59*(2), 71–82.

Kennedy, K. N., Goolsby, J. R., & Arnould, E. J. (2003). Implementing a customer orientation: Extension of theory and application. *Journal of Marketing, 67*(October), 67–81.

Khlebovich, D. I. (2012). Client oriented approach-research theory and practice. *Clienting and Management of the Customer Portfolio, 3*, 170–187.

Kotler, P., Rackham, N., & Krishnaswamy, S. (2006). Ending the war between sales and marketing. *Harvard Business Review, Special Double issue, 52*(84), 7–8.

Laughlin, P. R. (2011). *Group problem solving.* Princeton, NJ: Princeton University Press.

Laughlin, P. R., Carey, H. R., & Kerr, N. L. (2008). Group-to-individual problem-solving transfer. *Group Processes and Intergroup Relations, 11*(3), 319–330.

Le Meunier-FitzHugh, K. P., & Piercy, N. F. (2007). Exploring collaboration between sales and marketing. *European Journal of Marketing, 41*(7/8), 939–955.

Leung, A. S. M. (2008). Interpersonal conflict and resolution strategies: An examination of Hong Kong employees. *Team Performance Management, 14*(3/4), 165–178.

Liang, D., Ma, Z., & Qi, L. (2013). Service quality and customer switching behaviour in China's mobile phone service sector. *Journal of Business Research, 66*(8), 1161–1167.

Liao, H., & Subramony, M. (2008). Employee customer orientation in manufacturing organisations: Joint influences of customer proximity and the senior leadership team. *Journal of Applied Psychology, 93*(2), 317–328.

Macaulay, S., & Cook, S. (1995). Practical teamwork for customer service. *Team Performance Management, 1*(3), pp. 35–41.

McKinsey Report. (2012). The rise of the African consumer. Retrieved 6 November 2019 from https://www.mckinsey.com/industries/retail/our-insights/the-rise-of-the-african-consumer

McLeod, P. L., Lobel, S. A., & Cox, T. H. (1996). Ethnic diversity and creativity in small groups. *Small Group Research, 27*(2), 248–264.

McManus, K. (2000). Do you have teams? *HE Solutions, 32* (April), 21.

Medina, F. J., Munduate, L., Dorado, M. A., Martínez, I., & Guerra, J. M. (2005). Types of intra-group conflict and affective reactions. *Journal of Managerial Psychology, 20*(3/4), 219–230. https://doi.org/10.1108/02683940510589019

Nurmi, R. (1996). Teamwork and team leadership. *Team Performance Management: An International Journal, 2*(1), 9–13. https://doi.org/10.1108/13527599610105484

Oerlemans, G. M., & Peters, C. W. (2010). The multicultural workplace: Interactive acculturation and intergroup relations. *Journal of Managerial Psychology, 255*, 460–478.

Opute, A. P., & Madichie, N. (2014). Integration of functional areas of business: A research agenda. *African Journal of Business and Economic Research, 9*(1), 29–54.

Opute, A. P., & Madichie, N. (2016). An interrogation of accounting-marketing interface in UK financial services organisations: Mixing cats with dogs? *Australasian Marketing Journal, 24*(3), 214–225.

Opute, A. P., & Madichie, N. (2017). Accounting-marketing integration dimensions and antecedents: Insights from a frontier market. *Journal of Business and Industrial Marketing, 32*(8), 1144–1158.

Opute, A. P. (2012). Maximizing effectiveness in team sports: The personal audit tool. *Team Performance Management an International Journal, 18*(1/2), 78–101.

Opute, A. P. (2014). Cross-functional bridge in dyadic relationship: Conflict management and performance implications. *Team Performance Management: An International Journal, 20*(3/4), 121–147.

Opute, A. P. (2015). Optimizing team and organizational performance in sports setting: A diversity management perspective. In E. S. Linton (Ed.), *Advances in sports research* (pp. 39–60). New York: Nova Science Publishers.

Opute, A. P. (2017). Exploring personality, identity and self-concept among young consumers. In A. Gbadamosi (ed.), *Young consumer behaviour: A research companion*. Routledge: Taylor & Francis Group.

Opute, A. P., Dedoussis, E., & Tzokas, N. (2013). Building blocks of accounting-marketing integration in UK financial services organization. *Journal of Marketing and Operations Management Research, 1*(4), 323–336.

Opute, A. P., Madichie, N. O., Hagos, S. B. and Ojra, J. (in press). Entrepreneurship behaviour of African minorities in the UK: Demystifying cultural influence. *International Journal of Entrepreneurship and Small Business*. Available at: https://www.inderscience.com/info/ingeneral/forthcoming.php?jcode=ijesb

Pazos, P. (2012). Conflict management and effectiveness in virtual teams. *Team Performance Management, 18*(7/8), 401–417.

Pekovic, S., & Rolland, S. (2016). Customer orientation and firm's business performance: A moderated mediation model of environmental customer innovation and contextual factors. *European Journal of Marketing, 50*(12), 2162–2191.

Rahim, M. A. (2002). Toward a theory of managing organisational conflict. *The International Journal of Conflict Management, 13*(3), 206–235.

Ross, R. S., & Ross, J. R. (1989). *Small groups in organizational settings.* Englewood Cliffs, NJ: Prentice Hall.

Tajfel, H., & Turner, J. (1986). The social identity of intergroup behaviour. In S. Worchel & W. Austin (Eds.), *Psychology and intergroup relations* (pp. 7–24). Chicago, IL: Nelson-Hall.

Tarricone, P., & Luca, J. (2002). Employees, teamwork and social interdependence – A formula for successful business? *Team Performance Management: An International Journal, 8*(3/4), 54–59.

The Netherlands Organisation for Scientific Research. (2007). Conflict: Functions, dynamics and cross-level influences, Proposal for NOW Strategic Theme 2007–2011.

Ting-Toomey, S. (1988). Intercultural conflicts: A face-negotiation theory. In Y. Kim & W. Gudykunst (Eds), *Theories in Intercultural Communication* (pp. 213–235). Newbury Park, CA: Sage.

Ting-Toomey, S., Yee-Jung, K., Shapiro, R. B., Garcia, W., Wright, T. J., & Oetzel, J. G. (2000). Ethnic/cultural identity salience and conflict styles in four U.S. ethnic groups. *International Journal of Intercultural Relations, 24,* 47–81.

Tjosvold, D. (2008). The conflict-positive organization: It depends on us. *Journal of Organizational Behavior, 29*(1), 19–28.

Tjosvold, D., Law, K. S., & Sun, H. (2006). Effectiveness of Chinese teams: The role of conflict types and conflict management approaches. *Management and Organization Review, 2*(2), 231–252.

Treacy, M., & Wiersema, F. (1995). *The discipline of market leaders: choose your customers, narrow your focus, dominate your market.* Boston. MA: Addison-Wesley Publishing Company.

Van Knippenberg, D., De Dreu, C. K. W., & Homan, A. C. (2004). Work group diversity and group performance: An integrative model and research agenda. *Journal of Applied Psychology, 89*(6), 1008–1022.

Wanki, E. N. (2019). *Social identity and consumer preference formation for high involvement Products: A case study of Nigerians in the UK.* London, UK: Doctoral Thesis submitted at the University of East London.

Wellemin, J. H. (1997). *Successful customer care.* New York: Baron's Educational Series.

Chapter 14

Customer Service Training

Benjamin Mwanzia Mulili

Contents

Introduction

Customer service training is the process of imparting employees with the right knowledge, skills and competences that help them to improve their interactions with customers. The importance of customer service training (CST) is uncontested. For instance, Sendawula et al. (2018)

argue that the skills gained through CST enables the employees to perform their tasks more effectively, which eventually leads to the provision of quality services, improved customer satisfaction, increased sales volumes and faster firm growth. Bulut and Culha (2010) opine that CST increases the commitment and motivation of employees. Such employees become proud advocates of the firm and go out of their way to delight customers (Wang et al., 2017). Phiri and Pillay (2017) are of the view that CST can lead to higher staff retention rates, increased morale and loyalty among those trained. It also increases the confidence and performance of the employees (Dagger et al., 2013) and enables them to do their jobs better with reduced management support. Yilmaz et al. (2016) associate CST with the acquisition of skills that enhance innovation, creativity and performance improvement. According to Matilu and K'Obonyo (2018), CST enables a firm to retain customers and sustain its competitiveness, while Mpofu and Hlatywayo (2015) associate it with decreased costs of doing business, which translates into higher profits.

In spite of its importance, there is limited knowledge on how to implement a CST programme and the items to include in such a training, particularly for firms in Africa. This chapter partly fills this gap by reviewing the extant literature and recommending the way forward for businesses in Africa. The chapter has a number of sections. After the introduction, the chapter examines the importance of customer acquisition and retention before defining CST. Thereafter, some of the key areas that should be included in a CST programme are discussed. The process involved in CST is discussed before making recommendations for businesses in Africa.

Customer Acquisition and Retention

The art of acquiring and retaining loyal customers is a key success factor for any firm (Wirtz, 2017). However, retaining customers is a major challenge considering that competitors also do their best to attract them. Moreover, customer tastes and preferences keep changing, and the contemporary environment is highly dynamic (Teece, 2018). Nevertheless, in spite of all the environmental challenges that firms are exposed to, it is easier to retain current customers than it is to recruit new ones (Ayed, 2019). On their part, customers are concerned with the way they are treated and the experiences they have while interacting with a firm. They are also concerned with the perceived value of a firm's offering, which is the ability of the firm to satisfy their needs. Further, customers tend to stick to firms that continually meet or exceed their expectations, meaning that firms in Africa need to develop customer retention strategies, such as the training of employees who are in contact with customers (Magut & Kihara, 2019).

Definition of Customer Service Training

Training consists of planned programmes designed to improve performance at the individual, group and organisational levels while development is targeted at managers and refers to the acquisition of knowledge and skills to be used for future jobs (Mustapha & Osho, 2018). Training seeks a relatively permanent change in an individuals' knowledge, attitudes, skills, social behaviour, working patterns and interactions with co-workers and supervisors, improving performance at individual, team and organisational levels. Mathis et al. (2016) define training as a learning process through which people acquire skills and knowledge necessary for the attainment of organisational goals. This chapter narrows down to CST. Ideally, CST refers to the process of imparting employees with the right knowledge, competences and skills required to increase customer satisfaction. Sharma et al. (2018) opine that CST helps employees to have a better understanding of service encounters, including how to deal with customers in stressful situations. Training becomes necessary when there is a gap between the desired and the actual level of performance.

Areas of Customer Service Training

There is no consensus on the areas that should be included in a CST programme. For instance, Mouawad and Kleiner (1996) recommend that firms should train their employees in the areas of effective telemarketing skills, customer retention practices and strategies, problem-solving skills, communication skills, emotional intelligence, and digital/IT skills and capabilities. Based on an extensive review of literature (Abidemi et al., 2018; Matilu & K'Obonyo, 2018; Oghenekaro, 2018; Shumba & Zindiye, 2018; Wambalaba et al., 2019; Yilmaz et al., 2016; Zolfagharian, 2018), some of the key areas included in CST are captured in Figure 14.1.

Figure 14.1   Components of customer service training. (Developed for this chapter.)

Product and Service Knowledge

Training that seeks to enhance the employees' knowledge of the products and services of the firm is important because customers expect to interact with employees who are well-informed and can meet their needs. A knowledgeable person is able to discuss the various characteristics, features and benefits of their offerings while differentiating it from that of competitors. This plays a key role in persuading the clients to purchase the firm's products and services. Furthermore, an understanding of how the products are made enables the employees concerned to understand their quality and reliability implications, and to explain this information to external customers in a better manner. Customers buy benefits, meaning that features should be explained in terms of the accompanying benefits. Shumba and Zindiye (2018) did a study in Zimbabwe on the training of franchise operators and their employees and found that product knowledge was a key area that determined the success of franchises. A wide variety of businesses operate in Africa, ranging from the larger firms originating from Asian and Western countries to the micro, small, medium and large firms that are owned locally. The foreign firms tend to adopt policies developed from their home countries, and these would include the element of CST. However, some of the businesses owned by Africans tend to be small and face problems, such as limited financial resources, globalisation, competition from foreign firms and inadequate managerial talent; all these factors combine to make them less competitive (Mavunga, 2014). On this basis, and as a way of improving their competitiveness, firms operated by Africans should adopt CST that enables their employees to acquire knowledge of the firms' products and services, including the features, benefits and uniqueness of the goods and services of each firm.

Knowledge of Competitors' Products and Services

Unless a firm is a monopoly, it is likely to have competitors. Knowledge of competitors' products and services enables employees to differentiate their offers from those of competitors, considering that some customers have knowledge of what competitors offer. An employee who has good knowledge of the firm's products or services will gain and maintain a reasonable market share over competitors (Matilu & K'Obonyo, 2018). Competitors also look for information about other firms, and they can use the information to attack their rivals. For instance, a competitor can exploit the weakness of a firm's products or services that falsely claim to satisfy the needs of customers to strategically position their own products and services in the minds of customers and thus gain a competitive advantage in the market. The implication here is that firms in Africa should train their employees to identify their key competitors, analyse the competitors' strengths and weaknesses, improve on the firm's weaknesses, and position the goods and services of the firm as the best for satisfying the needs of the customers.

Communication Skills

Communication skills is an important component of any CST programme. Communication skills training helps to develop the communication skills of employees, which then enables the firm to reap the associated benefits. Effective communication with customers is associated with improved customer service, performance and sustainability (Abidemi et al., 2018). Through communication skills training, employees will be better placed to understand the needs of the customers. The employees should be trained to listen and respond appropriately to the customers. They should also be trained to actively listen to their clients, which means focussing attention on the clients and avoiding any forms of distractions. The employees should also be trained to maintain eye contact with the customers, as this increases the customers' trust and makes the customers have confidence that the employees are out to listen and to help them. Similarly, the employees should be trained to use confirming statements, which make the customers believe that the employees are interested and understand the needs of the customers. In the process of communicating with the customer, the employees should be trained to allow the customer to ask questions in order to clarify what they may not have understood. The employees should then reflect or rephrase what the customers said and respond to them in an appropriate manner.

Aside from listening, the training should include an element of talking, which is an important aspect of communication. The employees should be informed that the primary goal of talking is to remain positive at all times, and to focus on what can be done rather than what cannot be done. Equally important is the tone with which they communicate because it conveys a lot about their enthusiasm, energy levels, interest and attitude while interacting with the customers. The training should emphasise the importance of a friendly and amicable tone since it produces better results, and the employees should not lose their temper. Body language, such as facial expressions and posture, should also be covered in the training because it supports positive messages conveyed to the customers. The employees should be taught the importance of smiling at customers, keeping a professional appearance, maintaining eye contact when talking to them, being professional but relaxed, and not violating their personal spaces. Similarly, they should be trained to shake customers' hands in a firm and professional manner.

When dealing with customers over the phone, the employees should be trained to be prompt, empathetic and act as if the caller was nearby. This means that they should subconsciously smile, be friendly, professional, introduce themselves and the company they work for, ask the caller how they could be of help to them, be audible, use the caller's name and offer to call back if they lack all the information required at that moment. Similarly, the training should emphasise prompt response to emails. The employees should also be trained to understand the communication style adopted by each customer and to respond appropriately. For instance, where the customer is direct and prefers not to waste time, it is prudent to deal with them by directly addressing their concerns; otherwise, they will get frustrated. According to Mavunga (2014), different categories of firms operate in Africa, such as the multibillion multinational enterprises in sectors such as mining and manufacturing as well as the informal or formal businesses operated by Africans. In spite of all the challenges that micro, small, medium and large firms operated by Africans face, it is still prudent for them to train their employees on effective communication skills because of the numerous benefits associated with such training (Abidemi et al., 2018). This will enable the employees to manage themselves better as they manage their interactions with the clients. The result will be more fulfilled employees, satisfied customers and increased firm profits.

Customer Service Skills

The service encounter is the point at which the customer interacts with the firm. The nature of the interaction determines whether the customer buys or does not buy, and how the customer will interact with the firm in the future. Ideally, employees should be trained to make the customers appreciate the interaction and return in the future. In order to enhance this experience, Deviney (1998) recommends that the employees should be trained to appreciate the customer's business, understand the customer's buying behaviour, ask the right questions, deal with the customer's objections, understand the customer's problem, close the sale and arrange for after-sales follow-up. These are core areas that should be included in a CST programme. Besides, the employees should be trained to dress well, greet the customers, respond to their concerns and, through communication, influence them to prefer the firm and its products or services. The training should also emphasise the need to develop relationships with the clients, and to delight them in the process. When the service encounter is managed effectively, it leads to customer loyalty, brand identification and positive word-of-mouth advertising (Zolfagharian, 2018).

As the business environment changes, the level of competition is bound to increase, especially due to the international trade liberalisation policies that have been adopted by many countries in Africa (Zahonogo, 2016). This means that firms operated by Africans, whether in the formal or informal sectors, should seek to continuously improve their service encounters (Wambalaba et al., 2019). This can be done by monitoring the business environment and making service encounter improvements part of a CST programme. On the one hand, the approaches for monitoring the environment include reading newspapers, listening to different radio stations, and watching different television channels, among many others. On the other hand, the approaches for improving service encounters include auditing customers to determine the extent to which their needs are being met, reviewing the distribution chains to determine how effective they are, finding out changes that the firm needs to make, implementing the changes and following up to ensure the plans are being accomplished. All these are elements that firms in Africa should include in a CST programme.

Handling Customer Complaints and Conflicts

Customer complaints arise when customers have some displeasure with an element of a firm, such as its goods, services or employees. If the complaint is sorted out well, the customers remain loyal (Yilmaz et al., 2016). While there is no consensus on how complaints can be handled, a starting point would be to train the employees to identify the source of the complaint. The employees should be trained to accept that the problem exists and tell the customer what can or cannot be done about the product. Further, the training should emphasise keeping ongoing communication with the customers, particularly where solving the problem is a process. Employees should also be trained to remain calm at all times while interacting with the customers. Once the problem is sorted out, the training should also emphasise the need for following up to ensure the customer was satisfied with the solution provided.

Emotional Intelligence

A CST programme should include an element of emotional intelligence, which is the ability to manage one's emotions and those of others (Salovey et al., 2002). Given that different categories of firms operate in Africa (Mavunga, 2014), firms operated by Africans should train their employees on emotional intelligence because employees and customers have emotions, and the improper handling of emotions can affect the level of job satisfaction and productivity of employees as well as the satisfaction of external customers. Employees who are trained to manage their emotions positively are better placed to influence external customers to not only purchase the firm's products but also to remain loyal and talk positively about the firm. The employees should be trained to provide suitable physical surroundings for interacting with the clients, reduce the time that clients have to wait to be served, listen to clients and be empathetic to the customers. That way, they reduce stressful encounters for clients.

Competency in Digital Capabilities

Contemporary businesses operate in a highly digitalised ecosystem that destroys traditional business models and creates new opportunities to exploit (Weill & Woerner, 2015). In some cases, disruptive technologies, such as the use of hybrid and electric-powered cars, change the dynamics of a whole industry. Firms operated by Africans should train their employees to monitor any changes in technology, to evaluate their relevance to the firm and take advantage of them. For instance, an increasing number of consumers use their mobile phones and computers to search for information before purchasing products or services. This implies that employees can be trained on how to engage in online marketing, or how to market on social media platforms, such as Facebook and WhatsApp. This will enable the employees to introduce products to clients, handle complaints and interact with the clients on a continuous basis.

Benefits of Customer Service Training

CST benefits a wide range of stakeholders, such as customers, employees, teams, organisations and the wider society.

Benefits to Employees

One of the purposes of CST is to educate the staff on the ever-changing customer service practices and dynamics that impact employee performance, and which reduce conflicts and disparity among employees. CST equips employees with the knowledge needed to perform their tasks more effectively, which eventually leads to the provision of quality services, improved customer satisfaction, increased sales volumes and firm growth (Sendawula et al., 2018).

Through CST, new employees can be introduced to their work environments, colleagues, core values of the firm and expectations of their employers. This kind of training can be done face-to-face or online through video chat, Zoom, GoToMeeting or Google Hangouts. CST also increases the commitment and motivation of employees (Bulut & Culha, 2010). Trained employees tend to be more motivated to excel at their workplaces, as they modify their behaviours and transfer their knowledge to others (Bulut & Culha, 2010). Such employees are proud to be associated with the firm; they become advocates of the firm and go out of their way to delight customers (Wang et al., 2017).

CST leads to higher job satisfaction and a better working environment among employees. In some cases, CST can lead to higher staff retention rates, improved morale and more loyalty among those trained (Phiri & Pillay, 2017). Well-trained staff tend to deal with customers in a more appropriate manner and are able to build strong customer relationships by virtue of their customer service skills, communication skills and knowledge of the firm's products or services. Employees who perceive their firms to be better employers may decline new job offers and opt to stick to their current employer. In turn, customers recognise the efforts of the employees and may become loyal to such firms (Veldman et al., 2014). Besides, employees who satisfy customers are likely to have lower stress levels and lower chances of burning out. Once customer's problems are resolved, the employees can concentrate on more productive activities as opposed to calming irritated customers and arguing or dealing with their own emotions. Moreover, solving a problem leads to a sense of satisfaction.

CST increases the confidence of the employees, thereby leading to improved performance (Dagger et al., 2013). Employees with a high level of confidence are better placed to analyse customer demands and provide the best solutions to the customers' problems. Managers in Africa should, therefore, empower employees to take ownership of the customer service process in order to build employees' confidence. CST enables staff to perform their jobs better with reduced management support. Moreover, Yilmaz et al. (2016), among others, associate CST with the acquisition of skills that enhance innovation, creativity and performance improvement. CST increases the ability of the employees to perform their jobs better, which translates into greater productivity for the organisation. At the same time, the employees' market worthiness increases since they can take advantage of new employment opportunities.

CST enables the employees to create positive first impressions while interacting with clients. The first impression matters a lot to customers, and it can be the only impression (Oghenekaro, 2018). This impression can be created for customers who visit the premises, call on the telephone, and through online interactions; it can be done by wearing clothes that match the business, grooming appropriately and maintaining a relaxed and open demeanour. Proper grooming means being clean, wearing professional attire and having a professional outlook. A positive first impression lays the foundation for a great customer service experience. In line with the recommendations of Oghenekaro (2018), firms operated by Africans just like those from other parts of the world should avoid creating a negative first impression because of its long-term negative effects. Maintaining a favourable attitude enhances the first impression. While it is not possible to control the attitudes of external customers, employees can learn to control theirs allowing them to handle even difficult customers, both internal and external. An employee who smiles, maintains eye contact and retains a friendly facial expression is likely to create a better first impression. This impression can then be turned into profits and growth.

Benefits to an Organisation

CST has numerous benefits to an organisation. For instance, it enables a firm to retain its customers and sustain its competitiveness (Matilu & K'Obonyo, 2018). CST is based on the premise that customers who positively perceive the services of an organisation are likely to remain loyal. Further, such customers are a valuable base for cross-selling and can be a source of new ideas for businesses.

Employee training improves the productivity and performance of an organisation. This is because training increases the intellectual capabilities of the organisation by enhancing the skills, motivation and knowledge of the employees (Jex & Britt, 2014). Organisations with trained employees incur less wastage, fewer accidents, lower rates of absenteeism and also lower rates of labour turnover. This implies that trained employees perform better and more efficiently, which is the basis for improved organisational performance and greater customer satisfaction. The benefits of increased efficiency also include better firm reputation, lower rates of product returns and fewer legal battles. Therefore, training is associated with decreased costs of doing business, which translates into higher profits (Mpofu & Hlatywayo, 2015). CST in such areas as customer relationship management, handling complaints and closing sales increase the skills of the employees and make them to be more customer-focused. As a result of the training, an organisation is likely to meet customer needs better, provide higher levels of services and reduce the number of customer complaints.

Developing a Customer Service Training Programme

The process of developing a CST program, while not standardised, can involve at least five activities, namely conducting a training needs analysis (TNA), establishing the training goals, selecting the training methods, conducting the training and evaluating the training programme (DeCenzo et al., 2015). These steps are briefly explained as follows.

Conducting a Training Needs Analysis

A need is an unfilled gap, or the difference between the desired and the current state. Before top managers approve the execution of a CST programme, they should begin by undertaking a customer TNA so as to determine what to train the workers on and the conditions under which to conduct the training. It also sets the goals of the training and prepares the employees for the training (Blanchard & Thacker, 2018). At this stage, managers should lower employee's anxiety towards the training, demonstrate the value of the training and engage the employees so that they get motivated for the training.

There are several ways of identifying the need for the training. Firstly, the managers can receive a request for training from the workers. This information can emanate from meetings, conferences, surveys, reports, interviews or even workers writing directly to managers making this request formally. Alternatively, a training and development committee may recommend workers to be trained after noticing their inefficiencies. Secondly, the managers can analyse some of the negative developments in the firm's operations, such as increased customer complaints, rise in the number of accidents reported and decreased productivity. Thirdly, managers can analyse changes in jobs that result from job redesigns, technological breakthroughs and political developments. Alternatively, managers can find a need to train workers after observing the employees as they work, analysing the requirements of each job and reviewing performance appraisal reports. In a nutshell, identifying training needs requires a task and performance analysis.

Some firms do not conduct TNA for a variety of reasons. Firstly, TNA can be a difficult and time-consuming exercise, and an organisation may be pressed by other needs. Secondly, organisational resources are limited, and managers may decide to use the limited resources to develop, acquire and deliver the training rather than conducting TNA. Thirdly, some managers inappropriately assume that conducting training needs assessment is not necessary because available information already specifies the organisation's needs. Moreover, some employees may resist the TNA exercise for personal reasons. For example, some may resist it because of the benefits they derive from their current positions, or because of lack of trust in the persons conducting the exercise. Such workers may sense that the training is being used as a scapegoat to transfer them to less-desirable locations, or to get them out of the way so that other people can occupy their positions.

The TNA exercise can be conducted at the organisational, task and individual levels. At the organisational level, it determines where the training is needed and the conditions under which it should be conducted. At a task level, it determines what must be done to perform the jobs more effectively, while at the individual level, it determines who should be trained and the kind of training that is appropriate for them.

Establishing the Training Goals

The aim of any CST programme is to bring about some desired change (Lloret, 2016). Therefore, before approving a CST program, managers should explicitly state the changes, or results, sought from each employee. The goals should possibly be tangible, verifiable, measurable and communicable to both employees and managers. The goals of a CST programme should depend on the initial problems that gave rise to the training. Where TNA recommended training is due to increased customer complaints, the goal of the training programme would be to reduce those complaints. The objectives should be communicated as concisely as possible using a language that all the interested parties can understand with ease.

Selecting the Training Methods

A selected training method should not only explicitly illustrate the skills that are desired by the employees, but it should also motivate the employees to improve their performance. Moreover, the method should be able to provide the employees with the opportunity to actively participate and apply the skills practically. A good training method should provide immediate feedback on the performance of employees during and after the training. Some of the CST methods include using lectures, seminars and workshops, among many others.

The lecture method should be supported by audio-visual aids, such as PowerPoint presentations. According to Jobber and Lancaster (2015), learning a new skill involves moving people from the stage of being unconsciously unable (where the employee is unaware of the skill and unable to perform it) to the stages of being consciously unable (where the person is aware of the skill but unable to perform it), consciously able (aware of the skill and able to perform it consciously) and finally to unconsciously able (aware of the skill and able to perform it without thinking about it). Audio-visual aids are better in moving people through these stages because they involve hearing and seeing, which increase the retention rate of the information provided (Chen & Wu, 2015). Further, the participants should be encouraged to actively participate in the lecture by asking questions, bringing new suggestions or seeking clarifications as a way of stimulating their interest and enhancing their learning.

As a training method, role-playing involves asking a trainee, or some employees, to interact in an acting capacity with other employees posing as clients. After the interaction, each trainee is given feedback on their strengths and weaknesses and areas of improvement. The use of case studies allows employees to analyse situations, identify problems and opportunities, and recommend the best way to deal with such situations. In some cases, an experienced person may spend time with those less-experienced so that he or she can train them on a wide range of areas through coaching and mentoring. E-learning, such as web-based training, implies conducting a training session over the Internet. By so doing, employees who are too busy or far away can benefit as well. Error management training occurs when managers encourage employees to make errors and to reflect on the errors in order to understand what causes them so as to avoid them in the future.

Conducting the Training

CST can be provided by a firm's staff or by external parties. This decision is made after considering the availability of the necessary expertise within the organisation, time limitations, number of employees involved, subject matter of the training, cost and size of the training department, among many other factors. In situations where a firm lacks the knowledge, skills and experiences needed in designing and implementing the program, it can rely on external parties. Besides, external experts and consultants may be better prepared to train workers within shorter time limits. Where many employees require training, it may be more cost-effective to draw on local expertise (in-house training) within the firm to conduct the training. It is also important to encourage in-house training, particularly when the training is centred on sensitive issues and helps to maintain trade secrets. Though it is relevant to evaluate the costs associated with the training, this should not be the overriding consideration. Other factors to consider include past experiences with external trainers, the geographical proximity of trainers, local economic conditions and the presence of government incentives to conduct the training.

External training is often provided by consultants and registered training firms. Each external training provider who tenders for the training is evaluated in terms of their training costs, credentials, experience, background, delivery methods, topics to be covered and expected results, among other factors. The selected trainers should be trained before they embark on the actual training. The training-of-trainers may involve briefing them on the need for the training and the organisation's policy towards training, expected outcomes, venue for the training, materials and equipment to be used in the training, and the preparation of elaborate lesson plans.

Evaluating the Training Programme

After a training exposure, it is necessary to evaluate it so as to determine the extent to which it achieved its objectives. There are many models that have been designed to explain the evaluation of training programmes, and these include the ones proposed by Kirkpatrick (2009) and Kraiger (2002). On the one hand, Kraiger (2002) suggests that a training programme should be evaluated on the basis of its ability to meet the needs of the intended audiences, such as the learners and the organisation. On this basis, a training programme is perceived positively when it contributes to the learners' knowledge acquisition and decision-making skills, and when the financial performance of the firm improves. On the other hand, Kirkpatrick (2009) argues that training programmes can be evaluated by measuring changes at four levels, namely reaction, learning, behavioural and results levels. The reaction level is the most basic and measures how well the participants liked or disliked the training programme, whether the programme was worth the time, and whether it was presented in a meaningful and interesting manner. Reaction can be obtained by having the participants complete a questionnaire or participant evaluation form.

The second level of evaluation measures the amount of learning that took place. In essence, it evaluates the extent to which the employees learnt and retained the materials and intellectually assimilated them. This is done by evaluating the skills or knowledge gained at the end of the programme. Alternatively, the evaluation can be done on a continuous basis by using tests. Since knowledge acquisition and attitude change can positively affect performance, employees who acquire considerable knowledge from a training programme are more likely to transfer the knowledge to the workplace and to positively change their attitudes towards the work.

Thirdly, evaluators measure the behavioural outcomes of a training programme. Training is supposed to modify the behaviour of employees towards a desired direction. At this level of evaluation, the concern is to determine the extent to which the modified behaviour causes positive results, such as better reaction to customer complaints. Behaviour ratings can be collected from superiors, peers, subordinates and the clients of the trained employees. When employees transfer the material learnt to the workplace, the results include improved customer relations and higher levels of organisational commitment.

The last level of evaluation measures the results that accompany a training programme, given that results are the ultimate value of training. The results level measures the extent to which a training programme produces cost-related behavioural outcomes, such as productivity or quality improvements, or reductions in turnover, accidents, customer complaints and labour turnover. Thus, using Kirkpatrick's four-level model, managers have options as to how most effectively evaluate the effects of training.

Practical Implications for African Firms

This chapter has reviewed literature on CST generally and more specifically in Africa. On the basis of the literature reviewed, a number of benefits have been associated with CST. These include better job performance by employees (Dagger et al., 2013; Sendawula et al., 2018), commitment and motivation of employees (Bulut & Culha, 2010), delighted customers (Wang et al., 2017) and decreased costs of doing business (Mpofu & Hlatywayo, 2015), among many others. Firms operated by Africans will reap these benefits if they invest in CST.

The African business landscape has been shown to comprise large multinationals originating from Asian or Western countries and micro, small, medium and large firms originating from the African continent. The foreign firms tend to adopt policies developed from their home countries, while firms operated by Africans tend to be small and face numerous challenges, such as inadequate managerial talent. Yet the African and foreign firms have to compete in the same marketplace. Having identified the benefits associated with CST, this chapter makes a number of recommendations for businesses operated by Africans. Firstly, as Ayed (2019) found in Tunisia, it is easier to retain existing customers than to attract new customers. It is, therefore, advisable for firms operated by Africans to invest in training on customer retention strategies, such as having loyalty programmes among many others. Secondly, a study by Sendawula et al. (2018), found that training improved the performance of employees in Uganda's health sector. This implies that firms operated by Africans should invest in CST so as to improve the overall job performance of their employees. Thirdly, a study by Oghenekaro (2018) in Tekena Tamuno's Library of Redeemer's University, Nigeria, strongly recommended the importance of a positive first impression. This implies that employees should be trained to groom well, as it affects the creation of a positive first impression. Fourthly, Shumba and Zindiye (2018) recommend that product and service knowledge should form part of a CST programme, while Matilu and K'Obonyo (2018) emphasise the need to understand competitors' strengths and weaknesses. Fifthly, given that Abidemi et al. (2018) associate effective communication skills with improved performance and sustainability, firms operated by Africans should train their staff on how to communicate effectively. Other important areas that should be included in a CST programme are emotional intelligence (Salovey et al., 2002), customer service skills (Zolfagharian, 2018), digital capabilities (Weill & Woerner, 2015) and handling complaints (Yilmaz et al., 2016). A CST programme has to be designed appropriately, and its results evaluated accordingly in order to document its benefits.

Conclusion

This chapter reviewed extant literature on CST with a bias to firms operated by Africans. Although there are numerous approaches to gaining sustainable competitive advantage, this chapter has emphasised improved customer interactions as one way of gaining this advantage. Firms operated by Africans will gain the benefits identified above if they invest in CST. These firms will need to train their employees to understand the products and services of their firm, the strengths and weaknesses of their key competitors, customer service skills, communication and human relations skills, emotional intelligence, digital capabilities and the ability to handle customer complaints and conflicts. Such training will lead to the creation of a sustainable competitive advantage.

References

Abidemi, B., Halim, F., & Alshuaibi, A. (2018). The relationship between market orientation dimensions and performance of micro finance institutions. *Journal of Marketing and Consumer Behaviour, 2*(3), 1–14.

Ayed, M. (2019). Impacts of COSER strength on service loyalty: Case of automobile repair service in Tunisia. *International Journal of Customer Relationship Marketing and Management (IJCRMM), 10*(1), 34–47.

Blanchard, N. P., & Thacker, J. (2018). *Effective training: Systems, strategies, and practices.* Upper Saddle River, NJ: Pearson Prentice Hall.

Bulut, C., & Culha, O. (2010). The effects of organisational training on organisational commitment. *International Journal of Training and Development, 14*(4), 309–322.

Chen, C., & Wu, C. (2015). Effects of different video lecture types on sustained attention, emotion, cognitive load, and learning performance. *Computers & Education, 80*, 108–121.

Dagger, T., Danaher, P., Sweeney, J., & McColl-Kennedy, J. (2013). Selective halo effects arising from improving the interpersonal skills of frontline employees. *Journal of Service Research, 16*(4), 488–502.

DeCenzo, D., Robbins, S., & Verhulst, S. (2015). *Fundamentals of human resource management.* New York: Wiley.

Deviney, D. E. (1998). *Outstanding customer service: The key to customer loyalty.* New York: American Media.

Jex, S. M., & Britt, T. W. (2014). *Organisational psychology: A scientist-practitioner approach.* New York: Wiley.

Jobber, D., & Lancaster, G. (2015). *Selling and sales management.* London, UK: Pearson.

Kirkpatrick, D. L. (2009). *Evaluating training programs: The four levels.* San Francisco, CA: ReadHowYouWant.

Kraiger, K. (2002). Decision-based evaluation. In K. Kraiger (Ed.), *Creating, implementing, and maintaining effective training and development: State-of-the-art lessons for practice* (pp. 331–375). San Francisco, CA: Jossey-Bass.

Lloret, A. (2016). Modeling corporate sustainability strategy. *Journal of Business Research, 69*(2), 418–425.

Magut, C., & Kihara, A. (2019). Influence of student retention strategies on performance of TVETs in Nairobi County, Kenya. *Journal of Business and Strategic Management, 4*(1), 1–24.

Mathis, R. L., Jackson, J. H., & Valentine, S. R. (2016). *Human resource management.* Mason, OH: South-Western Cengage Learning.

Matilu, C., & K'Obonyo, P. (2018). Competitive strategies and human resource management practices adopted by the insurance companies in Nairobi, Kenya. *International Journal of Innovative Finance and Economics Research, 6*(3), 34–52.

Mavunga, G. (2014). Practicing customer service by trial and error: An investigation into the extent and nature of customer service training/education received by owners of small business enterprises in central Johannesburg. *Mediterranean Journal of Social Sciences, 5*(20), 1475–1485.

Mouawad, M., & Kleiner, B. (1996). New developments in customer service training. *Managing Service Quality: An International Journal, 6*(2), 49–56.

Mpofu, M., & Hlatywayo, C. (2015). Training and development as a tool for improving basic service delivery: The case of a selected municipality. *Journal of Economics, Finance and Administrative Science, 20*(39), 133–136.

Mustapha, A., & Osho, M. (2018). The impact of manpower development on organisational efficiency in national Inland waterways authority of Nigeria (NIWA). *International Journal of Arts and Humanities (IJAH) Ethiopia, 8*(1), 102–114.

Oghenekaro, A. (2018). Deployment of soft skills for effective customer service in the 21st century library. *Journal of Computer and Communications, 6*(3), 43–50.

Phiri, M., & Pillay, S. (2017). Customer perceptions of service quality at small medium micro enterprises (SMME): The case of crossley holdings, Durban South Africa. *Journal of Economics, 8*(1), 1–17.

Salovey, P., Mayer, J., & Caruso, D. (2002). The positive psychology of emotional intelligence. In C. Snyder & S. Lopez (Eds.), *Handbook of positive psychology* (pp. 159–171). New York: Oxford University Press.

Sendawula, K., Kimuli, S., Bananuka, J., & Muganga, G. (2018). Training, employee engagement and employee performance: Evidence from Uganda's health sector. *Cogent Business & Management, 5*(1), 1–12.

Sharma, P., Tam, J., & Wu, Z. (2018). Challenges and opportunities for services marketers in a culturally diverse global marketplace. *Journal of Services Marketing, 32*(5), 521–529.

Shumba, K., & Zindiye, S. (2018). Success factors for franchise entrepreneurs operating in a volatile business environment. A case of the fast food industry Harare, Zimbabwe. *The Social Sciences, 13*(4), 908–915.

Teece, D. (2018). Business models and dynamic capabilities. *Long Range Planning, 51*(1), 40–49.

Veldman, J., Klingenberg, W., Gaalman, G., & Teunter, R. (2014). Getting what you pay for – Strategic process improvement compensation and profitability impact. *Productions and Operations Management, 23*(8), 1387–1400.

Wambalaba, F. W., Namada, J. M., & Katuse, P. (2019). Strategies and effectiveness of experiential and service learning towards mission achievement. In B. Smith (Ed.), *Mission-driven approaches in modern business education* (pp. 161–192). Hershey, PA: IGI Global.

Wang, Y., Luo, C., & Tai, Y. (2017). Implementation of delightful services: From the perspective of front-line service employees. *Journal of Hospitality and Tourism Management, 31*, 90–104.

Weill, P., & Woerner, S. (2015). Thriving in an increasingly digital ecosystem. *MIT Sloan Management Review, 56*(4), 27–34.

Wirtz, J. (2017). *Managing customer relationships and building loyalty.* London, UK: World Scientific Publishing.

Yilmaz, C., Varnali, K., & Kasnakoglu, B. (2016). How do firms benefit from customer complaints? *Journal of Business Research, 69*(2), 944–955.

Zahonogo, P. (2016). Trade and economic growth in developing countries: Evidence from sub-Saharan Africa. *Journal of African Trade, 3*(1–2), 41–56.

Zolfagharian, M. (2018). Customer response to service encounter linguistics. *Journal of Services Marketing, 32*(5), 530–546.

THEME E: CUSTOMER SERVICE CULTURE

Chapter 15

Organisational Culture and Customer Service Delivery

Thomas Anning-Dorson, Ishmael Ofoli Christian
and Michael Boadi Nyamekye

Contents

Introduction

Excellent service delivery is non-negotiable for the firm that seeks to attract, develop and retain a loyal customer base and profit from it. Customer service has become the basis for long-term relationship development for both B2B and B2C industries the world over. The success of enterprises is shaped by how well service providers understand the value needs of customers and adequately meet these needs. Firms that understand this basic principle always compete favourably. Competition in the marketplace is won by enterprises that set the customer at the centre of all organisational activities, decisions and strategies. Increasingly, customers are becoming disloyal to brands due to lack of proper and clear differentiation of value offerings on the market. Innovations and new products are being copied and imitated at greater speed than before, leading to unsustainable competitive advantage development. Relying on internal structures and processes to offer added customer benefit beyond the core product provides a more sustainable way of competing in the turbulent business environment.

Considering the important role customer service plays regarding enterprise survival, firms would have to develop an organisation-wide culture that engenders excellent service delivery on all fronts

(Elsbach & Stigliani, 2018). Such an endeavour would ensure strict adherence to sets of conduct that aim at satisfying every customer. A great organisational culture supports excellent customer service and induces both employee and customer satisfaction (Zhang & Li, 2013; Jung & Yoon, 2015). The rationale is that how an organisation is run is predicated on the culture (beliefs, values and attitude), which affects the quality of service delivery. It is therefore important that companies and organisations have organised structures and a distinctive set of rules to be able to deliver quality customer service to keep their customers and employees happy as well as improve upon their image.

The alignment of firm-level culture with customer service orientation provides the necessary strategic tools for competitive advantage development (Anning-Dorson, 2018a). Organisational culture shapes the overall competitive orientation of the firm and determines the strategic contours through its leadership. Customer service excellence is, therefore, an offshoot of organisational culture. The service customers receive the end product of the cultural orientation of the entire firm. Hence, discussing issues of customer service in isolation as many scholars have attempted is just scratching the surface of an important subject. Customer service is a firm-level orientation borne out of the ethos of brands, entities and organisations. The discussion should centre on firm-level culture as the basis for an organisation-wide customer service orientation. This chapter attempts to share some insights on how firms can develop excellent customer service orientation through the firm-level culture. We also discuss some basic strategies of customer service that favourably position the firm in the turbulent business environment.

Building a Service Culture

Building and developing firm-level service culture should make the organisation customer focussed, capable of creating good customer service delivery processes, and increase firm-level productivity and efficiency. Specifically, customer-oriented firm-level culture brings firms closer to customers and helps to narrow firm strategic orientations towards specific customer needs and preferences. Organisations that are close to customers and which show identifiable firm-level cultural patterns (unique corporate values, beliefs and attitudes that place emphasis on customers) demonstrate superior strategic marketing effectiveness (Sin & Tse, 2000; Dai et al., 2018) and greater signs of higher levels of growth capabilities. Since service in itself has a higher degree of intangibility, the creation of organisational culture that facilitates the creation of long-term relationships with customers, specifically one that attracts, retains and develops a loyal customer base, as well as profits from same, cannot be overstressed (Kang & Busser, 2018). The need, therefore, arises for firms to align their overall organisational culture to their specific customer service orientation efforts, especially where they (the firms) desire to survive and compete favourably in the contemporary turbulent business environment.

We consider firm-level culture as patterns of shared organisational values and beliefs, which over time produce behavioural norms that are adopted in solving organisational problems (Deal & Kennedy, 1982; Schein, 1990; Pătraş et al., 2018). The idea is that shared values and organisational norms, in part, define organisational brands and highlight the overall specific purposes for which organisations exist. Effective corporate branding makes a memorable impression on consumers and allows clients to even know what to expect from the companies that serve them. Organisations exist primarily to serve customers, be it public or private customers. Hence, developing customer-oriented values and belief systems aimed at meeting customer expectations should be the focus of the firm. Such orientation helps gain and maintain strategic competitive advantage in today's competitive markets. The rationale is that once customers perceive the existence of an organisational culture that fosters service excellence, it serves as a key differentiator in the competitive market. The customers' own perception of the favourable customer service experience enhances the opportunity to create a loyal customer base (Schirmer et al., 2018). Satisfied customers could serve as invaluable strategic assets to all firms and act as a great influence on overall firm performance and long-term firm survival. Reichheld and Teal (1996) note that satisfied customers (those who express themselves as very satisfied with a product or service) are six times more likely to repurchase, recommend a brand or return to a brand than customers who merely express themselves as satisfied. We assert that without a pool of satisfied customers, the long-term goals of organisations could not be realised, as satisfied customers have been shown to have a positive correlational effect on long-term firm profitability, growth and survival. This is a more important reason why organisations must not practice their customer service activities in isolation, but must align their customer service efforts with the overall firm-level cultural orientations.

Additionally, firms can build an excellent service culture when they have a clear understanding of the concept of service and how that can be appropriately operationalised to benefit both the firm and the customers they serve. The rationale is that the proper understanding of service and its relationship with identifiable organisational service orientations of competing firms is one of several ways to champion the path to long-term enterprise success and the proper alignment of customer service orientation with customer-focussed firm-level cultural patterns and processes. The service-dominant logic paradigm sees all economic exchanges to be service based, and value in this paradigm is service driven (Vargo & Lusch, 2004). This proposition put forward by Vargo and Lusch (2004) helps us to understand and appreciate the concept of service in terms of various processes, patterns and benefits of exchange, relative to the units of economic outputs (e.g. goods) in the economic exchange encounter. Since various organisational processes, belief systems, norms and patterns of behaviour are the recognisable cultural elements that define specific firm-level cultural orientations, fittingly understanding service as an element of culture is justifiable and can wield a determining force for developing sustainable competitive advantage strategies that profit both firms and customers.

Service can be viewed as an element of culture, precisely firm-level culture. Service characteristics such as unique organisational patterns, processes, norms and heuristics that define various aspects of firm-specific cultural orientations are foundational elements that also help us to understand the core meaning of service, and its true application in any business environment. Understanding service as an aspect of culture could establish the grounds upon which internal structures and processes could be streamlined to better connect with the value needs of the customer (Groysberg et al., 2018). Having such perspectives helps firms to know what customers expect from any service encounter. In consequence, a clear understanding of the needs of customers is a prerequisite for delivering higher quality through effective customer service. As a case in point, Peeler (1996) notes that perceived product or service quality is one of the most important factors that lead to firm competitiveness. The discussion, therefore, of the importance of understanding customer needs and service quality becomes more rewarding when juxtaposed with the understanding of the nature and right applicability of service itself.

Realising the uniqueness of service in terms of its meaning and application as well as the provision of suitable internal structures and processes that support the provision of stupendous customer experiences that are capable of inuring benefits both to the focal firm and customers is a strategic source of building an excellent and enviable service culture that proffers sustainable competitive advantage development and sustenance benefits over the long term. Since excellent customer service is an off-shoot of organisational culture, the strategic adoption of firm values that centre on bringing convenience to customers, the creation of innovative processes that help serve customers better, the establishment of organisational norms and standards that seek the interest of customers, and the transformation of workforce conduct and practices in the light of meeting and, or exceeding, customer expectations are significantly suitable building blocks for excellent firm-level culture building and development.

Influencing Customer Service Engagement through Organisational Culture

Engagement with customers is an essential process for gathering innovative ideas that help serve customers better. Customers are recognised as active participants in the co-creation of (Prahalad & Ramaswamy, 2000), and in some cases collaborators in, the customer value management process. The important role customers play in the value creation process has been demonstrated in a study by Vargo and Lusch (2004). Vargo and Lusch (2004) assert that the economy has moved from a 'creating for' to 'creating with' logic where customers and suppliers team up to co-create value. This also indicates that value co-creation hinges on the notion that value exchange is explained both in terms of the provider and in terms of the interaction between providers, users and other stakeholders. This emphasises the important role customers play in the current business environment making them an enviable participative factor for value creation as dynamic participants in the value delivery process as well as active players in the entire value consumption and management process.

While many early researchers admit that the task of integrating customers into value creation and delivery of services comes with implications that are particularly critical for marketers of technical products, some believe that cognitive fit is likely to play an indispensable role in their ability to understand and contribute immensely to the success of effective service delivery processes (Alba & Hutchinson, 1987, 2000; Johnson & Russo, 1984; Mason & Bequette, 1998; Payne et al., 2008; Ng et al., 2019). Consequently, customers with skills and expertise are more confident in assessing technical outcomes and questioning service providers' explanations than neophytes do when it comes to decision-making. The link indicates that businesses need their customers as much as customers need the firms. The right collaboration and involvement of customers is a strategic resource for strategic competitive development and sustenance. Consequently, the provision of excellent customer service thus cannot be done in isolation without the involvement and participation of the customer. Firms that create the cultural orientation of involving the customer are able to meet the needs of the customer better (Anning-Dorson, 2018b). Customer engagement is critical to co-creating value (Anning-Dorson & Nyamekye, 2018). As a case in point, it has been demonstrated in some studies that customers who recognise more value through their co-creating services tend to be more satisfied (Grissemann & Stokburger-Sauer, 2012; Prebensen & Xie, 2017; Anning-Dorson et al., 2018; Clauss et al., 2019). This, thus, highlights the important act of involving customers in the creation of customer value and how that affects organisational success.

The phenomenon of customer engagement and customer participation in value creation and service delivery has attracted some academic attention. While many academic terms have been used to describe the concept in literature, for instance, 'Prosumer' (Ritzer & Jurgenson, 2010), 'Co-producer' (Wikström, 1996), and 'Coproduction' (Prahalad & Ramaswamy, 2004; Hoyer et al., 2010), customers still participate at three levels in any customer engagement process. Customers participate either on a low level, moderate level or in a high-level manner. Customer participation is the role customers play in the exchange of service delivery. Firms can meet individual customer needs when they are able to tailor their cultural orientations to the various levels of customers' participation capacities. Fostering a climate that allows customers to be involved at every stage in the firm-customer engagement process is a source of differentiation that creates competitive advantage. At every level – whether at the low level, the moderate level or the high level – the customer can provide valuable information to enhance value creation and delivery. Today's customer is able to freely express concern about the current nature of services being rendered to them and how it meets their expectations or even make suggestions on future service expectations (Nasr et al., 2018). The argument is that customers are a major source of innovative ideas (Li et al., 2019). Interestingly, innovation is a tool for sustainable competitive development and a major component of excellent customer service delivery. Innovation in service processes, service products and customer service behaviours induce both employee and customer satisfaction. The idea is that satisfied customers, whether internal customers or external, have a positive influence on firms' performance (financial and non-financial). This essentially highlights the need for firms to strategically align their cultural orientations to foster customer-firm collaborations in order to create and deliver excellent customer experience.

Firm-level cultural elements such as identifiable communication channels and media artefacts that ensure the exchange of accurate, reliable and timely information between firms and customers, the adoption of customer-focussed behavioural patterns among service employees that allows convenient customer participation and engagement, and the establishment of customer-focussed patterns of personnel conduct and organisational processes all promote firm competitiveness and stimulate desirable customer experience. Since customer value is the end product of an entire organisational cultural orientation, it is important for firms to build strong cultures that centre on the customer. Customer-centred cultures allow for active participation and involvement of the customer and allow the customer to direct the value creation process (Anning-Dorson et al., 2015; Anning-Dorson, 2016). Firms must, therefore, strive to develop an organisation-wide culture that sets the customer as the centre and brings about excellent service delivery across all touchpoints and along the customer journey to create enhanced customer experience and competitive advantage.

There are a number of areas where this idea makes a substantial contribution by demonstrating in practical terms the relevance of fusing firm-level cultural orientation with overall firm-level customer service orientation. From the stage of idea generation all the way up to the provision of follow-ups and after-sale services, the integration of firm-level culture with customer service orientation can determine relevance both to firms and the customers they serve. Organisations that successfully do this are influenced in the choices they make at each level of these stages, thereby focussing their decision-making efforts on matters that enhance the overall customer value delivery process as well as the total customer experience.

Positioning the Contemporary Service Firm in the Turbulent Business Space

Some attempts have been made in literature to discuss the importance of positioning brands and the methods employed in doing so (see Blankson, 2016; Coffie, 2018; Lynn, 2019). The conclusion we draw from the literature is that effective brand positioning is one of many factors that drive sustainable competitive advantage and increase firm success. Positioning brands in the minds of customers engenders repeat purchase decision behaviours among customers and enhances effective customer level brand communication efforts for, and on behalf of, firms. Effective communication is key to achieving exceptional customer service, as it creates a better way of understanding what customers expect from their companies and how companies offer and communicate value to the customers they serve. Effective customer service delivery is an antecedent to gaining positive brand positioning in the minds of customers (Keller, 2016). When the service encounter is memorable, it enhances easy brand recall as well as fosters easy resonation of brand attributes in the customer's mind's eye. The foundation upon which stupendous customer service can be hinged is firm-level cultural orientation, which is customer-centred, emphasising great service to the customers. Service firms that aim at gaining sustainable competitive advantage through the provision of breathtaking customer services should ensure that standards, patterns, norms, values and belief systems that promote customer service excellence form their firm-level cultural orientation.

Furthermore, considering the important role customers play in the life of organisations, building the right firm-level culture that places the service promise on customers is an important tool that could lead to firm success in both B2B and B2C industries. Service is intangible meaning that customers will likely need to depend more on subjective impressions in the assessment of the value they receive (Kuada & Hinson, 2014). The psychological assessment of the value derived from service starts at the first point of contact customers have with firms. Organisational culture can play an important role in the success of enhancing the subjective value customers derive from the service encounter. Essential cultural elements such as the existence of listening customer service personnel, the presence of service intermediaries, the presence of the right communication channels and media, and the appropriate choice of organisational colours and logos enhance the subjective measurement of customer value. In advertisement, for instance, some empirical evidence suggests that the kind of colours organisations choose in their advertisement campaigns influence customers' feelings of excitement and relaxation (Gorn et al., 1997; Puzakova et al., 2016). Factors such as the physical location of firms (Kotler, 2003) also enhance the image of organisations and help to communicate quality brand image and customer value to customers.

The key factors to consider in developing excellent customer service orientation through firm-level culture include knowing and understanding the target market in terms of what they expect from the overall customer experience, what the firm's strengths and weaknesses are, as well as the influence of external forces that compete for resources. These factors have a huge influence in building a customer-friendly organisational culture that is in sync with firm-level customer service delivery orientation efforts. These factors should consider whether the desired firm-level culture and the firm's customer service delivery orientation can together generate the level of customer service that enhances the customer experience and culminates into firm-level sustainable competitive advantage.

Recommendations

Following the discussions above, we make the following recommendations in the light of the relevance attached to the proper alignment of firm-level cultural orientation with overall customer service delivery processes of contemporary firms. At the outset, we recommend that firms need to have a clear understanding and an apt description of the service they offer in line with their total corporate cultural orientation. This will give them vision and direction on best practices that enhance the overall customer experience. Since service in its entirety has dimensions (more or less) of specific firm-level cultural elements, the clear understanding of the kind of service that specific firms offer will set the tone for the proper alignment of firm-level culture with firm-specific customer service orientations. Once organisations are able to identify what is important to them and what their vision is as far as delivering on specific service promises that place constant emphasis on the customer is concerned, they are positioned to develop and maintain an organisation-wide culture that stimulates exceptional service delivery on all fronts.

Second, organisations must make customer service a priority in line with their entire cultural orientation. Making customer service a priority is the first step to creating a culture that facilitates the delivery of excellent customer service that yields repetitively stunning customer experiences. Firms need stunning customer experiences to grow and stay in business. When customers are stunned by the service firm's offer, they become satisfied, and in most instances, become loyal. Making customer service a priority for firms helps firms to be able to learn appropriate ways of developing and building an excellent service climate that stimulates the provision of spectacular customer experiences and firm competitiveness. Firms that are able to prioritise their customer service orientation are in a better position to properly take care of their customers at all times.

Third, firms must learn to properly align their firm-level cultural orientations with their overall customer service delivery positioning strategies. Gaining an appropriate brand positioning in the minds of customers is an essential element that enhances easy brand recall and increases recurrent purchase behaviour among customers. The true blend of a firm-level culture that places great emphasis on customers and an entire organisational customer service orientation sets the tone for serving customers better while meeting firm-specific goals and objectives. Culture enables firms to differentiate themselves from one another, hence when appropriately affixed into the core corporate vision and spread along the entire contour of an organisation's leadership and followership, it can help to enhance competitive advantage development through service differentiation. Culture sets organisational norms, rules and service standards. These cultural elements enable service employees to function in organisations by serving as foundational stones that teach and guide both employees and management proper behaviours that help meet organisational goals and objectives. Since service employees are also customers to the firm, the focus on developing customer-focussed firm-level culture and organisation-wide best practices that prompt the provision of the right customer service should not be overemphasised in any industry, across both B2B and B2C contexts.

Conclusion

The chapter concludes that both culture and customer service delivery are very closely related, and their interplay cannot be overemphasised under any market condition. We argue that organisations without the right customer-focussed cultural mindset can neither please their customers nor deliver any quality customer service that meets or exceeds the expectation of the customers they serve. The right understanding of service alongside the creation of firm-level culture that places emphasis on the provision of stunning customer service are factors that can help to enhance the overall customer service experience and increase firm competitive advantage development and sustainability. In consequence, organisations must, in line with developing and fostering a culture that excellently focuses on the overall customer service experience, also learn to align what they determine as customer with what customers themselves term as value in order to be able to make it easier to deliver on superior service promises that benefit both the firm and customers. Building a service-oriented culture entails a lot of hard work, whether in B2B contexts or B2C contexts, and organisations, both services and manufacturing, ought to strive to incorporate the drive at building and championing the course of an organisationally cultured customer service mindset into their overall corporate vision, as well as putting in efforts to clearly understand their target market in order to serve them better. Organisations must learn to have unique and identifiable sets of values and rules which do not just benefit them, but which are also convenient for their customers.

Customers must have a voice, and they must feel like their service provider is interested in what they have to say to better the services and to increase their satisfaction. All these create a great brand for a firm or organisation, as placing a firm's customers first and making customer service a priority is the best way for an organisation to grow.

References

Alba, J. W., & Hutchinson, J. W. (1987). Dimensions of consumer expertise. *Journal of Consumer Research*, *13*(4), 411–454.

Alba, J. W., & Hutchinson, J. W. (2000). Knowledge calibration: What consumers know and what they think they know. *Journal of Consumer Research*, *27*(2), 123–156.

Anning-Dorson, T. (2016). Interactivity innovations, competitive intensity, customer demand and performance. *International Journal of Quality and Service Sciences*, *8*(4), 536–554.

Anning-Dorson, T. (2018a). Innovation and competitive advantage creation: The role of organisational leadership in service firms from emerging markets. *International Marketing Review*, *35*(4), 580–600.

Anning-Dorson, T. (2018b). Customer involvement capability and service firm performance: The mediating role of innovation. *Journal of Business Research*, *86*, 269–280.

Anning-Dorson, T., & Nyamekye, M. B. (2018, April). Customer engagement capability for service innovation and firm performance: The moderating role of competitive intensity. In *The 2018 annual conference of the emerging markets conference board* (p. 110). Johannesburg, South Africa: Wits Business School.

Anning-Dorson, T., Hinson, R. E., & Amidu, M. (2015). Environmental moderators and performance effect of interactivity innovation: Study of the services sector of an emerging economy. In *Proceedings of 2015 annual conference of the emerging markets conference board* (pp. 31–32). Dubai, UAE: Institute of Management Technology.

Anning-Dorson, T., Hinson, R. E., Amidu, M., & Nyamekye, M. B. (2018). Enhancing service firm performance through customer involvement capability and innovativeness. *Management Research Review*, *41*(11), 1271–1289.

Blankson, C. (2016). Positioning a brand. In *Riley, F. D. O., Singh, J., & Blankson, C (Ed), The Routledge companion to contemporary brand management* (pp. 196–217). Abingdon, UK: Routledge.

Clauss, T., Kesting, T., & Naskrent, J. (2019). A rolling stone gathers no moss: The effect of customers' perceived business model innovativeness on customer value co-creation behavior and customer satisfaction in the service sector. *R&D Management*, *49*(2), 180–203.

Coffie, S. (2018). Positioning strategies for branding services in an emerging economy. *Journal of Strategic Marketing*, 1–15. https://doi.org/10.1080/0965254X.2018.1500626.

Dai, J., Chan, H. K., & Yee, R. W. (2018). Examining moderating effect of organizational culture on the relationship between market pressure and corporate environmental strategy. *Industrial Marketing Management*, *74*(October), 227–236.

Deal, T. E., & Kennedy, A. A. (1982). *Corporate cultures: The rites and rituals of organisational life* (Vol. 2, pp. 98–103). Reading, MA: Addison-Wesley.

Elsbach, K. D., & Stigliani, I. (2018). Design thinking and organizational culture: A review and framework for future research. *Journal of Management*, *44*(6), 2274–2306.

Gorn, G. J., Chattopadhyay, A., Yi, T., & Dahl, D. W. (1997). Effects of color as an executional cue in advertising: They're in the shade. *Management Science*, *43*(10), 1387–1400.

Grissemann, U. S., & Stokburger-Sauer, N. E. (2012). Customer co-creation of travel services: The role of company support and customer satisfaction with the co-creation performance. *Tourism Management*, *33*(6), 1483–1492.

Groysberg, B., Lee, J., Price, J., & Cheng, J. (2018). The leader's guide to corporate culture. *Harvard Business Review*, *96*(1), 44–52.

Hoyer, W. D., Chandy, R., Dorotic, M., Krafft, M., & Singh, S. S. (2010). Consumer cocreation in new product development. *Journal of Service Research*, *13*(3), 283–296.

Johnson, E. J., & Russo, J. E. (1984). Product familiarity and learning new information. *Journal of Consumer Research*, *11*(1), 542–550.

Jung, H. S., & Yoon, H. H. (2015). The impact of employees' positive psychological capital on job satisfaction and organisational citizenship behaviours in the hotel. *International Journal of Contemporary Hospitality Management*, *27*(6), 1135–1156.

Kang, H. J. A., & Busser, J. A. (2018). Impact of service climate and psychological capital on employee engagement: The role of organizational hierarchy. *International Journal of Hospitality Management*, *75*(1), 1–9.

Keller, K. L. (2016). Reflections on customer-based brand equity: Perspectives, progress, and priorities. *AMS Review, 6*(1–2), 1–16.

Kotler, P. (2003). *Marketing for Hospitality and Tourism, 5/e.* Bengaluru, Karnataka: Pearson Education India.

Kuada, J., & Hinson, R. (2014). *Service marketing in Ghana a customer relationship management approach.* London, UK: Adonis Abbey Publishing an CSED.

Li, M., Jia, S., & Du, W. D. (2019). Fans as a source of extended innovation capabilities: A case study of xiaomi technology. *International Journal of Information Management, 44*(2), 204–208.

Lynn, M. (2019). How hospitality brands grow: What hospitality marketers should know about Andrew Ehrenberg's work (invited paper for 'luminaries' special issue of International Journal of Hospitality Management). *International Journal of Hospitality Management, 76*(1), 70–80.

Mason, K., & Bequette, J. (1998). Product experience and consumer product attribute inference accuracy. *Journal of Consumer Marketing, 15*(4), 343–357.

Nasr, L., Burton, J., & Gruber, T. (2018). Developing a deeper understanding of positive customer feedback. *Journal of Services Marketing, 32*(2), 142–160.

Ng, S. C., Sweeney, J. C., & Plewa, C. (2019). Managing customer resource endowments and deficiencies for value cocreation: Complex relational services. *Journal of Service Research, 22*(2), 156–172.

Pătraș, L., Martínez-Tur, V., Estreder, Y., Gracia, E., Moliner, C., & Peiró, J. M. (2018). Organizational performance focused on users' quality of life: The role of service climate and "contribution-to-others" wellbeing beliefs. *Research in Developmental Disabilities, 77*(June), 114–123.

Payne, A. F., Storbacka, K., & Frow, P. (2008). Managing the co-creation of value. *Journal of the Academy of Marketing Science, 36*(1), 83–96.

Peeler, G. H. (1996). *Selling in the quality era.* Cambridge, MA: Blackwell Business.

Prahalad, C. K., & Ramaswamy, V. (2000). Co-opting customer competence. *Harvard Business Review, 78*(1), 79–90.

Prahalad, C. K., & Ramaswamy, V. (2004). Co-creation experiences: The next practice in value creation. *Journal of Interactive Marketing, 18*(3), 5–14.

Prebensen, N. K., & Xie, J. (2017). Efficacy of co-creation and mastering on perceived value and satisfaction in tourists' consumption. *Tourism Management, 60*(June), 166–176.

Puzakova, M., Kwak, H., Ramanathan, S., & Rocereto, J. F. (2016). Painting your point: The role of color in firms' strategic responses to product failures via advertising and marketing communications. *Journal of Advertising, 45*(4), 365–376.

Reichheld, F. F., & Teal, T. (1996). *The loyalty effect: The hidden force behind growth. Profits, and Lasting Value.* Boston, MA: Harvard Business School Press.

Ritzer, G., & Jurgenson, N. (2010). Production, consumption, prosumption: The nature of capitalism in the age of the digital 'prosumer'. *Journal of Consumer Culture, 10*(1), 13–36.

Schein, E. H. (1990). Organisational culture. *American Psychological Association, 45*(2), 109.

Schirmer, N., Ringle, C. M., Gudergan, S. P., & Feistel, M. S. (2018). The link between customer satisfaction and loyalty: The moderating role of customer characteristics. *Journal of Strategic Marketing, 26*(4), 298–317.

Sin, L. Y., & Tse, A. C. (2000). How does marketing effectiveness mediate the effect of organisational culture on business performance? The case of service firms. *Journal of Services Marketing, 14*(4), 295–309.

Vargo, S. L., & Lusch, R. F. (2004). Evolving to a new dominant logic for marketing. *Journal of Marketing, 68*(1), 1–17.

Wikström, S. (1996). The customer as co-producer. *European Journal of Marketing, 30*(4), 6–19.

Zhang, X., & Li, B. (2013). Organisational culture and employee satisfaction: An exploratory study. *International Journal of Trade, Economics and Finance, 4*(1), 48.

Chapter 16

Cultural Influence on Customer Service Delivery

Ogechi Adeola, Isaiah Adisa and Abolaji Adewale Obileye

Contents

Introduction

In recent years, digital technologies have placed new demands on business organisations' customer service delivery, as they no longer compete solely with markets within their location but must operate on a global scale (Grönroos & Ravald, 2011; Lodorfos et al., 2015; Ngacha & Onyango, 2017). For organisations to attract a culturally-diverse market, they must adopt strategies that recognise the role of culture in customer satisfaction (Endara et al., 2019; Hopkins et al., 2009), beginning with the first point of customer contact – the workers who act as customer service representatives (Chase et al., 2004; Hopkins et al., 2009; Nyangau, 2017). It is at the point-of-service encounter that organisations must begin to meet the cultural needs of customers (Hopkins et al., 2009; Stewart & Jackson, 2003).

The importance of national or societal culture on customers' behaviour and service delivery expectations has been rigorously studied by reputable scholars using different country-case scenarios and industry-case scenarios as evaluation measures (De Mooij & Hofstede, 2011; Endara et al., 2019; Farayibi, 2016; Hoang et al., 2010; Ngacha & Onyango, 2017; Odor, 2018; Rivera et al., 2019). These studies collectively revealed the need for businesses to understand and incorporate cultural diversities into their business strategies if they are to thrive in a multicultural environment. Yoo et al. (2011) emphasised that organisations that observe and adopt the cultural characteristics specific to nations or social entities are able to meet the need of the customers and achieve organisational goals.

Each society has cultural features that distinguish it from all others. In studies by Winsted (1997) and Tsoukatos and Rand (2007), respect for culture has been found to be a determining factor in measuring customer satisfaction. Winsted identified cultural factors that influence customer satisfaction in the United States and Japan. Both nations valued civility, personalisation and conversation, but predominant cultural values in the United States included remembering, congeniality, prompt delivery and authenticity; while in Japan, formality and concern were found to positively affect customer satisfaction.

According to Voon (2011), an excellent customer service delivery plan requires a broad organisational strategy centred on providing professional, high-quality service from the initial encounter until the service request is resolved to the customer's satisfaction. There is evidence from extant literature on the role of culture in customer satisfaction. This chapter, therefore, focuses on how organisations can enhance business performance by understanding societal culture as it applies to customer-oriented culture and customer service delivery outcomes in Nigeria.

The Concept of Culture

The culture of a continent defines the distinguishing characteristics of its people (Idang, 2015). Even as access to nations around the world is enhanced by technology, human societies cling to their cultural identities; a set of beliefs, norms and values that shape human behaviour and determine the extent to which human behaviours are either acceptable or unacceptable (Ngacha & Onyango, 2017). Culture is a pattern of life for which a specific set of people are known, a pattern that separates them from every other group of persons. Culture creates a brand by which individuals are identified.

Africa is known for its unique culture and values (Idang, 2015). Africa's wide range of cultural ideologies shape its people and how they manage interpersonal transactions. An example is the concept of Ubuntu in South Africa. Ubuntu is a philosophical term that captures the expression of compassion, dignity, reciprocity, harmony and interest in building justice for humanity (Nussbaum, 2003). Nussbaum opines that this has become an African ideology:

> Your pain is my pain
> My wealth is your wealth
> Your salvation is my salvation

The Ubuntu ethic is to be as interested in others as much as you are in yourself. This ideology, when observed by business organisations, attracts customers within the continent. It is embedded in a cultural language that cuts across all life endeavours as a patterned set of behaviour, beliefs, values, knowledge and traditions (Hopkins et al., 2009; Parhizgar, 2001).

An organisation's culture is defined by the characteristics and traditions that originate from within (Morcos, 2018). The cultural attributes of an organisation are reflected in its mission statement, workplace attitudes, written and unwritten protocols, social relations within the workplace, and values (Odor, 2018). As a rule, organisational culture cannot be quantified; it can only be discussed in the abstract. In the banking sector, for instance, culture can be reflected in the architectural design of its buildings, a visual aspect that conveys a message to customers (Zaal et al., 2019). More so, the mode of dress of a bank's employees and the way they receive and attend to customers are all evidence of culture. The organisation that understands the culture of the market in which it operates will delight customers, thereby creating a bond characterised by trust and confidence.

Culture is also conceptualised as a collection of common beliefs, behaviours and values held and displayed within the workplace (Agwu, 2014). Organisations set cultural norms that regulate the behaviour of employees and dictate how they relate to customers. These corporate cultures exist within the larger society that itself informs how the organisation operates and what is expected from employees. A strategy that gives customers a satisfactory experience will motivate a revisit intention (Groysberg et al., 2018).

Regardless of the quality of an organisation's product or service, if the human elements that are involved in customer service do not reflect cultural expectations, it will be difficult to retain customer loyalty. Cultural sensitivity distinguishes extraordinarily successful companies because they create an image of exceptional service in the minds of customers.

Customer-Oriented Culture

To create a customer-oriented culture, business organisations must align their service strategies with their immediate business environment (Ngacha & Onyango, 2017). Human resources departments should be responsible for devising strategies to reach out to customers that patronise the firm in ways that demonstrate respect for the customers' culture. In doing so, the cultural influences of the immediate environment of an organisation define the corporate culture of that organisation. An understanding of the dynamism of a current business environment will help tailor cultural practices that attract, satisfy and retain customers (Iriana & Buttle, 2006).

A customer service-oriented culture expects workers to go the extra mile to satisfy customers – to treat each customer like royalty – giving them a pleasant experience that will spur revisit intentions. Customers are an organisation's most important asset. They are the reason for the existence of the business, and their satisfaction must not be taken for granted. All business strategies must be channelled towards delivering services that create a positive experience for the customers. Examples of this can be seen in Nigerian organisations' mission statements that emphasise a core interest in customers. The mission statements of some organisations include the following:

- FirstBank: *To remain true to our name by providing the best financial services possible*
- MTN: *To make our customers' lives a whole lot brighter*
- NASCO: *To enrich the lives of customers by providing them with products of superior quality and value... always!*
- DT Autocafe: *To offer value-based, high quality and convenient one-stop vehicle repair services to meet customer needs.*

These mission statements are meant to be reflected in the actions, attitude and behaviour of their employees. Organisations should put in place appropriate mechanisms to continuously communicate and deliver superior customer service.

Customer Service Delivery

Service delivery is a business component that describes the relationship between service providers and service consumers, and the quality of that relationships is based on the value that is obtained for the service rendered (Joseph, 2019). In recent years, organisations are able to enhance their customer service delivery process using an information technology infrastructure library (ITIL)

(Barafort et al., 2002). Through this medium, businesses define their service and product, as well as the responsibilities of the consumers. ITIL resources set standards for service quality, expectations, timeliness and availability. Organisations articulate their plans for service delivery designed to assure that customer satisfaction is the end product of every service delivery process (Adesina & Chinonso, 2015). To achieve success, organisations must maintain a consistent and dynamic means of achieving customer satisfaction by providing value-added services that assure a positive outcome (Adesina & Chinonso, 2015; Leon & Lestlie, 2000). The workers' mandate is to consistently adhere to the strategic service delivery process laid out by the management of their organisations. Customer service employees play a key role in service delivery interactions because customers will assume that the employees' attitudes and abilities reflect the culture of the entire organisation.

An organisation's service delivery policies denote the rendering of a product or service to the customer as stipulated and expected (Martins & Ledimo, 2015). It centres on when, where and how a service is rendered to the customer and if the service is considered fair or not. The scope of the service delivery understanding serves to reconcile the organisation's strategic intent and the customer's need (Goldstein et al., 2002; Martins & Ledimo, 2015). A service delivery system is a strategic process whereby the organisation puts in place necessary plans to meet the needs of customers by providing feedback mechanisms and creating a positive experience (Martins & Ledimo, 2015).

A wide range of service delivery activities is driven by the pursuit of customer satisfaction with the service or product rendered by the organisation. A successful service delivery process is aimed at giving customers a good experience through every medium encountered, either online or offline (Adesina & Chinonso, 2015; Shergill & Sun, 2004). A service delivery interaction can easily cut across all departments at multiple levels in an organisation, from the initial contact person through all core services, resulting in a customer's level of satisfaction with the organisation as a whole (Adesina & Chinonso, 2015; Shergill & Sun, 2004). It is, therefore, imperative that organisations become cognisant of some basic service delivery elements, including cultural awareness, when developing their service delivery systems.

Culture and Service Delivery Outcomes in Nigeria

Nigeria's native population numbers over 150 million people (Federal Government of Nigeria, n.d). The country operates a presidential system of government with a dual economic system of traditional agriculture and the trade sector. The country is endowed with both human and natural resources that drive its economic activities and industrial growth. Nigeria is rich with cultural heritage and is home to more than 250 ethnic groups with different values, norms and religious practice. Consequently, Nigeria is a culture-sensitive nation but provides a large market for organisations to tap into and make a profit. To be successful, business organisations in Nigeria must offer products and services that attract and sustain customer patronage in a multi-cultural society.

Understanding the nexus between culture and customer service delivery outcomes in Nigeria is best discussed using Hofstede's five metrics of culture: power distance, uncertainty avoidance, individualism vs collectivism, short-term orientation vs long-term orientation, and masculinity vs femininity (Hofstede, 2001).

Power distance relates to the unequal roles and positions occupied by people in a society, namely between elected or appointed county or local representatives and the general population. The understanding of this power distance, as defined by status and class, and alignment with the demands of those groups enables organisations to achieve effective customer service delivery in Nigeria. The Nigerian culture tends towards high power distance (Okeke, 2017) and it respects hierarchies in the workplace and society. It is important to design an effective customer service strategy to reflect an appropriate level of consciousness of social stratification within the market.

Uncertainty avoidance describes a situation in which people feel threatened by, and try to avoid, ambiguity. Nigeria's cultural tradition leans towards intolerance of ambiguous processes, so businesses must communicate a position of trustworthiness to consumers if they want to attract and sustain customers' patronage. Consumers in such a society will avoid products and services with unclear terms which they perceive to have some element of risk as they have been acculturated to avoid uncertainty.

Individualism vs collectivism stresses the cultural belief and orientation that questions which is more important, the group or the individual. Individualism is a social theory that the 'self/person' is more important than the collectivist 'group/we'. The 'group/we' concept holds that an in-group member's values are developed, promoted and protected by all. The Nigerian society reflects more of collectivism dimension than individualism, and this is demonstrated by their strong group ties (Okeke, 2017).

Short-term vs long-term orientation: Hofstede (2001) explained that the cultural orientations of a society inform the plans, objectives and goals of individuals in that society. A society and its members are categorised as having long-term orientation when they focus on the future and are willing to delay short-term success or gratification to achieve future satisfaction/ goals, exhibiting perseverance, persistence, saving and adaptability. Short-term orientation is a characteristic of individuals who seek immediate gratification; present or past traditions are more important than consideration of future outcomes.

A society and individuals with short-term orientation will hold in high esteem traditions, current social hierarchies and the fulfilment of social obligations. Organisations must be aware of the ways target customers' cultural orientations shape their lives, actions, plans, goals and objectives and how that orientation influences the design and marketing efforts of their product or service. For example, a market dominated by individuals with short-term orientation will find it difficult to accept an innovation that erodes their experience and current belief systems. For example, if a fabric designer introduces a trending Western cloth to women in a society that cherishes traditional attire and is not receptive to change, it will be difficult to gain market share in that short-term culture.

Masculinity vs femininity is a cultural concept that addresses the nature of a society's assigned gender roles. Masculinity emphasises the importance of achievement and material rewards; femininity is associated with caring for others. A culture with a masculine orientation will differentiate work-related assignments for males and females, unlike a feminine culture that is less gender-conscious in the workplace. Nigeria is a masculine society (Okeke, 2017), with material success held in high esteem. Organisations must consider the societal structures within which they operate and take into consideration the cultural values of the society in designing their customer service programmes and strategies.

Nigeria's Cultural Identity

Failure to recognise the culture of a social environment will turn customers away. A customer service delivery system designed to identify and blend in with culture of the society will create deep connections with the consumers, increase customer retention, and enhance organisational performance. In addition to Hofstede's five dimensions of cultural value, Commisceo Global Consulting (2019) found cultural influences unique to Nigeria which are language and communication dynamics, religion, family, hierarchy, etiquette and customs.

Language and Communication Dynamics: Nigeria has over 500 languages among 250 different ethnic groups. With this number of languages and ethnic group variations, it is difficult to have a generally accepted lingua franca, though most Nigerians have adopted English as its general spoken and written language for official purposes and business transactions. It would be detrimental to a business if a customer service representative or the business management themselves decide to adopt a local language as their means of communication with customers, except in an area where it is certain that the locals do not understand English. Customer service representatives must, therefore, be careful not to send the wrong message to customers by trying to communicate in languages that others cannot understand. This justifies the need to understand and apply individualism or collectivism metrics in different geographic contexts.

Also, the nature of the environment should decide what language a business should adopt. In Nigeria's urban areas, English is best for the majority, while another language or dialect will be appropriate in areas far from the urban centres. Rural dwellers who speak a local dialect could feel embarrassed or annoyed if a business attempts to communicate with them in English, making a purchase unlikely. The same could be said in the case of urban dwellers who are not fluent in a local dialect and thus uncomfortable with companies that conduct business in local languages. The customer service process must be cognisant of language dynamics to attract and retain customers in different areas.

Religion: The most prominent religions in Nigeria are Christianity, Islam, and worship of traditional deities, institutional allegiances which the majority of the population do not take lightly. Organisations have to take into consideration, the religious hours, days, or observances if they expect to appeal to certain categories of customers. Products and services that are controversial among certain religious groups should not be displayed or otherwise marketed in places where a strong religious influence is evident; the result will be fewer sales and even alienation to the company.

During the Ramadan period (the Muslim fasting period), products such as alcohol, when marketed indiscriminately in a Muslim-dominated environment, can be seen as culturally ignorant and insulting and may lead to chaos. However, after Ramadan, the Muslim population may be less sensitive to the matter. Likewise, the times of worship for the different religious groups (i.e. Friday afternoon for Muslims, Sunday morning for Christians, and various seasons for traditional worshipers) must be respected. In essence, products and services that conflict with religious beliefs and traditions must be avoided. Similarly, the dress code of an organisation's representatives should conform to the customs of the locals. That is why organisations in some states in Nigeria wear the environment's local attire on Fridays to communicate oneness. Businesses that wish to appeal to the entire population of their market area must not be perceived to be biased for or against any religious group, or they risk alienating potential customers from their organisations' goods and services.

The Family: Businesses that hope to attract and retain customers must enforce policies that will correctly assess family needs and provide benefits for the entire family. Collectivism, as a metric of culture (Hofstede, 2001), is applicable because it prioritises meeting the needs of a group over self-interest. Collectivism describes the aspect of culture that seeks the satisfaction of group members, meeting their needs and putting smiles on their faces. When an organisation provides customer-centred services that focus on the whole family across generations, it will boost sales and enhance customer satisfaction. Telecommunications companies in Nigeria, for example, offer special packages for families to connect with each other at reduced rates. Banks provide accounts for families to save for their infant children. Offering special programmes and promotions that meet the needs of the family will attract patronage, enhance customers satisfaction, and improve business performance.

Hierarchy: Respect for elders is woven into Nigeria's cultural fabric. The elderly occupy a social status that signifies wisdom, and abundant knowledge which calls for respect. Even a local adage from Nigeria's Yoruba tribe says, *'ti omode ba ni aso bi agba, kole ni akisa bi agba'* meaning 'a child can have clothes like the elders, but not rags like the elders'. In Isoko, it is said *'Omaha te who ewun whoho okpako, osa who eno efa no who ho ekpako na ha'* and in Igbo the saying *'Nwata kwo aka, osoro okoye rie nri'*, both translate to 'If a child washes his/her hands, he/she will dine with elders'. These cultural proverbs reinforce the idea that the wisdom of the elderly cannot be comprehended by the young and emphasises the sanctity of hierarchy.

The elderly should be treated with special care and respect. In a situation where the old and the young are in a service delivery queue, an organisation's employee is wise to attend to the elderly customer first, an action that will be perceived as cultural sensitivity to the customers, both young and old. This scenario confirms the power distance metric of culture (Hofstede, 2001), because the awareness and acceptance of the unequal power of a social group allows for preferential treatment between the young and the old without any chaos. Thus, as an element of building customer satisfaction, an organisation must recognise in its customer service delivery, the culture of power preference, which must be respected and observed.

Etiquette and customs: Organisations doing business in Nigeria should understand that there are basic etiquette rules that should be observed when attending to customers in person. In addition to the generally accepted standards of polite conduct, Nigerians expect the following:

■ Greet customers at every point of contact with a welcoming smile and eye contact. It is rude to rush the greeting process.
■ Ask about the individual's health and well-being as well as his/her significant other and family; this is considered to be a sincere and friendly interaction.
■ Shake hands, but be aware that some religions and cultures do not allow any physical contact, including handshakes, between members of the opposite sex.
■ Acknowledge a customer's title or honorific (Alhaji, Pastor, Imam, Chief Priest, Prophet) and name; a sign that they are held in high regard.
■ Bow to greet someone who is older; this is considered a sign of respect.

A customer service delivery plan should instil in employees the importance of understanding local etiquettes and customs when engaging with customers. This strategy aligns with masculinity and femininity metric of culture (Hofstede, 2001). Such practices are gender-specific, respectful of religion, and culturally-bound to distinguish the nature of the society. Excellent customer service delivery understands the importance of greetings; gender-related sensitivity and the use of appropriate religious titles vary in different societies, but must be identified, observed and respected. For instance, societies that value masculine characteristics hold titles in high esteem, while the values of feminine societies have less concern for titles but rather for care and concern for the quality of life (Hofstede, 2011).

Gift-giving etiquette is worth special consideration by businesses. The presentation of gifts is seen as a way of showing love and care in Africa. The customer service delivery system should include gift promos for customers during festive seasons as well as give honour and awards to repeat customers. These acts communicate care and love to the customers and give them the feeling that their patronage is appreciated. Varying categories of gifts can be created for different customers in such a way that the gifts can be apportioned to all customers depending on the value of their purchase. Gift-giving could be a unique aspect of the customer service delivery system if properly utilised to create a long-lasting experience with the customers.

A graphic representation of cultural influence on customer service which organisations in Africa must take into consideration in designing service delivery systems, is shown in the following figure.

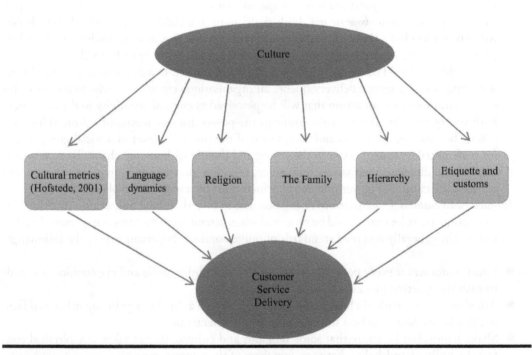

Source: Courtesy of Authors.

Conclusion

Culture is an integral part of every social institution and cannot be neglected by business organisations if they wish to become successful. Customers are the main focus of every business, and meeting their needs should be the centre of any business plan. Developing a customer service delivery system that will align with the culture of the people is critical to ensuring customer satisfaction.

Hence, the understanding and application of the five metrics of culture and other identified factors that influence culture in different contexts are imperative for excellent customer service delivery.

In Africa specifically, businesses should study the culture of a target audience, then design customer service programmes that align the standards and expectations of the business with those of the people it hopes to serve.

Business managers, when designing customer service delivery processes, must ensure each interaction built into those processes take cognisance of the language, religious allegiances and gender-related customs of the people in order not to cause unintended offense. By acknowledging and respecting these attributes, companies can also use this knowledge to their advantage by building bonds with customers through appreciation of their cultural norms. Respect for persons, especially the elderly, is a cultural norm that a service delivery process must exhibit at all times if positive customer experiences are to be created where the culture of a society values offering gifts, developing customer loyalty programs, and organisations should include promos, gifts and freebies.

Finally, to achieve customer satisfaction and increase customer loyalty and retention, businesses in Nigeria and the continent of Africa must put into consideration, the culture of the society, in designing customer service delivery systems.

References

Adesina, K. I., & Chinonso, I. (2015). Service delivery and customer satisfaction in hospitality industry: A study of the divine fountain hotels limited, Lagos, Nigeria. *Journal of Hospitality Management and Tourism, 6*(1), 1–7.

Agwu, M. O. (2014). Organisational culture and employees performance in the national agency for food and drugs administration control (NAFDAC) Nigeria. *Global Journal of Management and Business Research, 14*(2):1–10.

Barafort, B., Di Renzo, B., & Merlan, O. (2002). Benefits resulting from the combined use of ISO/IEC 15504 with the information technology infrastructure library (ITIL). In *International conference on product focused software process improvement* (pp. 314–325). Berlin, Germany: Springer.

Chase, R. B., Aquilano, N., & Jacobs, F. R. (2004). *Operations management for competitive advantage* (10th ed.), Boston, MA: Mc-Graw Hill.

Commisceo Global Consulting Ltd. (2020). Nigeria business & culture insight report. Retrieved from https://www.commisceo-global.com/resources/country-insight-reports/nigeria-insight.

De Mooij, M., & Hofstede, G. (2011). Cross-cultural consumer behavior: A review of research findings. *Journal of International Consumer Marketing, 23*(3–4), 181–192.

Endara, Y. M., Ali, A. B., & Yajid, M. S. A. (2019). The influence of culture on service quality leading to customer satisfaction and moderation role of type of bank. *Journal of Islamic Accounting and Business Research, 10*(1), 134–154.

Farayibi, A. (2016). Service delivery and customer satisfaction in Nigerian Banks. Available at SSRN: *SSRN 2836963*. http://dx.doi.org/10.2139/ssrn.2836963.

Federal Government of Nigeria (n.d.). Retrieved from http://nigeria.gov.ng.

Goldstein, S. M., Johnston, R., Duffy, J., & Rao, J. (2002). The service concept: The missing link in service design research? *Journal of Operations Management, 20*(2), 121–134.

Grönroos, C., & Ravald, A. (2011) "Service as business logic: Implications for value creation and marketing." *Journal of Service Management, 22*(1), 5–22.

Groysberg, B., Lee, J., Price, J., & Cheng, J. (2018). The leader's guide to corporate culture. *Harvard Business Review, 96*(1), 44–52.

Hoang, H. T., Hill, S. R., & Lu, V. N. (2010). The influence of service culture on customer service quality: Local vs. Foreign service firms in emerging markets. In P. Ballantine, & J. Finsterwalder (Eds.), 'Doing more things less. *Proceedings of the Australian and New Zealand Marketing Academy Conference (ANZMAC 2010)* (pp. 1–12). Christchurch, New Zealand.

Hofstede, G. (2001). *Culture's consequences: Comparing values, behaviors, institutions, and organizations across nations* (2nd ed.), Thousand Oaks, CA: Sage.

Hofstede, G. (2011). Dimensionalizing cultures: The Hofstede model in context. *Online Readings in Psychology and Culture, 2*(1). doi:10.9707/2307-0919.1014.

Hopkins, S. A., Nie, W., & Hopkins, W. E. (2009). Cultural effects on customer satisfaction with service encounters. *Journal of Service Science, 2*(1), 45–56.

Idang, G. E. (2015). African culture and values. *Phronimon, 16*(2), 97–111.

Iriana, R., & Buttle, F. (2006). Customer relationship management (CRM) system implementations. *Journal of Management, 6*(2), 136–147.

Joseph, C. (2019). *What are the benefits of delivering excellent customer service?* Retrieved from https://small-business.chron.com/benefits-delivering-excellent-customer-service-2086.html.

Leon, S., &Lestlie, K. (2000). *Consumer behavior* (7th ed.), Washington, DC: Institute of Management Consultant, pp. 47–53.

Lodorfos, G., Kostopoulos, G., & Kaminakis, K. (2015). The impact of service delivery system effectiveness on service quality: A hierarchical approach. *International Journal of Business Performance Management, 16*(2–3), 169–181.

Martins, N., & Ledimo, O. (2015). The perceptions and nature of service delivery among government employees: An exploratory study. *Journal of Governance and Regulation, 4*(4), 575–581.

Morcos, M. (2018). *Organisational culture: Definitions and trends.* Rotterdam, Netherlands: Author.

Ngacha, W. J., & Onyango, F. E. V. (2017). The role of a customer-oriented service culture in influencing customer retention in the hotel industry. *African Journal of Hospitality, Tourism and Leisure, 6*(4), 1–19.

Nussbaum, B. (2003). African culture and Ubuntu. *Perspectives, 17*(1), 1–12.

Nyangau, J. (2017). Effects of customer service delivery on customer satisfaction in micro finance industry in Nairobi County. *Journal of Marketing and Communication 1*, 1–15.

Odor, H. O. (2018). Organisational culture and dynamics. *International Journal of Scientific Research and Management (IJSRM), 6*(1), 31–39.

Okeke, O. J. P. (2017). Nigerian culture: A barrier to the career progress of women in Nigeria. *Global Journal of Human Resource Management, 5*(5), 1–11.

Parhizgar, K. D. (2001). *Multicultural behavior and global business environments.* Binghamton, NY: International Business Press.

Rivera, D. E., Fa, M. C., Sampaio, A., & Villar, A. S. (2019). Exploring the role of service delivery in remarkable tourism experiences. *Sustainability, 11*(5), 1382, 1–19. doi:org/10.3390/su11051382.

Shergill, G. S., & Sun, W. (2004). Tourists' perceptions towards hotel services in New Zealand. *International Journal of Hospitality & Tourism Administration, 5*(4), 1–29.

Stewart, D. M., & Jackson, E. C. (2003). Matching customer scripts and service encounter designs. *Proceedings of the Decision Sciences Institute National Conference.*

Tsoukatos, E., & Rand, G. K. (2007). Cultural influences on service quality and customer satisfaction: Evidence from Greek insurance. *Managing Service Quality: An International Journal, 17*(4), 467–485.

Voon, B. H. (2011). Measuring culture of service excellence: The development-validation journey. In *The 2nd International Research Symposium in Service Management at the University of Pembangunan Nasional (UPN)* (pp. 86–93). Yogyakarta, Indonesia.

Winsted, K. F. (1997). The service experience in two cultures: A behavioural perspective. *Journal of Retailing, 73*(3), 337–360.

Yoo, B., Donthu, N., & Lenartowicz, T. (2011). Measuring Hofstede's five dimensions of cultural values at the individual level: Development and validation of CVSCALE. *Journal of International Consumer Marketing, 23*(3–4), 193–210.

Zaal, R. O., Jeurissen, R. J., & Groenland, E. A. (2019). Organizational architecture, ethical culture, and perceived unethical behavior towards customers: Evidence from wholesale banking. *Journal of Business Ethics, 158*(3), 825–848.

Chapter 17

Reward and Recognition Systems in Customer Service Organisations

Thomas Katua Ngui

Contents

Introduction

Business enterprises globally have been revolutionised by new computer systems that capture, organise, optimise and partly automate business processes (National Academies of Sciences, Engineering and Medicine, 2017). The African continent is expanding very fast as an economic region (Chironga et al., 2011). The rapid technological advancement and globalisation of businesses have led to increased competition for customers. The customer base in any country is dependent on population size and the ability of citizens to buy products or services. Over the last 20 years, the African continent's population has grown rapidly and in 2011 exceeded the 1 billion mark (African Development Bank, 2014). With the rapid population growth, there has also been increased urbanisation. This rising trend of urbanisation in Africa serves to put pressure on an already inadequate infrastructure and demonstrates the urgent need for greater investment if living standards for Africa's growing population are to rise (Makhubela, 2018). The number of organisations competing for the limited number of customers has also increased tremendously over the past decade courtesy of advances in technology. Today, every organisation is in competition not just with local firms, but with all organisations globally. Technology has also led to the existence of virtual organisations which also compete for customers.

In the current competitive environment, therefore, it is prudent that customer service organisations motivate all their stakeholders (employees, customers and suppliers) in order to retain them and harness their full support towards the achievement of the organisational goals. Organisations should shift their actions towards customer centricity. Customer centricity is the idea that organisations should not only serve their customers, but also get 'close to them' – understand what they value, deliver exceptional experiences and memories, and work to build relationships (Glynn, 2017). The key focus towards the success of customer service organisations lies on how they handle all the people that they deal with. One important element of people management strategy is reward and recognition for the key elements of performance (West et al., 2005). The African market is unique compared to other global markets. The uniqueness of the African market is majorly based on poor infrastructure, linguistic diversity, low literacy rates, a fragmented retail market, differences in consumer behaviour, low data availability and quality, growing population, massive expansion of the consumer pool, urbanisation and the rise of mobile communications. Reward and recognition programmes always come in many different forms (both financial and non-financial), and therefore customer service organisations in Africa should choose what fits their needs.

Africa must take steps to secure its own share of global economic growth (Makhubela, 2018). Managers in African companies should, therefore, strive to create a service-oriented culture. This calls for a rethink of customer management strategies. According to Wellington (2017), the characteristics of a customer-service-oriented company include a customer-first approach, universal buy-in, high levels of empathy, exceptional follow-through and follow-up, and the willingness to make it easy for the customer to access and use its products and services. This calls for improvement in the African infrastructure which has remained poor. The African Development Bank estimates the continent would need to spend an additional $40 billion a year on infrastructure to turn around its current deficits and keep pace with economic growth (Makhubela, 2018).

Customer service organisations must ensure that staff are rewarded and recognised for delivering high-quality customer service (West et al., 2005). Customers should be rewarded for their loyalty to the organisation and its products and/or services, while suppliers should be rewarded and recognised for offering timely and quality goods and services that support product quality despite the poor infrastructure in Africa.

Africa is characterised by political troubles, wars, natural disasters and poor policies. The African markets are different from high income, industrialised markets such as those in America, Asia and Europe, and hence require a slightly different approach to reward and recognition. Political turmoil in countries like Algeria, Egypt, Libya, Morocco, Sudan, Zimbabwe, South Sudan and Tunisia and the civil war in Ivory Coast have dramatically reminded executives of the enormous uncertainty that businesses must cope with in Africa (Chironga et al., 2011). Many countries in the developed world currently focus their efforts and resources inwards as a result of challenging economic times (Makhubela, 2018). There is a danger that a shift away from emerging markets like Africa will negatively impact the global economy's ability to grow in the future (Makhubela, 2018).

Due to the low-income levels in Africa, organisations may not afford the huge financial budgets required to engage in massive financial rewarding. It is, therefore, necessary for managers in Africa to engage more in the use of recognition and non-financial rewards to motivate employees and customers. In determining how to reward and recognise employees, companies should consider their life stage and industry saturation level (Chinje, 2010). As Africa's economies progress, opportunities are opening in sectors such as retailing, telecommunications, banking, infrastructure-related industries, resource-related businesses and the agricultural value chain.

This chapter introduces a new perspective in ensuring the success of customer service organisations by introducing a reward and recognition programme for the suppliers in order to encourage improved performance of the organisational suppliers, which in turn will lead to improved product and service quality, ensuring customer retention and encouraging the appropriate customer service behaviours that organisations today need in order to thrive. Previous approaches have not considered rewarding and recognising suppliers, even though suppliers play a key role in the organisation/employee-customer relationship. According to research conducted by Grosso et al. (2000), Giannini et al. (2007), and Wang (2012), there is a positive relationship between raw material quality and product quality. The quality of the product manufactured and/or the service offered by an organisation will depend to a very large extent on the quality of raw material provided by the supplier. This, therefore, calls for more investment to ensure that suppliers provide high-quality raw materials in a timely manner. Supplier reward and recognition will, therefore, prove very important in motivating the suppliers to deliver timely high-quality products and services.

The African Market/Context

Africa is a very vast continent with a huge potential for business. However, various challenges have hindered its economic progress. In Africa, infrastructure is still poor; talent is scarce; and poverty, famine and disease afflict many nations (Chironga et al., 2011). The continent, now home to more than 1.1 billion people, will account for one-fifth of the world's population by 2025. More and more Africans are entering the consumer class, with tens of millions emerging from poverty in recent years (Boateng et al., 2015). Countries like Gabon, Botswana and Angola are small and dynamic; their income levels are growing, and their retail markets are unsaturated – offering ample opportunity for the enterprising retailer (Tshabalala, 2015). Most Western executives, unsure of the size of Africa's consumer markets, prefer to invest in Asia's dragon and tiger economies rather than in Africa's economic lions (Chironga et al., 2011). African countries such as Sudan, Zimbabwe, South Sudan and Egypt among others have been having politically related problems in recent years, thus impacting negatively on economic growth. It has also become a common trend that political and economic instability is witnessed in African countries whenever there are presidential elections. This greatly affects the business environment.

Aims of Rewards

Customer service staff are critical to the success and overall corporate image of an organisation. Employees, customers and suppliers have very critical roles to play towards the success of the organisation. All organisations should consider coming up with strategies that will help to motivate the people involved in its business activities. This, therefore, calls for the adoption of a multifaceted and multipronged approach to reward and recognise all the players. If only one category of the players is rewarded and the rest left out, success may not be achieved.

Reward and recognition programmes should lead to a higher level of satisfaction and engagement with employees, customers and suppliers while at the same time providing a solid return on investment. Rewards and recognition lead to increased employee engagement and encourages them to unleash their full potential to the organisation. Effective reward systems attract new employees and motivate them to perform at high levels. A reward system is, therefore, important for increased employee and organisational performance.

With increased competition, companies have to lure good quality employees to their organisation. This requires the adoption of very competitive reward and recognition programmes among other strategies. Reward and recognition, if well used, helps retain good quality employees due to increased job satisfaction. Various research studies have supported the existence of a positive relationship between reward and recognition and employee/organisational performance. For instance, a research conducted by Ndungu (2017) on the effects of rewards and recognition on employee performance in public educational institutions with reference to Kenyatta University, Kenya showed a significantly positive relationship between reward and recognition with employee performance.

Ibrar and Khan (2015) had earlier researched on the impact of rewards on employee performance at Malakand private school in Pakistan and concluded that there is a positive relationship between rewards (extrinsic and intrinsic) and employee's job performance. This, therefore, provides sound support for organisations that have the desire to improve on both people (employees, customers and suppliers) and organisational performance to invest more in reward and recognition. Most people prefer financial rewards and other nonfinancial rewards that give them the opportunity to take on important tasks and/or projects. They also appreciate the attention and encouragement given to them by the senior leadership of the organisation. In this way, employees feel that they are valued by the employers and that the company is seriously involved in the people's (customer, suppliers and employees) development. When employees, customers and suppliers are valued, their satisfaction and productivity improves, and they are motivated to maintain or improve their good work.

Reward Theories

This chapter will discuss four theories of rewards: Maslow's hierarchy of needs theory, Herzberg's two-factor theory, McGregor's theory X and Y, and Adams' Equity theory.

Hierarchy of Needs Theory – Abraham Maslow

This theory was developed by Abraham Maslow in 1943. According to Maslow, human needs are arranged in order of importance from the most important basic needs at the base of the pyramid to the least important self-actualisation needs at the apex of the pyramid. From the bottom of the hierarchy upwards, the needs are: physiological, safety, love and belonging, esteem and self-actualisation. Maslow argued that all humans will address the basic needs before moving to satisfy the higher-level needs and that the sense of well-being increases as people go higher up the hierarchy. According to the theory, different people will actualise at different levels or points. The self-actualisation may also go higher as an employee gets new higher expectations.

Basic Needs

These are the physiological needs that are necessary for human existence. These categories are biological requirements for human survival; therefore, if these needs are not satisfied, the human body cannot function optimally. They include food, shelter, clothing, water, air, sex, sleep and warmth. Humans will first attempt to satisfy these physiological needs, and once they are satisfied, they will now move to the next level.

Safety/Security Needs

These include the protection from danger, security, order, law, stability and freedom from fear/pain. These needs are fulfilled through job security, medical insurance, employee pension, etc.

Social Needs/Love Needs

The third level of human needs is social needs and involves feelings of belongingness. The need for interpersonal relationships motivates behaviour. Intimacy, trust and acceptance are very important in this level. There is a strong desire to love and feel loved and engage in social activities and group membership. This includes being members of both formal and informal groups, such as family groups and workgroups amongst others.

Esteem Needs

Maslow classified esteem needs into two categories: esteem for oneself (dignity, achievement, mastery, independence) and the desire for reputation or respect from others (e.g. status, prestige). These needs create a desire for self-respect and esteem for others, desire for self-confidence and achievement, as well as recognition and appreciation. Maslow indicated that the need for respect or reputation is most important for children and adolescents and precedes real self-esteem or dignity.

Self-Actualisation

This is the desire to achieve full potential with the premise that 'What a man can be, let them be'. This is about realising full personal potential, self-fulfilment, seeking personal growth, and peak experiences. A desire 'to become everything one is capable of becoming'.

According to Maslow, once the lowest available need in the hierarchy is satisfied, the next available need in the hierarchy becomes a motivator. Therefore, once a human being has satisfied a need to a considerable level, they now direct their efforts towards achieving the next available need. He argued that a satisfied need is not a motivator; only an unsatisfied need can motivate. Maslow argued that self-actualisation stimulates the desire for more.

Motivation-Hygiene Theory

Also referred to as Hertzberg Two-Factor theory, the Motivation-Hygiene theory is based on the premise that people's job satisfaction depends on two factors, namely:

1. Motivators/satisfiers
2. Hygiene factors/dissatisfiers

According to this theory, motivators cause job satisfaction and motivation, while hygiene factors cause dissatisfaction. The two factors are not the opposite of each other. Only motivation factors can motivate us. However, at the same time, we need the lack of dissatisfactions to achieve more efficient work.

Motivating factors can increase job satisfaction, and motivation is based on an individual's need for personal growth. If these elements are effective, then they can motivate an individual to achieve above-average performance and effort. Herzberg's factors of job satisfaction (motivating factors) include achievement, recognition, work itself, responsibility and advancement.

Hygiene factors – deficiency needs, for example, salary, working conditions, work environment, safety, and security are unsuitable (low level) at the workplace. This can make individuals unhappy, dissatisfied with their job. Other factors of job dissatisfaction (hygiene factors – deficiency needs) include company policy and administration, supervision and interpersonal relationships. Hygiene factors do not motivate, but if there is a problem with them, then they demotivate.

Adams' Equity Theory

The theory was suggested by Adams in 1965 stating that people will be motivated if they feel that they are treated equitably and fairly for their efforts in relation to others in the organisation. According to this theory, people will consider and compare their efforts (contribution to work), costs of their actions and benefits that will result from their contributions in relation to the reference person while determining if they are treated fairly and equitably. If the people perceive that the ratio of the reference persons input to output is not equal, then they will be motivated to reduce the inequity.

At the workplace, employees expect outcomes such as salary, rewards, promotions, verbal recognition, and interesting and challenging work commensurate with the inputs (time, education, experience and effort) that they offer the job. They also expect these outcomes to be equitably offered to all employees relative to their inputs to the organisation. When inequity exists, a person might reduce his/her inputs: efforts, quantity or quality of his/her work; increase his/her outputs (ask for pay raise) or even quit the situation if they feel that equity cannot be realised. Inequity, may also affect the relationship between the affected employee and the reference person.

The equity theory does not take into account differences in individual needs, values and personalities. For example, one person may perceive a certain situation as inequitable while another does not. All the same ensuring equity is very essential to motivation.

The McGregor Theory X and Theory Y

This theory was developed by Douglas McGregor in 1960. It is a leadership theory about organisation and management in which he represented two opposing perceptions about people. He refered to these two perceptions as Theory X and Theory Y. From his research, he concluded that the style of leadership adopted by the leader/manager depends on his/her perception of the people he leads.

Theory X

In Theory X, McGregor summarises the traditional view of management in a number of characteristic assumptions in which autocratic leadership style, close supervision, and the hierarchical principle are the key elements. Theory X starts from the assumption that people are naturally lazy, want to avoid work as much as possible, do not wish to take responsibility, have no ambition and prefer to be supervised. The authoritarian leadership style is, therefore, the most appropriate leadership style in Theory X. According to this theory, pure work motivation consists of financial incentives. People want to avoid work, and they must be continually coerced and controlled. Therefore, the system of rewards and punishments works best for them. Furthermore, their tasks and how these should be executed must be laid down in detail. According to this theory, people definitely do not wish to bear any responsibility for their work. The management implications for Theory X workers are that, to achieve organisational objectives, rewards of varying kinds are likely to be the most popular motivator.

Theory Y

In this theory, McGregor starts from the assumption that people have different needs. According to this theory, people consider effort at work the same as rest or play; they are ordinary people who do not dislike work. Depending on the working conditions, work could be considered a source of satisfaction or punishment. Individuals in this category seek responsibility (if they are motivated). According to McGregor, Theory Y people are naturally happy to work and have high motivation to pursue and achieve objectives. These people are ready to take personal responsibility for what they do. Such people take a creative problem-solving approach in their work. The challenge for management with Theory Y workers is to create a working environment (or culture) where workers can show and develop their creativity.

Components of a Reward System

People want to know that they matter to others and also want to feel important and appreciated. In order to convey a message of appreciation to your employees for the extra effort they give towards ensuring high customer satisfaction levels, it is necessary for organisations to invest in employee recognition and reward programmes. The rewards in these programmes may include pay raises, bonuses and gift cards, which are financial rewards, also referred to as monetary or extrinsic rewards. Recognition (intrinsic rewards), on the other hand, involves the psychological rewards gained by doing a job well. This includes initiatives like using the picture of deserving staff as the cover for a company newsletter or giving award plaques, certificates, or personalised jewellery, amongst others, including congratulatory mails from top management.

It is important that the elements of reward should be internally equitable, externally competitive, transparent, consistent and linked to competitive performance (Armstrong, 2002).

This is what the organisation should strive to achieve for the employees, customers and suppliers. The emphasis should be on a contingent pay. There are three basic reasons for using contingent pay: motivation, message and equity (West et al., 2005). Equity involves ensuring that employees feel fairly treated. It is right to relate pay to an individual's effort and performance. An employee will always compare what they earn with what their colleagues in the organisation earn, while at the same time comparing their performance with the performance of their colleagues. If based on these comparisons the employee feels that they are not fairly compensated in relation to their colleagues, then a feeling of inequity arises. This inequity can result in loss of motivation and increased job dissatisfaction, which may eventually negatively affect the employee's performance.

Reward and Recognition Systems

Employee reward and recognition is widely viewed as a major factor in motivating employees to improve performance. Reward and recognition programmes come in many different ways depending on factors such as availability of finances, industry and culture of the organisation. This can either be cheap or expensive. However, these programmes do not have to be costly. Valuing employee performance individually and in teams/groups can help create a culture of customer service. Most people are motivated not only by monetary rewards, but also because they are appreciated and treated with dignity as valued members of the team/organisation. Therefore, leadership styles adopted by supervisors/managers are very important in any employee recognition programme. Simple strategies such as the use of text messages, a card of recognition, a formal letter, a memo to all staff, or recognition in meetings, to appreciate an employee or team that has performed exemplary, can go a long way in improving their performance.

The reward and recognition programmes can be done publicly or privately, formally or informally, as well as individually or collectively in teams. This should, however, not be delayed for long unless it is absolutely necessary since they are most effective when offered immediately after the desired result or behaviour. Managers should always provide positive, accurate and timely feedback to employees about their performance. Rewarding and recognising employee behaviour that aligns with the essentials of great service: promptness, courtesy and knowledge, immediately after it happens or soon after helps the employee or team to improve the behaviour even further. This will, in turn, increase organisational performance.

It is important to use customer feedback in recognition programmes. Using only managers' appraisals to reward and recognise customer service employees is usually limited despite the fact that managers interact with employees on a more regular basis (daily) as opposed to the customers who only interact with the employee on occasional instances. Biases normally result from appraisal errors such as halo effect, horns effect, strictness error, same-as-me error, leniency errors and central error. Using feedback from many different employees, customers and suppliers may help to solve the biases. If employees learn that they get rewarded and recognised whenever they are involved in providing exceptional service to customers, then their focus changes and they improve their interaction with customers, which in turn helps improve the customer experience.

Reward Programmes

According to Anku et al. (2018), a reward is the total amount of financial and non-financial compensation or total remuneration provided to an employee in return for labour or service rendered at work. For an organisation to excel, it is important to retain employees, create motivation and increase job productivity through diverse strategies like rewards. Therefore, it is necessary for companies to design reward systems based on employees' skills and capabilities as well as organisational goals so as to improve performance and motivation (Korir & Kipkebut, 2016). A reward system consists of a number of interrelated processes and activities which combine to ensure that reward management is carried out effectively to the benefit of the organisation and the people who work there (Armstrong, 2010). This includes financial rewards (extrinsic rewards) like job promotions, pay raises, bonuses, commissions, gift cards or any other tangible reward that is given in recognition of good performance. Non-financial rewards mostly consist of social recognition, appreciation, working condition and meaningful work responsibility, among others. Therefore, rewards normally extend beyond the salary which is used to compensate the employee for the effort and time they give to the company.

In order for a reward system to be ideally motivational, the reward ought to fulfil various criteria: have value, be large enough to have an impact, be understandable, be timely, have a durable effect and be cost-efficient (Anku et al., 2018). Financial rewards have a cost component and therefore may be expensive for companies in a developing continent like Africa. It is, therefore, important for such companies to invest more in recognition programmes. Financial rewards, especially those given on a regular basis such as bonuses, profit sharing, gift cards, increased compensation, free food, football tickets, etc. should be tied to an employee's or a group's performance. Leaders have to leverage the right motivators to validate the behaviours they are trying to create, such as supporting other representatives, adding to the knowledge base and generating excellent customer feedback. While rewards play a role, they may also have some shortcomings. They can lead to a sense of entitlement and may not be effective over the long-term. Recognition and reward programmes should maximise the power of relationships, both internal and external to the company. An organisation should ensure that the programmes put in place are valuable, correctly designed and professionally executed to deliver significant and measurable results. Combining recognition and money is the formula for a very powerful reward. Nearly everyone responds well to praises of appreciation, but the response becomes even more positive when the praises have monetary value. It is best to award some money or something of value alongside recognition.

Use of Staff Reward and Recognition to Improve Customer and Supplier Loyalty

Human resource management theory and literature has supported the feeling that a motivated workforce is an asset for an organisation, while a workforce that lacks motivation is a liability. Employees who are personally invested in their work deliver better experiences to customers, who then return higher satisfaction and loyalty (Glynn, 2017). The challenge for managers is how to create and maintain a motivated spirit for the employees to put the best efforts in their jobs. Apart from their usual and contractual salaries, they can be rewarded for offering customer service at its best. Research has shown that in organisations where recognition occurs, employee engagement, productivity and customer service are better than in companies that do not reward and recognise employees. Recognition is more effective if done publicly as opposed to when done in private. It should also be done with proper identification and communication for its justification.

Recognition should be done every time the employee does something extraordinary towards the achievement of the company's goals. This should be done by employees at all levels and not necessarily by the chief executive officer (CEO). Employees can be included in the recognition equation so that an employee can recognise the good work of a colleague. This sends a signal to the employee that their peers also value the effort they put towards the achievement of organisational goals. It also sends a message of respect among employees. The top leadership of the organisation have a role to play in creating an environment where recognition comes from all directions in the company hierarchy. They should create a customer service-oriented team.

The leadership must, therefore, intentionally build a culture in which reward and recognition is not a predictably top-down movement, but rather a 360° experience. It should be continuous and offered at any time when it is deserved. Managers should keep in mind that recognition is not always effective on its own; it can be used in conjunction with other methods of boosting employee performance to improve their results. Small events/parties and gift packs/cards can be very valuable to an employee who has performed well. Opportunities for training can also be used as a reward for good customer service performance. Therefore, offering money isn't the only way to recognise outstanding or excellent service by employees; there are other ways to recognise and reward them besides cash. This could include promotions, time off, prizes, etc. Companies that excel in employee recognition are more likely to achieve strong business results, including higher profitability and better market leadership.

Employees value recognition programmes that focus on tangible accomplishments, that is, quantifiable aspects that are related to the company goals. It is important to offer employees recognition programmes that they value. This, therefore, calls for a thorough analysis to establish what the employees' value. Employees want to receive rewards that are of high quality, have high financial value, and that they can choose. Reward can be costly to sustain, especially if the financial rewards have to be offered to employees constantly. They can also lead to competition among employees, therefore negatively affecting teamwork, if the rewards are not team-based. In some other cases, employees may only focus on goals that are factored in rewards while avoiding/neglecting goals that are important in the company but are not rewarded. Although rewards are effective in offering short-term commitment and motivation; they are mostly devoid of the long-term engagement required with the organisation.

According to Fisher (2015) to claim the reward and recognition dividend, employees need to be treated like customers and communicated in a brand-consistent way. Loyalty reduces recruiting costs and requires the employer to train fewer people than its competitors. If employees know their corporate values, they do not need to waste time asking what they should do when it comes to making decisions (Fisher, 2015). Managers should make employees feel valued, respected and supported. They should also monitor employee satisfaction and implement practices and values that ensure employees are fairly treated and valued. Managers should adopt a warm and supportive style and encourage staff to go the extra mile in service of customers. This will encourage high levels of employee satisfaction and commitment and, thereby, customer satisfaction. Managers must also ensure staff have the skills to provide services that meet and exceed customer demands.

Reward and Recognition for Customers

Customers are current and would-be consumers of goods and services. Increasing competition has forced organisations to focus more on satisfying customers. According to Czepiel et al. (1974), customer satisfaction is the consumer's evaluation of the extent to which the product or service fulfils their complete set of wants and needs. A customer service-oriented company has the ability to help people, regardless of the challenges (Wellington, 2017). Studies have shown that there is a positive effect of customer satisfaction on customer commitment (Tonder & Beer, 2018). Customers voluntary behaviours contribute to an organisation's competitive position. Customers play a variety of roles in the company, both expected (paying for services/goods) and unexpected (providing feedback, referring other customers amongst other roles) for which they are not paid.

Organisations in the current competitive environment need to investigate customer needs, build relationships with both existing and potential customers, and also satisfy customers' needs (Rootman, 2006). Customers are the lifeblood of any business and thus need to be taken care of, treated well, recognised and rewarded for giving the company an opportunity to serve them. Competition among organisations has taught customers to be more discerning and more demanding in relation to customer service (West et al., 2005). Customers today are more informed and knowledgeable and will, therefore, demand value for their money. With increased competition, organisations must come up with customer attraction and retention strategies that will enable them to maintain their customers, staff and suppliers and keep them loyal at all times. Customer-centred organisations should serve their customers and get close to them; they should know what customers value, deliver experiences and memories, and build positive relationships with them. This is a unique approach to improve customer loyalty and boost staff morale.

Another approach to increasing customer loyalty and maintaining a sustained competitive advantage is to focus on human resources, which in turn, help attract and retain customers. This will also introduce a service culture to the organisation's stakeholders. Other efforts that will improve customer loyalty include rewarding staff, empowering customers and providing them with feedback, as well as offering vouchers and royalty points exchangeable for goods and services. Customer compliments should be posted in public places for the staff to see and appreciate. This can be done through social media, company website and advertisements, amongst others. If the company can develop relationships with the print and electronic media, they can also have such recognitions posted in the mainstream media. This strategy may be expensive, but its overall effect is far better than when the recognition is done only internally.

The loyal customers can be rewarded by being offered special treatment like special points of service (e.g. prestige customers in banks), extended hours of services, and access to certain benefits and events/services that are not accessible to other customers. Customers who have a long-standing relationship with the company, introduce new clients and provide substantial business to the company should be recognised and rewarded.

One benefit of recognition is that it can be offered on a daily basis through appreciations and congratulatory messages, therefore, creating daily motivation for customers. Conversely, rewards have to be planned for and done at specific periods. Recognitions are inexpensive and therefore can be used effectively to reinforce the actions and behaviours employers' value in their organisation. Recognition encourages other customers to partner with you by buying your products and services, hence leading to higher chances of brand and market success.

Reward and Recognition for Suppliers

The desire to increase supply chain performance has necessitated organisations to recognise and reward good performing suppliers so as to motivate them to ensure long and rewarding relationships. Giving suppliers incentives can be a great way to deliver extra value, but this needs to be managed effectively if it is to be successful. This exercise requires to be seen and be done fairly to eliminate the effects of a wrongly done rewarding system, which can be counterproductive. The company needs to understand its suppliers as well as take a holistic view of the business. Suppliers, who have performed well, can be recognised with certification, prizes and awards from the company. There should be discussions between the procurement departments, the production department and the supplier in order to ensure that needs are met by each party. The intention is to create motivation for all towards the achievement of the company goals and objectives. Motivation is also hierarchical depending on the person or organisation involved. The reward system should be structured in a way it will be fair to all and also be seen to be fair.

Effective Employee Recognition

According to Harrison (2005), employee recognition involves the timely, informal and/or formal acknowledgement of a person's behaviour, effort or business result that supports the organisation's goals and values beyond normal expectation. Nyakundi et al. (2012) as cited in Amoatemaa and Kyeremeh (2016) highlighted the aim of employee recognition as to allow individuals to know and understand that their work is valued and appreciated, provide a sense of ownership and belongingness, improve morale, enhance loyalty and increase employee retention rate in the organisation. Therefore, employee recognition helps appreciate any achievements from an individual or team that exceeds the normal expected performances. For recognition to be effective, organisations should recognise all the actions, behaviours, approaches and accomplishments that will make the organisation more productive and efficient. Recognition has a psychological base and influences better performance through improved satisfaction. Fairness, clarity and consistency should be taken seriously in recognition programmes. People need to see that each person or organisation (for customers and suppliers) that makes the same or a similar contribution has an equal likelihood of receiving recognition for their efforts. Policies (guidelines) on recognition should be developed and publicised so that everyone is aware of what constitutes a recognisable action. Feedback should also be given; this should be done as soon as possible after the event. People should be made aware of why they have been recognised so that positive behaviour can be reinforced.

Benefits of Employee Recognition

A recognition programme shows a business's appreciation for the departments, teams and individual employees who contribute to the organisational goals. The benefits of recognition programmes are many; they fulfil the intrinsic need that can be appreciated, and they illustrate an employer's commitment to its employees. Employee recognition in any form also increases employee engagement and raises morale. Employees can be rewarded by giving them higher levels of responsibility and more challenging and exciting roles. This effectively recognises, and thus, motivates the employees and raises the overall image of the organisation. A positive company image enables the organisation to attract the best employees and suppliers as well as more customers. Low turnover rates and high employee retention rates are also benefits of such employee recognition programmes. This is consistent with the arguments of scholars such as Empey et al. (2013) who argue that an effective reward and recognition strategy facilitates the alignment of reward and recognition elements with company goals, delivers consistent messages about business goals and organisational values and enhances the organisation's ability to attract and retain talent. Recognising people for their good work, thus, sends an extremely powerful message to the recipient, their work team and other employees through the grapevine and formal communication channels that their contribution/achievement is appreciated.

Conclusion

Reward and recognition programmes play a very critical role in the performance of all organisations; public and private, profit and non-profit, big and small. It is therefore, important for all managers and supervisors to take reward and recognition for employees, customers and suppliers seriously if the organisations are to succeed in achieving their goals. Managers should invest a lot of energy/effort in understanding the organisational culture due to its importance in reward and recognition programmes. Reward and recognition programmes are more effective in organisations where employees feel valued, respected and supported. This calls for managers to create the right organisational culture.

It is important that employees receive praise, recognition and reward for performing to, and beyond, the levels expected. Reward and recognition should be done at both team and individual levels. However, the emphasis should be more on team-based rewards due to its importance in improving the performance of customer service organisations. The rewards and recognition should extend to customers and suppliers, both individually and collectively. In developing countries, more emphasis should be on recognition programmes, especially in companies that have low budgets for reward and recognition purposes.

References

African Development Bank. (2014). *Tracking Africa's progress in figures*. Denmark: Phoenix Design Aid.

Amoatemaa, A. S., & Kyeremeh, D. D. (2016). Making employee recognition a tool for achieving improved performance: Implication for Ghanaian Universities. *Journal of Education and Practice, 7*(34), 46–52.

Anku, J. S., Amewugah, B. K., & Glover, M. K. (2018). Concept of reward management, reward system and corporate efficiency. *International Journal of Economics, Commerce and Management, 6*(2), 621–637.

Armstrong, M. (2002). *Employee reward* (3rd ed.), London, UK: Chartered Institute of Personnel and Development.

Armstrong, M. (2010). *Armstrong's essential human resource management practice: A guide to people management*. London, UK: Kogan Page Ltd.

Boateng, Y. A., Benson-Armer, R., & Russo, B. (2015). *Winning in Africa's consumer market*. Retrieved from https://www.mckinsey.com/industries/consumer-packaged-goods/our-insights/winning-in-africas-consumer-market.

Chinje, N. (2010). Customer relationship management (CRM) implementation within the banking and mobile telephony sectors of Nigeria and South Africa (Doctoral Thesis), Johannesburg, South Africa: University of the Witwatersrand. Retrieved from https://www.researchgate.net/publication/282322693.

Chironga, M., Leke, A., Lund, S., & Wamelen, A. (2011). The globe: Cracking the next growth market: Africa. *Harvard Business Review, 89*(5), 117–122.

Czepiel, J. A., Rosenberg, L. J., & Akerele, A. (1974) Perspectives on consumer satisfaction. In R. C. Curhan (ed.), *Marketing's contribution to the firm and society. AMA Educators' Proceedings* (pp. 119–123). Chicago, IL: American Marketing Association.

Empey, K., Cushen, J., Byrne, L., & Watson, T. (2013). *The essential guide to reward and recognition: How to get value in changing times*. Dublin: IBEC Human Resources Management Series.

Fisher, J. (2015). *Strategic reward and recognition. Improving employee rewards through non monetary incentives*. London, UK: Kogan Page.

Giannini, D., Parin, M.A., Gadaleta, L., Carrizo, A., & Zugarramurdi, A. (2007). Influence of raw material quality on quality of iced and frozen white fish products. *Journal of Food Quality, 24*(6), 527–538.

Glynn, K. (2017). *Customer-to-employee recognition: A revolutionary approach to engagement*. Retrieved from https://www.maritzcx.com/blog/general/customer-employee-recognition-engagement/.

Grosso, N. R., Nepote, V., & Guzmán, C. A. (2000). Chemical composition of some wild peanut species (*Arachis hypogaea* L.). *Journal of Agricultural and Food Chemistry, 48*(3), 806–809.

Harrison, K. (2005). *Why employee recognition is so important.* Retrieved from www.cuttingedgepr.com.

Ibrar, M., & Khan, O. (2015). The impact of reward on employee performance (A Case Study of Malakand Private School). *International Letters of Social and Humanistic Sciences, 52*(1), 95–103.

Korir, I., & Kipkebut, D. (2016). The effect of reward management on employees commitment in the universities in Nakuru county-Kenya. *Journal of Human Resource Management, 4*(4), 37–48. doi: 10.11648/j.jhrm.20160404.12.

Makhubela, K. (2018). *Africa's greatest economic opportunity: Trading with itself.* Retrieved from: https://www.weforum.org/agenda/2018/01/why-africas-best-trading-partner-is-itself/.

National Academies of Sciences, Engineering, and Medicine. (2017). *Information technology and the U.S. workforce: Where are we and where do we go from here?* Washington, DC: The National Academies Press. doi:10.17226/24649

Ndungu, D. N. (2017). The effects of rewards and recognition on employee performance in public educational institutions: A case of Kenyatta University, Kenya. *Global Journal of Management and Business Research, 7*(1), 42–68.

Nyakundi, W. K., Karanja, K., Charles, M., & Bisobori, W.N. (2012). Enhancing the role of employee recognition towards improving performance: A survey of Keyatta National hospital Kenya. *International Journal of Arts and Commerce 1*(7), 95–108.

Rootman C. (2006). The influence of customer relationship management on the service quality of banks. Unpublished MCom dissertation. Port Elizabeth, South Africa: Nelson Mandela Metropolitan University.

Tonder, E., & Beer, L. T. (2018). New perspectives on the role of customer satisfaction and commitment in promoting customer citizenship behaviours. *South African Journal of Economics and Management Science, 21*(1), 1–11.

Tshabalala, S. (2015). *The most promising retail markets in Africa are in countries people rarely talk about.* Retrieved from https://qz.com/africa/497066/the-most-promising-retail-markets-in-africa-are-in-countries-people-rarely-talk-about/.

Wang, L. (2012). *Study on processing characteristics and quality evaluation of peanut protein.* Beijing, China: Chinese Academy of Agricultural Sciences.

Wellington, E. (2017). *What does it mean to be 'customer service oriented?* Retrieved from https://www.help-scout.net/blog/customer-oriented/.

West, M., Fisher, G., Carter, M., Gould, V., & Scully, J. (2005). *Rewarding customer service? using reward and recognition to deliver your customer service strategy.* London, UK: Chartered Institute of Personnel and Development.

Chapter 18

Reward Systems and Customer Service Delivery among Small and Medium Enterprises in Lagos State, Nigeria

Dumebi Anthony Ideh

Contents

Introduction

There has been a shift from the manufacturing of products to service provision as the main focus of business organisations in Nigeria. Competition among organisations has made management and stakeholders become more concerned about service delivery. Organisations now compete not only in terms of product quality, but also with the level of customer service. There are indications that both reward systems and customer service delivery could affect the performance and competitiveness of organisations. The success or otherwise of an organisation may be attributed to how organisations manage their reward and recognition systems and how well employees deliver on their promises to customers. According to Armstrong (2006), reward systems consist of policies that guide the approaches to management practices that provide financial and non-financial rewards, maintain reward systems and ensure that these systems operate efficiently, flexibly and cost effectively.

In other words, a reward system consists of interrelated processes and practices that combine to ensure that reward management is carried out effectively for the benefit of both the organisation and the employees (Armstrong, 2012a). The purpose of reward systems is, therefore, to formulate and implement strategies and policies that reward employees fairly and consistently in line with the organisational values. The reward systems are important and should be aligned with the goals of the employees and those of the organisation. According to Armstrong (2012b), employees have become the most important determinants of organisational performance, as the economy is based largely on service and knowledge. Employees are a critical resource of any organisation, and their satisfaction on the job is greatly affected by the reward system (Chepkwony, 2014). Management should, therefore, ensure that the reward system is effective and competitive enough to influence employees to perform better.

It is important to note that managing service personnel is a major challenge in service provision because of their important role in quality service delivery. Although quality customer service is one of the greatest keys to long-term business success, excellence in service delivery is rare because organisations fail to reward workers for giving excellent service (LeBoeuf, 1987). In a competitive business environment, organisations that enjoy long-term prosperity are those that consistently pay attention to customer service by reexamining and improving those factors that are critical for improved customer service experience. This chapter, therefore, focuses on examining how reward systems affect customer service delivery among small and medium-scale enterprises (SMEs) in Lagos State, Nigeria.

SMEs play important roles in the development of national economies, especially in the developing nations and effort to examine what goes on therein is necessary. One of the major challenges faced by SMEs that goes unnoticed is that of service delivery. Despite the efforts being made at unravelling the factors working against good customer service delivery and the measures put in place by organisations to improve customer service experiences, the challenge of service failures still persists among SMEs. Many customers go through harrowing experiences in the course of getting served as a result of the actions of customer service personnel in the workplace. It is observed that some of the employees in this sector are paid wages that are far below the national minimum wage benchmark. It is, however, unclear whether there is a linkage between the service delivery experiences among SMEs and the reward system in that sector.

Reward systems could be argued to be at the heart of employee performance. This assertion as noted by Ejumudo (2011) is premised on the understanding that reward systems have the potency of engendering higher levels of performance in organisations through the stimulation and direction of employees along the path of goal accomplishment. If managers understand the preferred rewards by employees, it will bring about better up-to-date and personalised reward strategies that will, in turn, lead to enhanced commitment and performance. Hoole and Hotz (2016) argue that reward packages are mostly offered by compensation managers as a one-size-fits-all solution to employees without much thought about which rewards are more effective for a particular organisation setting.

Abduljawad and Al-Assaf (2011) state that staff reward is becoming the norm in most successful organisations in the USA and worldwide. It is observed that a recognised employee is a loyal employee, and a loyal employee is a dedicated employee. This implies that dedicated employees will perform at a higher level and that when such dedication is not recognised, the employees involved may lose their enthusiasm. It is believed that a happy employee is one who not only innovates, but also competes with others to be among the best. A dedicated employee will impact positively on both his/her organisation and other stakeholders. Employee dedication is critical for sustainability and continued success of any organisation.

As stated above, scholars (Abduljawad and Al-Assaf, 2011; Nthebe et al., 2016) have contributed to the research on the relationship between reward and customer service delivery across countries and in different industries. In Nigeria, the studies on reward systems are focussed on schools and other large corporate organisations (Ejumudo, 2011; Osibanjo et al., 2014; Wasiu & Adebajo, 2014). Despite the contributions of SMEs in the nation's economic development and the importance of the subject matter to organisational success, there is still a dearth of literature and studies that focus on the two critical areas of reward and customer service delivery among SMEs. It is on the strength of the identified gap in literature that informed this study to examine the nexus between the reward system and customer service delivery among SMEs in Lagos State, Nigeria. Although the study was conducted in Lagos State, Nigeria, its findings would be relevant to other African nations, as most of the developing nations are dominated by SMEs.

The aim of this chapter is to examine the relationship between reward systems and customer service delivery among SMEs in Lagos State, Nigeria.

The specific objectives of the chapter are as follows:

1. To establish the relationship between opportunities for learning and development and provision of good customer service
2. To examine the correlation between appreciation of employees and the quality of customer service rendered
3. To establish whether or not rewarding employees with promotion or advancement at work relates to employees' quality of service
4. To determine if payment of bonuses or incentives to customer service employees has a relationship with good customer service

The following hypotheses are formulated from the above objectives:

Ho1: There is no significant relationship between opportunities for learning and development and provision of good customer service.

Ho2: There is no significant correlation between appreciation of employees and the quality of customer service rendered.

Ho3: Rewarding employees with promotion or advancement at work does not significantly relate to employees' quality of service.

Ho4: Payment of bonus or incentives to customer service employees does not have a significant relationship with good customer service.

The remaining parts of this chapter would be presented under the following sections with their relevant subsections: conceptual and theoretical review of literature, research methodology, results and interpretation and conclusion.

Conceptual and Theoretical Review of Literature

This section focuses on the review of the existing literature on the subject matter of this chapter and in line with the research objectives. The review is presented in four main headings: the concept of rewards, an overview of service quality, rewards and service delivery and theoretical framework.

The Concept of Rewards

One of the important elements required by organisations to manage innovation is the reward system. It is necessary for organisations to reward performers for their contributions, those that collaborate in teams and also individuals that excel beyond expectations. Employees can be rewarded in different ways. For example, a profit-sharing programme allows employees to be rewarded for improving the organisations' earnings and profitability. Reward practice is made up of different recognition programmes that are both intrinsic and extrinsic. Organisations that intend to achieve high levels of performance and remain competitive usually relate short- and long-term bonus awards to the level of performance achieved.

Total rewards are described as the sum of the values of each element of an employee's reward package and may include everything that employees view as important and of value within their jobs (Bussin & Van Rooy, 2014; Fernandes, 1998; Nienaber, 2010; WorldatWork, 2006). As noted by Reilly and Brown (2008), total rewards is viewed in terms of the value proposition an organisation has to offer to the employees, and this includes direct and indirect financial rewards, positive features of the work, opportunities for career advancement in the organisation, social activities that are encouraged in the workplace and a range of other amenities and services provided by the employer.

Ohene-Danso (2015) opines that rewards play a key role in providing an incentive for employees to work hard. The view that employees recognise that rewards play such an important role agrees with the position of Metzer (2001) who asserts that a reward is an incentive that influences the repeat of positive behaviour or serves as an incentive for a repeat of that behaviour because the outcome has been pleasing. The study by Ohene-Danso (2015) reveals that most of the employees whose efforts are recognised are encouraged to work harder. However, it should be cautioned that the successful implementation of a reward strategy may not necessarily lead to enhanced performance on the job because aside from rewards, there are several other factors that influence an individual's performance.

Neckermann and Kosfeld (2008) identified two basic types of rewards. These are intrinsic and extrinsic rewards. Intrinsic rewards, also referred to as non-financial rewards, are inbuilt in an activity and the administration is not reliant on the presence or actions of any other person or thing. Intrinsic reward is about the feeling of being recognised and praised for a job well done and participation in whatever someone does. Extrinsic rewards do not follow naturally or inherently from the performance of activity but are administered to a person by some external agents. Extrinsic rewards are motivations normally in the form of money, retirement benefits, health insurance, compensation, salary or a bonus, amongst others.

In a similar vein, Armstrong (2012a) asserts that reward recognises an employee's contributions. Total rewards, according to Armstrong (2012a), refer to a combination of financial and non-financial rewards paid to employees. Financial rewards consist of job-based pay and person-based pay; while job-based pay relates to the value of the job, person-based pay provides rewards that recognise the individual's contribution, competence or skill. On the other hand, non-financial rewards include extrinsic rewards such as recognition and praise, opportunities for the development of new skills and intrinsic rewards that are received from the work itself. Non-financial rewards, unlike financial reward, do not involve payment of salaries, wages or cash (Armstrong, 2012a).

As noted by Fajana (2002), reward can be classified into three components: basic/base pay, benefits and incentives. Basic/base pay represents the fixed part of employees' remuneration that is directly attached to grade levels. Employees receive this based on availability, qualification and experience. Benefits, on the other hand, are viewed as indirect rewards, and they are what an employee gets for being a member of an organisation. Such benefits include medical allowances, leave bonus, study leave pay and subscriptions for recreational facilities and professional bodies, among others. Incentives vary in relation to the performance of the employees. The essence of incentives or variable pay is to encourage employees to perform above normal expectations. Incentives include bonuses, commissions and profits sharing, etc.

Reward systems, according to Armstrong (2010), consist of an organisation's integrated policies, processes, procedures and practices for rewarding its employees in accordance with their contribution, skill and competencies and their worth. The reward system is developed within the framework of the organisation's reward philosophy, strategies and policies and consists of policies, processes, practices, structures and procedures that may offer and sustain suitable types and levels of pay, benefits and other forms of reward. The reward systems as explained include the following components of reward philosophy: Policies that give guidelines on ways of managing rewards; Practices that offer financial and non-financial rewards; Processes that are concerned with evaluating the relative worth of jobs and assessing the individual performance (performance management); and Procedures operated in order to maintain the systems and to ensure that it operates efficiently and flexibly and provides value for money.

What these explanations by Armstrong (2010) reveal is that managers should make a conscious effort not to reward employees based on the managers' own discretion but rather a guideline should be set and followed in rewarding employees. The guideline should state clearly a defined size of an employee's job and standard for assessing the employee's performance on the job. More so, the reward system should equally contain established methods used to regulate the reward system such that the reward system can be easily adjusted according to changes in both the external and internal environment.

An Overview of Service Quality

Quality of service could be described as an attitude towards the available service that emanates when one's expectations are compared with perceptions (Cüliberg & Rosjek, 2010). According to the five-factor SERVQUAL Model of Parasuraman et al. (1988), service quality is made up of five dimensions: assurance, empathy, reliability, responsiveness and tangibility (Sharabi, 2013). Assurance is the knowledge and courtesy of employees and the employees' abilities to express trust and confidence. Empathy expresses how employees in an organisation care and give personalised attention to the customers, such that the customers feel valued and important. Reliability means the ability of an organisation to render the promised service unfailingly and accurately.

Responsiveness is the willingness of employees to assist customers and to render prompt service. Tangibility means the appearance of physical facilities, equipment, personnel and communication materials.

Liao and Chuang (2007) assert that good organisational leaders articulate a compelling and insightful vision for their organisation's customer service so that they inspire optimism and enthusiasm for winning their customers' loyalty in a continuous manner. It is equally important to state that good leaders serve as charismatic role models in service delivery for their employees in such a way that such leaders encourage new ways of serving customers (Liao & Chuang, 2007). Hui et al. (2007) point out that good managers can develop their service delivery by persuading and inspiring their employees through setting the objective, granting the employees the authorisation to take independent decisions, giving them rewards for achieving the objectives and making the service process thrive. It could be assumed from the study of Davis and Gautam (2011) that rewards form a part of the motivation, helping to bring changes by developing service employees, and indirectly affecting service giving behaviours (orientation), effort and competency.

Rewards and Service Delivery

According to Hazra et al. (2018), the commitment of employees to an organisation is related to rewards and recognition. In the opinion of Lawler (2003), the prosperity and survival of organisations are determined by how the organisation's human resources are treated. Most organisations previously studied have shown to have made significant progress by implementing a well-balanced reward and recognition programme for employees. While recognition is about saying 'thank you', reward is about pay and compensation.

According to Armstrong (2012a), reward makes a positive impact on performance when it contributes to the development of a high-performance culture. This signifies that if customer-interfacing employees are rewarded well, their performance will increase, and they will provide a high-quality service. According to Sigh (2007), incentives encourage employees to give their best efforts so that the average productivity level of workers increases. Reward systems motivate employees to do their best in performing assigned tasks (Gohari et al., 2013).

Nacinovic et al. (2009) state that organisations that aim at developing a corporate culture that will support and foster innovation should be supported with reward systems that are appropriate. This is because it is the reward system that defines who gets rewarded and why and that acts as a statement of an organisation's values, beliefs and norms. The study by Wasiu and Adebajo (2014) used data collected from selected secondary schools to establish a connection between employee reward system and job performance. The findings showed that there is a significant correlation between employees' performance and salary package, employee job allowances and in-service learning.

Bailey (2004) states that when employees are 'caught' doing something right (at exceptional levels), it is important for supervisors or managers to provide immediate recognition. It is necessary to reward the behaviour that is expected to be repeated and to note that if the reward is immediate, the benefits that would be realised might be even more significant. It is argued by Bailey (2004) that forms of rewards for immediate recognition do not have to be expensive or complex to administer. For example, shopping raffles or gift certificates to popular event centres or shopping malls are examples of rewards that are both immediate and simple to implement.

Yussuf et al. (2018) in their study in Wajir County, Kenya, found that fair systems for all employees and adequacy of the compensation/reward scheme affect service delivery to a great extent. The implication of this finding is that reward systems have a significant effect on service delivery. Similarly, Bernardin and Russell (1993) have also established that rewards and compensation has a way of motivating employees into overall performance to work. This means that providing employees with rewards that are commensurate with their work efforts enables them to function more efficiently (Yussuf et al., 2018).

Theoretical Framework

Expectancy theory propounded by Victor Vroom (1964) explained that motivation to perform may increase if employees are aware of what they have to do to get a reward, that they will be able to get the reward, and expect that the reward will be worthwhile. In other words, expectancy theory describes how individual's motivation to achieve a set performance target can be explained in terms of the outcomes that would be beneficial to the employee as a result of achieving that goal and the value placed on that outcome. Banjoko (2002) stated that the tendency for an individual to perform is a function of the expectation that the performance of an action will be followed by a certain outcome, and the attraction of that outcome to the individual. This can be presented using the following equation:

$$A = f\left(E \times V\right)$$

where A = action or effort, E = expectation that certain actions would lead to the attainment of an outcome, and V = valence of the outcome.

Expectancy theory is relevant to this chapter because it justifies why customer service employees will render high-quality service when there is a positive reward systems in the organisation.

Research Methodology

The unit of analysis for the study is SMEs in Lagos State, Nigeria. Lagos State, according to Ogunyomi (2014), has the highest number of SME enterprises in Nigeria. The study population comprised customer interfacing employees of SMEs in Lagos State. The survey research design was used for data collection and Bartlett et al. (2001). A sample size determination table was utilised to determine the 384-sample size for the study. Therefore, 384 copies of questionnaire were administered. Out of the copies of questionnaire returned, 221 (58% of total copies of the questionnaire distributed or 93% of the copies of the questionnaire returned) were found valid and therefore used for the analysis.

The instrument was designed using opinion and closed-ended statements. The study adopted the Likert 4-point scale that ranges from strongly agree (4) to strongly disagree (1) for opinion statements to gather information from respondents. The research instrument was subjected to face and content validity and reliability testing. For validity, the questionnaire was given to other experts for their review and comments. The Cronbach's Alpha reliability coefficient of the instrument was 0.79, which is considered satisfactory. Descriptive and inferential data analyses were carried out with the use of Statistical Package for the Social Sciences (SPSS) software version 20.

Frequency distributions showing absolute frequencies and relative frequencies, or percentages were adopted. Pearson's Product Moment Correlation was used to further analyse and test the formulated hypotheses.

Results and Interpretation

Respondents' Views on Reward and Recognitions

While 46.2% of the respondents disagree or strongly disagree with the statement that they are rewarded fairly for the amount of work they do, others are of the opinion that they are fairly rewarded by their organisations. From Table A18.1 (see Appendix), it is observed that 55.7% of respondents are of the opinion that they receive adequate praise for the quality of customer service they render while 44.3% hold a contrary opinion on the statement. It is noted that 75.6% of the respondents hold the view that employees are demotivated by lack of praise for good service rendered, while 24.4% of the respondents disagree and strongly disagree with the statement. It is observed that 89.1% of the respondents support the statement that the praise employees receive for good customer service makes them feel valued. It is the opinion of 77.8% of the respondents that customer service employees rewarded with opportunities for learning and development will provide good quality service. Also, all the respondents hold the opinion that customer service employees will provide better quality service if their efforts are appreciated.

Furthermore, only 13.6% of the respondents disagreed or strongly disagreed with the statement that employees will render quality service if they are rewarded with promotion or advancement at work. On whether the system of reward by their organisation motivates them, 59.3% of the respondents either disagree or strongly disagree with the statement. A total of 68.8% of the respondents disagreed or strongly disagreed with the statement that the salaries they are paid by their employers are linked to their quality service delivery. Out of the 221 sampled respondents, 64.2% of them either agreed or strongly agreed that the praise they receive in their organisations is meaningful to them. Only 48% of the respondents either disagreed or strongly disagreed with the statement that the respondents are not encouraged to pursue company objectives by the existing reward system. Approximately 52.5% of the respondents either strongly disagree or disagree that their respective organisations give incentives such as bonuses to employees to improve their quality service delivery.

Equally, 68.3% of the respondents are not in agreement that their organisational reward system is fair at rewarding people who accomplish their company's objectives. In the same vein, 50.7% do not agree or strongly agree that their reward system recognises the people that contribute the most to their organisation. On whether employees will provide better quality service if additional benefits are given to them by their organisation, 76.5% of the respondents either agree or strongly agree to the statement. It is observed from Table A18.1 (see Appendix) that 53.4% of the respondents either agreed or strongly agreed that the existing reward system does not encourage them to focus on providing good services to their customers. A total of 83.7% of the respondents either agreed or strongly agreed with the statement that rewarding customers service employees with bonuses or other incentives would affect their quality of service delivery.

Respondents' Views on Customer Service

It is the opinion of 91.8% of the respondents that employees would deliver quality service if they are adequately rewarded, while 62.9% of the respondents support the statement that the expected levels of customer service are clearly stated in their organisations, and 37.1% of the respondents have a contrary opinion to the statement. The majority of the respondents (84.1%) indicated that they understand how to deliver effective customer service. Additionally, 96% of the respondents support the statement that good customer service is important for the growth of their organisations, and 87.7% of the respondents stated that the nature of their job makes them constantly relate with the customers.

Test of Hypotheses

- Ho1: There is no significant relationship between opportunities for learning and development and provision of good customer service.
- Ho2: There is no significant correlation between appreciation of employees and the quality of customer service rendered.
- Ho3: Rewarding employees with promotion or advancement at work does not significantly relate with employees' quality of service.
- Ho4: Payment of bonuses and incentives to customer service employees does not have a significant relationship with good customer service.

The Pearson's Product Moment correlation coefficient result shows that the correlation between opportunities for learning and development and provision of good customer service is positively and statistically significant ($r = 0.201$, $n = 221$, $p < 0.003$). Therefore, the hypothesis that there is no significant relationship between opportunities for learning and development and provision of good customer service was not accepted. This supports the views of Demerouti et al. (2014) that employees who are compensated in terms of career development opportunities are able to perform better on the job.

Also, the Pearson's Product Moment correlation coefficient result shows that the correlation between appreciation of employees and the quality of customer service rendered is positively and statistically significant ($r = 0.437$, $n = 221$, $p < 0.05$). Therefore, the hypothesis that there is no significant correlation between appreciation of employees and the quality of customer service rendered is equally not accepted. This finding is in agreement with Bailey (2004) that when employees are 'caught' doing something right, it is important for them to be provided with immediate recognition. Recognition in the form of appreciation may not be expensive or difficult to implement. For example, a 'thank you' note or public verbal praise or commendation is an acceptable form of appreciation that is effective and still not complex to administer.

In the same vein, the Pearson's Product Moment correlation coefficient result shows that the correlation between rewarding employees with promotion or advancement at work and employees' quality of service delivery is positively and statistically significant ($r = 0.218$, $n = 221$, $p < 0.05$). Therefore, the hypothesis that rewarding employees with promotion or advancement at work does not significantly relate with employees' quality of service is not accepted. This is in line with the views of Sigh (2007) that giving incentives motivates employees to put forth their best efforts and increases the average productivity level of such employees.

The Pearson's Product Moment correlation coefficient result shows that the correlation between payment of bonuses or incentives to customer service employees and good customer service delivery is positively and statistically significant ($r = 0.420$, $n = 221$, $p < 0.05$). Therefore, the hypothesis that the payment of bonuses and incentives to customer service employees does not have a significant relationship with good customer service delivery is not accepted. This result agrees with findings from several studies (Ashraf et al., 2014; Osibanjo et al., 2014) that have established that both financial and non-financial rewards have a strong relationship with job performance. The overall implication of these findings is that reward and recognition have a significant relationship with customer service delivery among SMEs in Lagos State, Nigeria.

Although Yussuf et al. (2018) in their study found that fair systems of reward and adequacy of the compensation/reward scheme affect service delivery to a great extent, from the results of the survey, it is doubtful if the sampled SMEs in Lagos State, Nigeria, have a fair reward system. For example, the response from Table A18.1 (see Appendix) shows that 53.4% of the respondents were of the opinion that the existing reward system does not encourage them to focus on providing good services to their customers, while 68.3% of the respondents were not in agreement that their organisational reward system is fair at rewarding people who accomplish their company's objectives. Also, the majority (52%) of the respondents hold the view that employees are not encouraged to pursue company objectives by the existing reward system.

Conclusion

This chapter examined the relationship between reward systems and the quality of customer service delivery in selected SMEs. The information provided in the chapter was based on a survey research design, and the data gathered from the respondents were analysed using descriptive and inferential statistics.

The reward systems and customer service delivery are two elements that SME owners should focus on to achieve the organisation's goals and objectives. One of the long-term driving factors of success in organisations or what distinguishes one organisation from the other is the quality of customer service delivery. A major outcome of the study survey is that most respondents have the opinion that SMEs do not have a fair reward system that can motivate the employees to provide quality service to their customers.

It is observed that customer service employees of SMEs will provide good customer service if they, among other things, are rewarded with opportunities for learning and development, have opportunities for promotions and are rewarded with bonuses and other incentives by the management. Based on the findings, it is recommended that for employees to provide quality service, which is a necessary ingredient for organisational performance, managers of SMEs in Nigeria and other African countries should endeavour to take a closer look at their organisations' reward systems with a view to improving on them by making them fair and equitable in terms of job inputs and outcomes. Managers of SMEs should create harmony between the organisational goal of providing excellent services and products and the reward systems adopted. Managers of SMEs in Africa should also reduce their focus on external factors (poor infrastructures, poor access to funding, harsh government policies, etc.) that hinder their performance and look inward on how to improve the performance of their organisations through better reward systems and quality service delivery, among other internal factors.

References

Abduljawad, A., & Al-Assaf, A. F. (2011). Incentives for better performance in health care. *Sultan Qaboos University Medical Journal, 11*(2), 201–206.

Armstrong, M. (2006). *Handbook of human resource management practice* (8th ed.). London, UK: KoganPage Limited.

Armstrong, M. (2010). *A handbook of human resource management practice*. London, UK: Kogan Page Limited.

Armstrong, M. (2012a). *Armstrong's handbook of human resource management practice* (12th ed.). London, UK: Kogan Page Limited.

Armstrong, M. (2012b). *Armstrong's handbook of reward management practice: Improving performance through reward* (4th ed.). London, UK: Kogan Page Limited.

Ashraf, N., Bandiera, O., & Jack, B. K. (2014). No margin, no mission? A field experiment on incentives for the public service industry. *Journal of Public Economics, 120*, 1–17. http://dx.doi.org/10.1016/j.jpubeco.2014.06.014

Bailey, C. (2004). Rewarding and incenting customer service representatives: A guide to help you keep your customer service teams happy and providing consistently high quality service. [White Paper]. Retrieved from Customer Centricity, Inc, www.customercentricity.biz

Banjoko, S. A. (2002). *Human resource management: An expository approach* (Republished ed.). Lagos, Nigeria: Pumark Nigeria Limited.

Bartlett, II, J. E., Kotrlik, J. W., & Higgins, C. C. (2001). Organisational research: Determining appropriate sample size in survey research. *Information Technology, Learning, and Performance Journal, 19*(1), 43–50.

Bernardin, H. J, & Russell, J. E. A. (1993). *Human resource management: An experiential approach*. New York: McGraw-Hill.

Bussin, M., & Van Rooy, D. J. (2014). Total rewards strategy for a multigenerational workforce in a financial institution. *South Asian Journal of Human Resource Management, 12*(1), 1–11. http://dx.doi.org/10.4102/sajhrm.v12i1.606.

Chepkwony, C. C. (2014). The relationship between rewards systems and job satisfaction: A case study at teachers' service commission-Kenya. *European Journal of Business and Social Sciences, 3*(1), 59–70.

Cüliberg, B., & Rosjek, I. (2010). Identifying service quality dimensions as antecedents to customer satisfaction in retail banking. *Economic & Business Review, 12*(3), 151–166.

Davis, R., & Gautam, N. (2011). *Conceptualising service culture. Leading applied business*. Retrieved 11 July 2012 from http://thedomm.com/2011/05/03/conceptualising service-culture-by-robert-davis-and-neil-gautam-2011

Demerouti, E., Bakker, A. B., & Leiter, M. (2014). Burnout and job performance: The moderating role of selection, optimisation, and compensation strategies. *Journal of Occupational Health Psychology, 19*(1), 96–107. http://dx.doi.org/10.1037/ a0035062

Ejumudo, K. B. O. (2011). Performance appraisal in the Delta State civil service. *Journal of Management, 5*(2), 21–28.

Fajana, S. (2002). *Human resources management: An introduction*. Lagos, Nigeria: Labofin and Company.

Fernandes, F. N. (1998). Total reward-an actuarial perspective. *Actuarial Research Paper, 116*, 23–45. Retrieved from http://www.cass.city.ac.uk/research-and-faculty/faculties/faculty-of-actuarial-science-and-insurance/publications

Gohari, P., Kamkar, A., Hosseinipour, S. J., & Zohori, M. (2013). Relationship between rewards and employee performance: A mediating role of job satisfaction. *Interdisciplinary Journal of Contemporary Research in Business, 5*(3), 571–597.

Hazra, K., Sengupta, P. P., & Biswakarma, S. K. (2018). Compensation: Policies & practices and its impact on employee commitment in the hospitality industry. *International Journal of Humanities and Social Science Invention (IJHSSI), 7*(4): 42–53.

Hoole, C., & Hotz, G. (2016). The impact of a total reward system of work engagement. *SA Journal of Industrial Psychology, 42*(1). http://dx.doi.org/10.4102/sajip.v42i1.1317

Hui, H., Chiu, W., Yu, P., Cheng, K., & Tse, H. (2007). The effects of service climate and the effective leadership behaviour of supervisors on frontline employee service quality: A multi-level analysis. *Journal of Occupational and Organisational Psychology, 80*(1), 151–172.

Lawler, E. E. (2003). Reward practices and performance management system effectiveness. *Organizational Dynamics, 32*(4): 396–404.

LeBoeuf, M. (1987). *How to win customers and keep them for life.* New York: The Berkley Publishing Group.

Liao, H., & Chuang, A. (2007). Examination of transformational leadership in building long term service relationships. *Journal of Applied Psychology, 92*(4), 1006–1019.

Metzer, R. L. (2001). *Reward systems in organizations.* Evanston, IL: Prentice-Hall Inc.

Nacinovic, I., Galetic, L., & Cavlek, N. (2009). Corporate culture and innovation: Implications for reward systems. *World Academy of Science, Engineering and Technology International Journal of Economics and Management Engineering, 3*(5), 376–381.

Neckermann, S., & Kosfeld, M. (2008). *Working for nothing? The effective of non-material awards on employee performance.* Frankfurt: Goethe University Germany.

Nienaber, R. (2010). *The relationship between personality types and reward preferences.* (Doctorial Dissertation). Johannesburg: University of Johannesburg. http://dx.doi.org/10.4102/ac.v11i2.153

Nthebe, K., Barkhuizen, N., & Schutte, N. (2016). Rewards: A predictor of well-being and service quality of school principals in the North-West province. *South Asian Journal of Human Resource Management/ SA TydskrifvirMenslikehulpbronbestuur, 14*(1), a711. http://dx.doi. org/10.4102/sajhrm. v14i1.711

Ogunyomi, P. O. (2014). Human resource management and organisational performance of small and medium enterprises in Lagos State, Nigeria. (Unpublished doctoral thesis). Lagos, Nigeria: University of Lagos.

Ohene-Danso, J. (2015). Reward systems and performance of sales: A descriptive study among the Ghanaian insurance industry. *Journal of Advocacy, Research and Education, 2*(1), 36–45.

Osibanjo, O. A., Adeniji, A. A., Falola, H., & Heirsmac, P. T. (2014). Compensation packages: A strategic tool for employee's performance and retention. *Leonardo Journal of Social Sciences,13*(25), 65–84.

Parasuraman, A., Zeithaml, V. A., & Berry, L. L. (1988). SERVQUAL: A multi-item scale for measuring customer perceptions of service quality. *Journal of Retailing, 64*(1), 12–42.

Reilly, P., & Brown, D. (2008). Employee engagement: What is the relationship with reward management? *WorldatWork Journal, 17*(4), 37–49.

Sharabi, M. (2013). Managing and improving service quality in higher education. *International Journal of Quality and Service Sciences, 5*(3), 309–320. http://dx.doi. org/10.1108/IJQSS-03-2013-0016

Sigh, B. D. (2007). *Compensation and reward management.* New Delhi: Excel Books.

Vroom, V. (1964). *Work and motivation.* New York: Wiley.

Wasiu, B. O., & Adebajo, A. A. (2014). Reward system and employees performance in Lagos State (A study of selected public secondary schools). *Kuwait Chapter of Arabian Journal of Business and Management Review, 3*(8), 14–28.

WorldatWork. (2006). *Total rewards model. Strategies to attract, motivate and retain employees.* Scottsdale: WorldatWork. Retrieved from http://WorldatWork.org/pub/total_rewards_model.pdf

Yussuf, S. K., Bichanga, J., & Mwencha, P. M. (2018). Effect of learning and reward system on service delivery in devolved governments in Kenya: A case of Wajir County, *European Journal of Business and Strategic Management, 3*(4), 1–14.

Appendix

Table A18.1 Respondents' Views on Reward and Recognition

Views on Reward and Recognition	Strongly Agree		Agree		Disagree		Strongly Disagree		N
	Frequency	%	Frequency	%	Frequency	%	Frequency	%	Total
I am rewarded fairly for the amount of work I do	18	8.1	101	45.7	79	35.7	23	10.4	221
I receive adequate praise for the quality of customer service I render	24	10.9	99	44.8	74	33.5	24	10.9	221
Employees are demotivated by lack of praise for good service	89	40.3	78	35.3	31	14.0	23	10.4	221
The praise I receive for good customer service makes me feel valued	75	33.9	122	55.2	9	4.1	15	6.8	221
Customer service employees rewarded with opportunities for learning and development will provide good quality service	72	32.6	100	45.2	30	13.6	19	8.6	221
Customer service employees will provide better quality service if their efforts are appreciated	157	71	64	29	0	0	0	0	221
Employees will render quality service if they are rewarded with promotion or advancement at work	106	48	85	38.5	25	11.3	5	2.3	221
The system of reward by my organisation motivates me	25	11.3	65	29.4	84	38	47	21.3	221
The salary I am paid is linked to my quality of service delivery	3	1.4	66	29.9	103	46.6	49	22.2	221
The praise I receive here is meaningful to me	33	14.9	109	49.3	54	24.4	25	11.3	221

(Continued)

Table A18.1 (*Continued*) Respondents' Views on Reward and Recognition

Views on Reward and Recognition	Strongly Agree		Agree		Disagree		Strongly Disagree		N
	Frequency	%	Frequency	%	Frequency	%	Frequency	%	Total
My organisation gives incentives (such as bonuses) to employees to improve their quality of service delivery	17	7.7	88	39.8	63	28.5	53	24	221
I am not encouraged to pursue company objectives by the existing reward system	28	12.7	87	39.4	88	39.8	18	8.1	221
The reward system in my organisation is fair at rewarding people who accomplish the company's objectives	7	3.2	63	28.5	107	48.4	44	19.9	221
Our reward system recognises the people who contribute the most to our company	36	16.3	73	33	67	30.3	45	20.4	221
I will provide better quality service if additional benefits are given to me by my organisation	88	39.8	81	36.7	35	15.8	17	7.7	221
The existing reward system does not encourage me to focus on providing good service to customers	25	11.3	93	42.1	87	39.4	16	7.2	221
Rewarding customer service employees with bonus incentives will affect their quality of service delivery	82	37.1	103	46.6	33	14.9	3	1.4	221

Source: Survey 2018.

Frequency = Frequency; % = Percent

Table A18.2 Respondents' Views on Customer Service

Views on Customer Service	Strongly Agree		Agree		Disagree		Strongly Disagree		N
	Frequency	%	Frequency	%	Frequency	%	Frequency	%	Total
Employees would deliver quality service if they are adequately rewarded	126	57	77	34.8	15	6.8	3	1.4	221
The levels of customer service expected here are clearly stated	18	8.1	121	54.8	63	28.5	19	8.6	221
I understand how to deliver effective customer service	69	31.2	139	62.9	10	4.5	3	1.4	221
Good customer service is important for the growth of this organisation	127	57.5	85	38.5	9	4.1	0	0	221
The nature of my job makes me relate constantly with the customers	77	34.8	117	52.9	17	7.7	10	4.5	221

Source: Survey 2018.

Table A18.3   Correlations Matrix

		Opportunities for Learning and Development	Appreciation of Employees	Promotion or Advancement	Bonus, Incentives to Employees	Good Customer Service
Opportunities for learning and development	Pearson Correlation	1	0.124	0.581[a]	0.208[a]	0.201[a]
	Sig. (2-tailed)		0.066	0.000	0.002	0.003
Appreciation of employees	Pearson Correlation	0.124	1	0.125	0.319[a]	0.437[a]
	Sig. (2-tailed)	0.066		0.063	0.000	0.000
Promotion or advancement	Pearson Correlation	0.581[a]	0.125	1	0.058	0.218[a]
	Sig. (2-tailed)	0.000	0.063		0.389	0.001
Bonus, incentives to employees	Pearson Correlation	0.208[a]	0.319[a]	0.058	1	0.420[a]
	Sig. (2-tailed)	0.002	0.000	0.389		0.000
Good customer service	Pearson Correlation	0.201[a]	0.437[a]	0.218[a]	0.420[a]	1
	Sig. (2-tailed)	0.003	0.000	0.001	0.000	
	N	221	221	221	221	221

[a] Correlation is significant at the 0.01 level (2-tailed).

THEME F: CUSTOMER SERVICE SKILLS

Chapter 19

Emotional Intelligence

Yvonne Ayerki Lamptey and Kenneth E. Parku

Contents

Introduction

The first formal mention of emotional intelligence (EI) appeared in the German article 'Emotional Intelligence and Emancipation' (Leuner, 1966). Subsequently, the term 'emotional intelligence' appeared in English literature, which was in an unpublished doctoral dissertation by Payne in 1986 (Matthews et al., 2002). Since then, EI has captured the interest of both the popular press and scientific researchers (Mayer et al., 2000; Lynn, 2004).

Emotions are involved in everything people do including their actions, decisions and judgements. Individuals who are emotionally intelligent use their thinking to manage their emotions rather than being managed by them. The concept of emotional intelligence (EI) has become a very important indicator of a person's knowledge, skills and abilities in the workplace, school and personal life in the last two decades. According to Mayer et al. (2004), EI is the ability to perceive, generate, access and understand emotions and to reflectively regulate emotions in ways that promote emotional and intellectual growth. Similarly, Bellack (1999) explains EI as the ability to acquire and apply knowledge from one's emotions and the emotions of others.

Research suggests that EI plays a significant role in job performance, motivation, decision-making, successful management and the leadership of organisations. A relationship has therefore been established between EI and customer service management in view of high performance and profitability of organisations (Gignac et al., 2012). It is not surprising that people prefer to be around individuals who make them feel better, and this is especially true when it comes to customers. They are constantly looking for services or product providers that give them satisfaction. Customers are particularly sensitive to hostile behaviours from organisations and would not hesitate in changing their perception of a business. This situation can be linked to employees whose duties are to provide quality service to customers. Most often, instances of dissatisfaction of customers arise from a worker who lacks the emotional awareness and interpersonal skills needed for a position that places them in direct contact with customers. Thus, there is the need for employees to be educated on EI and how that can improve their customer service. For instance, coming into contact with angry customers can be a real test of EI (Cherniss & Adler, 2000). Nonetheless, it forms an integral part of dealings between the worker and the client, and it can determine if the customer will decide to repurchase the organisation's products or services. Therefore, managing emotions of customers in an organisation is a vital part of customer service, which can either make or break the organisation.

Providing EI training to employees would be valuable in assisting customer service representatives to cope with the stress of emotional labour and feel relaxed. A relaxed employee, in turn, will be in the best position to build a positive emotional state in themselves and in the customers that they interact with. They may even be in a better frame of mind to build a positive connection with customers (Brackett et al., 2011). This chapter will aid in establishing a positive relationship between EI and customer service.

The subsequent sections of this chapter will provide an in-depth discussion on the evolution of EI, theories underpinning EI, and the components of EI. It will also focus on establishing the relationship between EI and customer service, and the implication of EI and customer service in organisations.

The Evolution of Emotional Intelligence

The roots of EI are traced to Darwin's earlier works on the importance of emotional expression for survival. In the 1900s, traditional definitions of intelligence emphasised cognitive aspects, such as memory and problem-solving, with the awareness of the non-cognitive aspects only gaining importance in later years. When psychologists began to think and write about intelligence, they focussed on cognitive aspects such as memory and problem-solving. However, there were researchers who understood that the non-cognitive aspects were also important in intelligence.

Though the field of EI is a fairly new one, the word itself was first coined and used in literary writing by Salovey and Mayer in 1990 (Bellack, 1999). The concept has become immensely popular, providing evidence that success is not determined by cognitive intellect alone (Goleman, 2003). Some of the forerunners in the research on EI outline various characteristics which determine a person's EI intelligence. While Mayer et al. (2008) consider EI as a purely cognitive ability, Goleman (2002) and Reuven Bar-On (2010) view it as a personality trait. Mayer and Saloveys' four-branch model of EI lays emphasis on emotional perception, emotional assimilation, understanding and management (Mayer et al., 2004) as the features of EI. Whereas Bar-On (2002) agrees that the qualities of emotional self-awareness, self-actualisation, interpersonal relationship, reality testing, stress tolerance, optimism, happiness, etc. are the factors that determine a person's EI. Similarly, Goleman (2003) mentions emotional self-awareness, self-control, empathy, problem solving, conflict management, leadership, etc. as the characteristics of an emotionally intelligent person. Again, the mixed ability model proposed by Reuven Bar-On emphasises how personality traits influence a person's general well-being, and Goleman's model focuses on the individual's workplace success (Stys & Brown, 2004).

Mayer et al. (2004) believe emotions and reasoning sometimes have been viewed in opposition to one another. The belief was that emotions were chaotic and dangerous to logical thought, and it may get in the way of rational decision-making. Researchers like Mayer et al. (2008), as well as Goleman (2003), provided views on how EI rose from a large body of literature to be a field of research on its own. Goleman argues that an emotion may be crucial to the survival of several factors whether in a social, biological or psychological context. Additionally, Mayer et al. (2004) suggest that emotions signal relationships between a person and a friend, a family, a situation or a society and internal relationship between a person and his or her memory.

Theories and Models of Emotional Intelligence

During the last two decades, EI researchers have developed three major models which include ability, mixed and trait EI models. Ability models regard EI as a pure form of mental ability. In contrast, mixed models of EI combine mental ability with personality characteristics such as optimism and well-being, while trait models of EI refer to an individual's self-perception of their emotional abilities.

An Ability Model of Emotional Intelligence was developed by John Mayer and Peter Salovey in 1990, and they have continued to conduct research on the significance of the construct. The theory of EI integrates key ideas from the fields of intelligence and emotion. It is emphasised that EI is based on a model of intelligence. It proposes that EI comprises two areas. The first area is experiential EI, which is the ability to perceive, respond and manipulate emotional information without necessarily understanding it. The second area is the strategic EI, which is the ability to understand and manage emotions without necessarily perceiving feelings well or fully experiencing them (Mayer et al., 2004). This model is further categorised into four branches. The first branch of emotional perception is the ability to be self-aware of emotions and to express emotional needs accurately to others. Emotional assimilation, which is the second branch, has the ability to distinguish among the different emotions such as feelings which identify those that are influencing their thought processes. The third branch, which is emotional understanding, refers to the ability to understand complex emotions. Lastly, emotion management, which is the fourth branch, has the ability to connect or disconnect from an emotion depending on its usefulness in a given situation (Mayer et al., 2008).

A Mixed Model of Emotional Intelligence by Reuven Bar-On (2006) developed the first measuring tool of EI that was used under the term 'emotional quotient'. Bar-On's model of EI relates to the potential for performance and success, rather than performance or success itself and is considered as process-oriented rather than outcome-oriented (Bar-On, 2010). In this model, five components of EI are outlined: intrapersonal, interpersonal, adaptability, stress management and general mood. Till date, most descriptions, definitions and conceptualisations of emotional-social intelligence have included one or more of the following key components, all of which are included in Bar-On's conceptual model. The components include the ability to understand emotions as well as express our feelings and ourselves, the ability to understand others' feelings and relate with people, the ability to manage and control our emotions, the ability to manage change and solve problems of an intrapersonal and interpersonal nature, and the ability to generate positive mood and be self-motivated Caruso et al. (2004).

The Trait EI model proposed a conceptual distinction between the ability-based model and a trait-based model of EI. The Trait EI model refers to an individual's self-perceptions of his emotional abilities. The Trait EI should be investigated within a personality framework. An alternative name for the same construct is trait emotional self-efficacy (Mayer et al., 2000).

Components of Emotional Intelligence

Emotional self-awareness, the first component of EI, emphasises the understanding of an individual's feelings. Patients with brain disorders that disconnect the amygdala from the prefrontal cortex, which are parts of the brain, are at a loss to give words to feelings, a hallmark of the disorder alexithymia (Bar-On, 2010). Self-awareness is the lead constituent of EI, which comprises having a thorough understanding of emotions, weaknesses, strengths, needs and drives of one's self. Individuals who possess a high degree of self-awareness are able to recognise their feelings and how these feelings affect them, other people, and their performance at work. Abraham (2007) also explains self-awareness as a person's ability to understand his or her feelings, bearing in mind changes in feelings from time to time. Without self-awareness, individuals cannot fully understand their weaknesses and strengths. Mayer et al. (2004) are of the view that emotions contain information which helps to signal us about paramount events happening in our world, our social or internal world, or our natural environment. Therefore, emotions need to be incorporated into our reasoning in an intelligent way to solve problems, our behaviour and sense of judgment.

The second component of EI, emotional self-management, is the ability to regulate distressing effects like anxiety and anger and to prevent emotional impulsivity. Positron-emission tomography (PET) measurements of glucose metabolism reveal that individual differences in metabolic activity are associated with levels of distress, which means that the more the activity, the greater the negative effect (Mayer et al., 2008). In contrast, metabolic activity in the left medial prefrontal cortex is inversely related to levels of activity in the amygdala, an array of inhibitory neurons in the prefrontal area. In humans, the greater the activity level in the left medial prefrontal cortex, the more positive the person's emotional state. Thus, a major locus of the ability to regulate negative effect appears to be the circuit between the amygdala and the left prefrontal cortex. Similarly, according to Mayer et al. (2008), EI is about the regulation of emotion in oneself. Goleman's (1995) model referred to self-regulation as self-management. Bar-On's (2010) model referred to self-regulation as the ability to understand oneself.

When self-regulation is combined with motivation, it can help in conquering setbacks in managing emotions. Motivation is a common attribute that most successful employees possess. Cooper (1997) defined motivation in three aspects. The first definition states that motivation relates to the drive or the energy behind one's actions. People have the tendency to be guided in their interest to make a good impression on other individuals, working interesting jobs and achieving success in what they do. The second definition refers to the choices people make and route that their behaviour takes. The last part deals with sustaining behaviour in a clear manner and having a distinct definition of how long individuals persist in their attempt to achieve their goals. Motivated employees are driven by commitment, passion and the desire to succeed in whatever they do. Goleman (2003) claims that those with the potential for leadership are motivated by a deeply held desire to achieve just for the sake of achievement. Such employees are highly optimistic, energetic, willing to discover and learn fresh methodologies, keen to take calculated risks and creative tasks, proud about their accomplishments, and are indifferent to external rewards, such as status, salary and power.

Empathy plays a pronounced part in relationship management. It is that quality of an employee that can win the support and trust of others. Empathy makes employees comprehend other peoples' perceptions and views better, making the work atmosphere more pleasurable and industrious. Empathy ensures that links ensue between individuals so that one and all are involved, and no employee feels sidelined, and as such, an empathic employee becomes an effective employee (Cockerell, 2009). To Marques (2010), to attain leadership effectiveness, employees must improve on empathy since it enriches a sense of leadership by equipping employees with the consciousness to heed, collaborate and have better comprehension of interrelationships among individuals. Empathy has become more and more significant to success at work because empathic employees are more probable to have a suitable amount of openness about diversity and the variances between cultures. The empathic attribute also plays an imperative role in increasing trust in employee-to-employee interactions. Similarly, empathy helps employees to have an optimistic approach towards adjusting to new environments and developments which generate a concerted atmosphere. Empathy gives employees the skill to read and be conscious of people's emotions, thus, employees are able to complete dire leadership activities (Skinner & Spurgeon, 2005). In addition to empathy, social skill is necessary in the use of emotions.

Goleman (2003) refers to social skill as sociability with a purpose. Similarly, Riggio and Reichard (2008) explain that social skills characterise a wider range of competencies that are most strictly connected to the concept of social intelligence. Social skills that are crucial constituents of social intelligence comprise the capacity to express oneself in social collaborations; sense and understand diverse social circumstances; understand social roles, customs and scripts; social role-play; and solve interpersonal problems. Singh (2007) expounds that social skill is the capacity to capitalise on associations towards the ideals and philosophies an employee wants to encourage through dependence, likeability and respect. But just as the line hazes among self-regulation, motivation, empathy, self-awareness and social skills, if social skills were removed, the other four dimensions of EI may drop flat. Individuals with social skills can have a collaborative network when the time for action arises (Goleman, 2003) in a person's life and for work.

Emotional Intelligence and Customer Service

Studies have indicated that there is a link between EI and customer service. However, the big question is how can EI contribute to effective customer service? Emotions are a vital element of our minds, and this aids us to improve, inspires us to act, and in a case of danger, helps us elude the hazard and survive (Brackett et al., 2011).

The recognition of the positive impact of EI on customer service is an essential tool in making organisations gain a competitive advantage in keeping clients. Workers who use their natural talents in the execution of their jobs yield meaningful outcomes more than average workers. This is to say that, customers acknowledge the passion and commitment workers feel towards them and cannot help but respond in an emotional way. This emotionally driven reaction forms a bridge between workers and customers that develops into a cordial relationship beneficial to the organisation. Therefore, elements of EI in customer service should be a major concern for organisations

(Walter V. Clarke Associates, 1996). Today's customers do not only look out for the price and innovativeness of a product or service before purchasing it. These customers are highly influenced by their emotional experiences with a particular brand. Fine-tuning attention to customers' emotional needs is a precondition for accomplishing an effective customer service Cobb & Mayer (2000).

Customers' emotions are not a 'one-size-fits all' situation. Therefore, workers and management adopt measures that will aid in the maximisation of their EI. The most difficult phase of dealing with the emotions of customers, whether positive or negative, is the fact that emotions are intangible, multifaceted and difficult to notice (Gignac et al., 2012). Nevertheless, it can be addressed by broadly categorising emotions as positive and negative to guide how emotions should be addressed. Positive emotions include surprise, happiness and gratitude from customers. If your customers exhibit these attributes, it is important to react to them and take advantage of it. Positive interaction tends to have an enormous effect on customers, such as raising the probability of them purchasing more of your products and giving recommendations (Zeidner et al., 2004). Contrarily, negative emotions include anger, frustration and disappointment. Customers who exhibit these traits need to be handled with care. It is important for employees to be open minded, patient and empathetic with the customers. Improving customer service skills of workers will require equipping them with knowledge on how to improve their EI. This can be done by teaching workers to enhance their ability to recognise and understand people's moods, understand emotions of other people, manage relationships and build networks, work for internal motives that go beyond money and status, and think before acting (Cherniss & Adler, 2000). This need cannot be overemphasised for customer service.

In Africa, corporate practices have not highlighted the amalgamation of EI and customer service in improving organisational performance. This situation is a matter of concern considering that the introduction of EI in organisations leads to effective customer service management. Consequently, organisations in Africa must begin to focus on their human capital. They must develop into emotionally intelligent organisations, acknowledging the importance of emotional capabilities within the organisations and stimulating employees to exhibit emotional competences when discharging their duties and tasks. This arouses improved work performance and eventually leads to improved customer service. In line with this, there is a need for building a new customer service training model which integrates EI competencies into the training model as a basis for the development of emotionally intelligent workers.

Developing EI in the Workplace

EI is critical in the workplace because the variety of emotions that are exhibited in workplaces on a daily basis are astounding (Bradberry & Greaves, 2005). People experience an average of 27 emotions each working hour. The understanding of an organisation's culture largely rests on how the organisation responds to emotions within it and how it deals with emotional management (Lynn, 2004). With nearly 17 working hours each day, an individual has about 456 emotional experiences from the time of waking up until bedtime. This suggests that more than 3,000 emotional reactions guide an individual through each week and more than 150,000 each year. Of all the emotions experienced in a lifetime, nearly two million of them happen during working hours. Weinberger (2002) comments about the value of using our EI in how we conduct ourselves and how we relate to others at the workplace. Therefore, workers should all be striving for an emotionally intelligent organisation in which the employees create a culture that uninterruptedly uses the skills and tools of EI.

According to Dulewicz and Higgs (2000) and Goleman (2003), EI makes a difference in terms of individual and organisational success. The application of EI at the workplace will make managers have a workforce with a high level of commitment and employees will inturn have managers who are approachable and open to their needs. Lynn (2004) is of the view that EI can make a huge difference in both our personal lives and workplace performance. EI is the peculiar element that decides if 'we make lemonade when life hands us lemons or spend our life stuck in bitterness'. Hence, EI enables us to have healthy, warm relationships, rather than cold and distant relationships at the workplace.

Since the initial development of the construct of EI, there have been intense assertions made about its contribution to organisational performance (Goleman, 2003). While the dramatic claims of some researchers have been roundly refuted (Zeidner et al., 2003), research has revealed that EI has incremental predictive validity over and above personality and verbal intelligence. The most important issue is that the overall contribution of EI on workplace outcomes and employee attitudes is an ongoing event (Dolan & Bradley, 2004). For instance, Bar-On (2010) established a link between EI and extraction perceptions of senior managers in a public sector sample. Managers with higher EI were able to manage stress and address issues that may cause them to resign. Additionally, Bar-On (2010) believes that EI can lead to increased turnover in workplaces and improve employees' sense of job security. Therefore, EI will result in lower turnover when employees are able to manage the emotions that emerge from the perceptions of job insecurity. In Africa, few studies have linked EI to the performance of an organisation. Therefore, research into the relationship between EI, labour turnover and organisational performance will be vital for the analysis of how EI is perceived and used in workplaces in Africa.

There are several research studies that have found EI to be both learnable and teachable. Studies including Goleman (2003) and Bar-On (2006) are of the view that EI can be improved through learning. A study by Sjölund and Gustafsson (2001) evaluated 29 adults' scores before and after attending a managerial skills workshop. In the workshop, several EI competencies were discussed and taught. Mean scores increased from 97 at pre-test to 106 at post-test. The question, according to Goleman (2003), is at which stage of life are EI interventions most effective? According to Dulewicz et al. (2003), teaching EI at later stages of life may be too late, and because EI capabilities are still being learned at young ages, training at young ages may be premature. As age increases the parent–child relationship shifts and the parents' roles may diminish while relationships with others (e.g. peers, colleagues, professors) increases. Therefore, perhaps, the time frame to begin targeting EI training is at the traditional college ages of 18–23 and at the beginning phases of career development (Zeidner et al., 2003). As academic and business studies (Sjölund & Gustafsson, 2001) have shown, EI appears to be learnable and teachable at least within certain contexts, because EI is still at the beginning of the learning curve. Mayer et al. (2004) believe that EI training, specifically its potential and effectiveness, is an important area for future research. A majority of the studies listed above used prescribed methods that included longer treatment time frames, some as long as one academic year (Freedman, 2003). EI training can be effective when looking at the dimensions of the training design. More specifically, EI training programmes targeted at developing EI need to focus on the four dimensions-self-awareness, self-regulation, awareness of others and regulation of others (Sadri, 2011).

Gender Differences in Emotional Intelligence

Competing evidence exists surrounding whether males and females differ significantly in general levels of EI. Goleman (1995) is of the view that gender differences in EI exist, admitting that while men and women may have different profiles of strengths and weaknesses in different areas of EI, their overall levels of EI are equivalent. However, studies by Mayer et al. (2004) and Cherniss and Adler (2000) found that women are more likely to score higher on measures of EI than men, both in professional and personal settings. A similar study found that women score higher than men on measures of empathy and social responsibility, but men outperform women on stress tolerance and self-confidence (Bellack, 1999). In other words, women and men are both intelligent in measures of emotional ability, but they are strong in different areas. Since patterns of EI are not fixed, men and women can boost their overall skills by building their abilities where they lack them (Goleman, 2002). A study exploring the concept of gender differences in EI in Africa will be very timely. It will aid in having a comprehensive debate about the issues of gender in EI and establish whether some of these findings prevail in the African context or whether there may be contrary views. The study will also assist in identifying what could possibly be the factors stimulating the gender imbalance in EI.

Dilemmas and Arguments on Emotional Intelligence

Although psychologists have studied aspects of EI in organisations for decades, it is still unclear about the nature of EI, in terms of its measurement and its impact on individual performance as well as organisational effectiveness. In some cases, the lack of clarity has led to conflict and controversy among researchers and practitioners. One of the most basic controversies involves the definition of the concept of EI. The term emotional quotient (EQ) as Goleman stipulated was first coined by Bar-On (1988) as a counterpart to intelligence quotient (IQ), which is a cognitive ability. Bar-On thought of EQ as a set of social and emotional abilities that help individuals cope with the demands of daily life. Mayer et al. (2004) had something different and more restricted in mind when they introduced the term EI several years later. EI was concerned with the way in which an individual processes information about emotion and emotional responses (Freedman, 2003).

A related area of controversy has to do with the measurement of EI. Several instruments are now available that claim to measure EI. All are of recent except for Bar-On's EQ-i, which was developed in the mid-eighties. All these instruments have their strengths and weaknesses. Mayer et al. (2008) clarify how the different instruments overlap and how they diverge in what they measure. Much progress has been made, and all the current measures show promising outcomes. However, there is still much work to be done in clarifying and refining measurement methodology.

The relationship between individual and group EI presents yet another unresolved issue. Group EI is not simply the sum total of the individual EI of group members. Having a few people with high individual EI is not enough to generate the conditions necessary for teamwork and group effectiveness. Groups also need norms and enduring processes that support awareness and regulation of emotion within the group.

Another dilemma stems from the fact that much of the research on which the field is now based has been conducted by firms that have little incentive to publish their work. For instance, much of the most exciting and compelling research comes from consulting firms that have been contracted to investigate a particular problem or issue. These firms conduct studies for corporate clients that use the research for their own purposes. These clients are not willing to pay the firms to prepare articles about the research findings for publication in scientific journals, and so it is difficult for the researchers employed at these firms to take the time to prepare such articles. Another problem is that the clients would prefer that the details of the research be known to as few as possible, especially not to their corporate competitors (Dulewicz et al., 2003).

Implications of EI for Customer Service Management in Organisations

Customer service is a very important concern for organisations trying to survive. If customers are satisfied, it will lead to their loyalty and their retention and a subsequent increase in the cost-effectiveness of the organisation (Helgesen, 2006). Customer service has become a powerful competitive tool in every business because it is a procedure that provides satisfactory services to customers. It can be perceived from two dimensions, the technical quality and relational quality. The technical quality refers to the benefits offered to customers, for instance, interest rate on a home loan as well as the length and security of the loan. The relational quality describes the interaction between the customer and the company, for instance, the relationship between customers and the service workers of the organisation (Mechinda & Patterson, 2011). As a result, millions of businesses are shaken and even devastated by their inability to provide effective customer service. A lot of organisations talk about how the customer is the driving force of an organisation and their concerns should, therefore, be prioritised. Most organisations refer to customer as 'king', 'number one' or 'the person who signs our paychecks'. Nonetheless, these praises of customers are not seen in practice. Most customers complain about organisations' inability to serve them effectively. Unsatisfactory customer service reduces the profitability of organisations (Tamilarasan, 2011). Having an effective customer service is the best device that attracts new customers and retains the existing ones. This is possible if an organisation pays attention to customer orientation, the employees' personal work values, and attitudes towards their customers. Workers will have to improve on their customer orientation to attract more customers, and hence increase the organisation's profitability (Brown et al., 2002). Customer loyalty is a deeply held commitment of a customer to repatronise a particular product or service, regardless of the alternative or substitute products and services that might be introduced in the near future (Oliver, 1999). When the service persons are able to discern the emotion of the customer and relate appropriately, the delighted customer will come along with others.

When an organisation focuses on effective customer service, it leads to the growth of labour productivity and reduces marketing costs due to a high level of recommendation by customers. Similarly, it aids in achieving higher returns on the marketing investments of a firm as a result of the high level of customer satisfaction. Effective customer service will also lead to an increase in positive word of mouth, increase in the quality of services provided to customers, and increase in high-quality communication channels. Likewise, it gives an organisation a better understanding of customers' needs. Finally, improved service reduces the gap between what the organisation provides and customer expectations (Chen & Chen, 2004).

Case Studies 1

A banking firm had a problem with its IT division; its productivity level was lagging compared to other units in the organisation. This was a worrying situation because the IT unit was responsible for designing new technologies that the organisation would use in interacting with its customers. These technologies were also aimed at gaining competitive advantage with the innovation. The new technology had the ability to revise the pattern in the entire banking industry, linking it with customers. Therefore, the progress of the bank was resting on the shoulders of the IT department.

Diagnosing the difficulties facing the IT department, the bank began to find out the factors stimulating the problem. The bank started by considering if there were incentives available to the workers, resources and skill level, as well as procedures in carrying out their tasks. The bank found that there were extra bonuses available, but it did not have any significant impact, even though skill level was high, the required resources were available, and the right processes were adhered to. However, the area of concern was the employees, specifically their 'employee commitment' scores.

The IT workers showed up to work as expected, but most of them were not actively involved with their tasks. They were not putting in enough effort or demonstrating the urgency that was required to design the technology needed to compete against some of the other big banks to improve on customer satisfaction scores.

With further inquiry into their side of the business, the bank discovered that the scores were being driven by strained employee–manager relationships within the division. The IT managers and leaders were good at getting things *(tasks)* done, but not very good at building relationships and creating connections and engagement across the IT division and with other departmental employees. They needed to consider inputs from other units in the organisation. They did not know how to identify, control, perceive and understand others' emotions and translate that into the development of the new technology to improve customer service management (Mayer et al., 2004).

Practice Questions

1. Do you think an introduction of EI into the organisation will improve its customer service? How?
2. Which EI competencies does the bank need to instil into the IT department?

Case Studies 2

A client signed up for an HR consultancy service based on its reputation in the industry. The client found out that the experience was not exactly what he expected. The consultants insisted he used a particular software that was recommended by management. However, the client consistently had difficulties using the software. On several instances, the client complained to the consultants and management about his difficulties with the software and how it was wasting his time in executing the duties. Every time he made complaints, the consultants ignored his concerns and woes. What made matters worse was that management and the consultants were not coordinating their efforts. Therefore, the client had to deal with them separately which was not supposed to be the case; hence, the client was frustrated. When the time came for the client to give a review on the firm's performance, he refused to give them a positive Google review when they requested one. The client had no option but to share his disappointing experience with a lot of their potential customers. What this means is that the firm will have a negative reputation in the public's eye. It is therefore imperative to invest in creating an exceptional customer service experience, especially in recent times where businesses are going global and have online audiences. A feedback on a firm's services and products will be public and visible to all target audiences. If the consultancy had paid attention to the client's emotions, they would have been well positioned to prevent the disaster and create a better customer experience.

Practice Questions

1. What do you think the consultancy could have done to prevent the situation with regard to EI?
2. Do you agree that EI would have played a key role in improving the customer service of the firm?

Conclusion

Since 1990, EI has garnered considerable attention from the academic community, applied settings and mainstream society. Three competing models of EI have emerged along with their own corresponding measurement strategies. While the pure model emphasises cognitive ability and relies on an objective, performance-based measure of EI, the mixed models assess both cognitive ability and personality traits using self-report measures. Interestingly, considerable debate remains regarding the legitimacy of the construct (one derived from the 'pure' model, the other from the 'mixed' model) and how it should be measured. Despite these, various studies have shown that success and happiness come when we have effective awareness, control, and management of one's own emotions, and awareness and understanding of other people. Consequently, it has been established that there is a relationship between EI and customer service management. In other words, EI is seen as the 'missing link' to effective customer service in organisations. Firms need to transform their workplaces into an 'emotionally intelligent' organisation and train their workers to build effective EI capabilities in discharging their duties. This will help to enhance customer service levels through improved employee attitude and performance. In the quest to build a continuing relationship with customers, organisations must focus on combining EI with three aspects of customers: the value in customer perspective, the quick response to the customer needs and the desires to achieve customer satisfaction. Once this is achieved, customer loyalty becomes the expected result of customer satisfaction and high profitability for organisations.

References

Abraham, A. (2007). The need for the integration of emotional intelligence skills. *The Business Renaissance Quarterly, 1*(3), 65–79.

Bar-On, R. (1988). *The development of a concept of psychological well-being.* Doctoral dissertation, Rhodes University, South Africa.

Bar-On, R. (2002). *EQ-I: Bar-On emotional quotient inventory technical manual.* Toronto, Canada: Multi-Health Systems.

Bar-On, R. (2006). The bar-on model of emotional-social intelligence (ESI). *Psicothema, 18*, 13–25.

Bar-On, R. (2010). Emotional intelligence: An integral part of positive psychology. *South African Journal of Psychology, 40*(1), 54–62.

Bellack, J. (1999). Emotional intelligence: A missing ingredient. *Journal of Nursing Education, 38*(1), 3–4.

Brackett, M. A., Rivers, S. E., & Salovey, P. (2011). Emotional intelligence: implications for personal, social, academic, and workplace success. *Social and Personality Psychology Compass, 5*(1), 88–103.

Bradberry, T., & Greaves, J. (2005). *Emotional intelligence quick book.* Translated by: M. Ganji. Tehran: Savalan Publications.

Brown, T. J., Mowen, J. C., Donavan, D. T., & Licata, J. W. (2002). The customer orientation of service workers: Personality trait effects on self and supervisor performance ratings. *Journal of Marketing Research, 39*(1), 110–119.

Caruso, D. R., Mayer, J. D., & Salovey, P. (2004). Relation of an ability measure of emotional intelligence to personality. *Journal of Personality Assessment, 79*(2), 306–320.

Chen, Q., & Chen, H. (2004). Exploring the success factors of E-CRM strategies in practice. *Journal of Database Marketing and Customer Strategy Management, 11*(4), 333–343.

Cherniss, C., & Adler, M. (2000). *Promoting emotional intelligence in organizations.* Alexandria, Egypt: ASTD.

Cobb, C. D., & Mayer, J. D. (2000). Emotional intelligence: What the research says. *Educational Leadership, 58*(3), 14–18.

Cockerell, L. (2009). Creating leadership magic. *Leader to Leader, 2009*(53), 31–36.

Cooper, R. K. (1997). *Executive EQ: Emotional intelligence in leadership and organizations.* New York: The Berkley Publishing Group.

Dolan, T., & Bradley, J. J. (2004). The effects of instruction on emotional intelligence as measured by the emotional competence inventory, perceived stress scale and symptoms of stress checklist. *Teaching Journal of the ooi Academy, 1*(1), 1–6.

Dulewicz, V., & Higgs, M. (2000). Emotional intelligence: A review and evaluation study. *Journal of Managerial Psychology, 15*(4), 341–368.

Dulewicz, V., Higgs, M., & Slaski, M. (2003). Measuring emotional intelligence: Content, construct and criterion-related validity. *Journal of Managerial Psychology, 18*(5), 405–419.

Freedman, J. (2003). Key lessons from 35 years of social-emotional education: How self-science builds self-awareness, positive relationships, and healthy decision-making. *Perspectives in Education, 21*(4), 69–80.

Gignac, G. E., Harmer R. J., Jennings, S., & Palmer. B. R. (2012). EI training and sales performance during a corporate merger. *Cross Cultural Management: An International Journal, 19*(1), 104–116.

Goleman, D. (1995). *Emotional intelligence: Why it can matter more than IQ.* New York: Bantam.

Goleman, D. (2002). *Primal leadership: Learning to lead with emotional intelligence.* Boston, MA: Harvard Business School Press.

Goleman, D. (2003). Apples and applesauce. *Issues and Recent Developments in Emotional Intelligence, 1*(3), 425–448.

Helgesen, Ø. (2006). Are loyal customers profitable? Customer satisfaction, customer (action) loyalty and customer profitability at the individual level. *Journal of Marketing Management, 22*(3–4), 245–266.

Leuner, B. (1966). Emotional intelligence and emancipation. A psychodynamic study on women. *Praxis der kinderpsychologie und kinderpsychiatrie, 15*(6), 196.

Lynn, A. (2004). EI and sound business practice. *Hoosier Banker, 88*(1), 24.

Marques, J. (2010). Spirituality, meaning, interbeing, leadership, and empathy: Smile. *Interbeing, 4*(2), 7–17.

Matthews, G., Zeidner, M., & Roberts, R. D. (2002). *Emotional intelligence Science and myth.* Cambridge, MA: The MIT Press.

Mayer, J. D., Caruso, D. R., & Salovey, P. (2000). Emotional intelligence meets traditional standards for an intelligence. *Intelligence, 27*(4), 267–298.

Mayer, J. D., Salovey, P., & Caruso, D. R. (2004). Emotional intelligence: Theory, findings, and implications. *Psychology Inquiry, 15*(3), 197–215.

Mayer, J. D., Salovey, P., & Caruso, D. R. (2008). Emotional intelligence: New ability or eclectic traits? *American Psychologist, 63*(6), 503.

Mechinda, P., & Patterson, P. G. (2011). The impact of service climate and service provider personality on employees' customer-oriented behavior in a high-contact setting. *Journal of Services Marketing, 25*(2), 101–113.

Oliver, R. L. (1999). Whence consumer loyalty? *Journal of Marketing, 63*(4), 33–44.

Riggio, R. E., & Reichard, R. J. (2008). The emotional and social intelligences of effective leadership. *Journal of Managerial Psychology, 3*(2), 169–185. doi:10.1108/02683940810850808.

Sadri, G. (2011). Emotional intelligence: Can it be taught? *Training & Development, 65*(9), 84–85.

Singh, S. K. (2007). Role of emotional intelligence in organisational learning: An empirical study. *Singapore Management Review, 29*(2), 55–74.

Sjölund, M., & Gustafsson, H. (2001). *Outcome study of a leadership development assessment and training program based on emotional intelligence. Educating people to be emotionally intelligent.* Sandton: Heinemann.

Skinner, C., & Spurgeon, P. (2005). Valuing empathy and emotional intelligence in health leadership: a study of empathy, leadership behavior and outcome effectiveness. *Health Services Management Research, 18*(1), 1–12.

Stys, Y., & Brown, S. (2004). *A review of the emotional intelligence literature and implications for corrections.* Ottawa, Canada: Correctional Service of Canada, Research Branch.

Tamilarasan, R. (2011). Customer relationship management in banking services. *Journal of Advances in Management, 4*(1), 23–34.

Walter, V. Clarke Associates. (1996). *Activity vector analysis: Some applications to the concept of emotional intelligence.* Pittsburgh, PA: Walter V. Clarke Associates.

Weinberger, L. A. (2002). Emotional intelligence: Its connection to HRD theory and practice. *Human Resource Development Review, 1*(2), 215–243.

Zeidner, M., Matthews, G., & Roberts, R. D. (2004). Emotional intelligence in the workplace: A critical review. *Applied Psychology, 53*(3), 371–399.

Zeidner, M., Matthews, G., Roberts, R. D., & MacCann, C. (2003). Development of emotional intelligence: Towards a multi-level investment model. *Human Development, 46*(2–3), 69–96.

Chapter 20

Presentation Skills

J. N. Halm

Contents

Introduction

The importance of communication to the proper functioning of any business setup can never be overemphasised. Sehgal and Khetarpal (2006) assert that 'communication is rightly called the lifeblood of a business organisation' (p. vii). No business will ever survive without communication. Charvatova (2008), in listing the three key factors that play a significant role in the management of any organisation, formulation of necessary strategies, and market performance, added *communication* to *corporate culture* and *human resources*. On a daily and consistent basis, individuals within the organisation have to communicate if the organisation is to achieve its raison d'être (reason for existence).

One common form of communication that organisations employ on a regular basis is presentations. Bradbury (2006, p. 2) argues that 'almost any kind of business transaction involves some degree of presentation skill'. Kauer (2011, p. 5) defines a presentation as 'the process of conveying ideas, insights, information and knowledge to a group of people'. Kogon et al. (2015) simply define presentation as sharing information between two or more people to inform or persuade.

Bradbury (2006) argues that presentations are employed during almost all kinds of business transactions. The business presentation is one of the most common modes of business communication employed within the organisation. For centuries, the traditional salesperson had been utilising this means of business communication to get wares into the hands of customers. In many African towns and villages, the traditional salesperson moves from house to house – hut to hut – doing sales presentations.

The success of an individual in the corporate world is very much dependent on one's ability to be able to present one's ideas in a manner that will bring people to understand and appreciate one's views. No matter how superior one's ideas are, if one is unable to present them effectively, others with inferior ideas but better presentation skills will be given the nod. Every individual must, therefore, have adequate knowledge of the dos and don'ts of effective presentations.

It is important to note that a business presentation does not necessarily have to involve a slide-show or PowerPoint presentation. Giving of status reports, demonstrating how a product works, pitching for a deal and rolling out a corporate strategy are all forms of presentations.

Presentations are used for meetings within departments and units, both vertically and horizontally. There are few staff meetings without one form of presentation or another. Presentations are expected of heads of departments when they have to face the Board. Beyond the more formal settings, this form of communication is also employed under not-so-formal conditions. For instance, when the Head of ICT is explaining the features of a new software, there must be a presentation. When new staff are being taken around the office, they are given a presentation.

Presentations also play an important role when an organisation has to communicate with external stakeholders. The chief executive is expected to make a presentation to shareholders at the Annual General Meeting. Various members of staff regularly give presentations to suppliers, distributors, wholesalers and retailers, amongst others. The sales presentation is very much part and parcel of any organisation's regular means of communication to customers.

A typical presentation is unique in the sense that it is one mode of communication that combines oral communication with written communication. This presents a unique challenge for the presenter whose presentation must follow the tenets of written communication, adhere to the dictates of a good oral presentation while at the same time remain visually appealing. It must, however, be stated that a presentation is markedly different from writing (Schwabish, 2017).

Types of Presentations

Broadly speaking, there are two main types of presentations based on the purpose of the presentation. These are *informative* presentations and *persuasive* presentations. In other words, presentations either *inform or persuade*. Kauer (2011) adds a third purpose, that is, *instruction* or training. However, it can be argued that training is primarily meant to inform. *Harvard Business Review* (2014) states that reasons for choosing to do a business presentation could be to inform, persuade or sell. As selling is an act of persuasion, it can be argued that all business presentations fall under either the *informing* or *persuading* categories.

Gilbert (2013), however, grouped business presentations into three broad categories: Speech, Standard Internal Presentation, and Senior Executive Presentation. This categorisation was based on a number of factors including the audience composition, the focus of the audience, the need for visual aids, the use of stories or data, an emphasis on emotion or logic, the use of humour and the duration of the presentation, as well as the participation or otherwise of the audience.

The Sales Presentation

Although the ultimate aim of every sales presentation is to persuade a customer to make a purchase, the uniqueness of the sales presentation could account for why some writers want to give it a separate category. This uniqueness is the fact that a typical sales presentation both informs and persuades at the same time. The information given in the sales presentation is mainly to persuade the prospect. In this sense, a sales presentation will differ from a presentation on a technical paper given by the research, engineering or product development departments.

A sales presentation can have an audience of one or an audience of one thousand. It can be an informal discussion by the wayside, in an elevator, or a formal presentation at a conference room in a five-star hotel. It can be done with or without visual aids.

Another way in which sales presentations stand alone is that a typical sales presentation might call for the handling of objections. When the prospect is engaged, it is expected that one would want to know more about the offering before making up their mind whether to take the sale forward. This is done by raising objections to some of the information the presenter provides.

Benefits of Presentation Skills

Key to Professional Growth

Every business professional must develop effective presentation skills because regardless of one's position or department, there will be a need to communicate one's thoughts or ideas to another person or persons. Yate and Sander (2003) assert that communication and presentations are among the core competencies that employers look seek. This calls for the development of the right presentation skills. For the customer service professional whose job involves dealing with customers on a daily basis, the need for good presentation skills can never be overemphasised. Aside from the daily dealings with customers on a one-on-one basis, there will be times when there will be a need to present the company's ideas to a group of customers.

Organisations would, as a matter of necessity, need to communicate their ideas to customers in very effective ways. Therefore, individuals with great presentation skills will be highly valued within the organisation or department. Those with well-developed presentation skills are able to hold their own in the presence of others and more often than not are those that will tend to rise through the organisation. As a matter of fact, those with good presentation skills are more likely to get employment than those who cannot communicate their ideas well enough.

Key to Personal Career Growth

On a personal basis, it is most important for individuals to develop effective presentations skills. Interpersonal communications require an ability to persuade others to one's point of view, and it will require good presentation skills to pull that off. Those who are able to win others to their side are those who eventually get ahead in the workplace. Developing the right persuasive skills ensure that the right career opportunities are opened up for the individual. Additionally, great presentation skills appearing on one's curriculum vitae (CV) or resumé can be a great added advantage when job hunting.

Vital for Personal Confidence

An ability to convey one's thoughts convincingly can confer a sense of personal confidence to the individual. This personal confidence can go a long way to helping one succeed in life.

Vital for Other Life Skills

Theobald (2013) argues that the skills acquired in becoming a good presenter or public speaker can be translated to other areas of the individual's life. For instance, acquiring good presentations calls for learning how to build effective arguments and delivering them effectively. This is a skill that one needs in life. Also, the planning and preparation needed to put together a good presentation also come in handy when planning one's life.

Qualities of an Effective Presentation

According to Brusino (2008), there are nine essential qualities that every effective presentation must possess. Effective presentations must have the following qualities: value, clarity, tailored to the specific audience, logical, appropriate duration/length, memorable, understandable, realistic and challenging. These qualities form a good basis for an in-depth evaluation of every presentation.

Wempen (2007) also stressed that for a presentation to be effective, the design and format had to be appropriate for the audience and the medium. An effective presentation also had to be focussed on the subject, leaving out or reducing to a minimum any extraneous information.

Phases in a Presentation

For a good appreciation of what it takes to put up a very effective presentation, it is helpful if the entire process is divided into three main parts, viz. pre-presentation, in-presentation and post-presentation.

The Pre-presentation Phase

Stack (2013) proposes five steps to take at the pre-presentation phase. These are

1. *Developing objectives*
2. *Analysing the audience carefully*
3. *Developing the body and the main ideas of the presentation*
4. *Creating supporting information*
5. *Developing the opening, closing and transitions of the presentation*

It is important to note that the last three steps can all be grouped under a broader step of Developing the Presentation.

Yate and Sander (2003), however, proposed a ten-step process which includes the following steps: *Take audience inventory, assess the situation, get organised, get your thoughts on the table, do the research, enrich the research, build the body, build the presentation, add visual aids as well as prepare, practise and present.* Bradbury (2006), in listing the seven basic steps to a successful presentation also stressed on the need for rehearsing the presentation before the actual presentation. Rehearsals are a must if presenters want to be on top of their presentations.

Evidently, there is no general agreement among researchers on whether the first step of the presentation process is an analysis of the audience or a development of the objectives. The best advice would, therefore, be to go with a particular context. If the audience is a group of customers that the customer service professional is already familiar with, there would be no need for an in-depth audience analysis as opposed to a situation where one has to present to a hitherto yet-to-be-engaged customer or customers.

Developing Objectives

Why is the presentation necessary? This is the question that should initiate the entire presentation planning phase. Sampson (2003) stated that key objectives for presentations could either be overt or covert. Examples of overt objectives are to sell a new idea, share a strategy or data, enthuse about changes, explain new systems and introduce procedures. Breaking down these objectives into smaller sub-objectives gives the presentation its main topic headings. Covert objectives include getting some presentation practice, building one's confidence, increasing one's visibility and positioning one's self for promotion, as well as influencing the right people (Sampson, 2003).

Zelazny (2000, p. 10) suggests that the way to define the objective of a presentation is to 'write, in one sentence, what, realistically, you want the members of your audience to do or think as the result of this presentation'. In his opinion, if more than a single sentence is needed to state an objective, then the presenter is not really clear about the objectives.

One of the key reasons why every presentation needs to have a clearly stated objective is to give the presentation a 'marking scheme'. Without a clearly stated objective, it would be difficult to determine the success or otherwise of the presentation. It is also important to clearly state one's objective because it helps bring focus to the preparation. Extraneous materials are quickly discarded, and only those aids and supporting materials that will help achieve the stated objectives are considered.

Analysing the Audience Carefully

Without an audience, there is no presentation. Even if the presentation is to an audience of one, there is still a need to seek to understand the audience and its needs. Audience analysis is the key to making better presentations (Hattersley, 1996).

For the customer service professional, in all likelihood, the audience will be customers – potential or current. Customers want to know that the business cares for them. Therefore, a good presentation is one that is tailor-made for that particular audience. Customers must be able to feel that the presenter has their best interest at heart. Reimold & Reimold (2003) refer to this as the audience-directed presentation attitude, as opposed to a self-directed attitude. The audience is likely to lose track if they are made to feel that the entire presentation is designed to suit the presenter and not the audience – in this case, customers.

The key to a good presentation, therefore, is to really know one's customers (audience), starting with their needs. Sidons (2003) categorised the needs of audiences into seven areas. These include, straightforward information, historical background, comparisons, interpretation, motivation, education and entertainment.

Nishiyama (2000) asserts that in audience analysis for a presentation, it is important to investigate the specific background of each member of the audience. Things to look out for include one's current status and position, preferences, interests, responsibility and authority, personal stake, attitudes and personality. Suffice it to say that undertaking such an analysis would be dependent on the size of the audience.

When researching an audience, it is important to consider the audience's reasons for attending the presentation, their level of knowledge of the subject and the past relationship with the presenter or presenter's company, as well as the audience's preferred method of information assimilation (Sidons, 2003). It is also important to know how the audience will receive the message and how they will accept it.

Reimold and Reimold (2003) suggested that the best way to get into the minds of the customers is to write out at least 20 questions you believe the customers could ask. The idea behind coming up with so many questions is to push the presenter to really get into the mind of the audience.

It is equally important that one considers the size of the audience. There is a vast difference between presenting to five colleagues in one's department and presenting to a large group of potential customers at a conference hall. The preparations must definitely be different.

If it is a presentation with an objective of convincing a group to take an action, such as doing business with your organisation, then it is important to know those whose opinions really carry weight in that audience. Who is the main decision-maker, who has the final word? This is an important question to answer. There are times when one person whose opinion matters about a particular subject might not even be in the presentation. What that 'influencer' would use to make a favourable or unfavourable decision will be second-hand information. It is not out of place for the chief executive to want to discuss things over with a board chairman who might not be at the presentation. It is also possible for one to discuss with a spouse before making a decision. A good presentation is one that takes into consideration all these other behind-the-scenes influencing personalities. The presentation must be crafted in such a way that the needs of these influencers who might not be at the presentation are also met.

In undertaking an analysis of the audience, it is also important to know what the audience knows about the subject of the presentation. This will go a long way in determining the kind of materials that are put together for the presentation. It will even determine the kind of language that the presenter has to use. Jargons and terms that the audience might be unfamiliar with are either explained or omitted from the presentation altogether. This is a critical aspect of audience analysis since it can be very embarrassing for the presenter. To present before a group who knows much more about the subject of the presentation than the presenter is as equally embarrassing as presenting to a group that gains absolutely nothing from the presentation because the presenter spoke 'above their heads'.

Another issue that needs to be tackled during audience analysis is about the feelings of the audience towards that particular subject matter. If it is a topic that generates strong positive emotions for the customers, then the presenter's job has been half done. An interesting topic might not be as difficult to deliver as an otherwise tough and uninteresting topic. However, if the emotions of the audience are negative towards the subject of the presentation, then the presenter has his or her work cut out for him or her. The way staff members would receive a presentation about management's plans to cut some allowances and benefits would not be the same way they would receive a presentation announcing a bonus package for all employees.

One of the clearest proofs that a presenter truly cares about the audience – their needs and interests – is to prepare well. If a customer-handling professional truly cares about the customers, he/she would put in the time to prepare well for any presentation. Any time and energy that is used to prepare the presentation must be seen as an investment into the business–customer relationship.

Developing the Presentation

With enough knowledge of the audience (or customers), the next thing is to develop the main presentation. A typical presentation has three main parts – the introduction, main body and the closing. The three main parts of the presentation correspond to the following: 'Tell the audience what you intend to tell them' (Introduction); 'Tell them' (Body); 'Tell the audience what you told them (Closing)'. This section includes the stages of developing the body and the main ideas of the presentation, creating supporting information, and developing the opening, closing, and transitions of the presentation as proposed by Stack (2013).

The Main Body

This is a formal presentation and is the section for the main points as well as all other supporting information. It is where "you tell them what you want to tell them." According to Lundberg (2011), the body is where the presenter's energy and knowledge come together to fully inspire, entertain, inform, educate, and sell or pitch to the audience. It is imperative that any fact that is presented is well-researched. Any figures or facts that are presented must come from reliable and verifiable sources. The main body of the presentation must have a logical pattern to enable the audience to follow the speaker's sequence of thoughts. In providing information on any subject, some patterns might be from simple to complex, general to specific, or past to present (INTELECOM, 1999).

If the subject lends itself to it, the main body of the presentation can be arranged in terms of timelines, such as what happened first, what happened thereafter, and the next. Also, a subject can be discussed by arranging the topics directionally – from one part of the subject to the next and the next, until the entire subject is exhausted.

For more complex subjects, it helps if the following arrangement is used: overview, details, background, immediate consequences, and further developments (Seifert, 2015).

Creating Supporting Information

Any piece of information that communicates and lends credence to the main ideas in the presentation must be gathered and sorted out appropriately. According to Stack (2013), these include product descriptions, photos, reports, quotations, questions, statistics, findings from recent surveys, etc. Collectively, this information can also be referred to as visual aids.

Visual Aids

Koneru (2008, p. 267) defined visual aids as 'forms of supporting material, which provide all forms of intellectual, technical, psychological, emotional and sensory reinforcement of ideas'. Visual aids include illustrations, tables, figures, graphs, charts, maps, drawings, photographs and video clips. Visual supports can also be real-life objects. Koneru (2008) insists that all aids other than tables are classified as 'figures'.

It has been estimated that members of the audience tend to retain only 10% of what they heard at a presentation when it is presented solely in words. However, when the presentation is a combination of words and visual aids, the audience tends to remember as high as 50% (Koneru, 2008).

According to Koneru (2008), when incorporating visual support into a presentation, there is an effective three-step approach that presenters must adopt. The first step is to introduce visual aid by mentioning the most important fact about the aid. After introducing the aid, the next thing is to display the aid then to discuss it in a more interpretative manner. The discussion is not just about repeating what the audience can already see or what they already know about the aid, but rather to state why the aid is significant to the point of the discussion.

The main body of the presentation is also the place where the presenter can make use of visual aids to help carry the audience step by step through the presentation. In persuading a customer to buy a particular gadget that the customer is not familiar with, any presentation on the gadget would best be served by having the gadget at hand. The customer can have a feel of how that gadget works in real life and real time. There is some information that is so complicated that they are best communicated with the use of visual aids. Attempting to explain these complex matters might require too much time and too much talking. This is where good visuals come in. Another reason for the use of visual support for presentations is that the use of visuals cut down the time for the presentation.

Blokzijl and Andeweg (2007) asserted that in presentations that tend to give out information, visual aids are vital for the learning and retention of the information presented. In an experiment involving students from the Delft University of Technology in the Netherlands, they discovered that students who sat in lectures where visual supports were employed did better in subsequent examinations than students who sat in lectures where no visual supports were used. They further discovered that those who engaged with visual support tended to recall the lecture better even after a week. Therefore, if certain information must be presented to have a lasting effect, it is best to do so with some visual aids.

Visual aids also create more interests in the presentation than one that is devoid of such visual support. Because the audience is not aware of what is coming up next, and they do not want to miss out, they tend to be more glued to the presentation. If they are aware that it is only words that they would be hearing, they are more prone to drift mentally because humans have the capacity to hear one thing and do something else at the same time.

Developing the Opening, Closing and Transitions of the Presentation

The Introduction

The purpose of the introduction of every presentation is to introduce the audience to the main purpose of the entire presentation and give the audience an overview of what they are to expect throughout the presentation. The key to a good introduction is to capture the attention of the audience. It behoves the presenter to find exciting and attention-grabbing ways to open the presentation.

There are a number of ways to introduce a presentation. A good question can set the minds of the audience in the direction of the presentation. Other devices include using an interesting short story related to the topic, an interesting quote or a humorous statement or joke. Jokes must, however, be treated with caution because a crude or sensitive joke can throw off the presentation. Another effective way to open a presentation is to start with a shocking fact that instantly throws the audience off their guard. Depending on the setup of the presentation, a short video can also be used to open the presentation. It is important to note that the opening device that is adopted must be related to the topic; otherwise, it would start the presentation off on the wrong note.

The Closing

The essence of the closing is to leave the audience in an enlightened or inspired state. A good presentation should end on a positive note. This is where the presenter summarises what has been presented in as few words as possible. A great presentation should close with a good summary. The summary is simply a recap of the main message and the key points. The audience must be reminded of the purpose of the presentation, as well as the key points that were made.

Reimold and Reimold (2003) are of the opinion that the summary should start with a phrase like 'In closing', or 'In summary', among others. This is because it is very possible that the presenter might have lost some part of the audience during the delivery. Therefore, summarising with a phrase that brings them back from any mental excursion they might have undertaken to the presentation is a major benefit. Closing can also be done with a memorable quote or story to hammer home the main point of the presentation.

The Closing should also include a call for action, especially if the presentation was meant to persuade the audience to take some form of action. It is the last thing you want the audience to take away so it must be well prepared.

Before the presenter finally pulls the curtain on a presentation, it might be important to inform the audience about what to do next. The Call to Action must not be ambiguous or else the audience will be left confused, which would mar an otherwise great presentation. This is most important for persuasive presentations.

Transitions

In linking the main points within the body of the presentation, transitions are employed. Transitions are the signposts that the audience follows during the presentation (McLean, 2010). Transitions give an indication of where the presenter is at any moment in the presentation. Transitions are the bridges between the significant points of the presentation. Examples of transitional statements are 'Having gone through A, let's now turn our attention to B' or 'With A out of the way, we now move on to B'. Transitions help to keep a presentation organised as logically as possible.

McLean (2010) provided a very exhaustive list of 14 transitional types that can be used in a presentation. These include Internal Previews such as 'We will next take a look at...'; Internal Summaries such as 'as I just said...'; Sequence such as 'First...second...third' or 'next, then, last' and Clarifications such as 'to put it another way', 'that is to say', 'to rephrase it', etc.

According to Lee and Nelson-Neuhaus (2002), transitions can also be non-verbal. A pause, a raised voice, a dropped voice, a step and various hand gestures can all indicate to the audience that one thought has been completed and the next thought is about to commence.

Practising (or Rehearsing)

It is not enough to have a great presentation on paper. The presentation must eventually be presented, making it is essential to take it for a 'dry run'. Evidently, the best kind of rehearsal should be the one done in the actual room where the presentation will take place and with the equipment that would be used for the actual presentation. However, the ideal rarely occurs, but this does not mean that the presenter should not rehearse. The essence of constant practice is to ensure that the presenter flows naturally during the presentation while at the same ensuring that one curbs any bouts of anxiety that might arise during the presentation.

Another advantage of rehearsing a presentation is to ensure that one gets the timing right. It is always critical that one is able to deliver a presentation within the time allotted. It will take the constant rehearsal to be able to get the timing spot on. On the issue of time, there are as many opinions as there are experts on how long a presentation should last. Kahrs (2000) is of the view that a presentation should generally not go beyond 20 minutes – the reason being that after 20 minutes, people start to tune out and their minds begin to wander. Rehearsals must be timed so that it falls in line with the expected time allotted for that particular presentation.

The In-presentation Phase

A good rehearsal is not a guarantee for a successful presentation. Practice might make perfect, but not always. No matter how well one rehearses, there is always that possibility that things will not go as planned. During the real delivery, there will still be some nerves to deal with. This is normal. Nerves serve a good purpose (Caplin, 2008). The anxiety and raised energy levels are needed for good performance during the presentation. The key is not to show the audience the tension. There are a number of relaxation techniques that can be used during the presentation to handle nerves.

One way to ease the tension and take control of the presentation is to make use of that first statement in the introduction. It is natural for the audience to size the presenter up within the first few seconds of the presentation. The audience will spend those first few seconds deciding if the presenter is worth listening to or not. The attention-grabbing opening, therefore, establishes the fact that the presentation is something giving attention.

Kaul (2005) asserts that the nervousness that the presenter feels during the presentation goes through phases. When the nerves hit, they steeply climb up for a few minutes beyond which they stabilise or plateau. Controlling oneself during the beginning of the presentation until the plateau stage is therefore of great importance since things usually get easier and more manageable after that. It must, however, be stated that controlling one's nerves is not the same as attempting to suppress one's nerves. The latter will end up in an eruption of the suppressed feelings at a point.

It is important to note that handling of objections or responding to questions can either be during the presentation or after the presentation is done. There are pros and cons for either going for the former or employing the latter.

Handling Objections and Q&A Sessions

If there is a Question and Answer (Q&A) session at the end of the presentation, it is important that the presenter clearly indicates when he or she will be ready. Sometimes, it is important that the Q&A is done before the conclusion so that the presenter gets to end the presentation as he or she had planned. Other times, it is best placed when the presenter is totally done with the entire presentation. The best time to handle the Q&A session will be dependent on the context of the presentation. If the time allotted for the Q&A is after the presentation, but the presenter is interrupted by a question, it is important to not lose focus. However, the presenter must be assertive enough to politely inform the questioner that the question will be addressed at the designated time.

Before answering a question, it helps to repeat the question for a number of reasons. First, it helps those in the audience who might not have heard the question the first time to get to hear it better. When answering a question from an individual in the audience, it pays to carry the entire audience along (Kahrs, 2000). Second, by repeating the question, the presenter takes a bit of time to think of what to say.

If a particular question is beyond the capacity of the presenter, it is proper for one to admit not knowing the answer, but to add quickly that he or she will try to get the proper response later on. It is improper to try to bluff. The audience will know when the presenter is struggling to come up with an answer, so it is best to admit and move on to another question.

When the Q&A session ends, it is a good time to share any documents, handouts or materials that the audience can take home. Unless the situation really calls for it, the best time to give out handouts of the presentation is after the presentation. When the audience has the handouts during the presentation, they are more likely to pay attention to the handouts than the presenter. It is important to do a good post-presentation evaluation to ensure that mistakes are not repeated. Feedback can be solicited from independent observers or members of the audience.

Body Language

During an actual presentation, the presenter must be conscious of his or her appearance and body language. The presenter's attire must be appropriate for the occasion and the audience. Distracting clothing might cause interference. A good body posture is important to an effective in-person presentation. Hand gestures must not be a distraction from the presentation. Body movement, if necessary, must be natural and controlled.

Eye contact must be made with the audience at all times, except when a pointer is being used to single out a specific point in a presentation. Kahrs (2000) goes further to declare that eye contact and eye movement are probably the most important components of all presentation skills. Eye contact must be seen as completely random by the audience for it to seem natural. It is unprofessional to enter a staring match with individuals in the audience. In answering the question of how long a presenter should look at an individual in the audience, Kahrs (2000) implied that the presenter should finish one thought or sentence with one individual at a time.

It is important that the presenter's voice is projected in such a manner that everyone in the audience hears clearly. The tone of voice must be varied so as to ensure a natural flow. A monotonous voice quickly becomes boring, and this might lead to the presenter losing the audience. Presenters are also advised to eliminate vocal fillers such as 'um', 'uh', 'okay', 'you know' and 'like' from their presentations. Confidence is an invaluable weapon in the arsenal of those who deliver effective presentations. Another of those weapons is enthusiasm.

The use of body language during a presentation has cultural implications. What would pass as professional in one cultural context could have devastating effects on the presentation in another context. In some African countries, looking directly into the eyes of someone older than you can be construed as an act of disrespect. Putting one's hand inside the pocket of one's trousers would be a serious infraction in some African cultures. There also various differences in the appreciation of the handshake in various cultures. The distance between the individual and the audience can even bring about challenges, if not handled appropriately. Therefore, it is imperative for customer-facing professionals to be wary of these seemingly insignificant but very important body language gestures.

The Role of Technology

Technology has always played an important role in presentations. Traditionally, devices such as flip charts, microphones, slide projectors with the use of transparencies, overhead projectors, laser pointers and various audio-visual equipment have helped in the creation of effective business presentations.

In the use of technology for presentation, it can be argued that Microsoft PowerPoint, one of the earliest acquisitions by Microsoft for its Office suite, has played a most remarkable role. As a matter of fact, PowerPoint is almost synonymous with business presentations in many parts of the world. It is estimated that the market share for PowerPoint is a staggering 95% of the presentation software market (Thielsch & Perabo, 2012).

In today's world, there is online presentation software that enhances any presentation. To eliminate the need for specialist designers to put together a professional presentation, many presentation software have been developed (Duarte, 2008). These include *Adobe Spark, Slidebean, Keynote, Microsoft Sway, Google Slide* and *Zoho Show*. This presentation software has helped transform ordinary presentations into great ones.

There are also applications that can be used to create animated video presentations. These days, there is even wearable technology that has enhanced the typical presentation. However, whichever type of presentation one opts for, whether in-person or technology-mediated, the right skills are required to make the right impact. Like every skill, constant effective practice is critical to success.

The Post-presentation Phase

Regardless of where the Q&A session is placed in the entire presentation – whether during the presentation or after the presenter is finished – it is important that the presentation ends with a good emphasis on the main theme of the presentation. The post-presentation phase kicks in when the presenter walks off the stage or when the curtains come down. Experts advise that a good presenter should take note of what he or she did right and what could have been done better. It helps to write these things down, if possible. This becomes important for future presentations. It also helps if one is able to get feedback from those who were present.

Conclusion

The professional salesperson must, first of all, know the kind of presentation that is required for a particular context. He or she must then take steps to ensure proper preparation for the said presentation. Proper preparation for a presentation begins with the development of the right objectives. This should be done in tandem with a good analysis of the unique characteristics of the audience. Regardless of how well-prepared a presentation is, there is always the need for the presenter to take time to practise before the day of the presentation.

During a presentation, the presenter is expected to consider both verbal and non-verbal aspects of the presentation. This is to ensure that the audience gets to receive the exact message that was intended by the stated objectives. Cultural nuances must also be considered so as not to offend any audience members. If the presentation calls for a Q&A session, it is important that the presenter factors in all possible scenarios to ensure a good ending to the presentation. The right technologies must be adopted to ensure a successful presentation.

In conclusion, presentations would continue to be a very important role in the communications efforts of businesses, regardless of the increasingly high-tech environment businesses operate in. The individuals who will master this mode of communication will remain essential to the fortunes of the organisation. To these individuals, many opportunities for leadership will open up, and they will eventually find themselves at the very top of the corporate ladder.

References

Blokzijl, W., & Andeweg, B. (2007). *The effect of text slides compared to visualizations on learning and appreciation in lectures*. Paper presented at IEEE International Professional Communication Conference, Seattle, WA. doi:10.1109/IPCC.2007.4464074.

Bradbury, A. (2006). *Successful presentation skills*. London, UK: Kogan Page.

Brusino, J. (2008). Great presentations. *Infoline, 25*(0809), 3.

Caplin, J. (2008). *I hate presentations: Transform the way you present with a fresh and powerful approach*. Oxford, UK: Capstone Publishing.

Charvatova, D. (2008). Relationship between communication effectiveness and the extent of communication among organizational units, *International Journal of Humanities and Social Sciences, 2*(5), 576–578.

Duarte, N. (2008). Slide: Ology – *The art and science of creating great presentations*. Sebastopol, CA: O'Reilly Media.

Gilbert, F. (2013). *Speaking up: Surviving executive presentations*. San Francisco, CA: Berrett-Koehler Publishers.

Harvard Business Review. (2014). *Presentations (20-Minute Manager Series)*. Boston, MA: Harvard Business Review Press.

Hattersley, M. (1996). *The key to making better presentations: Audience analysis*. Boston, MA: Harvard Business School Publication.

INTELECOM Hazardous Materials Training and Research Institute. (1999). *Communication skills for the environmental technician*. New York: John Wiley & Sons.

Kahrs, T. K. (2000). *Enhancing your presentation skills*. Bloomington, Indiana: iUniverse.

Kauer, M. (2011). *The Do's and Don'ts of delivering a presentation*. Berlin, Germany: epubli GmbH.

Kaul, A. (2005). *The effective presentation: Talk your way to success*. New Delhi: Response Books.

Kogon, K., England, B., & Schmidt, J. (2015). *Presentation advantage: How to inform and persuade any audience*. Dallas, TX: BenBella Books.

Koneru, A. (2008). *Professional communications*. New Delhi: Tata McGraw-Hill Publishing.

Lee, D. G., & Nelson-Neuhaus, K. (2002). *Presentations: How to calm down, think clearly, and captivate your audience*. Minneapolis, MI: Personal Decisions International.

Lundberg, D. (2011). *Presenting Powerfully*. Tampa, FL: Debbie Lundberg.

McLean, S. (2010). *Business communication for success*. Boston, MA: Flat World Knowledge.

Nishiyama, K. (2000). *Doing business with Japan: Successful strategies for intercultural communication*. Honolulu, Hawaii: University of Hawaii Press.

Reimold, C., & Reimold, P. M. (2003). *The short road to great presentations: How to reach any audience through focused preparation, inspired delivery, and smart use of technology*. Hoboken, NJ: John Wiley & Sons.

Sampson, E. (2003). *Creative business presentations: Inventive ideas for making an instant impact*. London, UK: Kogan Page.

Schwabish, J. (2017). *Better presentations: A guide for scholars, researchers, and wonks.* New York: Columbia University Press.

Sehgal, M., & Khetarpal, V. (2006). *Business communication.* New Delhi: Excel Books.

Seifert, J. W. (2015). *Visualisation, presentation, facilitation: Translation of the German classic* (30th ed.), Norderstedt, Germany: BoD – Books on Demand.

Sidons, S. (2003). *Presentation skills.* London, UK: CIPD (Original work published in 1998)

Stack, L. (2013). *Creating an effective presentation: Preparing for success, controlling the environment and overcoming fear.* Littleton, CO: The Productivity Pro.

Theobald, T. (2013). *Develop your presentation skills: Creating success* (2nd ed.), London, UK: Kogan Page.

Thielsch, M. T., & Perabo, I. (2012). Use and evaluation of presentation software. *Technical Communication, 59* (2), 112–123.

Wempen, F. (2007). *PowerPoint 2007 Bible.* Indianapolis, Indiana: Wiley Publishing.

Yate, M. J., & Sander, P. (2003). *The ultimate business presentations book: Make a great impression every time.* Avon, UK: Kogan Page.

Zelazny, G. (2000). *Say it with presentations: How to design and deliver successful business presentations.* New York: McGraw-Hill.

Chapter 21

Professional Grooming

J. N. Halm

Contents

Introduction

The importance of communication between individuals within an organisation, by whatever means, is crucial. Sethi and Seth (2009) described interpersonal communication within the organisation as 'an inseparable, essential and continuous process just like the circulatory system in the human body' (p. 32); clearly emphasising on how important communication is to the survival of the organisation just as blood is to the body.

Ruesch and Kees (1969) categorised non-verbal forms of communication into three broad classes. These are sign language, action language and object language. Sign language includes all forms of communication in which gestures replace words, numbers and punctuations. Action language includes all intended and unintentional physical signals that an observer can make inferences from. The final category is the object language which embraces all forms of non-verbal communication where material things are displayed, intentionally or unintentionally. In this last group, we find the meaning obtained from the display of things such as buildings, machines, art objects and construction works, as well as the human body and whatever is used as a covering.

Murphy et al. (1997) state that in oral communication, the outward appearance of the individual conveys a non-verbal message that affects the message being spoken. Feijoo et al. (2013) further argued that while an individual can decide whether to communicate verbally or not, non-verbal communication is very difficult to hide since the individual would constantly be sending out messages through the face and the body. Parasuraman et al. (1988) in listing the ten dimensions of service quality, highlighted tangibles, which they defined as including physical facilities, equipment and appearance of personnel.

Sharma (2018) stated that an individual's professional appearance, which is a combination of both the attire and grooming, sends out a message which either attracts or repels others. Additionally, a person's appearance is usually the first thing a customer sights, thereby creating a positive or negative first impression. Chaney and Martin (2007) assert that dressing and appearing right 'lends credibility to one's ideas and accomplishments' (p. 33). However, to get the appearance right to send the right message across, the individual must be groomed right.

The term 'professional grooming' cannot be easily defined as can be seen from the dearth of academic work on the term. In many instances, professional grooming actually relates to the proper cleaning and conditioning by professionals of animals such as dogs, horses, rabbits, cats and other such domesticated animals. However, for the purposes of customer service management, professional grooming can be defined as the act of properly preparing and maintaining one's body and appearance in order to communicate the right message, especially in the workplace setting. For individuals whose jobs predominantly involve dealing with customers on a regular basis, the need to communicate effectively is greatly emphasised.

Personal Grooming

Personal grooming refers to all the ways and means by which individuals manage their personal hygiene and appearance. It is about keeping the outward appearance appropriate at all times. It is expected of anyone whose job involves being in contact with customers on a daily basis to ensure that their personal grooming is always top-notch. Whatever is left unattended to will be noticed by customers, and thus, create a negative image for the customer service professional in particular and the organisation as a whole.

As an example, a customer might rate a particular experience of poor quality, not because of the quality of the product or service per se, but simply because a customer-handling professional appeared unkempt. The quality of grooming of the customer-handling professional, therefore, has a telling effect on the quality of the customer's experience.

Personal Hygiene

General personal hygiene practices are an essential part of any discussion on professional personal grooming. Grooming and personal hygiene are actually referring to the same practice, with the former being the older generic term (Smith, 2007). These two terms can sometimes be referred to as *personal care*.

For centuries, human beings have been engaged in various forms of grooming for a number of reasons – chief among them being the need to maintain good health. A healthy customer service professional is an asset to both the organisation and the customers. Therefore, any action that would enhance the health of the customer service provider must be heeded.

Grooming is the way the body defends itself against all forms of attack from the outside environment on the exposed parts of the human body (Smith, 2007). However, beyond the obvious health implications of proper grooming, it must also be stated that grooming communicates a message. It is a way of telling the world to take an individual seriously since they take themselves seriously enough to do personal grooming.

Poor grooming habits denote a lack of respect for one's self, which will translate to a lack of respect for one's customer. Good grooming affects one's self-image and confidence. Santos (1995) argues that a person's self-confidence is directly proportional to one's physical appearance and grooming. Good personal hygiene also indicates an individual who takes pride in what he or she does. Those who take time to properly groom themselves send out signals that they are detail-oriented and therefore can be trusted.

Key aspects of personal grooming for the customer service personnel include, but are not limited to, the hair (cuts and styles), face, makeup, facial hair, skin, fingers and nails, feet, toes and toenails. Good grooming also deals with clothing – including shoes, belts, ties, socks, handkerchiefs, accessories, etc.

Hair Care

The hair on the head of an individual plays a very important role in the self-image and self-esteem of that individual. Although it is particularly important for women, hair matters for both genders. It is claimed that a significant number of men fear losing their hair (Dingwall, 2010). Customer service professionals should ensure that they always keep their hair properly cleaned. The right shampoos should be used to ensure that hair looks healthy at all times.

The appearance of dandruff in an individual's hair negatively affects the appearance of the individual. It is worse if dandruff drops on one's clothing. Aside from the use of shampoos to banish dandruff, there are several homemade remedies that an individual can use to solve any dandruff problems. These involve the use of items such as olive oil, aloe vera, salt, lemon and coconut oil, among others.

Whatever hairstyle an individual decides to wear to work, the rule is that it must not be too eye-catching (Santos, 1995). The keyword in describing a hairstyle that is meant to be worn to the workplace is 'appropriate'. It is important to consider one's features and assets before going for a particular hairdo or hairstyle since not all hairstyles befit an individual's face.

Face

The face is always on display; therefore, it must always be as clean and as clear as possible. The use of makeup is must always be given serious consideration. Too much makeup has its own connotations. The professional look must be as natural as possible, with minimum application of makeup. In other words, good makeup is the one that does not call attention to itself.

Facial massage and treatment should not be the reserve of only ladies. Busy professionals can undertake their own facial treatments at home if they so wish. It is important that the face is properly cleaned to remove all traces of sweat, grease and dirt that build up during the day.

Facial Hair

Too much hair around the eyes, on the ears, or coming from the nostrils is unsightly, to say the least. There are those with hair growing between their eyebrows, giving them what people derogatorily refer to as a 'unibrow'. It makes the individual look very unkempt. Hair at the wrong places on a person's face can make even a well-groomed individual look hideous. The issue with hair on ears, between brows, and sticking out of the nostrils is that a good nose hair trimmer, tweezers and a bit of attention are all that it will take to get rid of the excess hair. For those who do not want to do this at home, a visit to the salon for a quick waxing job will do the trick. Since it does not require much effort to get rid of unsightly facial hair, a customer service representative who appears unsightly sends out a message that he or she could not be bothered about what anyone thinks.

For those who decide (or are allowed) to keep beards and moustaches, as is the case in many parts of Africa due to religious persuasions, the rule of thumb is to keep them regularly trimmed and neat. Moustaches must not be so long as to cover the upper lip. The rule for keeping beards and moustaches also apply to sideburns. They must be properly trimmed at all times.

Some organisations have strict rules against men keeping facial hair. Disney is one of such organisations. At Disney, men's hair is not allowed to cover their ears or touch the collar (Poisant, 2002). There is even an infamous 'No Facial Hair' policy for players of the American professional baseball team, New York Yankees. It is claimed that this particular policy has been in place since 1973 (Barbarisi, 2013). Facial hair for the military is dependent on the nation in question. There are some countries where servicemen are allowed to grow full beards while other nations strictly prohibit any facial hair. For some organisations, such as construction firms and oil refineries, banning facial hair is more for safety precautions rather than the aesthetics.

Oral Health

Oral health is currently perceived as being 'multi-faceted and includes the ability to speak, smile, smell, taste, touch, chew, swallow and convey a range of emotions through facial expressions with confidence and without pain, discomfort and disease of the craniofacial complex' (Glick et al., 2016, p. 916). From the above definition, it is clear that oral health involves more than just taking care of one's teeth.

Oral hygiene practices must be kept throughout the day. It is not enough to brush one's teeth in the morning and evening. Food particles that hide between the teeth can be removed through flossing. The tongue should also be well brushed because lots of bacteria reside on the tongue.

During the day, it is important that one is on guard regarding the quality of one's breath. It is a serious infraction against professional grooming for customers to detect a strong odour of spices such as onion, garlic or even a whiff of alcohol in one's breath. A customer-handling professional must always have breath mints and minty gums readily available.

Skin

The skin, being the largest organ of the human body means that it plays an integral role in any discourse on professional grooming. It is estimated on average, an adult has 18 square feet of skin covering the entire body, and this weighs about six pounds (Feibleman, 2012). Others have given the weight of the skin of an average to be approximately nine pounds (Engler & Arndt, 2010). The skin serves the unique purpose of being the organ that protects all internal organs from harmful substances within the environment.

The skin is in layers; with the topmost layer, the epidermis, consisting of cells that are in a constant state of regeneration. As the outermost cells wear off, new cells emerge from underneath to take their place. It is estimated that this process takes between a month and two months. The advantage in this is that an individual can always correct most skin conditions with the right management.

Knowing one's skin type is one of the first steps in maintaining great skin. Fitzpatrick, as cited in Butler (2000), provides a common way of identifying skin types. He categorises skin types into six groups according to their reaction to ultraviolet rays. These include I (always burns easily, never tans); II (burns easily, tans minimally); III (burns moderately, tans gradually); IV (burns minimally, tans easily); V (rarely burns, tans profusely); and VI (never burns, deeply pigmented). Bartky (2008), however, identified four skin types – dry, oily, normal and a combination of the first three.

For many people, the single most important thing they can do to maintain good and healthy skin is to reduce exposure to sunlight. It is also important to ensure that the skin is kept hydrated at all times. The skin must always be treated gently and with the utmost care.

Hands

Hands, just like the face, are almost always in view of customers. Therefore, the state of one's hands constantly communicates a message to customers. It is true that the condition of one's hands says a lot about the person. The hands are also one of the most easily contaminated of all the body organs. They, therefore, require constant grooming to ensure that they are always neat. For a customer service professional, hand care is most important because of the constant shaking of hands that is associated with the role.

A typical customer-handling professional might shake the hands of as many customers that he or she comes across within a typical day. According to Santos (1995), if your hands are not the kind of hands you would love to hold, then you must work on them daily. If the individual has rough skin, it helps to have hand lotion handy.

Fingernails

Dirt under the fingernails is one of the clearest signs of an improperly groomed customer service professional. This is why it is advisable to keep the nails short-clipped and well-filed. Weekly trimming of one's nails should be the least that can be done to create a positive impression in the minds of customers. Nails that are not filed well and left jagged can scratch the skin, accidentally causing injuries that can become infected. Unfiled fingernails can even rip clothing.

Feet

People, in general, tend to take good care of their bodies. However, the feet are one of the most ignored when it comes to personal hygiene. Most people will only begin to care for their feet and toes when they are faced with health challenges (Dingwall, 2010). In spite of their importance to our mobility and overall well-being, the feet are not given as much attention as the other parts of the body.

The role of air in keeping one's feet odour-free is well-known. This is because the feet have the tendency to sweat profusely when placed in shoes and socks for a long time. Aside from the possibility of bad odour emanating from one's shoes, fungal infection such as athlete's foot (tinea pedis) could occur. It is worth noting that in a work environment, personal grooming is more than a personal or private matter because one person's lack of proper hygiene can have an adverse effect on every other person in the workplace.

Toenails must be properly and regularly clipped and filed properly. Just as with fingernails, clipped toenails must not be left jagged so as to avoid injuries, which can be infected.

Clothing

Clothes introduce an individual to the world. It is one of the clearest statements an individual can make about his or her personality. Kudesia and Elfenbein (2013) assert that regardless of whether an employee faces customers constantly or deals only with colleagues internally, an employee's clothing is a strong brand indicator for an organisation. There is a good reason why the cabin crew of an airline always looks properly fitted and well-groomed. The message is that the crew takes care of itself, and so can be trusted to take care of their customers. It is expected of professionals in a particular field or industry to look like professionals from that field or industry. Customers would stay away from banks where the employees are shabbily dressed because bankers are expected to have a certain professional look. Most patients would not be too comfortable getting into a surgical theatre if the surgeon going to operate on them is shabbily dressed and looking unkempt.

The power of dressing right influences more than just the external customer. Even within the organisation, the kind and quality of clothing an individual wears to the workplace has a profound effect on whether or not he/she will be accepted by colleagues. Sharma (2018, p. 177) defines professional dressing as 'dressing in such a manner as to enhance your authority, command respect, and promote your advancement in the workplace'. It is true that the clothes a person wears may not be a good indication of who he/she is, but it actually leaves a lasting impression about who the person is.

In purchasing clothes for the workplace, regardless of the formality, Sabath (2000) advocated for what she referred to as the 'Four C's'. She stated that clothes for work must be *Correct* and appropriate, *Crisp* and clean, must have *Coordination*, and must be *Complementary*.

Colour can be added to this list of Cs since different colours have different meanings, and the wrong application of colours can send the wrong message. Andres and Ilada-Andres (1997, p. 23) state that 'color properly used is a joy to both the wearer and the beholder.'

Santos (1995) likens one's clothing to a frame around a picture with the picture being the individual. In choosing this frame, therefore, simplicity should be the watchword. If the frames overshadow the picture itself, then there is a problem.

Dress Codes

To ensure that the message that is transmitted from the attire of employees is consistent with the aspirations of the organisation, some organisations prefer to institute dress codes. Walt Disney in creating the Disney World brand was very strict on all customer-facing employees (referred to as 'cast members') having to present a uniform look. Walt Disney insisted that a uniform look eliminated any distraction for customers (referred to as 'guests') (Poisant, 2002).

There is another message that having a dress code communicates. It is a way of levelling the field for employees – regardless of the socioeconomic background of any employee. Florida and Kenney (1991) in promoting this idea cited the examples of firms in Japan where it was not unusual for top management to be dressed in the same manner as middle-level managers and even workers on the shop floor.

It is of importance to note that the way an individual dresses has a profound effect on the way he/she feels, and this goes a long way to affect the way he/she behaves. It was discovered that when individuals wore formal business attire, they felt more in command, trustworthy and competent. These individuals were at their friendliest when they were dressed in business casual or casual clothing (Peluchette & Karl, 2007).

The 2007 findings of Peluchette and Karl have serious implications for customer service, since in many parts of the world, organisations tend to adopt day-specific dress codes. In some countries, Mondays to Thursdays are mostly used for formal business attires while Fridays and weekends are for business casual or strictly casual attires. The implication, therefore, is that staff might tend to be friendlier towards customers as the weekend approaches than from the few first working days of the week.

Morem (2005) traced the trend of dressing casually to work from the 1990s. She stated that it did not take long before employees started taking advantage of the once-a-week occurrence to turn it into an everyday affair. Morem (2005) claims that there is a rise in a reversion to the times of more formal dress code because business leaders feared that the relaxing of the dress code was leading to relaxed attitudes towards work. Also, customer perceptions are leading to a departure from the casual to the more formal way of dressing to work. However, it is interesting to note that for some companies such as California-based global media-services provider, Netflix, there is not a dress code. This is because 'freedom' is one of the core beliefs of the organisation (Morgan, 2014). It seems, therefore, the best advice would be for employees to dress according to the atmosphere created by the vision and mission of the organisation.

Solomon and Schopler (1982) found that individuals perform better in roles when they feel their attire is appropriate for that role. This is why business leaders must ensure that employees come to work in the right attire. Even in organisations where there is no strict adherence to a dress code, individuals who desire to be taken seriously on the job would do well to dress according to the code of their managers. Following the lead of top management is an indication that the individual takes the position seriously and has plans to get ahead on the job (Andrews, 2008). Additionally, managers will not only notice such an individual, but will be more comfortable with him/her. Such an individual will most likely be recommended for higher responsibilities.

Andrews (2008) further differentiated between a dress code and a fashion code. He added that although many organisations have a dress code, very few have a clearly written-out fashion code. Therefore, it was possible for an individual to adhere to a dress code, but be off on the unwritten fashion code of the organisation. For instance, the dress code for men in an organisation might be a white shirt, a particular colour of necktie, dark suit and matching shoes. A customer service staff might come to work meeting all these standards, but the trousers (pants) length would be short enough for the one's socks to be visible when the one is standing upright. If the men in that organisation are used to having the fabric above the bottom of the front of the pant leg slightly creased over the shoe, a fashion code would have been defaulted.

It might be a personal choice, but the style of clothing should also be considered since appropriateness is a key aspect of communication. Right communication must be appropriate for a specific context. In other words, an individual can be well-dressed but not appropriately dressed. Attire that might be acceptable for a dinner might be out of place in the office setting. It is therefore important that customer-facing employees are made aware of the difference in the various attires. For example, employees must know the difference between a tuxedo and a suit. It is important to know what occasion calls for what type of attire.

Footwear

This is one item of clothing that can easily make or mar an individual's appearance. Category, colour and comfort should be the three main determinants of the business professional's choice of footwear.

Colour of the footwear must match the attire. This does not imply that clothing and shoes must have the same colour. However, certain colours do not match and take away from the appearance of the business professional. Any colour combination that becomes a distraction during a customer interaction should be avoided.

Shoes are made to be walked in, so it is important that the feet are comfortable in them. The size of a shoe must be just right. Too big or too small sizes can cause much embarrassment and affect the confidence and composure of the customer-facing professional. It would be very difficult to give a customer the best of smiles when the shoes are squeezing the life out of one's feet.

Shoes can also be a source of bad odour and must be properly aired after wearing them. This is especially true if the wearer's feet are allowed to sweat inside the shoes. Shoes must also be in good repair and always cleaned. Leather shoes must always be shined. A single smudge or speck of dirt on one's shoes can take away from an otherwise perfect look.

Body Odour

Regardless of how a customer service representative appears, an unpleasant odour becomes an infraction against personal grooming. A customer service professional must always consider the effect their body odour will have on the customer. Bathing is a universal method of ensuring that one's body is clean and fresh. Bathing can be a daily affair. Although, in warmer climates such as in Africa, it must be more than a once-a-day affair. Perineal care, the bathing of the private parts, is essential to personal hygiene. Bad body odour usually comes from the presence of bacteria breaking down the protein in the sweat produced by the apocrine glands (van Hoepen & Verster, 2008). The use of deodorant is a must for every business professional, although care must be taken to ensure that strong scents are used minimally. Bacteria are most active in the moist and warm areas of the body, such as the armpits and groin areas (Novick, 2000). These areas must, therefore, be properly washed daily and also be shaved well. A good aftershave can complement the use of perfume and leave the user with a fresh fragrance all day long.

A decent perfume or cologne can leave a positive impression on the minds of one's customers (Baron, 1988). In choosing a good fragrance, it is important to note the various kinds available. Lynch (2009) lists five categories of fragrances. These are floral, fruity, woody, green and oriental. A combination of these fragrances can create very memorable scents.

Proper Diet

If we are what we eat, then diet has a role to play in professional grooming. It is proven that carbohydrates are the body's first choice for energy, and this should be part of a healthy diet. Carbohydrates are also good for the proper functioning of the brain. As an important macronutrient, fats are essential for the maintenance of healthy hair and skin. The effect of a good balanced diet on the skin is well-known. What an individual eats shows in the skin so to look good, one must eat well.

Drinking enough water also adds to the well-being of the individual. It is true that more than half of the body is made up of water. Therefore, when the body lacks sufficient water, the skin suffers the most. The skin needs adequate water to be able to regenerate. Therefore, when starved of water, the effects begin to show and thereby affect the appearance of the individual. Skin moisturisers, lotions and creams work by helping to maintain moisture on the skin, which is why the skin glows when adequately moisturised.

Exercise

The body needs exercise to function properly. Much has been written about the benefits of regular exercise. Aside from increasing metabolism, helping to build stronger joints and bone density, lowering bad cholesterol, regulating blood sugar levels and lowering blood pressure, regular exercise also improves the mental capacity and mood of the individual (Lang, 2007). The latter benefit is one of the main reasons why customer service professionals should engage in regular exercise, especially in the morning. The demands of facing customers every day require that customer-handling professionals always try to maintain a good mood.

Those whose jobs involve sitting for long hours receiving and serving customers need to exercise well and regularly, as there are serious health implications in such work environments. According to Jebb and Moore (1999), there is evidence that those engaged in low levels of physical activity have a higher risk of weight gain and obesity.

Rest

A lack of rest can take away from the appearance of an individual. The lack of rest will show on the face, in the gait, and in the attitude of employees towards customers. Although the figures vary, it is well-accepted that the average person needs a lot of sleep at night. Walker (2017) stated that regularly sleeping less than six to seven hours a night affects the body's immune system and even doubles the person's risk of developing cancer.

Some experts have argued that the best mode of rest for the human body is to divide the rest during the day into two phases as opposed to the monophasic approach that is widely practised. Some tribes whose habits have not been affected by modernity tend to take the usual long night of seven to eight hours of sleep and also an afternoon half-an-hour to one-hour nap (Walker, 2017). This might explain the origin of the 'power nap'.

Influence of Culture and Religion on Personal Grooming

As personal as it might seem, personal hygiene really does not occur in a vacuum. Individuals live with others within a community and the way the community behaves – norms, beliefs, etc. – tends to affect the individual. In other words, even an individual's personal hygiene practices can be affected by the individual's culture and religion.

For instance, a number of the world's most prominent religions have specific rituals for washing of the hands and some other parts of the body. Strict adherence to these rules has implications for personal grooming practices of the individual adherent. A good example is the Islamic practice of washing the hands, face, forearms, ears, nose, mouth and feet, three times each as well as moistening one's hair with water.

In some cultures, individuals do not shave certain parts of their body, such as their armpits or even beards. In many cultures, the shaving of a woman's legs is not commonly practised. The challenge with the influence of culture and religion on personal hygiene is treading the thin line between religious conformity and professional grooming. Customer service professionals within certain establishments are torn between adhering to the dictates of their religious beliefs and the rules of the establishment.

From a traditional African perspective, grooming has been largely confined to a feminine activity. Many African men would not be too bothered about certain aspects of grooming such as skin and nail care. However, it can be said that attitudes are changing as the traditional distinct lines between the gender roles become increasingly blurred. These days, it is not out of place to see upwardly mobile gentlemen visit beauty parlours all over the continent for manicures and pedicures.

Conclusion

Employees represent an organisation; therefore, it is expected that the organisation takes a keen interest in the appearance and grooming of all employees. The culture of the organisation also has an effect on the grooming practices of employees. Organisations must put in place the right systems and structures to ensure that all employees adhere to the right professional grooming guides. Company dress code and personal hygiene policies must be strongly adhered to by all employees. Nickson, Warhurst and Dutton (2005) insist that it is a legitimate managerial strategy for service organisations to control the attitudes and appearance of employees for customer service purposes.

Customers will make decisions about doing business with a particular company based on the appearance of its staff. Professional grooming goes a long way in ensuring that the individuals who are the face of the organisation always put their best foot forward.

References

Andres, T. Q. D., & Ilada-Andres, P. C. B. (1997). *How to become a successful secretary Vol. 1 – Personality development*. Manila, Philippines: Rex Book Store.

Andrews, C. J. (2008). *Why didn't somebody tell me this stuff?* Morrisville, NC: Lulu Press.

Barbarisi, D. (2013, February 23). No beards – And that's final. The Yankees have no intention of ever dropping the boss's rules on facial hair. *The Wall Street Journal*, Retrieved from https://www.wsj.com/articles/SB10001424127887324048904578320741510151474.

Baron, R. A. (1988). Perfume as a tactic of impression management in social and organisational settings. In S. Van Toller & G. H. Dodd (Eds.), *Perfumery: The psychology and biology of fragrance* (pp. 91–106). Amsterdam, the Netherlands: Springer.

Bartky, D. S. (2008). *Grooming secrets for men: The ultimate guide to looking and feeling your best*. New York: iUniverse.

Butler, H. (2000). *Poucher's perfumes, cosmetics and soaps* (10th ed.). Berlin: Springer.

Chaney, L. H., & Martin, J. S. C. (2007). *The essential guide to business etiquette*. Westport, CT: Praeger.

Dingwall, L. (2010). *Personal hygiene care*. Chichester, UK: Wiley-Blackwell.

Engler, N., & Arndt, K. A. (2010). *Skin care and repair*. Boston, MA: Harvard Health Publications.

Feibleman, J. K. (2012). *Technology and reality*. Hague, the Netherlands: Martinus Neijhoff Publishers.

Feijoo, H. M. P., Hernández, J. M. P., Gonzalez, L. L., & Bravo, C. C. (2013). *Communication & customer service: Advanced vocational training*. Madrid: McGraw-Hill Interamericana de España, S.L.

Florida, R., & M. Kenney. (1991). Transplanted organization: The transfer of Japanese industrial organizations to the US. *American Sociological Review, 56*(3), 381–398.

Glick, M., Williams, D. M., Kleinman, D.V., Vujicic, M., Watt, R. G., & Weyant, R. J. (2016). A new definition for oral health developed by the FDI world dental Federation opens the door to a universal definition of oral health. *Journal of the American Dental Association, 147*(12), 915–916.

Jebb, S. A., & Moore, M. S. (1999). Contribution of a sedentary lifestyle and inactivity to the etiology of overweight and obesity: Current evidence and research issues. *Medicine & Science in Sports & Exercise, 31*(11), S534.

Kudesia, R., & Elfenbein, H. (2013). Nonverbal communication in the workplace. In J. A. Hall & M. L. Knapp (Eds.), *Nonverbal communication* (pp. 805–832). Berlin: De Gruyter Mouton. doi:10.13140/RG.2.1.2270.6325.

Lang, A. (2007). *Morning strength workouts*. Champaign, IL: Human Kinetics.

Lynch, L. (2009). *Romance cooking: Unlocking the secrets of seducing Mars or Venus*. Bloomington, IN: AuthorHouse.

Morem, S. (2005). *How to gain the professional edge: Achieve the personal and professional image you want* (2nd ed.). New York: Ferguson.

Morgan, J. (2014). *The future of work: Attract new talent, build better leaders, and create a competitive organization*. Hoboken, NJ: John Wiley & Sons.

Murphy, H. A., Hildebrandt, H.W., & Thomas, J. P. (1997). *Effective Business Communications* (7th ed.). Boston, MA: McGraw-Hill.

Nickson, D., Warhurst, C., & Dutton, E. (2005). The importance of attitude and appearance in the service encounter in retail and hospitality. *Journal of Service Theory and Practice, 15*(2), 195–208. doi: 10.1108/09604520510585370.

Novick, N. (2000). *Skin care for teens*. Lincoln, UK: iUniverse.

Parasuraman, A. P., Berry, L. L., & Zeithaml, V. A. (1988). SERVQUAL: A multiple- Item Scale for measuring consumer perceptions of service quality. *Journal of Retailing, 64*(1), 12–40.

Peluchette, J. V., & Karl, K. (2007). The impact of workplace attire on employee self-perceptions. *Human Resource Development Quarterly, 18*(3), 345–360.

Poisant, J. (2002). *Creating and sustaining a superior customer service organization: A book about taking care of the people who take care of the customers*. Westport, CT: Quorum books.

Ruesch, J., & Kees, W. (1969). *Nonverbal communication: Notes on the visual perception of human relations*. Berkeley, CA: University of California Press.

Sabath, A. M. (2000). *Beyond business casual: What to wear to work if you want to get ahead*. New York: ASJA Press.

Santos, A. E. (1995). *Office management in a computerized office*. Manila, Philippines: Rex Book Store.

Sethi, D., & Seth, M. (2009). Interpersonal communication: Lifeblood of an organization. *The IUP Journal of Soft Skills, 3*(3/4), 32–40.

Sharma, P. (2018). *Soft skills personality development for life success*. New Delhi: BPB Publications.

Smith, V. (2007). *Clean: A history of personal hygiene and purity*. Oxford, UK: Oxford University Press.

Solomon, M. R., & Schopler, J. (1982). Self-consciousness and clothing. *Personality and Social Psychology Bulletin, 8*(1), 508–514.

Van Hoepen, L., & Verster, V. (2008). *Client services and human relations – Level 2 (FET College Series)*. Cape Town: Pearson Education.

Walker, M. (2017). *Why we sleep: Unlocking the power of sleep and dreams*. New York: Scribner.

Chapter 22

Twenty Traits of Customer Service Champions

J. N. Halm

Contents

Introduction

With the increasingly competitive environment many businesses find themselves in, any advantage – no matter how small – would be welcome by many business owners, leaders, managers and supervisors. That excellent customer service confers an unmatched advantage for businesses is a fact that few would debate. Tomes have been written about the unique advantages that businesses that are known to provide the best services have over those whose service is unsatisfactory.

    Although every organisation provides some sort of service to customers, within every organisation, there are those who directly deal with customer requests and serve customers on a daily basis. It is important to note that being in any such position in an organisation is not an automatic qualification for being someone who is adept at providing the kind of customer service that can be described as 'excellent'.

To find out what makes these individuals great at championing the cause of excellent customer service, it is important to start from the basics by finding out what customer service is all about.

Defining Customer Service

It is difficult to find a universally accepted definition of the term *customer service* in spite of the fact that it is one of the most discussed business topics. Customer service has been simply defined as including the service provided in support of a business core product (Zeithaml et al., 2010). Another simple definition stresses on an organisation's ability to supply the wants and needs of its customers (Chinunda, 2013). However, Gibson (2012, p. 6) defined customer service as 'the process of satisfying the customer, relative to a product or service, in whatever way the customer defines his or her need, and having that service delivered with efficiency, compassion, and sensitivity'. Hudson and Hudson (2013, p. 5) defined *customer service* as 'the practice of delivering products and service to both internal and external customers via the efforts of employees or through the provision of an appropriate servicescape'. For others, it is a matter of 'treating customers with respect and dignity at all times, trying to determine the best and most equitable way of giving the customer what he or she is seeking, and trying to view the situation from the perspective of the customer' (Rask, 2008, p. 31).

Others have simply defined customer service as anything that touches the customer (Coyle et al., 2008).

It is one thing to offer service to one's customers, and it is a totally different ball game to offer the kind of service that customers would mark as 'excellent'. There are a number of factors that must be present to make a particular customer service excellent.

The first quality of customer service that makes it excellent is that it must be 'constant'. It is not enough to provide great service occasionally. It must always be present. Customers must not be made to worry about the quality of service they are going to receive at each visit. They must know and trust that the quality would always be great. That is what excellent customer service is about.

The second quality that makes customer service excellent is that it must be 'consistent'. It is important to distinguish between constant and consistent. The word 'constant' in this context, refers to the quality of being unchanging. However, being 'consistent' is when the thing is, in addition to being constant, also behaves, in the same manner, each time. Brands are built on the consistency of their actions. Therefore, if a business wants to be known for providing excellent customer service, then it must ensure that the quality of service is the same every single time. The quality of service on Monday morning in a certain week should be the same, if not better, the following Monday. One disadvantage of inconsistent customer service is the confusion it creates for customers. Customers would always be in a state of anxiety since they can never be too sure of the kind of service they would be receiving during each encounter.

The third quality of customer service that makes it excellent is that it must exceed customer expectations. Customer service is really about managing expectations. In the end, it is the customer who has the 'marking scheme' for what actually constitutes excellent customer service. It is the customer who decides whether a particular service has been up to the standards or not. To get the customer to give the organisation or the experience the highest marks that constitute excellence, there is a need for the one handling the customer to possess certain traits.

The actions of customer-handling professionals that ensures that customers find a certain quality of service as being very impressive are mostly things these individuals do out of their own will.

These seemingly insignificant things that customer service professionals do that win the hearts of customers are not forced out of these professionals. They do those things because they know it is just right to do so. Coercion is not behind these acts.

Hence, *Excellent Customer Service* must be defined as the provision of consistent feats of volition that constantly exceed customer expectations.

Customer Service and Handling People

A common theme running through most definitions of customer service is people. It takes people to serve people. Customer service is really about managing people and their expectations. Excellent customer service is about handling people comprising of colleagues in the office or external paying and non-paying customers. Without people, there will be no customer service.

Humans are inherently social beings (Baumeister & Bushman, 2017). We crave the attention of fellow humans. Customers – being human as they are – prefer to be served by people, even in this increasingly tech-saturated environment businesses find themselves in. More than half of customers (57%) who place calls to organisations for business do so because they prefer to talk to a real person (Google LLC, 2013, p. 8). There seems to be an inherent desire for human-to-human contact without any, or with minimal, technological mediation.

Handling People and Leadership

Handling people and handling them well is one of the key mandates of a great leader. Leadership has been defined as the ability to enthuse others to follow a definite goal. It has also been said to be the ability to get individuals to work together as a group to achieve a common goal. To several others, leadership is about wielding influence and using it for the common good. Yet, others have defined it as the ability to motivate the actions of other people. Leadership is also that quality of having the kind of confidence in one's ability that attracts others to follow. Leadership is also a process of eliciting the greatness that already exists in other people and putting it to good use.

A definition of a good leader, therefore, must necessarily include one's ability to handle other people (Cribbin, 1981; Pattar, 2017; Tannenbaum et al., 1961; Donelly et al., 1985; Cohen, 1990). In other words, a person is called a leader because he/she leads people.

If both leadership and customer service are about handling people, then it will be safe to surmise that those who will excel at customer service must be those who possess the necessary leadership qualities.

Leaders and Champions

Cavitt (2007) refers to those individuals within an organisation who are committed to the delivery of excellent customer service as 'Customer Service Superstars'. They are those employees who are very committed to delivering an excellent service experience, constantly ensuring that the voice of the customer is always heard within the organisation. In their interactions with customers, these service champions are able to communicate effectively with their customers, leading to the formation of very strong and long-lasting relationships with these customers.

A customer service champion is, therefore, a leader of service excellence – a leader in every sense of the word. Through the provision of great customer service, these individuals, regardless of their job titles, provide leadership at the workplace. They are those who will eventually grow through the organisation to prominent leadership positions. Unsurprisingly, *customer service champions* happen to be great leaders. Great leaders are great because they are great at handling people. They know what to say, when to say and how to say the right things. They are able to carry others along towards a common goal.

A *customer service champion* must also know what to say to customers, at what time to say it and how to say it. On a regular basis, those whose job it is to champion the cause of great customer service are required to provide good leadership in whatever situation they find themselves. It takes leadership to win a customer and to maintain the relationship. It takes leadership to solve a customer's problems. When a customer is aggrieved and needs an issue handled professionally, it calls for leadership. In fact, it takes leadership to get a customer to fall in love with the product-service offering as well as the experience for the customer to keep coming back repeatedly. In that light, it can be argued that those who must serve customers well, must actually lead them.

The Quintessential Customer Service Champion

Hudson and Hudson (2013) used the example of Walt Disney to stress the point that it takes one very committed individual to drive the customer service philosophy of an organisation. Undoubtedly, Walt Disney was the quintessential Customer Service Champion. Walt Disney's business philosophies and his unbridled desire to focus attention on the customer's experience led to the creation of a multi-million dollar business. Disney University, the global training programme for Disney employees, is recognised as one of the world's leading customer service training programs. Disney Institute, the professional development and external training arm of The Walt Disney Company, is also known for offering some of the highest-quality training and advisory services to organisations worldwide based on the tenets of Walt Disney. The sheer number of books written about 'The Walt Disney way' of doing things is enough proof that Walt Disney was indeed a *customer service champion*.

What makes a Walt Disney? What makes a *customer service champion*? What makes an individual becomes so committed to always ensuring that the customer's experience is always positively memorable? What specific qualities stand out in the *customer service champion*? These are the questions that must be answered in any quest to unearth more of those who will champion the cause of great customer service in any organisation.

Leadership: Nature or Nurture, Traits or Skills

If customer service champions are truly leaders within the organisation, then the age-old question of whether leaders are born or made springs up. Are certain individuals born with the traits to be great at offering excellent customer service? Is there a genetic predisposition that makes some individuals more adept at being customer service champions?

Although the purpose of leadership has remained constant over the years, there has been an evolution of leadership over the years, and this has gradually affected the conceptualisation and definition of what leadership is and what it constitutes. The leaders of yesteryears, effective as they might have been, might fail woefully in these rapidly changing times. Leadership styles that were hailed in centuries gone by would, at best, be seen as crude in this present dispensation.

Rauch and Behling (1984) asserted that there were four broad theories used by most research on the nature of leadership. These are *Universal Trait, Universal Behaviour, Situational Trait* and *Situational Behaviour*.

The earliest thoughts on leadership centred on the idea that some individuals were born with the gift of leadership. Up to the mid-nineteenth century, these theories held sway and gained much support. This line of thinking meant that some people had an early advantage in life right from birth. Regardless of how hard others worked, if they were not meant to be leaders, they were never going to be leaders. Unsurprisingly, many leaders were viewed as divine beings and not mere mortals.

Subsequently, however, the so-called Great Man Theory of Leadership gradually gave way, albeit not drastically, to a new line of thought about leadership. The new argument was that leaders were born leaders because they were born with traits that made them leaders. This slight departure from the Great Man Theories became known as the Trait Leadership Theories. The mainstay of this newer leadership thought was that individuals were not necessarily born as leaders. However, those born with certain traits were likely to become leaders. Therefore, by identifying these traits, it was assumed that leaders could undoubtedly be identified. The Universal Trait Theories, which postulated that great leaders are born and not made and that all great leaders will have certain common characteristics, have obviously not stood the test of time. There are no universal traits found that are common to all leaders.

The Trait Leadership Theories also fell short in one very important detail – the conditions available to the leader. The environment in which an individual is placed has a bearing on whether that individual grows to become the leader that they were 'born' to be. For instance, the kind of colleagues around the individual would determine, to a large extent, the way the individual would react to circumstances. From this line of thinking came a realisation that rather than being identified by certain traits, leaders were to be identified by what they do under the circumstances they find themselves in. The ideas that emanated from this line of thinking were referred to as Contingency Theories.

Acceptable as the Contingency Theories of Leadership sound, there is another predominant thought pattern on leadership that followed from after it. This is referred to as the Behavioural Theories. The advocates of this thought pattern argue that great leaders are not born; rather, great leaders train themselves to be great. This school of thought proposed that, regardless of one's genetic predisposition, if one puts in considerable effort and patience with time, one would eventually display the necessary leadership qualities.

From the preceding discourse, it is clear that after centuries and centuries of this debate, the growing consensus is that leaders are more 'made' than 'born'. *Customer service champions*, must, therefore, be made and not born. The Walt Disneys of our time put in the time and effort to become what they became. In other words, what made them customer service champions were not traits, but rather skills developed over time.

Blank (2001), who was of the view that leaders were not born, catalogued 108 skills that leaders had to develop to enable them to perform as leaders. The possession of these skills by certain individuals is what gives people the impression that these 'special' people were born leaders. Blank (2001) separated the skills into Foundational Skills, Leadership Direction Skills and Leadership Influence Skills. Foundational Skills have to do with self-awareness and establishing rapport with others. Direction Skills have to do with charting a course as a leader and developing leadership in others. Influence Skills have to do with how to create the kind of atmosphere that engenders the creation of a core of committed and willing followers.

Farlow (2012, p. 5) stated that there was no 'genetically determined mould' from which leaders sprung. Farlow (2012) listed as many as 40 simple skills that individuals can develop that would make them the leaders they want to be. These include Having a Vision, Being Action-Oriented, Accepting Responsibility, Being Creative, Having Respect for Ethics and Developing People, amongst others.

Melecio (2014) noted that for a leader to become great, he or she must get two main things right. The individual must first, be good with people and situations, and secondly, the person must be good with the tasks at hand. If there are any top qualities that are needed by leaders in general, and by extension, customer service champions, then they might include *People Skills, Situational Awareness* and *Technical Skills.*

The analysis of Melecio (2014) regarding the necessary leadership qualities are similar to those postulated by Katz (2009). The major difference between the two is that whereas Melecio (2014) refers to the fact that the leader must be good with situations in addition to People Skills and Technical Skills, Katz (2009) added *Conceptual Skills* to the mix. Conceptual Skills go beyond just being situationally aware. It is about seeing the big picture, not only in a particular situation at a time, but from the perspective of the entire organisation. Schermerhorn, Jr. (2010) indicated that the three skills were of different importance depending on the level of the individual within the organisation. Technical skills were more important than the other two skills to lower level managers, whereas top-level managers would need a lot more conceptual skills than they would need technical skills. It is of interest to note that regardless of one's level in the business, human (people) skills were needed in equal measure.

Human (People) Skills

A customer service champion must necessarily possess great people skills, in addition to all other skills. To handle customers successfully requires good interpersonal skills, otherwise known as people skills. These are the competencies that aid the interaction and communication with others within a social setting. Interpersonal skills can, therefore, be referred to as social skills.

Social skills are the 'tools that enable people to communicate, learn, ask for help, get needs met in appropriate ways, get along with others, make friends, develop healthy relationships, protect themselves, and in general, be able to interact with the society harmoniously' (Dowd & Tierney, 2005, p. 1). It is easy to see how these functions relate to the role of a customer service champion. Customer service champions must communicate with customers, get along with customers – both outside and inside the organisation, make friends with customers and develop a healthy relationship with them.

Some authors contrast hard skills, that is, technical knowledge and ability, with intrapersonal and interpersonal skills, which they refer to as soft skills. Klaus (2007, p. 2) described soft skills as those that 'cover a wide spectrum of abilities and traits: being self-aware, trustworthiness, conscientiousness, adaptability, critical thinking, attitude, initiative, empathy, confidence, integrity, self-control, organizational awareness, likability, influence, risk-taking, problem-solving, leadership, time management, and then some'.

Due to the fact that these skills are vital for lubricating human-to-human interactions, they are therefore a prerequisite to success for those whose daily tasks involve dealing with people. Due to their importance, people skills are in such high demand that the probability of prospective employees getting hired is in direct proportion to the level of people skills they possess. Even in fields where technical knowledge is most prized, such as medicine, there is a growing awareness of the need for interpersonal skills (Barakat, 2007). Hargie et al. (1994) asserted that training programmes on interpersonal skills had been reported in the literature for a wide range of professions, including firemen, policemen, engineers, pharmacists and librarians, among others.

Thompson (1996) delineated 20 skills he found to be useful in ensuring the personal effectiveness of individuals, especially in dealing with people. These skills were grouped into three broad categories, namely *Personal Effectiveness Skills, Interaction Skills* and *Intervention Skills*.

According to Thompson (1996), personal effectiveness skills are those that are necessary for helping the individual manage his or her own self. They can also be referred to as intrapersonal skills. Interaction skills are the skills needed for maximising the interactions between the customer-handling employee and the customer. Intervention skills are the skills used to directly counter the common problems that customers face during a service interaction or in the process of experiencing a service. These skills are essential for a good performance of individuals on the job.

Personal Effectiveness Skills include

- *Self-Awareness*
- *Time Management*
- *Stress Management*
- *Assertiveness*
- *Using Supervision*
- *Continuous Professional Development*

Interaction Skills are

- *Dealing with Diversity*
- *Verbal Communication*
- *Non-Verbal Communication*
- *Written Communication*
- *Interviewing*
- *Handling Feelings*
- *Handling Conflict*

Intervention Skills are

- *Anti-Discriminatory Practice*
- *Being Systematic*
- *Assessment*
- *Planning*
- *Review and Evaluation*
- *Termination*
- *Reflective Practice*

A careful study of these skills in relation to customer service reveals a direct correlation to the skills exhibited by those referred to as *customer service champions*. Thompson's broad categorisation, therefore, forms the foundation on which to discover the traits of customer service champions.

Schermerhorn, Jr. (2010) argues that those who have great human or people skills are also more likely to have high emotional intelligence. Mayer and Salovey (1997, p. 5) define emotional intelligence as 'the ability to perceive emotions, to access and generate emotions so as to assist thought, to understand emotions and emotional knowledge, and to reflectively regulate emotions so as to promote emotional and intellectual growth'.

Situational (Situation) Awareness

Although the concept has its roots from military strategy, situational awareness (SA) has usefulness in any setting that deals with people. Endsley (1995, p. 35) defined situation awareness as 'the perception of the elements in the environment within a volume of time and space, the comprehension of their meaning, and the projection of their status in the near future'.

It is about being aware of what is going on around you at any point in time and understanding what that information means to you now and in the future. Flin et al. (2008, p. 17) defined SA as 'the cognitive processes for building and maintaining awareness of a workplace situation or event' or 'knowing what is going on around you'. It is seeing the big picture and acting in a manner that is right. Situation awareness is sometimes used interchangeably with the term 'situational awareness' (Flin et al., 2008).

SA is that ability to walk on to the shop floor or customer reception area, take a quick glance around and notice that something is wrong without being told. SA is a skill that can be developed over a period of time. The three main elements of SA are gathering information, interpreting the information and anticipating future states (Flin et al., 2008).

At the first level, the individual is expected to gather information from the environment using all the senses. For instance, observing the behaviour of colleagues, hearing what others are saying around you and even picking up the odour in the office. To be able to quickly gather information in a situation, the customer service champion must fully develop his or her powers of observation.

With the information gathered, the next phase is to make meaning of it. The information will be interpreted based on what is stored in the individual's long-term memory. The brain works in such a way that any information that is processed is stored up for later use. Therefore, when new information is gathered which looks like something previously encountered, the brain quickly deciphers it and a corresponding decision is made. This makes a lot of our decisions seem routine. Our past experiences, therefore, directly affect our interpretations of current events. However, sometimes the mind's interpretation of a piece of information can be erroneous.

The final level in SA is in anticipating what will happen next. Individuals with high levels of SA seem to be able to see things ahead of time. For the customer service champion, this is a very crucial aspect of the SA skill set. An ability to anticipate the customer's needs, wants and concerns before the customer verbally expresses a request does a lot of good for the relationship. Customers appreciate it when their requests are anticipated ahead of time.

Technical Skills

Besides people skills and SA, Melecio (2014) stated that the leader must be skilled at the task at hand. In other words, technical skills are very important for the success or otherwise of the customer service champion. Schermerhorn, Jr. (2010, p. 12) defined a technical skill as 'the ability to use a special proficiency or expertise to perform particular tasks'.

Regardless of how skilled the individual is at dealing with people and being aware of whatever is going on around, if one is not adept at the task at hand, the quality of customer service will still be adversely affected. A bank teller must, in the very least, be adept at handling customers' money. If one fumbles often, mixes up customers' money, and cannot do simple arithmetic, the quality of service delivery will not be regarded as excellent – regardless of how well she handles people and how situationally aware she is.

In the past, having the right technical skills relating to one's specific job was enough for the individual to thrive on the job. However, the current dispensation of a digitally-saturated workplace calls for individuals to have the requisite skills to effectively make use of the digital technologies that have become part and parcel of the workplace. Many of these skills are almost second nature to the younger and more tech-savvy generation who are appropriately referred to as 'digital natives' (Di Giacomo et al., 2018, p. 4). However, for the older generation, there must be a conscious attempt to unlearn the old ways of doing things and to learn new ways.

van Deursen and van Dijk (2008) enumerated four distinct types of digital skills. These are: *Operational Skills* or the skills needed to operate digital media; *Formal Skills* or the skills needed to handle the special structures of digital media; *Information Skills* or the skills needed to search, select, and evaluate information in digital media; as well as *Strategic Skills* or the skills needed to employ the information contained in digital media.

As customers become more tech-savvy and as technology becomes more sophisticated, the need for the customer service champion to possess the aforementioned skill set would become more important. The individuals who will thrive in providing superior service to customers would be those who will proactively upgrade their skill set in these areas. The job market would become increasingly unfriendly to those without these skills.

The need for digital skills has far greater implications than just for the customer service professional and the organisation involved; digital skills are needed if organisations in Africa are to provide the kind of service that is truly exceptional. The truth is that customer service is not very high on the agenda of many organisations on the continent. Chinunda (2013) painted a very bleak picture of the quality of customer service by companies in Africa. However, with the ability of digital technology to personalise the customer's experience, companies in Africa have the perfect opportunity to improve the experiences of their customers. With the right technologies, organisations can easily recognise customers by name, remember the preferences of these customers and employ that information to help customers make the best purchasing decisions. It must be stated, nevertheless, that all this will be possible if those charged with serving customers have the right digital skills.

Conceptual Skill

Katz (2009) explained conceptual skill as that ability to find the interrelationship between all parts and functions of the organisation. It deals with how changes in these different parts and functions affect one other. Conceptual skills also involve having an idea of how the organisation relates to all other stakeholders, such as industry players, regulatory bodies and the community in which the organisation operates. It is about how external factors affect the fortunes of the organisation. The ability to see the big picture helps the leader make the decisions that best serve the purpose of the organisation. For the *customer service champion*, conceptual skills help in understanding how policy changes will affect the relationships with customers.

Since these are skills that can be acquired, it behoves on organisations to ensure that employees, particularly those whose job schedules require direct dealings with customers, are taken through the kind of orientation, training and coaching that equips them with these skills. Training must go beyond just emphasising on skills around a job function but must incorporate a lot of human-to-human interactions (Chakraverty, 2018). Obakpolo (2015) recommends that the management of organisations intervene to promote friendships at work by initiating activities both within and outside the workplace.

It is therefore evident that skills, rather than genetic traits, are what customer service champions would need to excel in their chosen line of work. However, with all these skills listed, which ones should the individuals who want to be *customer service champions* concentrate on? What are the top 20 skills that distinguish a normal customer service representative from a customer service champion? Taking into consideration all that has been discussed on the skills needed for leadership, the following list has been compiled.

Top 20 Skills Needed by Every Customer Service Champion

As earlier stated, customer service is a people business. Therefore, it would be expected that of the most important 20 skills needed by customer service champions, a greater portion would involve interpersonal skills. However, it is imperative that individuals who aspire to be customer service champions first work on themselves before engaging with their customers. This accounts for the first set of skills – the intrapersonal skills.

- **Intrapersonal Skills**
  1. *Self-Awareness*: To know oneself, strengths and weaknesses alike, is the foundation of greatness. *Customer service champions* have a good idea of who they really are. They know their own capabilities and limits and so are hardly overtaken by circumstances. Those with highly developed self-awareness are not very judgemental on themselves when things do not go according to expectations.
  2. *Intrapersonal Communications*: It has been established that customer service is about communicating with customers. However, before one can effectively communicate with others, one must know how to effectively communicate with oneself. *A customer service champion* can apply self-talk to calm his or her nerves down before reacting to a situation. Self-talk can be used to rehearse what one intends to say to another person before one says it.
  3. *Time Management*: The ability to manage oneself and one's activities so that an apparent lack of time is not a challenge is an attribute of a *customer service champion*. Such individuals ensure that they are not overwhelmed with duties that will adversely affect their commitments to their customers. They understand the importance of prioritisation of tasks.
  4. *Self-Confidence*: Knowing one's ability is one thing and having confidence in that ability is another thing. Dealing with different customers from different socioeconomic backgrounds requires a high sense of self-confidence. Customer service champions cannot be intimidated by a customer.
  5. *Inner Drive for Excellence*: The role of volition in the creation of excellent customer service cannot be disregarded. The most amazing examples of excellent customer service were mostly as a result of individuals acting on their own accord without being prompted. *Customer service champions* must, therefore, be individuals who seek and practice excellence in all their dealings on their own accord.
- **Human (People/Interpersonal/Social)Skills**
  6. *Interpersonal Communications*: This is the bedrock of great customer service. An ability to communicate well lubricates the business–customer relationship. Customer service champions know what to say to customers, how to say it and when to say it, whether in writing, over the phone or in-person. When they are before a customer, they are conscious of their body language as well as their words. Customer service champions are conscious of their appearance because they are aware of the implications of the way one presents oneself to the customer.

7. *Questioning*: To serve customers well, it is imperative that one needs to know what is going on in the mind of that customer. To get into the minds of customers calls for asking the right questions at the right time and in the right way. *Customer service champions* possess the requisite skills to ask the right questions to unearth customer concerns.

8. *Listening*: Listening goes beyond hearing. When customers have something to say, it pays to listen. Customer service champions know this and therefore have developed the right listening skills to employ when necessary.

9. *Empathy*: To step in the shoes of a customer and to feel his/her pain is a trait of a customer service champion. It is important to feel someone's pain. It is a natural unconscious response that every right-thinking human being has. However, customer service champions have the ability to consciously relate with a customer's situation and therefore go to great lengths to proffer appropriate solutions.

10. *Open-Mindedness*: A customer service champion must not be myopic in his or her views. Dealing with different people from different backgrounds calls for a non-discriminatory attitude. Individuals who are judgemental and prejudiced will struggle to deal with the attitudinal, cultural, racial, socioeconomic and individual diversities that different customers come along with.

11. *Stress Management*: Dealing with customers on a daily basis is emotionally draining. Those who are unconscious of this fact and therefore do nothing about it are those who end up losing their temper in the presence of customers or even worse, get into fights with customers. A *customer service champion* stays above the fray and has a variety of ways to manage the stress that comes with the job.

12. *Conflict Management*: Those who serve customers regularly know that conflicts are a staple of the job. Things sometimes go wrong – sometimes in the most spectacular fashion. Customer service champions know what to do when these unpleasant situations occur.

13. *Assertiveness*: Indeed, many customers tend to take advantage of an organisation's desire to please them. Some customers have the capacity to cause untold damage if they are not kept in check. This is why *customer service champions* must be assertive, and yet professional when they encounter such customers. When a customer demands something that is unethical or even criminal, assertiveness is needed to reject such demands. Customer-handling professionals should not be afraid to lose a customer if they become assertive.

14. *Creativity*: Not all solutions to customer service challenges would be found in a manual or policy document. Some problems require creative thinking on the part of the *customer service champion* to find an amicable solution. Individuals who always apply the rules to the letter tend to come across as robotic and inflexible. A customer service champion must be able to think outside the box to come up with solutions that would be mutually agreeable to both the organisation and the customer.

15. *Flexibility*: The current state of the work environment calls for individuals who can adapt to changing circumstances, embrace new ideas and be resourceful enough to take advantage of the changing situations. The *customer service champion* must be adaptable to customer demands and conditions without defaulting in any rule of the organisation.

16. *Decisiveness*: Decisiveness is one of the qualities of excellent customer service. As activities continue to increase within the same 24-hour period, time will become 'scarcer' for customers. Those who aspire to be *customer service champions* must, therefore, have the ability to make decisions quickly and effectively. The risk of losing a customer is high if too much time is wasted in making a decision.

17. *Teamwork*: A customer service champion knows that it takes the entire organisation to offer the best of services to a customer. Even a one-man organisation still needs others to make things work. A *customer service champion*, therefore, develops the right teamwork skills to enable one to thrive within the organisation.

■ *Conceptual Skills*

18. *Conceptual Skills*: Dealing with different customers with different mindsets and attitudes sometimes presents very abstract challenges that require an ability to see through the challenges and to formulate concrete solutions. This is a skill required of *customer service champions*. They must be able to instantly see how one decision would be able to impact future interactions with other customers.

■ *Situational Awareness Skills*

19. *Situational Awareness*: A *customer service champion* must have the capacity to scan the environment, make meaning of happenings and make accurate projections about future events. The individual must be able to detect customer dissatisfaction 'a mile away' and take decisions to nip any negative situation in the bud. This particular skill requires the individual to have an eye for minute details.

■ *Technical Skills*

20. *Continuous Professional Self-Development*: *Customer service champions* understand that though they might be employed by an organisation, they are actually their own 'bosses'. They are therefore willing to always upgrade themselves on the job. They know that their competence on the job can open up future opportunities, so they use their own resources to improve themselves. They buy books, read and study broadly about their job and industry. They learn of the latest developments about their job before the average employee does. Individuals who stagnate on the job because the organisation refuses to send them for training cannot become *customer service champions*. As discussed previously, in a rapidly evolving digital era, an individual must constantly upgrade his or her digital skills to survive and thrive on the job.

Conclusion

Customer service will continue to remain critical to the fortunes of businesses as competition increases and as customers become more knowledgeable. As technology improves, the playing field will continue to be levelled. More advanced software and mobile applications will ensure that even micro businesses will have a fighting chance against their more established competitors. A major area where organisations can outperform competition is in the quality of service they provide. This is where the need for *customer service champions* will play out, and as the competition increases, this need will only continue to grow. Those individuals with the right skill set will become most sought-after, both within and from outside their organisations.

References

Barakat, N. G. (2007). Interpersonal skills. *Libyan Journal of Medicine, 2*(3), 152–153. doi:10.4176/070620

Baumeister, R. F., & Bushman, B. J. (2017). *Social psychology and human nature, Comprehensive edition* (4th ed.), Boston, MA: Cengage Learning.

Blank, W. (2001). *The 108 skills of natural born leaders*. New York: AMACOM.

Cavitt, C. (2007). *Customer service superstars*. New York: Bowker.

Chakraverty, J. (2018, September 24). *Why your company should prioritise soft skills.* Retrieved from https://www.forbes.com/sites/voicesfromeurope/2018/09/24/scaling-soft-skills-to-submit/#40a8b7ca1466.

Chinunda, E. D. (2013). *Customer service: The kingpin of business success in Africa.* Bloomington, IN: Xlibris.

Cohen, W. A. (1990). *The art of a leader.* Englewood Cliffs, NJ: Prentice Hall.

Coyle, J. J., Langley, C. J., Gibson, B., Novack, R. A., & Bardi, E. J. (2008). *Supply chain management: A logistics perspective.* Mason, OH: South-Western Cengage.

Cribbin, J. J. (1981). *Leadership: Strategies for organizational effectiveness.* New York: AMACOM.

Di Giacomo, D., Vittorini, P., & Lacasa, P. (Eds.), (2018). Digital skills and life-long learning: Digital learning as a new insight of enhanced learning of the innovative approach joining technology and cognition [Editorial]. *Frontiers in Psychology 9*(2621), 4. doi:10.3389/fpsyg.2018.02621.

Donelly, J. H., Ivancevich, J. M., & Gibson, J. L. (1985). *Organizations: Behavior, structure, processes* (5th ed.), Plano, TX: Business Publications Inc.

Dowd, T., & Tierney, J. (2005). *Teaching Social Skills to Youth.* Boys Town, NE: Boys Town Press.

Endsley, M. R. (1995). Toward a theory of situation awareness in dynamic systems. *Human Factors, 37*(1), 32–64.

Farlow, M. J. (2012). *Leaders are made not born: 40 simple skills to make you the leader you want to be* St. Louis, MI: LinkUp Publishing.

Flin, R., O'Connor, P., & Crichton, M. (2008). *Safety at the Sharp End: A Guide to Non-Technical Skills.* Hampshire, UK: Ashgate Publishing.

Gibson, P. (2012). *The world of customer service* (3rd ed.), Mason, OH: South-Western, Cengage Learning.

Google LLC. (2013). *The role of click to call: In the path to purchase.* Retrieved from https://think.storage.googleapis.com/docs/click-to-call_research-studies.pdf.

Hargie, O., Saunders, C., & Dickson, D. (1994). *Social Skills in Interpersonal Communication.* New York: Routledge.

Hudson, S., & Hudson, L. (2013). *Customer Service in Tourism and Hospitality.* Oxford: Goodfellow Publishers.

Katz, R. L. (2009). *Skills of an effective administrator.* Boston, MA: Harvard Business Press.

Klaus, P. (2007). *The hard truth about soft skills.* New York: Harper Collins.

Mayer, J. D., & Salovey, P. (1997). What is emotional intelligence? In P. Salovey & D. J. Sluyter (Eds.), *Emotional development and emotional intelligence: Educational implications* (pp. 3–34). New York: Harper Collins.

Melecio, N. (2014). *Leading past perception: Helping leaders make a difference.* Morrisville, NC: Lulu Publishing Services.

Obakpolo, P. (2015). Improving interpersonal relationship in workplaces. *IOSR Journal of Research & Method in Education (IOSR-JRME), 5*(6), 115–125.

Pattar, V. (2017). *Be a leader, not a follower.* India: Vikhyath Publications.

Rask, R. L. (2008). *Work ethics and the generation gap! Which ethical track are you on?* Bloomington, IN: AuthorHouse.

Rauch, C. F., & Behling, O. (1984). Functionalism: Basis for an alternate approach to the study of leadership. In J. G. Hunt, D. M. Hosking, C. A. Schriesheim, & R. Stewart (Eds.), *Leaders and managers: International perspectives on managerial behavior and leadership* (pp. 45–62). New York: Pergamon Press.

Schermerhorn, Jr, J. R. (2010). *Exploring management* (4th ed.), Hoboken, NJ: John Wiley & Sons.

Tannenbaum, R., Weschler I. R., & Massarik, F. (1961). *Leadership and Organization. A behavioral science approach.* New York: McGraw-Hill.

Thompson, N. (1996). *People Skills.* London, UK: Macmillan Press.

van Deursen, A., & van Dijk, J. (2008). *Measuring digital skills. Performance tests of operational, formal, information and strategic internet skills among the Dutch population.* Paper presented at the ICA Conference, Montreal, Canada, May 22–26, 2008. Retrieved from https://www.utwente.nl/en/bms/vandijk/news/measuring_digital_skills/MDS.pdf.

Zeithaml, V. A., Bitner, M. J., & Gremler, D. D. (2010). *Services marketing strategy.* Chichester, UK: Wiley International Encyclopedia of Marketing.

THEME G: CUSTOMER EXPERIENCE – ADVANCING CUSTOMER SERVICE IN AFRICA

VII

Chapter 23

Advancing the Services Sector's Potential in Africa through Customer Experience: A Conceptual Perspective

Isaac K. Arthur, Ebenezer G. A. Nikoi and Samuel Benagr

Contents

Introduction

Recent studies point to a rapidly burgeoning service sector that is contributing significantly to gross domestic products (GDP), employment, trade, foreign direct investments and income, among others globally (UNCTAD, 2017; Melvin, 2016). In Africa, where rapid economic growth and substantial reduction in poverty have been recorded in recent decades (Ncube & Lufumpa, 2014; Rodrik, 2018), many economies are being transformed and expanded through services-oriented activities (UNCTAD, 2017). Services, such as transport, energy, finance, telecommunication and business, are on the rise in Africa and are contributing directly and indirectly to economic growth, productivity, poverty reduction and job creation (Dihel & Goswami, 2016). The exploding service sector marks the largest economic sector in Africa, as it has outpaced the agricultural, manufacturing and extractive sectors in terms of growth and accounts for over 50% of the continent's GDP (ADB, 2016; AGRA, 2017). The sector offers promising opportunities for export diversification (Dihel & Goswami, 2016) and is the key to Africa's structural transformation for development (ADB, 2016). This development can linger on given the emergence of many activities that potentially promise tradeable services for the continent.

However, Africa's service sector lags well behind Western and some emerging economies in terms of scale and performance (Bridges Africa, 2016; Lee & McKibbin, 2018). Furthermore, many small-sized service providers have been forced out of business due to competition from large multinational service companies (see Kragelund & Carmody, 2016). Consequently, African service-oriented companies must draw on innovative ways to add value to their businesses in order to bridge the performance gap and to establish a unique identity. Addressing this concern is crucial, particularly when customer loyalty remains key to the success of every business. What then are the potential innovative strategies and how can they be operationalised to win customer loyalty?

Pine and Gilmore (1999) suggest that staging experiences provide answers to businesses searching for new ways to add value to their enterprises. Additionally, Srivastava and Kaul (2016) argue that businesses must focus on customer experience in order to build loyalty in the market. Shamah et al. (2018) also argue that customer loyalty is key to marketing in a competitive environment, and therefore, an organisation's ability to generate loyalty results in positive outcomes, such as repeated purchases, positive word of mouth and the willingness of customers to pay higher prices. With the current state of increasing consumerism in society and in the globalised competitive market, what gives service business organisations in Africa a competitive edge? In other words, in their delivery of services, how can organisations create value to foster customer loyalty and grow customer relationships for their organisations' sustainability and potential expansion? Although many scholarly works have dealt with customer experience in the service sector (see Melvin, 2016), there is a gap in conceptual focus on the potential for innovative activities to improve customer loyalty that harnesses the advantages of the experience economy in the service sector.

Given the dearth of research on the potential of the experience economy for the service sector in Africa, this paper sets the stage for future empirical studies. Moreover, the rising affluence characterised by the emerging middle class and democratisation of technology in Africa makes this timely (Ncube & Lufumpa, 2014). Using the experience economy as the conceptual framework, this paper argues that service-oriented activities stand a chance of attaining robust customer loyalty in Africa. Specifically, we draw on Pine and Gilmore's (1999) four-part typology of experience realms as a framework for analysis, situating the arguments within the Ghanaian business space and examples from other African subregions.

The paper is organised as follows. The first section conceptually discusses building loyalty through customer experience. This is followed by an overview of the African service sector. It goes on to examine the prospects of customer experience in Africa's service sector. Thereafter, the paper provides recommendations for an experience-based model for customer service delivery in Africa based on the four realms of experience as advanced by Pine and Gilmore (1999). The paper concludes that experiences in Africa's service sectors must be designed tactfully to appeal to consumers.

Building Loyalty through Customer Experience

The term 'experience' has been used in different ways, and academics from diverse backgrounds, including psychology, philosophy, marketing, media and performance, have shaped its multiple meanings (see Schmitt, 2011; Hirschman & Holbrook, 1982; Long & Wall, 2009). One way to understand experience from a marketing perspective is through Pine and Gilmore's (1999) definition, which is the commercialisation of events attached to goods and services that engage individuals in a personal way. The attached experiences to goods and services also reveal to the consumer idealistic, aesthetic and symbolic meanings (Arthur & Damoah, 2015). Examples of experience include attaching a themed or storytelling event to banking services to create a memorable experience for customers (Pine & Gilmore, 1999).

However, experiences as add-ons only characterise a secondary sector, since some experience(s) constitute primary output(s) on the market (Sundbo & Darmer, 2008). The latter is thus referred to as an experience industry or primary experience sector (Nielsen & Dale, 2013). Examples of such core experience offerings include leisure events, museums, arts, festivals, cityscapes, sporting and music events (Sundbo & Darmer, 2008; Richards, 2001). Some of these core experiences are produced and distributed through the Internet, television and mobile phones.

The consumption of goods and services was traditionally for utilitarian purposes, but has now gravitated towards experiences due to their high value to consumers (Schmitt, 2011). Consequently, consumers are willing to pay high prices for experiences, thus making the commercialisation of experiences lucrative for businesses (Sundbo & Darmer, 2008). The demand for experience reflects a change in consumer behaviour (Hirschman & Holbrook, 1982), which fulfils Toffler's (1970) prediction that the post-service economy will be marked by the creation and consumption of experience in affluent communities where disposable incomes are high. Given the growing global scale of affluence, which corresponds with the consumption of experience, consumers are increasingly searching for identity or self-realisation (Lorentzen, 2009). This development points to the importance of the experience economy as a concept in the contemporary market space and a vital ingredient in building customer loyalty.

Pine and Gilmore (1999) categorised experience into four groups: entertainment, education, escapism and aesthetic. These types of experiences feature different levels of intensity and engagements from consumers and therefore provide an essential framework for analysing how businesses can design specific experiences for customers (Arthur & Hracs, 2015). Education is obtained through absorption while actively participating in an activity. For entertainment, the consumer passively absorbs the events through his/her senses. Whereas aesthetic experience takes place when the consumer is immersed in an event but remains active, escapism reflects the consumer's active participation in an immersive environment (Pine & Gilmore, 1999).

An entertainment experience could involve listening to music/story while receiving medical treatment in a hospital. The specific music/story could have a symbolic meaning for the patient and in effect, engage his/her mind. An educational or escapist experience may entail taking a tour of a heritage site (slave route in Ghana or Senegal) or playing an active role in creating an entirely new service product. The latter could take the form of allowing a customer to create his/her own recipe at a restaurant. Such experiences engage consumers mentally (cognitively) or physically as they absorb the unfolding event. An aesthetic experience may entail the environment or ambience in which a service is provided.

Interestingly, such activities may blur the boundaries of experience realms, as it could provide educational/informative experience to diners (Boateng et al., 2018). Pine and Gilmore (1999) argue that most specific experiences cross boundaries, and therefore, businesses must exploit that in their dealings since the richest experiences entail aspects of all four experiences indicated above. The boundaries of experience creation are blurred further, as customers can actively co-create experiences while interacting with service providers (Melvin, 2016; Prahalad & Ramaswamy, 2004). For example, a touring experience could be fashioned and co-constructed with the tour guides (Boateng et al., 2018). The four types of experience can develop memories of consumers, which can ultimately influence their loyalty behaviours (Ali et al., 2014).

Africa's Services Sector: An Overview

In this section, we aim to provide an overview of the services sector in Africa while emphasising analogies between the performance of key services-oriented activities in Ghana and other African countries. According to UNCTAD (2009), in various developing countries, the outpacing of the agricultural and industrial sectors by the service sector has been appraised as a positive driver of economic growth and development. Following the general trend of growth in the service sector in developing economies, Africa's service sector grew by 3.2% between 2004 and 2012 (UNCTAD, 2015).

Although the rapid growth of the service sector in Africa has been attributed to internal demand, education and technical advancement (Zamfir, 2016), the thriving of the sector dates to the offshoring of basic service activities by multinational corporations in the early 1990s. By the end of the first decade of the twenty-first century, increasingly sophisticated services were performed for these firms by operational centres in a growing number of Africa countries (Fernandez-Stark et al., 2011). The establishment of such offshore services was credited to 'key competitive advantages, particularly in low human resource costs, language proficiency and technological skills' (Fernandez-Stark et al., 2011, p. 208). By 2010, the offshore service sector accounted for U.S. $252 billion in revenues and employed over 4 million people globally dominated by developing countries, of which Africa formed a part. UNCTAD (2015) observed that overall, the service sector provided one-third of formal employment during 2009–2012. Furthermore, in some countries in Africa, as much as two-thirds of the workforce is engaged in services.

The service sector in sub-Saharan Africa (SSA) contributes significantly to the region's GDP. It accounted for 58.0% of GDP in 2015, up from 47.6% in 2005. This shows a rapid growth of the sector's share of GDP in SSA (World Bank, 2015). South Africa and Nigeria, the two largest economies of the region, dominate the SSA service economy, providing 29.9% and 27.8%, respectively, of the SSA services in 2015 (Powell, 2017). The main drivers of this growth include the financial services, transport, telecommunication and tourism (Zamfir, 2016). However, estimates suggest that SSA's overall informal services sector activities account for a substantial share of its output and employment (Powell, 2017).

It is therefore unsurprising that the 'Ghanaian government has actively encouraged the development of the country's services sector, whose rapid expansion has broadened overall economic growth and contributed to low unemployment in Ghana. However, several factors limit the service sector's impact on the economy' (Powell, 2015, p. 1). This quotation is an apt summation of the services sector in Ghana, and by extension, in most economies in Africa (see Uwitonze & Heshmati, 2016).

According to Powell (2015), services accounted for almost 50% of Ghana's GDP and a substantial share of trade. For nearly a decade (2005–2013), the service sector took over from agriculture as the biggest contributing segment of the economy, with GDP rising from 32.2% to 48.8%. In the area of job creation, it has been a leader too, with 43.1% of Ghanaian jobs attributed to the sector in 2010. This trend reverberates in most economies on the continent, such as those of Rwanda, Kenya, Ethiopia, etc. For instance, Uwitonze and Heshmati (2016) report that in 2014, the service sector was the largest and most dynamic in the Rwandan economy. According to UNECA (2015), Rwanda's service sector is globalising at a faster pace, as well as offering the possibility for economic transformation. Riding on the back of this sector, the Rwandan economy, in a fierce global competitive space, has since 2001 recorded averagely 8% annual GDP growth with a corresponding increase in per capita income, from US$211 in 2001 to US$718 in 2014 (Uwitonze & Heshmati, 2016). In Ethiopia, the situation is no different. The service sector has effectively dislodged the primary sector – agriculture – to become the leading contributor to the country's share of GDP and employment. Figures for 2014/2015 stood at 46.6% of GDP for the service sector (Kabeta & Sidhu, 2016).

Given the pro-business attitude of the Ghanaian government, there has been an increase in both road and air transportation business over the last decade. Powell (2015, p. 2), in her USITC report, submits that 'the government has made significant investments in road expansion and repair, and port operations have been enhanced through automation and the introduction of electronic and technological improvements to surveillance, security, data interchange, and cargo handling'. In the case of information and communication technology (ICT), between 2009 and 2013, the information and communication sector in Ghana witnessed an appreciable growth rate. The annual average growth rate was recorded at 26.5%. Its share of total Ghanaian GDP over the period rose from 1.8% to 2.4% (Powell, 2015). In the area of television broadcast services, as at the third quarter of 2016, the total number of TV operators authorised by the National Communications Authority (NCA) in Ghana was 83, out of which 35 TV stations are operational (NCA, 2016).

Over the years, the banking industry in the country has undergone some transformation. Innovative offerings including e-banking, automated teller machines (ATMs), telephone banking, and SMS banking contributed to the growth and job creation. Notwithstanding, the sector had issues of non-performing loans, elevated interest rates, and high maintenance costs of ATMs and branches in rural areas, which had a multiplier effect on other sectors. Ghana is endowed with a wide range of natural, cultural, heritage and historic attractions. Over the years, governments have sought to prop up the sector for it to increase its quota. In doing this, the government is promoting growth in the tourism industry through public–private partnerships to boost investment infrastructure, promote Ghanaian travel to new audiences, and support worker training. Focuses include business travel, ecotourism, cultural tourism and domestic travel (see Powell, 2015).

Although the service sector contributes significantly to overall GDP in Africa, several subsectors have declined in growth rates (Cinyabuguma et al., 2017). In Ghana, for instance, the fall in the sector's growth can be attributed to poor performance in community, social and personal service activities (–38.1%), hotels and restaurants (–25.8%), financial intermediation (–23.5%) and trade, repair of vehicles, household goods (–16.1%) (ISSER, 2015). All these subsectors occasioning the slow growth have a direct human factor and element to them.

It is worth asking why the principal actors (customers) in these subsectors failed to engage with the service and the resulting negative growth? It is such probing that lends lots of credence to the core mission of this chapter – customers getting added benefits by way of the experience they get while patronising a service, which in turn becomes a booster for future repeat patronage. This thinking is consistent with the core elements of the definition provided by Pine and Gilmore (1999) for the experience economy indicating that companies stage meaningful events to engage customers in a memorable and personal way. Moreover, staging to engage in a manner that leaves an impression on customers means that they get more than just the product. For example, in marketing their organic meat products, farmers in Danish rural areas use storytelling about their sheep grazing on local, historic and protected sites (Arthur & Hracs, 2015). This leaves an impression of learning experience on their consumers. It may appear that the service sector in Africa has peaked and perhaps missed the opportunity of moving to the next economic transformational level, the experience economy.

Prospects of Customer Experience in Africa's Services Sector

Indeed, efforts by businesses to modify their operations from the mere offerings of goods and services to memorable customer experiences marks a step towards business success and addressing the needs of experience consumers (Arthur & Hracs, 2015). According to Chua (2018), in South Korea, music and entertainment companies have become objects of emulation by Japan, China and many other Asian countries, as they have moved away from just selling music products to selling experience to stand out from their saturated music industry. Specifically, companies are selling to fans experiences they can have with their favourite groups and singers. These companies interact with fans in ways such as creating fan clubs, meeting fans and posting videos on their channels and social media accounts. In Japan, maid cafes are making use of the advantages of the experience economy by offering experiences targeted at *anime*[1] (Anime, n.d.) fans, where servers are dressed in maid outfits and acting like *anime* characters. These examples seem to create an impression that the experience economy thrives in wealthier countries where innovations on the market are pervasive and fashioned to meet consumers' demands.

While many business ventures in Africa are perceived as subsistent and less innovative, there is evidence to suggest that the experience economy is not new in Africa as many service-related companies across the continent are selling experiences as an added value to their outputs. For example, at the Gold Coast Restaurant in Accra, diners experience decorations of historic photos of individuals (usually Ghanaian and international celebrities), places, and events on the walls. Another experience is that Azmera Restaurant, close to the Gold Coast in the locality, makes female attendants dress traditionally like queens. As an add on to the tourist experience at the Ngorongoro Conservation Area in Tanzania, tourists can stay in a safari lodge (The Ngorongoro Crater Lodge) designed in the form of a Maasai mud-and-stick homestead. With large windows to enable clear viewing of wildlife and nature, and colonial-style interior – crystal chandeliers, Zanzibar wall panelling, and antique furniture, among others – visitors are immersed into an aesthetic experience.

Furthermore, apart from the traditional customer usage of mobile phones for communication, mobile phone companies in Ghana are providing information, financial and entertainment experience to customers such as mobile money. Moreover, in order to develop a workforce that is able to service the ICT sector, companies, both public and private, have invested in ICT parks, healthcare call centres and Internet cafes. These services are helping to stimulate customer experiences in the ICT and health sectors. Additionally, some transport operators in Ghana, like OA, VIP, VVIP, and Intercity STC Coaches have introduced add-on services such as screening of video films on board. Some drivers on the long-distance routes even buy ice cream/yoghurt for their passengers. However, as experience-related strategies become more ubiquitous and saturated, there is the need to differentiate and enhance customer loyalty through the creation of new experiences (Arthur & Hracs, 2015). In effect, the question is, under what conditions can businesses become innovative to create new and sustainable experiences?

---

[1] Anime are Japanese animated productions featuring hand-drawn or computer animation. Anime includes animated television series, short films and full-length feature films. The word is the abbreviated pronunciation of 'animation' in Japanese (see Anime, n.d.).

Recent developments on the continent give reasons to be optimistic for the customer experience to harness loyalty in the continent's service sector. As suggested in Deloitte and Touche (2013), Africa is equally subject to the new consumer impulses and consumption stimuli; therefore, African consumers want the same as consumers elsewhere. However, this will be dependent on individuals' spending power and preference (McEwan et al., 2015). Consumer spending in Africa has skyrocketed in the last few years, recording a growth of $1.4 trillion in 2015, with South Africa, Nigeria and Egypt contributing more than half of that total (Hattingh et al., 2017). This figure is expected to reach $2.5 trillion by 2030 (Signé, 2018). According to Oteng-Ababio and Arthur (2015), Africa is extolled as the ultimate frontier for investment and marketing opportunities for international investors. The key motivations for all these ventures are the existing market and purchasing power of consumers. The continent is seeing the proliferation of service activities such as hospitality and tourism, banking, real estate, health business, transportation and shopping malls.[2] Many of these activities have been established through foreign direct investments (FDI), and local and intra-African investments (CFAO, 2015; Kragelund & Carmody, 2016).

The existing consumption trajectory or consumerism, coupled with structural fundamentals such as increasing income levels and affluence, urbanisation, growth in population and younger demographic groups, and the democratisation of technologies in the continent, will potentially play a key role in driving customer experience production by service companies (Hattingh et al., 2017; Signé, 2018). This echoes Amos's (2017) view that Africa has the potential to become a new production and consumption hub in the twenty-first century, as was the case with Asia in the late 20th century.

The continent's population is growing and expected to increase by 20% in 2025 and will be attended with a falling dependency ratio and expanding the workforce. An additional 190 million people are expected to be living in urban areas, where per capita consumption is higher than the national average (Hattingh et al., 2017). Rising incomes, resulting in the upsurge of the middle and upper classes and affluence in the continent are of immense importance. This is in view of their willingness to pay more for quality goods, feeding investment in production and marketing (McEwan et al., 2015).

The consumption of such quality outputs includes experiences that could be attained from services such as entertainment, health care and private education (Ncube & Lufumpa, 2014). There are 330 million middle-class Africans, representing about a third of the continent's total population. While Egypt and Gabon have the largest middle classes based on income, the middle class of most West African and Southern African countries – along with Cameroon, The Democratic Republic of the Congo and Kenya – fall within the average of between 25% and 75% of their population. Central and East African countries have the smallest middle class in percentage terms (CFAO, 2015).

Technology adaptation, particularly the use of mobile phone and Internet services, which was previously viewed as tools to embellish the comfort of the privileged urban class, is now ubiquitous on the continent, as its usage knows no class and locational boundaries (Njoh, 2018). According to GSMA (2018), mobile phone subscription in SSA totalled 444 million in 2017, equivalent to around 9% of subscribers globally, with a penetration rate forecast to reach the 50% level by the end of 2023, and 52% by 2025. The mobile phone and Internet are now widely used for providing services in the hospitality, tourism, banking, real estate, health and transportation sectors.

---

[2] Within the last decade, Africa has seen a record bourgeoning of shopping malls in urban regional centres such as Accra in the west, Nairobi in the east, Casablanca in the north and Lusaka in the south. These malls are attached with various experiences targeted at attracting the high-earning middle class (see Oteng-Ababio & Arthur, 2015).

Currently, Africa is attracting many expatriates to benefit from recent economic activities. These expatriates, mostly workers and investors are usually higher-income earners and are, therefore, potential consumers of experience. In Sekondi-Takoradi, Ghana, for example, expatriates working in the international oil companies are notable consumers of experiences provided at the various hotels and amusement centres (Fiave, 2017). According to Kragelund and Carmody (2016), Zambia has become a tourist attraction for Chinese migrants, mostly in the middle and upper classes. China in 2012 was adjudged the single biggest market for Zambian tourism (Ministry of Tourism and Arts 2014, as in Kragelund & Carmody, 2016). The recent growth in infrastructural investments in Africa also provides a good source of customer experience production.

In Ghana, the recently developed 'Accra Airport City', a miniature commercial business centre within the vicinity of the Kotoka International Airport, offers travellers and non-travellers alike a wide range of experiences (Arthur, 2018). In Livingstone, Zambia, there has seen South African multinational investments in hotel chains, fast-food outlets, petrol stations, telecommunication and supermarkets that also provide varied potential sources for customer experience creation (Kragelund & Carmody, 2016). These impulses point not only to the existence of the experience economy in Africa, but also their potential to succeed in the service sector given the increasing economic growth and globalisation of markets, changing dynamics of population, urbanisation, rising income and the increasing consumer-driven capitalism in many countries on the continent. These experiences have the potential to significantly contribute to the transformation of Africa's economy, though they need to be scaled up in order to achieve this.

Recommendations for an Experience-Based Model for Customer Service Delivery in Africa

Service providers must understand that experience is crucial for customer satisfaction and competitiveness since enduring experience affects customer emotions and consequently influence behaviours (Manthiou et al., 2014). Consumers globally are becoming ethically, environmentally and politically correct in the choices they make in the wake of rising consumer savviness, demands and brand awareness (Arthur & Yamoah, 2019). There are unmet needs of personal branding or self-staging, getting value for money amid stiff competition, and promise of discounts coming by the Internet and its offshoots. The game-changer becomes the uniqueness of one's offerings. The opportunity for this next level of economic transformation abounds in all manners of business endeavours both in the private and public sectors in Africa. Seizing these opportunities requires that the stakeholders understand the terrain and its idiosyncrasies. Leke et al. (2018) contend that Africa's growth opportunities in the twenty-first century are so vast and complex that one may easily lose sight of the obvious if care is not taken.

This section, therefore, proposes ideas for enhancing customer experiences in selected service sectors in Africa, based on the four experience realms. This is targeted at companies that have no knowledge of the experience economy concept and those that have not consciously implemented the concept as part of their overall competitive strategy. This concept when properly engineered and orchestrated will deliver that added value that customers will take away with them, talk about, have the urge for the repeated encounter of same, and tell the story to others; thus, increasing patronage. There are myriad of service-related businesses that can benefit from the experience economy. In this section, we limit our attention to hospitality and tourism, banking, real estate, health business and transportation. Arguably, these activities feature prominently in Africa's economic geography.

Educational Experience

Sophisticated consumers are interested in knowing the sources of what they consume on the market. In response, service-related businesses can adapt their market orientation by creating an educational experience for them. Consumers can also derive quality from the details of the raw materials, their history, processing and presentation (Cawley et al., 2003). Consequently, public and private organisations can commercialise their details through compelling storytelling events to passively engage consumers. Transport operators can educate passengers on the competencies of drivers/pilots, the nature and design of carriers, safety information, organisation of check-in, interesting facts about destinations and key locations along their routes, companies' details, safety records and route connections. Real estate developers can provide narratives of history, location, design details, ethical information and the nature and sources of building materials of properties. These could be made via educational tours with prospective owners.

Hospitality and tourism organisations can also provide narratives about their history, operations of specific businesses, types and sources of food (e.g. key players such as chefs, service delivery and operational philosophy), locational accessibility and proximity to other services, and pricing of services. To assure patients of quality, health service providers may provide patients with prior information of health personnel in terms of skills and competencies, explain treatment procedures and other forms of information, leading to the co-creation of treatment processes with patients. In the wake of customers losing their investments with financial institutions, as in the recent cases of Ghana (Banahene, 2018), educating customers to assure them of secured investments and returns is key. Consequently, banks must create customer experiences by informing them about the processes of investments, opportunities and various financial security tips. Organisations can provide most of these experiences through themed events, of using social media – one of the most democratised means of disseminating knowledge and information. It could also take the form of drama which provides edutainment experiences for customers. Organisations can make consumers actively participate in this experience by using feedback from consumers to educate them in a more compelling manner.

Escapist Experience

As consumers prefer to move away from their comfort zone to different locations, businesses should be in the position to create an escapist experience for them. In the health sector, for example, patients could be nursed outside the hospital premises in therapeutic landscapes, which are simultaneously health promoting and disease preventing. Therapeutic landscapes have achieved a lasting reputation for physical, mental and spiritual healing (Williams, 2010). For instance, in Ghana, prayer camps like Edumfa, Hebron and Aburi have gained a reputation as sites of healing partly due to their milieu that blends natural and built elements associated with rural geographies, thus providing escapist appeal.

In contrast to the city environment replete with angry, stressed people, and built-up streets depleted of nature, the therapeutic qualities of rural natural settings offer fresh air, medicinal plants and herbs, fresh and natural food, extensive scenery, and genuine and committed social relationships, which are health promoting (Williams, 2010, p. 215). The transport sector can immerse passengers by way of getting them to actively participate in all manner of activities on board. This may include passengers using their laptops, reality headsets, and playing games such as cards. Hospitality and tourist operators can organise agro-tourism trips where people visit farms and participate in farming activities (see Arthur & Hracs, 2015). Banks could occasionally offer services to clients outside the banking hall. This could take place at special or themed events to make banking services more memorable. Real estate developers may take into consideration the specific needs of clients citing properties at places with qualities, such as thematic, serenity, rurality and spaciousness. In this regard, clients would actively participate in the choosing of such locations and properties.

Aesthetic Experience

Given the fact that 'consumers are reflexive individuals who consume signs to recreate individual identities which are not fixed, but rather "self-images" of the moment' (Firat 1992, quoted in Burton, 2002, p. 729), service providers can take advantage of this to offer consumers aesthetic experiences. These providers must use their services as props to allow customers to experience rich interior decorations in an immersive fashion. Consequently, they ought to prioritise investing in ambience or servicescapes and sightseeing activities to serve as key marketing strategies to foster customer loyalty (Manthiou et al., 2014). This echoes Kotler's (1973) view that an organisation must keep a good physical atmosphere to create a positive image. Such images can be boosted by 'using symbolism (e.g. flags, corporate banners and association logos), music and sensory stimulation (e.g. lighting, sounds, smells, textures, colours, flowers and art)' (Manthiou et al., 2014, p. 29). Transport operators can, for example, focus on immersing people in the design of carriers and terminals. The interior designs must include accessibility to WIFI, phone-charging units and restrooms. They may take into consideration locating rest stops at serene, picturesque historic environments.

Entertainment Experience

Entertainment, particularly in the form of music and dance, marks a key feature of African cultural heritage. In a globalised world characterised by other forms of technologically driven entertainment, African service providers must combine traditional and modern forms of entertainment to make their interactions with customers more pleasant and memorable. The transport industry, for example, can provide music appealing to specific customers (e.g. ethnic groups/race, age groups, social classes), movies, infotainment systems, entertainment news and live performances. Real estate developers can factor in parks and recreation areas in the design of buildings (residential and non-residential) for customers to entertain themselves. The hospitality and tourism industry may focus on music and other forms of themed entertainment events. In Ghana, for example, popular music appears to be overshadowing indigenous and folkloric music and dances. These can be revitalised through the experiences provided by the hospitality and tourism services operators. Health-related businesses can also create entertainment experiences for patients through music, dance and storytelling therapies.

Conclusion

For businesses to provide all the experiences outlined above, they must develop effective themes that are concise and compelling, complement the themes with consistent positive cues to create the expected indelible impressions for the consumer, eliminate negative cues (by avoiding anything that diminishes, contradicts or distracts from the theme), provide memorabilia that will keep the consumers' memories of the experience and engage all five senses of the consumer to intensify the experience (Pine & Gilmore, 1999). An example of such experience engaging the five senses could be a touring service at a brewery where visitors have the experience of smelling baileys, touching and feeling objects, seeing the production process, hearing stories from the tour guard while at the same time hearing the sounds of machinery and having a taste of drinks produced at the brewery (Arthur & Damoah, 2015). However, Pine and Gilmore (1998) caution that combining some senses together may not be the best since they may not be mutually complementary, implying that experiences must be designed tactfully to appeal to consumers.

References

ADB. (2016). *African development report 2015-growth, poverty and inequality nexus: Overcoming barriers to sustainable development*. Abidjan, Côte d'Ivoire: African Development Bank Group.

AGRA. (2017). *Africa agriculture status report: The business of smallholder agriculture in sub-Saharan Africa, Issue Number 5*. Nairobi: Alliance for a Green Revolution in Africa (AGRA).

Ali, F., Hussainb, K., & Ragavan, N. A. (2014). Memorable customer experience: Examining the effects of customers experience on memories and loyalty in Malaysian resort hotels. *Procedia – Social and Behavioral Sciences, 144*, 273–279.

Amos, I. (2017). *The ongoing democratisation of technology is fuelling grassroot innovation in Africa*. Retrieved from https://www.iafrikan.com/2017/01/17/the-ongoing-democratization-of-technology-is-fuelling-grassroots-innovation-in-afrika/

Anime. (n.d.). *Definitions.net*. Retrieved from https://www.definitions.net/definition/anime

Arthur, I. K. (2018). Exploring the development prospects of Accra Airport City, Ghana. *Area Development and Policy, 3*(2), 258–273.

Arthur, I. K., & Damoah, O. B. O. (2015). Exploring the resource and capabilities of food related enterprises in rural Denmark: Implications for rural enterprises in Ghana. *Ghana Journal of Geography, 7*(2), 58–78.

Arthur, I. K., & Hracs, B. J. (2015). Experience the difference: The competitive strategies of food-related entrepreneurs in rural Denmark. *Geografiska Annaler: Series B, Human Geography, 97*(1), 95–112.

Arthur, I. K., & Yamoah, F. A. (2019). Understanding the role of environmental quality attributes in food-related rural enterprise competitiveness. *Journal of Environmental Management, 247*, 152–160.

Banahene, K. O. (2018). Ghana banking system failure: The need for restoration of public trust and confidence. *International Journal of Business and Social Research, 8*(10), 1–5.

Boateng, H., Okoe, A. F., & Hinson, R. E. (2018). Dark tourism: Exploring tourist's experience at the Cape Coast Castle, Ghana. *Tourism Management Perspectives, 27*, 104–110.

Bridges Africa. (2016). Harnessing the potential of the services sector in Africa. *International Centre for Trade and Sustainable Development, 5*(4). Retrieved from https://www.ictsd.org/sites/default/files/Bridges%20Africa_May2016.pdf.

Burton, D. (2002). Postmodernism, social relations and remote shopping. *European Journal of Marketing, 36*(7–8), 792–810.

Cawley, M. E., Gaffey, S. M., & Gillmor, D. A. (2003). A role for quality rural tourism services in rural development? Evidence from the Republic of Ireland'. In K. B. Beesley, H. Millward, B. Ilbery & L. Harrington (Eds.), *The new countryside: Geographic perspectives on rural change* (pp. 143–154). Brandon, Canada: Brandon University Rural Development Institute.

CFAO. (2015). *The middle class in Africa: Realities and challenges*. White Paper. Retrieved from ww.cfaogroup.com/static/2017/12/08/CFAOWhite%20Paper%20The%20middle%20classes%20in%20Africa%20UK%20april2016.pdf?qA3g3_m5sGX6zBNHJgp4PQ:qA3g3_m5sGX6zBNHJgp4PQ:fIcrNtDaj1kHsdVnXP2w9g

Chua, F. (2018, July 8). *Should companies undergo transformational growth to succeed in the experience economy?* (Blog Post). Retrieved from http://customerthink.com/should-companies-undergo-transformational-growth-to-succeed-in-the-experience-economy/

Cinyabuguma, M., Ndoye, D., & Taiwo, O. (2017). Leveraging the potential of the services sector to support accelerated growth in Senegal. *Policy Research Working Paper 8031*, Africa Region: World Bank Group.

Deloitte & Touche. (2013). The rise and rise of the African middle class. Deloitte on Africa Collection, Issue 1. Johannesburg, South Africa: Deloitte. Retrieved from http://sabc.ch/wp-content/uploads/2017/12/Deloitte-study-May20131.pdf

Dihel, N., & Goswami, A. G. (Eds.) (2016). *From hair stylists and teachers to accountants and doctors: The unexplored potential of trade in services in Africa*. Washington, DC: World Bank.

Fernandez-Stark, K., Bamber, P., & Gereffi, G. (2011). The offshore services value chain: Upgrading trajectories in developing countries. *International Journal of Technological learning, Innovation and Development, 4*(1/2/3), 206–230.

Fiave, R. E. (2017). Sekondi-Takoradi as an oil city. *Geography Research Forum, 37*, 61–79.

GSM Association. (2018). *The mobile economy sub-Saharan Africa 2018*. London, UK: GSMA Head Office.

Hattingh, D., Leke, A., & Russo, B. (2017). Lions (still) on the move: Growth in Africa's consumer sector. *Perspectives on retail and consumer goods, 6*. Retrieved from https://www.mckinsey.com/industries/consumer-packaged-goods/our-insights/lions-still-on-the-move-growth-in-africas-consumer-sector

Hirschman, E. C., & Holbrook, M. B. (1982). The experiential aspects of consumption: Consumer fantasy, feelings and fun. *Journal of Consumer Research, 9*(2), 132–140.

ISSER. (2015). *The state of the Ghanaian economy in 2014*. Legon, Ghana: Institute of Statistical, Social and Economic Research.

Kabeta, Z. E., & Sidhu, I. S. (2016). Service sector: The source of output and employment growth in Ethiopia. *Academic Journal of Economic Studies, 2*(4), 139–156.

Kragelund, P., & Carmody, P. (2016). The BRICS' impacts on local economic development in the Global South: The cases of a tourism town and two mining provinces in Zambia. *Area Development and Policy, 1*(2), 218–237.

Lee, J-W., & McKibbin, W. J. (2018). Service sector productivity and economic growth in Asia. *Economic Modelling, 74*, 247–263.

Leke, A., Chironga, M., & Desvaux, G. (2018). *Africa's business revolution: How to succeed in the World's next big growth market*. Boston, MA: Harvard Business School Press.

Long, P., & Wall, T. (2009). *Media studies: Texts, production and context*. London, MA: Pearson Longman.

Lorentzen, A. (2009). Cities in the experience economy. *European Planning Studies, 17*(6), 829–845.

Manthiou, A., Lee, S., Tang, T., & Chiang, L. (2014). The experience economy approach to festival marketing: Vivid memory and attendee loyalty. *Journal of Services Marketing, 28*(1), 22–35.

McEwan, C., Hughes, A., & Bek, D. (2015). Theorising middle class consumption from the Global South: A study of everyday ethics in South Africa's Western Cape. *Geoforum, 67*, 233–243.

Melvin, J. (2016). Customer value facilitation: The service experience within a heritage tourism context. In U. Altinay & S. Poudel (Eds.), *Enhancing Customer Experience in the service industry: A global perspective* (pp. 8–24). Cambridge, UK: Scholars Publishing.

NCA. (2016). Quarterly statistical bulletin on communications in Ghana. *National Communications Authority, 1*(3). Retrieved from https://www.nca.org.gh/assets/Uploads/stats-bulletin-3-final-08-06-17.pdf

Ncube, M., & Lufumpa, C. L. (Eds.) (2014). *The emerging middle class in Africa*. New York: Routledge.

Nielsen, B. T., & Dale, B. E. (2013). Defining and categorizing experience industries. In J. Sundbo & F. Sorensen (Eds.), *Handbook on the experience economy* (pp. 65–83), Cheltenham, UK: Edward Elgar.

Njoh, A. J. (2018). The relationship between modern information and communications technologies (ICTs) and development in Africa. *Utilities Policy, 50*, 83–90.

Oteng-Ababio, M., & Arthur, I. K. (2015). (Dis)continuities in scale, scope and complexities of the space economy: The shopping mall experience in Ghana. *Urban Forum, 26*(2), 151–169.

Pine, B. J., & Gilmore, J. (1999). *The experience economy: Work is theatre and every business a stage*. Boston, MA: Harvard Business School Press.

Powell, J. (2017). The sub-Saharan African services economy: Insights and trends. *Working Paper ID-046*, Washington: U.S. International Trade Commission.

Powell, J. B. (2015). *Factor affecting growth in Ghana's services economy*. Working Paper ID-046. Washington: U.S. International Trade Commission. Retrieved from https://www.usitc.gov/publications/332/executive_briefings/powell_ghana_ebot10-15-2015.pdf

Prahalad, C. K., & Ramaswamy, V. (2004). Co-creation experience: The next practice in value creation. *Journal of Interactive Marketing, 18*(3), 5–14.

Richards, G. (2001).The experience industry and the creation of attractions. In G. Richards (Ed.), *Cultural attractions and European tourist* (pp. 55–69). Cambridge, MA: CABI Publishing.

Rodrik, D. (2018). An African growth miracle? *Journal of African Economies, 27*(1), 10–27. https://doi.org/10.1093/jae/ejw027

Schmitt, B. (2011). Experience marketing: Concepts, frameworks and consumer insights. *Foundations and Trends in Marketing, 5*(2), 55–112.

Shamah, R. A. M., Mason, M. C., Moretti, A., & Raggiotto, F. (2018). Investigating the antecedents of African fast food customers' loyalty: A self-congruity perspective. *Journal of Business Research*, 86, 446–456.

Signé, L. (2018). *Africa's consumer market potential: Trends, drivers, opportunities, and strategies.* Washington, DC: Brookings Institutions' Africa Growth Initiative Report. Retrieved from https://www.brookings.edu/wp-content/uploads/2018/12/Africas-consumer-market-potential.pdf

Srivastava, M., & Kaul, D. (2016). Exploring the link between customer experience–loyalty–consumer spend. *Journal of Retailing and Consumer Services, 31*, 277–286.

Sundbo, J., & Darmer, P. (Eds.). (2008). *Creating experience in the experience economy.* Cheltenham, UK: Edward Elgar.

Toffler, A. (1970). *Future shock.* New York: Random House.

UNCTAD. (2009). *Information economy report 2009: Trend and outlook in turbulent times.* New York: United Nations Conference on Trade and Development.

UNCTAD. (2015). *Economic development in Africa 2015: Unlocking the potential of Africa's services trade for growth and development.* New York: United Nations Conference on Trade and Development.

UNCTAD. (2017). *The role of the services economy and trade in structural transformation and inclusive development.* Geneva: Multi-year Expert Meeting on Trade, Services and Development, Fifth session. Retrieved from https://unctad.org/meetings/en/SessionalDocuments/c1mem4d14_en.pdf

UNECA. (2015). *Economic report on Africa 2015: Industrializing through trade.* Addis Ababa: United Nations.

Uwitonze, E., & Heshmati. A. (2016). Service sector development and its determinants in Rwanda, IZA Discussion Papers, No. 10117, *Institute for the Study of Labor* (IZA), Bonn.

Williams, A. M. (2010). Therapeutic landscapes as health promoting places. In T. Brown, S. McLafferty, & G. Moom (Eds.), *A Companion to Health and Medical Geography* (pp. 207–223). Malden, MA: Wiley-Blackwell.

World Bank. (2015). *Africa's pulse: An analysis of issues shaping Africa's economic future.* Working Paper, No. 95729, Washington, DC: World Bank Group.

Zamfir, I. (2016). *Africa's economic growth, taking off or slowing down?* European Union: European Parliamentary Research Service.

Index